THE LIST

—Harvey Jackins

RATIONAL ISLAND PUBLISHERS
SEATTLE, WASHINGTON, USA

THE LIST

Second edition. Copyright © 1997 by Harvey Jackins. All rights reserved. No part of this book may be used or reproduced in any manner whatsoever without written permission except in the case of brief quotations embodied in critical articles and reviews. For information, address Rational Island Publishers, P.O. Box 2081, Main Office Station, Seattle, Washington 98111, U.S.A.

Jackins, Harvey.
    The list / Harvey Jackins — 2nd ed.
        p.   cm.
    Includes bibliographical references.
    1. Re-evaluation Counseling. I. Title.
BF637.C6J3226   1997
158'.9—dc21
ISBN 1-885357-48-6   97-8536

Manufactured in the United States of America

FOREWORD

Re-evaluation Counseling is now forty-seven years old. It began in Seattle in the United States in 1950 and did not begin to spread very widely until the 1970s. It has become known mainly through personal contact between people rather than through any widespread publicity. People have learned to use it person-to-person, in small classes, and increasingly through workshops and conferences that have grown out of personal contacts.

Re-evaluation Counseling has some of the aspects of a "movement." People are welcome to explore it and, on the basis of their own experiences, join in its activities and become teachers and leaders of it. People are, however, forbidden to use its name for their activities unless what they are doing is consistent with the guidelines which the Community as a whole has established.

Respect for Re-evaluation Counseling as a movement has grown with people's experience in using it. Important theoretical advances and breakthroughs to more effective practice occur with increasing frequency.

At this point groups of Re-evaluation Counselors, united in the theory that they embrace, use, and teach, are functioning in eighty-six countries.

As the theory has developed, many books, pamphlets, and journals have been published to communicate different portions of it. Increasingly, it has seemed that a general summary is needed.

As a person who has been associated with Re-evaluation Counseling from its beginnings, I was asked to produce such a summary. A preliminary version was circulated to a small number of leaders four years ago. The results were very encouraging. Now this greatly expanded version of *The List* has been produced. I welcome correspondence about the ideas summarized within it.

—Harvey Jackins

THE LIST

(What I Think I Know)

Second Edition

1. How "Re-evaluation Counseling" Began—pages 1-5

2. Background Insights into Reality and Humans—pages 7-13

the universe and its nature	7
life	7
knowledge	8
source of difficulties/pseudo-reality	8
human beings—the broad view	8
intelligence	9
vulnerable to distress; able to recover	10
rational needs/instincts	11
good, caring, cooperative, loving, communicative, seeking closeness	11
zest	12
responsibility	12
freedom of decision	12
power	13
other characteristics	13

3. Distress Patterns—pages 15-22

inherent human behavior versus distress patterns	15
sources of distress patterns	16
intermittent versus chronic	16
thinking, feelings, distress patterns	16
some characteristics of distress patterns	17
"restimulation"	19
"acting out" distress patterns	19
varieties, similarities, of distress patterns	20
dealing with distress patterns	20
distress patterns are addictive	21
rational needs and "frozen" needs	21

4. The Discharge Process—pages 23-27

the eliminating-distress process	23
re-evaluation/re-emergence	23
order of/indications of/kinds of discharge	24
discharge indications and sequence chart	25
goal of discharge process	26
discharge spontaneous, eagerly sought, often inhibited	26
"storage" of patterns	27
interaction between "deciding" and discharge	27

5. How to Counsel—pages 29-78

- the large context 29
- beginning/ending sessions 32
- phenomena during sessions 33
    - who's in charge of the session? 33
    - safety/confidentiality 33
    - no "bad" feelings 34
    - apparent non-cooperation 34
    - identifications 34
    - "dramatizing"/"rehearsing" 35
    - re-evaluation 35
    - physical distress/yawns 36
    - first thoughts/"flash answers" 36
    - inhibition of discharge/"control patterns" 37
    - "protection of patterns by patterns" 38
    - "cafeteria-tray-dispenser syndrome" 38
    - challenges to the client 38
    - exhaustion 39
    - dreams 40
    - getting lost in distress 41
- understanding being a counselor/attitudes/actions 42
- client understandings/attitudes/actions 50
- modes of counseling 52
- rapid review of related experiences 53
    - counseling as a tool for freeing a person of particular distress symptoms or particular kinds of non-survival behavior 53
- telling the story/early memories 55
- occluded memories 56
- contradictions 57
- organized contradictions 61
    - directions 61
    - planning/keeping notebooks 62
    - commitments/frameworks/synopses 63
    - the Frontier Commitments 64
- goals 67
- "techniques" 67
- counseling on oppressed/oppressor roles 71
- building and taking care of a Co-Counseling relationship 73
- improving sessions 76
- group activities/group attention 78

6. Ideas Which Can Be Helpful to One's Living Rationally and Re-emerging Rapidly as a Client—pages 79-85

- some elements of reality 79
- rational attitude/action 79
- thinking 79
- problem-solving/reaching agreement 81
- death 81
- no obligations or "shoulds" 81
- freedom to choose viewpoint/freedom of decision 81
- human-to-human 82
- "no ancestors, no descendants" 83

loving/being loved 83
blame 84
mistakes 84
"all for one and one for all" 85
beauty and order 85

7. The Modes of Re-evaluation Counseling—pages 87-107

processes of freeing intelligence 87
the primary modes 87
using transcendental forces 89
writing and using written material 90
movies, etc. 90
rational re-emergent activities/the need to client 90
permissive and directive counseling 91
strategizing for re-emergence 92
teaching Re-evaluation Counseling 92
demonstrations 93
wrestling 93
"news and goods" 94
validation circles 94
casual/committed Co-Counseling relationships 94
discussion groups/topic groups 94
coming to a decision 95
reaching others with Re-evaluation Counseling 95
support groups 95
workshops 95
sports at workshops 96
song fests at workshops 96
creativity at workshops 97
conferences 97
gather-ins 97
Community meetings 97
think-and-listens 97
thinking on a topic 98
written communication between Co-Counselors 98
audio cassettes and videocassettes 99
speak-outs about oppression/"panels" 99
some early unworkable techniques 100
introductory lectures 100
"self-estimation" 101
"counseling the leader" 101
intensive counseling 102
Re-evaluation Counseling in schools 102
work with families 103
"relationship sessions" 103
counseling with a stranger 104
the Community Passover Seder 104
Co-Counselors together at non-Re-evaluation Counseling events 105
prepared to be counselor 105

  publications 105
  translation 106
  the "pilot plant" idea 106

8. Specialties in Counseling—pages 109-128

  the complexity and variety of distress patterns 109
  distress patterns as addictions/addictions 109
  pre-natal distress/birth 111
  improving relationships 112
  learning 113
  how the learning process operates 114
  counseling on sexual distress/sexuality/sexual abuse/sexual preference 115
  aging/immortality/death 117
  discharging distresses about death 118
  suicide compulsions 119
  pain/anesthesia/healing 120
  disabilities/illness 122
  men/women counseling each other 123
  different ages/counseling across age barriers 124
  play/work 125
  creativity 126
  money 127
  decision-making 127
  communication/language 128

9. Teaching Re-evaluation Counseling—pages 129-130

  how and when to teach Re-evaluation Counseling 129
  requirements for teachers 129
  the relation of the Re-evaluation Counseling teacher to the
   Re-evaluation Counseling Community 130

10. Leadership—pages 131-136

  what leadership is 131
  everyone can be a leader and, to re-emerge, needs to be a leader 131
  patterns and leadership 132
  tips about leading 133
  assisting leaders to lead well 133
  mistakes are okay 134
  attacks are not okay 134
  "pseudo-democracy" versus democracy 135
  to find out more 136

11. Other Theories of Human Behavior Cannot in General Be Reconciled
  with the Insights of Re-evaluation Counseling—pages 137-138

12. Theory and Policy—pages 139-140

  theory 139
  policy 139

13. Phenomena for Which Most Humans Do Not Have a Satisfactory Explanation and Need to Be Offered Such an Explanation—pages 141-149

> apparent "mystical" and "psychic" experiences 141
> confusions about sexuality 141
> other common confusions 142
> dreams 143
> talented/not talented 144
> the damage of hypnosis 144
> vocal difficulties 145
> attitudes towards "super" entities 146
> the general natures of change 146
> "sleepiness" 146
> inattention 146
> discipline 147
> memory 147
> "painful" emotions 147
> allergies 148
> menstrual cycles 148
> tickling 148
> every age is a good age 149
> deliberately view any situation from many different viewpoints 149

14. Oppression—pages 151-175

> overview 151
> oppression and distress patterns 151
> the different oppressions 152
> internalized oppression 156
> counseling/discharging on the oppressed role 157
> the oppressor role 158
> modes of tackling oppression 161
> general liberation/wide world change 163
>> the necessity, the possibility, and the possible procedures for transforming the current owning-class-working-class society 163
>> overview 164
>
> propositions for human liberation 166
> effective organizing 169
> nuclear war 170
> pacifism and "non-violence" 171
> the environment 171
> nationalism and patriotism 171
> cultures 173
> religion 173
> non-oppressive societies 173

15. It Is Possible to Build a Fellowship, Sisterhood, or Community of the People Who Take Responsibility for the Use of Re-evaluation Counseling Insights, for the Re-emergence of the Peoples of the World, for the Liberation of All People from All Oppressions, and for the Achievement of a Rational, Cooperative, Peaceful, Non-Exploitative Society—pages 177-182

16. Recent Developments in Counseling—pages 183-186

- the complete, logical distinction between the past and the future 183
- some universal, or nearly universal, oppressive patterns 183
- extended understatements 186
- integrity and courage 186

17. Rational Human Health Care—pages 187-191

- our bodies, our intelligence, and our environments 187
- health and well-being are rational concerns 187
- there are positive factors, also 188
- the experiences of RC Community members 188
- nutrition 188
- medicine and surgery 189
- the cost of "profiteering" hospital care 189
- re-examine the assumptions made in the past about health care 190
- staying healthy 190
- no mysticism in the RC attitude 190
- opposing aging and death 191

18. Information to Which Every Young Person Should Have Access—pages 193-210

- adults 193
- existence and the universe 193
- human capabilities 195
- nerve cells, nerve systems, quantitative complexity, qualitative changes in our functioning 196
- the evolution of our central nervous system 197
- interference 198
- you are all right 198
- learning, acquiring information 198
- interruption of thinking 199
- the recovery process 200
- complete recovery from distress is possible 201
- it is okay to be curious 201
- it is okay not to "believe" 201
- this society is not good 202
- past societies have been even worse 202
- young people are oppressed 203
- you have been mistreated 203
- people are still okay underneath 204
- how to understand, handle, and help the people around you 205
- in the present oppressive society, learning is not the primary function of the schools 207
- human beings of any gender are much alike 208
- it is possible to be your real self 208
- helping people younger than yourself 209
- refuse to accept any oppressions 209
- don't participate in oppressing anyone else 209

19. The Role of Religion in Human Affairs—pages 211-212

    there are understandable reasons why people create religions 211
    painful-emotion recordings enter the picture 211
    ways in which existing religions can be useful to conforming "believers" 212

20. The Prospect of Completely Identifying Oneself With Reality
    and Completely Rejecting the Pseudo-Reality of Distress—pages 213-214

    the complete "all-rightness" of oneself 213

21. How to Begin Re-evaluation Counseling in a New Location or
    With New People—pages 215-216

    situation: you have learned Re-evaluation Counseling in an already-organized
        Community and are familiar with some of the benefits of using it 215
    situation: you have heard about Re-evaluation Counseling from a friend or
        from reading some literature and want to find out how to "get started"
        and try to use it with your neighbors 216

22. Completely Intelligent Functioning—pages 217-218

APPRECIATIONS—page 219

APPENDIX

    Goal Chart 1
    Commitments 3
    How to Begin "Re-evaluation Counseling" 15
    Postulates 21

RESOURCES

    Books 1
    Pamphlets 3
    Journals 5
    Literature in Languages Other Than English 7
    Videocassettes 11
    Audio Cassettes 14

The long detour from reason we have wandered
Was not our choosing. Evolution's seeking
For more and greater complex interactions
Arose within reality itself.

So when intelligence at last appeared
It's understandable that it was fragile
And could break down and lapse to previous function
As humans labored on, half-smart, half-stupid.

But talk and tears and laughter, yawns, and shaking
Became recruited to a healing process
And, slowly, re-emergence made its way,
Becoming, more and more, a conscious effort,
More planned and organized, and more united,
Reaching to all the regions of our planet.

This book's a summary, a firm step forward.

Seeing the outcome certain now, I glow.
My precious fellow humans, struggling still,
Will make it all the way. I helped a little.

1. HOW "RE-EVALUATION COUNSELING" BEGAN

1.001 The activity now known as "Re-evaluation Counseling" began almost as an "accident." A friend of mine, Eddie, with whom I had been a co-leader of shipyard workers during World War II and who had also been a business agent for an A.F. of L. union following the War, had, as a result of the wave of reaction that assaulted the labor movement after the War, been forced to become a painting contractor in order to try to evade the "blacklisting" of all progressives that was organized to keep such people out of work. Eddie had taken a younger man on as a partner, whose name was Merle. Merle was, I think, in his late twenties, was married, and had two children. I knew him slightly and liked him as far as I knew him.

1.002 I was in a somewhat similar position to that of Eddie. After I left the shipyards I had also been a business agent for an A.F. of L. union until a wave of reaction led to purges of the local leaderships by the international union leaders. I also lost my job and faced a blacklist wherever I attempted to secure a new one. I, too, had finally organized a contracting firm where I did most of the work myself but hired other victims of the blacklists to work with me when I could afford to do so. Times were very difficult. Both Eddie and I were working hard to endeavor to earn a living and saw each other only infrequently.

1.003 Early one Saturday morning Eddie called me on the telephone and said he needed my help. He said the problem was with Merle, his partner. He said Merle had become increasingly irrational over a period of months, that he had taken him to several psychiatrists who had said they could do nothing to help him, and that their judgment was that he was a "hopeless case" and would have to spend the rest of his life in mental institutions. Eddie said he had kept him at his house for long periods but that his wife was afraid to have him around the children and that she would not permit Eddie to bring him home any more. He said that Merle had driven his own family away several months before with his irrational behavior and for the past weeks had been sitting in his empty apartment not sleeping, not eating, and, increasingly of late, screaming at himself at all times of the day or night.

Eddie said he did not know what else *he* could do but he hoped that *I* would do something to help. He said that Merle's neighbors had called that morning and said that if Eddie did not come and take Merle away, they would call the police and have him arrested. Eddie said he counted on me to do something to try to help Merle or at least keep him out of the hands of the police. He reminded me that we both knew that the state hospitals in our state were at the time assembly lines for electric shock "treatment" and that this was destructive of people. I protested my lack of knowledge of what to do and my desire to avoid getting involved, but Eddie said he had no alternative place to turn, and I finally agreed to try to see what I could do and at least get Merle away from the threat of arrest.

1.004 I drove across town to Merle's apartment, pounded on the door until he finally let me in, and "threatened" him until he agreed to come home with me. He would not look at me. Apparently he could not talk coherently, but I succeeded in driving home with him, trying to think on the way of what possibilities were open to me. (My most realistic hope was that a social-worker friend of mine could perhaps tell me of a psychiatrist who would not give up on people as easily as the ones Eddie had consulted and that meantime I could keep Merle out of the hands of the police. I also thought that if he had not been eating, I would force him to eat. Since he had not been sleeping, I would make him sleep, and I had vague thoughts of giving him vitamin pills in large quantities.)

When we arrived at my home I tried all of these but succeeded only with the vitamin pills. When I fiercely told him that he must sleep, he said he couldn't, once, and then refused to talk. When I forced him to lie down in a bedroom and ordered him to sleep, he said that he couldn't, and when I left to call my social-worker friend, he sneaked out the back door and started to run away. Hearing the back door close, I went back and captured him, and he was so weak that I had little difficulty in carrying him in and throwing him on the bed again. When I once again ordered him to sleep, he said, "I can't," in a desperate voice.

I decided to "bluff" since I did not know what else to do. I told him we would "start fixing him up right away." I got an old psychology book of my wife's out of the bookcase (I think it was called "Typical Sessions in Psychotherapy"), found a chapter where some therapist was questioning a patient, warned Merle that he would have to "cooperate" with me, and asked him whatever stupid question was listed in the book.

Merle grew very tense, looked at me, and burst into tears. I immediately told him that crying would not do any good, that he must cooperate better than that, and when he indicated that he would try, I asked him the same question. Once again he became very tense and burst into tears. Once again I scolded him and demanded better cooperation from him.

1.005 This happened perhaps fifteen times, to my increasing frustration. I was upset by Merle's crying. I felt sure that it was "wrong" but simply did not know what else to do. Finally, the thought appeared in my mind, "Maybe he needs to cry." Since I could not get anything else to happen anyway, I decided to allow him to cry, and the next time he began, I did not interrupt him right away. After he cried for a few minutes, however, I became restimulated and "forgot" that I had decided to let him cry, and stopped him once more. *Once the sound of his crying died away, however, I was able to remember that I had decided to allow his crying* and was able to start him crying again easily. This series of events was repeated at least four or five times.

1.006 Finally, I was able to allow him to continue crying. Soon Merle began interrupting his crying himself every few minutes and apologizing, saying, "I don't know why I'm crying. I don't know why I'm crying. I'm sorry." When I told him (somewhat disgustedly, I'm sure) to "go ahead and cry," Merle's crying would burst out afresh. This series of events was repeated many times.

1.007 After several hours, a burst of very violent crying took place followed by Merle saying, "I know now why I'm crying. I know now why I'm crying. It's my sister. We were very close, and she died about eight months ago. I never realized until just now that it had bothered me." Merle then resumed crying, occasionally mixing in talk about his memories of his sister.

Altogether this continued for about twelve hours. At this point I refused to listen any further because it was about 12:30 a.m. and I was very sleepy and, although I didn't know it, I was, of course, very restimulated and upset. I made Merle promise not to run away during the night, which he promised. He said that he felt a little sleepy. He told me later that he slept until about 3:30 and then sat and chain-smoked cigarettes the rest of the night.

After noon the next day, the crying resumed. After several hours a new violent outburst of crying came, and when it tapered off he reported suddenly seeing with great vividness the scene of his mother's burial in North Dakota when he was eight years old. He then cried on until midnight, talking a little about both his mother and sister.

I called Eddie at midnight and reminded him I had to go to work the next day. Eddie said he would have a house-painting crew come by with the painting truck and pick Merle up and keep him with the crew during the day's shift (which he did). Eddie called me at work at lunch time, very excited, very pleased. He described Merle as "weak, shaky, unable to work," but said, "You can talk to him. It's the first time in months I've been able to talk to him. Whatever you're doing, don't give up."

1.008 For the next two weeks I sat with Merle every evening and all through the weekends. For several days he cried steadily, hour after hour after hour.

1.009 Toward the end of the first week Merle began to shake and tremble, at first mixed with the crying, but then more and more by itself. After several evenings, shaking and trembling replaced the crying. At first I had tried to make Merle return to crying since he was obviously changing as a result of that, and he tried and would succeed temporarily, but very soon the shaking and trembling would begin again. I finally stopped interfering and listened to him talk about all the things that had frightened him and watched him tremble on and on and on. These sessions continued all evening every evening and most of the following weekend.

1.010 The trembling continued every evening into the second week, when Merle began to laugh. By then it seemed obvious that the trembling had been having the same kind of good effect as the crying had previously, so it seemed to me that he was being silly to waste his time with laughter when the crying and shaking had worked so well. He tried to respond as I requested but soon burst into laughter again. I found myself involuntarily joining in the laughter and assumed we were both "wasting our time."

1.011 Eddie reported that Merle was easily doing "two men's work" on the painting crew and with great enthusiasm. He whistled and sang while he worked. He told the other painters that he was feeling better than he ever remembered feeling before in his life.

1.012 He came to me and said he felt he had imposed on my family long enough by living there, that he had left his old apartment and taken a room at the Y.M.C.A. He showed me letters that he had begun writing to his wife, reassuring her and inviting her and the children to rejoin him. He said that he had signed up for swimming and dancing lessons which he had always wanted but never had a chance to take when he was younger. Except for one or two brief contacts with him and a reassuring note from him in California later reporting that all was well, this was the last contact I had with him.

Eddie and I were very interested in what had happened to Merle, but Merle himself was simply busy enjoying life.

1.013 Eddie and I discussed at some length what we had observed happen to Merle. We agreed that one possibility was that "something cyclical" had simply been worked through with Merle and that the crying and the shaking and the laughter had not been significant. We also agreed, however, that there was a possibility that we had stumbled upon something very important about people that wasn't generally known. We were very curious to find out if the good things that had obviously happened to Merle could perhaps happen to other people who were also listened to well.

1.014 We agreed that the question was, "Will what happened to Merle work with other people in general?" Since Eddie and I were the only ones who were very interested as yet, we decided to try it with each other. This was the beginning of Co-Counseling.

1.015 For the first session I became the counselor and tried to listen to Eddie. He wanted to talk, and his talking seemed very dull after all the emotional discharge that I had gotten used to with Merle. Eddie reported later, however, that the insomnia that he had been experiencing early every morning had disappeared after being listened to the first time.

My first session as client seemed very disappointing and uncomfortable to me. Eddie continued to talk enthusiastically about his sessions, however, and I was not quite willing to give up.

1.016 The second time that Eddie attempted to counsel me he asked me to tell him about an experience he knew that I had had. This was the time when I was part of the group of workers at Boeing Aircraft Company who were trying to organize the union there for the first time. The workers had stayed united against pressure from the international union to settle for a very poor contract with the Boeing Company and had finally achieved the beginnings of a decent labor contract. Naively we celebrated our victory and assumed the struggle was mostly over, but instead of course, the international union officers, who felt threatened in their offices by this huge new local, contacted the Boeing Company. A campaign was launched to drive all the leadership of the local out of the union and out of Boeing under charges that they were "communists." A gang of thugs was organized, sensational charges were filed in the newspapers, and between beatings and propaganda, the original leadership of the union was eventually driven out of the industry. The local union was taken over by appointed puppets of the company and the international union officers.

I had been one of the first casualties of the "goon squad" (the gang of hired thugs). While the international union president kept me from leaving at the end of a local meeting until everyone else had gone, fourteen men with brass knuckles and lead saps gathered outside the door and attacked me when I emerged. Before they were through every bone in my face was broken, there was blood in my spinal fluid, and I had a "black eye" that covered my whole face.

Eddie asked me to remember the scene of the attack and tell him about it. At first I refused. I insisted that I had been too busy to remember what was going on and I felt very uncomfortable. Eddie, however, patiently coaxed me to remember and talk about minute after minute of the beating scene. I felt very uncooperative, but I did continue to talk about it, hoping that each time I answered one of his questions it would "shut him up" and I could change the subject.

What happened instead was that my feet began to shake, my knees began to shake, everything about me began to shake, and the cot on which I was lying in Eddie's attic began to bounce about the floor from my vibrations. I was a most uncooperative client, but Eddie patiently persisted for an hour and a half until I finally revolted, refused to talk any more, and left the scene. I felt "terrible" at that point and was full of resentment at Eddie for making me feel these feelings.

I had to drive four miles to get home from Eddie's house and half way there I suddenly realized that *the entire world had changed*, that I felt differently about everything around me. This change has lasted the rest of my life since then. I don't think that since that time I have ever felt as bad as I had apparently been feeling every day up until that time without realizing it.

1.017 With Eddie already enthusiastic and me newly won over to the benefits of people listening to each other, we began to experiment with counseling a much greater variety of people. Our wives had sessions. People who had seen the changes in Merle volunteered for sessions. Not every session worked well every time, but many of them resulted in spectacular improvements in the lives of people we worked with.

1.018 This counseling of each other and of volunteer "guinea pigs" continued for several months. We worked at it nearly every evening. All this was carried on in addition to regular, hard, full-time jobs. Exhaustion finally led me to decide that this must be explored full-time and because no one else was interested as much as I was, I decided that I would pursue it and attempt to teach others to do it. Forty-six years of teaching and practicing Co-Counseling had begun.

1.019 A *theory* began to be assembled from the results of people's sessions. A firm decision was made to include nothing in this theory that came from existing theories of psychology or other theories of human behavior, but to only include results personally experienced by those of us who were practicing Co-Counseling. The name "Re-evaluation Counseling" was chosen to describe what we were doing because of the obvious "re-evaluation" which followed discharge in most people's sessions.

1.020 The dependable indications of the discharge process were slowly identified, and the order in which these processes tended to occur was recognized. People who could, began with tears (sobbing, crying), and then proceeded in a rough order with shaking (trembling, perspiring from a cool skin, sometimes very active kidneys), and after much of this had gone on, would begin laughter associated with a cool skin. Following this came storming and raging, laughter associated with a warm skin, reluctant talk, eager talk, and relaxed laughter. Eventually there would be "forgetting" of the distress experience as a distress experience. Yawning, sometimes accompanied by stretching and scratching, was identified as a dependable indication of the discharge of pain or physical discomfort. We found that yawning would tend to occur at any point in the series of emotional discharges.

Each of these stages would tend to take place over a few hours or weeks if the person began working on one particular distress experience or one particular difficulty. If the person set out to improve his or her entire life or entire functioning, each stage typically would last through months or years of very satisfying progress.

1.021 Approximately twenty years of slow, determined growth of the use of Re-evaluation Counseling in Seattle followed. The growth was punctuated by occasional vicious attacks, launched or organized by very distressed people looking for something to hate, or by government agencies. (I was charged with contempt of Congress in 1955 based on my past activity in the labor movement and was sentenced to six months in prison. I was the target of much intense hostile publicity. [I won on appeal.]) It was financially almost impossible to keep going, but somehow a growing recognition by people who had used Co-Counseling for themselves brought just enough loyalty and support that the group survived. We had organized a counseling firm of Personal Counselors, Inc., and taught classes through it and prepared and issued publications.

In spite of all the difficulties, the counseling effort survived and continued to deepen and broaden its effectiveness.

1.022 About 1969 or 1970, people who had learned to Co-Counsel in Seattle began to move to other cities in some numbers and began, with our support, to spread the knowledge of Co-Counseling to other places. In the twenty-six years following 1970, Co-Counseling practice on some level or other has begun or become established in eighty-six countries besides the United States. The pattern of attacks being mounted upon it has continued, but the attacks have been surmounted or endured, and the project has survived.

1.023 At present, Re-evaluation Counseling is an increasingly deliberate attempt to uncover the reality of the universe, the real nature of humans, the nature of humans' difficulties, and workable ways for correcting the difficulties.

1.024 At present, the goals of Re-evaluation Counseling are the re-emergence to their real natures of all human beings, the exploration of the universe, the acceleration of the upward trend, and the thorough enjoyment of what we are doing while we are doing it.

1.025 Parts of the literature have been translated into thirty-two languages. Barriers of nationality, language, race, culture, and political antagonism have been overcome. *The commonality of the discharge, re-evaluation, and re-emergence experience for all humans* has been established. It has been clearly revealed that a deeply passionate hunger for the use of this process exists for people everywhere in the world and remains intact even within the most distressed (and apparently uncooperative) individual.

1.026 In 1996 the concepts of Re-evaluation Counseling are spreading widely and are being reached for as possible solutions to the problems of survival in a period of societal collapse. This eager interest is noticeably intensifying at present.

1.027 The overall direction and goal of Re-evaluation Counselors is to seek complete re-emergence for *every* individual (and ultimately *all* individuals) from *all* past distresses.

1.028 Re-evaluation Counseling goals, attitudes, and philosophy are useful to the individual all the time, not just during a session or two a week, or a support group or a class once a week, but as a guide to living every moment of every day. If the individual is not "living Re-evaluation Counseling," she or he is almost certainly "living out" her or his chronic distress pattern.

1.029 Often people come to participate in Re-evaluation Counseling with attitudes they have picked up from the society, such as hoping that Re-evaluation Counseling is an emergency measure that they can use to attain "normalcy." It certainly can be used in this way, but it is much better to realize that Re-evaluation Counseling is an ongoing process, a continuing tool for living, and a path toward eventual "complete re-emergence" to full functioning as a human individual. Other ways of looking at Re-evaluation Counseling include seeing it as a process for gaining an ever-more-accurate picture of reality and as a way of freeing all the people of the world from the effects of distress so that the entire world can function elegantly—for all living creatures, for the total environment, and for all human beings.

1.030 Basically, any good theory is the summary of successful experiences. On its growing edge, it includes informed conjectures and inspired guesses (which should remain labelled conjectures and guesses until they have been confirmed). Re-evaluation Counseling theory has developed this way.

1.031 Re-evaluation Counseling attempts to be constantly self-correcting and proclaims all its policies to be draft policies.

1.032 The one-point program, support of which is required for one to be a member of the Re-evaluation Counseling Community, is to use Re-evaluation Counseling to recover one's occluded intelligence and help others to do the same. During the period which seemed to be most threatening of a drift toward nuclear holocaust in world affairs, the Community temporarily added a second subsidiary point—to prevent nuclear holocaust in order to give time for the one-point program to work.

2. BACKGROUND INSIGHTS INTO REALITY AND HUMANS

the universe and its nature

2.001 An objective universe exists.

2.002 The universe which we can take notice of and be aware of, which we can grasp, manipulate, treasure, and enjoy, spreads out from us individually in every direction. It is the nature of the human being at its center to be intelligent, to take charge.

2.003 The universe is dynamic. This dynamism operates at widely-differing rates. There is no stasis anywhere in the universe. Any appearance of stasis is a superficial appearance or is a projection of a human's distress pattern.

2.004 The universe is benign. Our survival and functioning are consistent with the universe's survival and functioning. We fit the universe well. Everything we require for meeting our needs exists in the universe.

2.005 An upward trend toward complexity, meaning, integration, and independence exists everywhere in the universe, counter to the "downward trends" of disorganization, randomness, passivity, monotony, etc., associated with entropy.

2.006 The existences of the upward trend and the downward trends are compatible and consistent with each other. In a sense, the upward trend is "fueled" by the processes of the downward trends.

2.007 The upward trend exists in the universe and will proceed in some way or other independently of our interference with it, assistance to it, or other interaction with it.

2.008 What is "evil" or "wrong" from the human viewpoint is the "slopping over" of the downward trends into the functioning of the upward trend (the destruction of a human being, the burning of a Stradivarius violin for fuel, the accretion of a rigid distress pattern on a flexible human mind).

2.009 Each event and phenomenon and human being and thought is unique.

life

2.010 In general, non-living matter is largely passive in its responses to its environment.

2.011 The responses of a human being to the environment resemble the responses of other living creatures more than they resemble the responses of non-living matter. The distinctive characteristic of living creatures is their active response to the environment. Living creatures tend to impose their organization on the environment.

2.012 Almost all living creatures with the exception of humans are able to respond actively to the environment only on the basis of pre-set patterns of response, which are fixed and limited in number for almost any one living creature other than a human. (A very few species of non-humans [chimpanzees, gorillas, orangutangs, possibly some species of octupi and squid] show the beginnings of the function which we define as intelligence in humans, that is, the ability to create brand new, accurate responses to new situations.)

2.013 Life is worth living. We are lucky to exist. We are even more fortunate to be alive. We are even *more* fortunate to be intelligent. We are even *more* fortunate to be engaged in re-emergence. We are even *more* fortunate to be part of the deliberate and aware Re-evaluation Counseling movement toward re-emergence.

2.014 It is much better to be alive, if only for one second and that second spent in agony, than never to have been alive at all.

2.015 Every moment is brand new. We have an unlimited supply of them.

knowledge

2.016 For any subject, the amount of knowledge that human beings do not yet possess about that subject is probably much greater than the amount which we do possess. We do, however, possess enough knowledge to act sensibly.

source of difficulties/pseudo-reality

2.017 The source of harms, difficulties, and hurts coming from the wide world does not seem to be inherent in our nature or in the nature of the wide world. These difficulties seem to flow from the accumulation of irrational social relations, irrational use of the environment, and the patterned organization of conflict between human beings. This implies that changing the wide world even in its broadest phases is desirable for our individual benefits, and necessary for the fulfillment of our goals.

2.018 The concept of "pseudo-reality" can prove useful in communicating between Co-Counselors and can often be helpful to a re-emerging client.

By "pseudo-reality" we mean the false descriptions of the universe, of our societies, of our oppressions, of our relationships, and of our own natures, which we have been given by other people who have been previously brainwashed to accept these false ideas, and by the educational and other oppressive institutions of the societies. Insights into the false natures of these previously-installed wrong ideas can be held onto by the client (and be brought more easily back to the client's attention when distracted from them) if viewed as a whole complex of false information and illusions created in order to secure our cooperation with, and our support of, the irrationalities and the institutions.

2.019 Present human traditions, relationships, institutions, politics, and educational and health care systems are all heavily contaminated by distress patterns.

human beings—the broad view

2.020 We accept no limiting definitions of a human being.

2.021 The human being (without patterns) is integrated, whole.

2.022 A human being functions in an integrated way. Mind and body are thoroughly interrelated and integrated with the universe.

2.023 The fundamental similarities between all humans in our sub-species are much greater than any differences.

2.024 All human beings are closely related to each other. We are all members of the same sub-species. All living things are intimately related and dependent upon each other. All living things "belong to" each other in a profound way.

2.025 Through our own living existence, we have an inherent connection to all other living things. We could not exist without their existence.

2.026 All presently-existing humans are very closely related to each other, are members of one sub-species. There are trivial physical differences based on blood type, size, right- or left-handedness, body shape, hair, skin color, etc. No such characteristics or group of characteristics combine to constitute a "race." There is only one race, the human race.

Each human is unique. Even identical twins have significant differences. The possession of vast intelligence, awareness, complete freedom of decision, and complete power over the universe around us is common to all and unites us all. Any apparent deviation from this arises from acquired *and removable* distress patterns.

2.027 Everyone is completely "all right" and always has been.

2.028 All human beings have the same capacity for feeling—love, joy, excitement, etc., or grief, terror, fear, embarrassment, anger, frustration, boredom, etc.

2.029 All human beings are inherently equal. Regardless of *any* differences, caused by *any* factors, including genetic distortions or accidents or any failures to develop completely, each human being deserves complete respect from all other human beings. To take any other attitude would itself be an inhuman pattern.

2.030 Recognized and admired strengths of particular groups in the human population are inherently potential in every person.

2.031 No human culture is intrinsically, in any overall way, superior or inferior to any other culture.

2.032 Every single human being, at every moment of the past, if the entire situation is taken into account, has always done the very best that she or he could do, and so deserves neither blame nor reproach from anyone, including self. This, in particular, is true of you.

2.033 Human beings inherently expect to be welcomed into, and cherished by, the universe.

2.034 The people that we think of as our ancestors or our descendants are not really such. The line of descent is from DNA molecule to DNA molecule. Each human being is a separate branch off that line of descent. So the people you thought of as your ancestors or your descendants are simply adjacent "branches." The huge mass of "obligations and duties" that has been attached to the notion of "descent from" or "ancestor to" is all patterned. These people can be or become good friends or allies but are never really one's ancestors or descendants.

intelligence

2.035 Every human being is inherently possessed of the capacity for vast intelligence and still possesses it unless severe mechanical damage has been done to the human's forebrain (or unless the development of the forebrain has been interfered with or prevented by genetic or other factors).

2.036 Human intelligence operates by receiving new information from the environment, by comparing and contrasting this new information with information from past experiences that has already been understood and stored in the memory, and by constructing a fresh, new, appropriate, and successful response to the specific situation at hand.

2.037 Human intelligence functions with great complexity and with at least thousands of parallel processing circuits in operation. It has been estimated that a human processes eleven trillion items of information every second in ordinary functioning. Every item of information evaluated is evaluated in dozens of different ways, and the results are checked and compared with each other. Most of this evaluation takes place below awareness.

2.038 *Conjecture*: This special ability of intelligence (as well as the ability to be aware, to have complete freedom of decision, and to have complete power to require the environment around us to respond in any way which we wish it to) arises as a *qualitative* development out of the enormous *quantitative* increase in the number of nerve cells and their interconnections in the human central nervous system. This development has taken place as part of the evolution of our species in the past.

2.039 *Conjecture*: Traces or beginnings of these flexible abilities appear in a few other species of living creatures. This probably indicates that these flexible abilities will tend to appear whenever the quantitative complexity of the central nervous systems of any line of living creatures becomes great enough.

2.040 *Conjecture*: All forms of life that we have any knowledge of will tend to change and evolve. These changes will take place in all possible directions. Some of these changes will tend to be in the direction of greater complexity and greater independence of the environment. Some of these evolutionary changes will tend to move the creature in the direction of becoming intelligent. It is intelligent human policy to support that evolution and to minimize the imposition of rigid patterns, particularly on fauna that are approaching the complexity which could convey rational ability. Reality will be enhanced by the existence of many kinds of rational intelligences. We need fear no competition with any other kinds of rational intelligence.

2.041 Theoretically and practically we see no limit to what the human mind can grasp, learn, understand, or remember.

2.042 There is nothing that a human mind can do that is alien to being understood by another human mind, although actions taken by *patterns* may at first *seem* baffling or completely alien.

2.043 Each person possesses abilities at least as great as those of the most outstanding people of past and present societies.

2.044 Human beings are inherently far more intelligent than our societies and our cultures have commonly recognized, taught, or publicized.

2.045 Humans handle the world optimally when they trust their own thinking.

2.046 What we usually call "logical" thinking is intelligent thinking carefully checked out to be free from any errors or patterns having crept into the process. What we call "intuitive" thinking is the same kind of thinking but which has been done rapidly and its tentative conclusions recognized and stated prior to careful checking. Such intuitive thinking is a valuable process and should be encouraged in every way. Any conclusions reached by thinking intuitively can afterwards be checked over carefully and, thus verified, become dependable and become what we call logical thinking.

2.047 Each young person, no matter what age she or he is, has a complete, independent, functioning intelligence. What distinguishes her or him from an adult is that she or he is at an earlier point in development in terms of acquiring information and experience, and in bodily growth and maturity.

vulnerable to distress; able to recover

2.048 Distress, physical or emotional, suspends human intelligence and causes the human to revert to a more primitive method of functioning. This requires the information input during the distress experience to become (at least temporarily) a rigid recording, a rigid pattern of functioning, keeping the information of the experience from being evaluated rationally. If not discharged and re-evaluated, it becomes a compulsive pattern of acting, feeling, sounding, and behaving rigidly.

Such a compulsive distress recording can be triggered later by a similarity in a new situation to the distress situation of the past, or it can be triggered by the intuitive (but usually unworkable in the past) attempt of the person wearing the distress pattern to display it and rehearse it. People tend to display and rehearse such patterns in the hopes that attention from another person or some fortunate contradiction to the recorded distress pattern in the new situation will bring about discharge and re-evaluation and re-emergence from the rigidity.

2.049 All of the complex processes which we summarize under the term "discharge" (dependably indicated by talking unrepetitively, by yawning, crying, shaking, laughing, raging, perspiring with cold skin, perspiring with warm skin) are attached to pre-rational physical functions, but the crucial releasing effects of them are by now inherent parts of our rational natures.

2.050 A rational response to a hurt might include: 1) interrupting the action that is hurting one, 2) discharging completely while still feeling the distress of the hurt, and 3) organizing and taking action to see that the hurtful event is not repeated.

2.051 We inherently have the ability (and can reclaim and use this ability in practice) to *simultaneously* discharge, act, feel, and think.

2.052 There are not two "kinds" of humans, the one kind "mentally defective" or "mentally ill," the other fully human; all humans can fully recover the functioning of their intelligence (unless there is severe physical damage to the forebrain).

rational needs/instincts

2.053 Humans have rational needs (including the need to love, be loved, rest, exercise, eat nutritious food, work, play, enjoy solitude, participate in physical movement), the meeting of which has a pro-survival effect. All these needs can be thought about, planned for, and met.

2.054 Rational needs vary at different developmental stages of an individual's life.

2.055 Humans have many instincts (to breathe, to eat, to sleep, to reproduce, etc.) which, in the absence of hurt, are quickly brought under and subordinated to our human capacity for rational thinking. It is only when distress becomes attached to these instincts that they resist the control of our intelligence. In the absence of distress recordings, a logical, pro-survival response which is not dependent on instinctual drives and is right for any current conditions can be chosen, or created.

good, caring, cooperative, loving, communicative, seeking closeness

2.056 Human beings are inherently "good" (kind, cooperative, merciful, compassionate, committed to justice). This "goodness" is another aspect of our intelligence, not separate from it. Our goodness exists independently of what we do or accomplish.

2.057 Human beings naturally care about each other, enjoy cooperating with each other, and enjoy living.

2.058 The survival of all human beings is enhanced by cooperation between us. All human beings should be allies, and anything that prevents us from being effective allies to each other should be subject to contradiction, discharge, and re-evaluation by agreement of both parties. Among the greatest individual triumphs is the conversion of a former "antagonist" into an ally.

2.059 Love is the way that human beings naturally feel about each other. Love and intelligent communication are not separate functions but are different aspects of the same relationship. If one intelligence can recognize the presence of another intelligence, that intelligence is predisposed toward, and will move in the direction of, loving the other intelligence. Apparently the only entity that we have knowledge of in the universe up to the present that is complex enough to be really deeply enjoyable to a human mind is another human mind. The prime directive for human intelligence (as apparently for all forms of life) is to survive. For an intelligent human it is quickly obvious that cooperation enhances survival more than competition. Even in circumstances where there is the appearance of intelligent competition between two human beings, closer examination will make it plain that the apparent competition is based on cooperation, with each person challenging and assisting the other to exceed previous limits and perform better and better and better. Everything in the universe is deeply interesting to a functioning intelligence. For two or more intelligences to share any particular such interests is thoroughly enjoyable.

2.060 Love is a general attitude. The content of love in any particular case is unique. It is specific to each relationship and, in detail, to each interaction.

2.061 Love is a word which can be correctly used to describe the human experiencing the integration and connectedness of all things in objective reality.

2.062 Humans naturally love themselves and are inherently deeply connected to themselves.

2.063 Humans inherently need both to love and be loved. It is a hurtful experience to not be loved. It is a hurtful experience to not have the opportunity to love. The lack of opportunity to love is the more hurtful of the two.

2.064 No one should participate in sex without the presence of and the expression of love. It is an inherent need of humans to participate in a great deal of expression of love, without sex or sexual feelings being involved.

2.065 Human beings inherently love to communicate with each other. Nothing is complex enough to fully challenge, interest, and engage a human mind except another human mind.

2.066 Individuals of the human species inherently need, enjoy, and seek to touch each other, to be physically close to each other. Such touching needs to be *aware*. Aware hugging can express and meet this inherent need.

2.067 We have a limitless capacity for closeness with one another and with a limitless number of people.

2.068 Humans are inherently closely connected with each other and the universe (environment, animals, etc.). Isolation and feelings of isolation exist only as distress patterns, the results of previous hurts.

zest

2.069 The inherent emotional tone of a human being is *zest*, an eagerness to observe everything, to learn everything, to deal with everything, and to enjoy everything that is going on.

responsibility

2.070 Complete responsibility for *everything* is the relaxed, unforced, unobligated inherent attitude of each human being.

2.071 As far as we can tell from previous observations, the feeling of complete, powerful responsibility is inherent in an unhurt human from the very beginning.

2.072 We are free to take full responsibility, each of us, for the farthest atom of the farthest star in the farthest galaxy. If we set any limit to our responsibility, then we have accepted a patterned attitude that is in conflict with our inherent attitude toward our surroundings.

freedom of decision

2.073 Nearly all decisions are simple choices between several options.

2.074 Human beings inherently have complete freedom of decision.

2.075 There are no limits to our freedom of decision. We are free to decide on a new viewpoint in any situation. We are even free to decide to act irrationally. We are free to make a "bad" decision. We are free to make decisions "in the teeth of the evidence." We are also free to always be rational in our decisions, but the important *complete* freedom of decision does not mean there is anything automatic about our being rational. "There are no guard rails on this cliff edge."

2.076 It is possible that freedom of decision for any individual is independent of discharge. The possibility is still being explored and discussed.

2.077 Every person is always free to choose for himself or herself the viewpoint that he or she will take towards any situation and is free to change that viewpoint whenever she or he wishes. (However, if one has made agreements for action or attitude with another person based on the viewpoint held before the change, then one owes the other person a notification and an explanation of the change of viewpoint and the reason for the change. One should ask the other person for agreement to release one from the previous agreement or negotiate the construction of a substitute agreement based on the new viewpoint. This should take place as a responsible act in relation to the other person.)

2.078 Complete freedom of decision offers us the opportunity to direct our *own* lives by making our *own* choices rather than being enforced by patterned behavior based on old recordings of distress or based on the operations of oppression in the oppressive society.

2.079 Any person of any age, given accurate information, can make a rational decision.

2.080 The apparent inability of people to decide or to act on a decision appears to usually be a result of powerlessness patterns laid in so early in our lives that it's difficult to find contradictions to them in our memories. One technique to discharge them is the systematic statement and application of the decision that "I can" (whatever we wish to do but have not done yet) and "I will."

power

2.081 Human beings inherently have complete power to have the universe around them respond to them in any way they wish it to respond. It may take a long time and much effort, it may require the attainment of immortality or the cooperation of future generations, but anything that a human being rationally wishes to accomplish can eventually be accomplished.

2.082 If even one person reclaims her or his power, and acts on it, that person can guarantee the future of the world.

other characteristics

2.083 The ability to give aware attention to others (to counsel others) is an inherent human characteristic.

2.084 Human beings are inherently aware of and interested in their environment.

2.085 The natural attitude of humans toward the land, the sea, and the air, and toward all other living things is one of respect, love, and a deep concern for the existence and welfare of each part of the web of life into which we are born. It is a deep hurt to have one's inborn sense of his or her relationship with nature denied or distorted by the culture he or she is born into.

2.086 The ability to lead is an inherent quality of all humans. The essence of leading is to organize other intelligences to cooperate with one's own intelligence toward a common goal.

2.087 Humans are inherently appreciative of their bodies and all their bodies' processes.

2.088 Inherent human rights include, but are not limited to: the right to exist, the right to feel worthwhile, the right to know one is connected to all other human beings and living things, and the right to know that one is limitless. Inherent human characteristics include, but are not limited to: feeling good about being who one is; feeling good, innocent, blameless, powerful, strong, tender, patient, generous, decisive, resilient, energetic, open, trusting, trustworthy, loving, loved, safe and secure, playful, responsible, expressive, competent, and hopeful.

2.089 Humans inherently feel safe and secure when safe. All humans are inherently courageous, gentle, sensitive, strong, playful, beautiful, creative, spontaneous, and also have every other positive aspect of any humans that we might list. These qualities are permanent, universal, limitless, and unconditional. They do not depend on one's gender, race, age, freedom from distress, or the absence of restimulation.

2.090 There are "no limits" for women.

2.091 Any newborn baby has already experienced a very complex past, is possessed of a great deal more knowledge than people usually assume, has a personal, complex history and a collection of at least some distress patterns that were installed before, during, and following birth.

2.092 It is our inherent human nature to view unsolved problems as interesting challenges rather than as insurmountable difficulties.

3. DISTRESS PATTERNS

inherent human behavior versus distress patterns

3.001 Irrational behavior is acquired, not inherent.

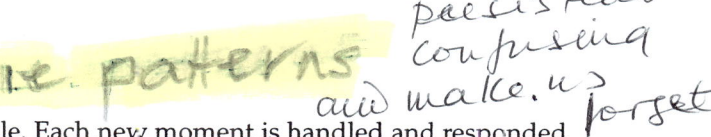
re. patterns — they are persistent, confusing, and make u forget

3.002 Inherent human behavior is fundamentally flexible. Each new moment is handled and responded to in a new, creative, successful way.

3.003 Flexible human intelligence compares and contrasts the information being received in the present with information stored in our memory from previous experiences and formulates responses which take the similarities and differences into account and are adapted to the specific, unique, present-time situation.

3.004 Inherently *all* human behavior is this flexible, this rational, this successful. Yet observably the behavior of all presently-existing adult humans contains certain areas or "patches" where the human being does not act with this flexibility or success. We have called these areas "distress patterns" or "distress recordings."

3.005 We do not know why, but human intelligence is inherently vulnerable to being shut down by physical or emotional hurts and becoming subject to the imposition of distress patterns. We don't know if intelligence would necessarily be vulnerable on any occasion when it developed anywhere in the universe. We don't yet know why people are "pulled" toward making wrong decisions.

3.006 The undischarged distress recording is the source of all human irrationality.

3.007 Because of distress patterns (and often also because of lack of sufficient information), we usually tap into only a small portion of our potential intelligence.

3.008 When a distress recording is operating, its rigid functioning tends to completely replace, partially replace, or influence and distort the actions which arise out of the flexible processes of the person's thinking.

3.009 Under present conditions, most human beings function at least partly on the basis of their distress patterns most of the time instead of functioning completely on the basis of their intelligence.

3.010 At the present, most human beings, in most situations, function as *composites* of flexible, rational thinking and behavior, and of rigid patterns.

3.011 There is a qualitative difference between the person and the irrational patterns which have become attached to the person, and each must be related to differently.

3.012 There are not *two kinds* of human beings. Each person is rational and flexible where unpatterned, and rigid where patterned.

3.013 There are no "bad" human beings, but only good human beings acting badly as a result of their distress patterns.

3.014 The human remains excellent no matter how obscured by patterns. The essential human is permanent. The distress is a temporary, extraneous accretion. The human deserves complete appreciation and complete self-appreciation, regardless of the accreted patterns.

3.015 A distress recording includes every bit of the content of what happened to the human being during the distress experience. It acts as a very detailed, literal, and complete *recording*. It can subsequently be triggered into acting as if it were the actual nature and functioning of the human by a similarity in the circumstances surrounding the human at the later period to the original circumstances when the recording was installed. It can also be triggered by an intuitive attempt on the part of the human to rehearse the recording in the hopes of finding a sufficient contradiction to turn the recording to discharge and become free of it. Without an understanding by the surrounding people of the processes of discharge, re-evaluation, and re-emergence, this contradiction and discharge does not usually take place, and instead the pattern gains in scope from being rehearsed, rather than becoming dissipated

3.016 We understand how to recover from these patches of inhuman, rigid functioning.

sources of distress patterns

3.017 There are three principal sources of distress recordings: 1) accidents, 2) "contagion," and 3) the semi-deliberate operations of the oppressive societies.

3.018 A distress recording or a "distress pattern" results from an experience of hurt and includes *everything* that was going on at the time the recording was made—all the visual, auditory, tactile, kinesthetic, and other contents of the experience, all the words and sounds present in the experience, all the feelings and emotions, and all the "thoughts" present in the person's mind at the time. These "thoughts" may have been the product of thinking then, but once congealed in and attached to the distress recordings are no longer flexible.

3.019 Human distress patterns arise through the congealing of certain pre-rational mechanisms of functioning which we inherited from our pre-rational ancestors. These are similar to the mechanisms in use by other mammals. These mechanisms are a very crude kind of learning for pre-rational mammals, and we use them in "training" our horses and dogs. These mechanisms no longer serve any useful purpose for *us* now that we have evolved to our present complexity and to our ability to be intelligent. The "conditioned learning" which allows a pre-intelligent mammal to change its rigid behaviors does not, in general, lower the *level* of functioning of the mammal. For human beings to relapse to this level of functioning, however, creates what we call a *distress recording* or *distress pattern* which enormously degrades our level of functioning until we have found a way to contradict, discharge, re-evaluate, and re-emerge from the area of distress to flexible thinking again.

intermittent versus chronic

3.020 Distress patterns may affect the person intermittently, dominating the human being when restimulated sufficiently, or influencing the human being as the restimulation becomes less intense. Each undischarged or un-understood restimulation of a distress recording adds to its effect upon the human being and tends to increase its domination of the human being. When the restimulation of the distress pattern has reached a certain point, it will become "chronic" and will tend to "play" all the time, to dominate the human being's behavior and feelings chronically.

3.021 Distress patterns which are still intermittent will "take over" and dominate the individual temporarily under conditions of restimulation. An example for many people is "stage fright," where the individual is relaxed until the situation reminds him or her of the feeling of being obligated to perform.

Chronic distress patterns operate as a nearly constant "background." An example would be a person who functions in many different ways but is always feeling and being influenced by the feeling, "I am stupid."

3.022 Clients will tend to view their *intermittent* distress patterns as "problems" but will tend to view their *chronic* distress patterns as their "personalities," "part of themselves," or "the way things are." With theory to guide them, and with experience, clients can notice and systematically contradict their chronic patterns as something separate from themselves.

3.023 A chronic pattern almost always began as a tense "desperate solution" to an "impossible" situation. As a result, these chronic patterns tend to *feel* as if they still have survival value to the person because the person "survived" during the original experience.

thinking, feelings, distress patterns

3.024 Feelings were the best guides we had to acting before we evolved to intelligence. We still have feelings. Some of them feel "good," and some of them feel "bad." Neither kind is a satisfactory guide to action. If one has what seem to be "good" feelings, one can discharge using them as contradictions to distress or one can "enjoy" them, but it is unwise to be guided by them in one's actions. If one has "bad" feelings, one should seek contradictions to them and discharge their content, but it is not safe to be guided by them in one's actions. Only logical thinking is acceptable as a guide for our actions.

Human beings operating in the grip of distress patterns are regressed to the kind of primitive functioning of other mammals where feelings are used as approximate pictures of reality and are used as guides to action. Feelings will not give one an accurate picture of reality and are not dependable, logical guides to action.

3.025 Because of the prevalence of patterns in our cultures at this historical period, it is "taken for granted" by most beginning Re-evaluation Co-Counselors that if one has a particular distress feeling, such as *embarrassment* or *fear* or *sadness*, that one must necessarily act upon it. Actually, there is no rational reason to translate any feeling into *action*. Feelings are not a satisfactory guide for effective action. Actually, people have tended to look up to and use as models the people who "go against their feelings" in their actions—the knight who moves into effective combat with the dragon that terrifies him, the performer stricken with stage fright or embarrassment who performs determinedly nevertheless, the person who refuses to be intimidated by any threats. It will be wise in communicating Re-evaluation Counseling theory to new people to communicate early in their instruction about this actual freedom from any *need* to act on one's distress feelings. It will expedite their re-emergence and save them much time that would otherwise be wasted in rehearsal of accumulated distresses.

3.026 What *seems* to be one's own thinking at any particular time can be intelligently suspected of being contaminated with patterns. However, that thinking, the best of one's own thinking available at that time, is the *only* thinking one has at that point. One can request information and opinions from others, and this can be valuable information, but it is not a substitute for one's own thinking. One should *trust* one's own thinking. Trusting one's own thinking and acting on it tends to leave one alert to and aware of any results of mistakes, and one will tend to correct them. If one trusts someone else's thinking instead of one's own, one has *quit* thinking and is likely to continue with the mistaken policy in spite of any bad results. Trust your own thinking, trust your own thinking, trust your own thinking.

Any distress pattern can be eliminated by the discharge process.

some characteristics of distress patterns

3.027 If we think of our flexible intelligence as if it were gear-and-cog computing machinery, then the information input during a distress experience acts as if it had been deposited onto this machinery when the machinery was not operating, and as if it had piled up on the gears and cogs in a certain area and "jammed" them.

In another way, this mis-storage behaves as if it were a rigid scar on what used to be a flexible surface. Information from a distress experience is not available bit by bit, but only in one big tied-together chunk. If this information is recalled at all, it all comes together, unevaluated, not understood.

The mis-stored information input from a distress experience also behaves as if it were a *recording,* a very literal, detailed, complete recording of everything that went on during that distress experience.

3.028 One effect of the residue of information mis-storage left by the distress experience is quantitative. We are not as functionally intelligent as we were before the distress experience left this mis-storage upon us.

The second kind of effect is qualitative and can be examined by viewing the distress mis-storage as a recording. Carrying this distress-experience recording, we are now "booby-trapped." Our excellent intelligence is no longer dependable. It can be "turned off" and replaced by rigid, unthinking behavior whenever anything acts to restimulate the distress recording.

3.029 Once distress patterns are having a sizeable effect upon an individual, they will tend to "snowball," that is, the rehearsal of existing irrationalities will add new layers of distress almost continually.

3.030 In ways that are difficult to understand and describe, distress patterns, particularly the ones that have become chronic, can *partially* affect the human's feelings and behavior later, even when some intelligence is again operating.

3.031 A distress pattern in another human may be distinguished from rational thought or rational behavior by its non-positive character, and even, sometimes, by our feelings of dislike or discomfort. The completely dependable characteristic of a distress pattern that can *always* be used to distinguish it is its *rigidity*. Any "thought," action, or feeling which does not vary when expressed repetitively, is a pattern and needs to be handled as a pattern rather than hoped-to-be-communicated-with, argued with, etc., as a thinking person might be responded to.

3.032 A distress recording has no power of its own. Any apparent power which it seems to possess is the power of the human, borrowed and subverted by the pattern. Through such subversion, however, a distress pattern has three "pseudo-abilities": 1) The distress pattern can *persist*. As long as it exists at all, as long as it is not completely erased, it will persist with its rigid content. 2) It can *confuse* the person to whom it is attached. It continues to sound a confusing contradiction to one's rational thinking and can substitute its message or irrational conclusions for the rational thinking which the human is attempting to do. 3) The distress pattern can make its victim *forget*.

3.033 Many patterned behaviors were originally relatively successful attempts to survive in hurtful situations (given limited resources and information). These have been "locked in" because of the lack of discharge. (For example, keeping quiet in the face of physical attack may have saved a young person from further injury in the past. Although this was not necessarily the best strategy in the past and may very well be a poor strategy in the present, it will still *seem* to be "necessary for survival" in the present as long as the pattern remains undischarged.)

3.034 Every distress pattern contains physical components which impose some kinds of physical rigidities upon the client. These rigidities can be contradicted by movement against them, and physical flexibility can be recovered with discharge. To contradict the physical rigidities is likely to lead to emotional discharge as well.

3.035 The pattern "feels" exactly the same to its victim whether it is one percent discharged or ninety-nine percent discharged. We have power against patterns because of our limitless flexibility. The pattern will persist as long as it exists at all, but regardless of how we may feel as we attempt it, we *are* always capable of out-persisting the pattern.

3.036 "Numbness" indicates that too much attention is involved in the distress pattern in a situation without enough contradiction to allow the distress to be felt and discharged. Sufficient contradiction (furnished by changing the environment, by actions and activities of the counselor, or by use of "directions" against the distress by the client) will convert numbness to discharge.

3.037 Distress patterns which were installed very early tend to become deep and persistent chronic patterns (because of the numerous opportunities they have had to become restimulated and reinforced). No matter how "permanent" or "timeless" they may seem to be, they must of necessity be only patterns which *can* be contradicted and discharged completely.

3.038 Even though we have not yet seen an adult attain complete freedom from chronic patterns of powerlessness, such patterns must of necessity be *only patterns* which *can* be contradicted and discharged completely.

3.039 There is an observable spontaneous tendency for people to "return to the scene of the hurt," i.e., to seek out repeats or approximate repeats of the situation where the hurt occurred. This often, or usually, results in additional hurt, either seriously, through a re-enactment of what had been damaging before or, more lightly, by adding a fresh layer of restimulation onto the existing distress recording. This behavior seems clearly non-survival, but it can be understood as risk-taking in an attempt to approach the distress, and hoping for, or counting on, enough contradiction that the original hurt will be discharged instead of being added to. Without the knowledge and resources of Re-evaluation Counseling theory, this has not usually worked well, but it has apparently been persistently pursued by people as the only way the people could think of for approaching the distress in the hopes of discharging it.

"restimulation"

3.040 What we mean by "restimulation" is the coming into activity and the dominating of the individual by a distress pattern. The appearance of its operation has been described "as if a button on an automatic phonograph is pushed and the recording of the distress pattern moves into operation" and begins to "play the individual."

3.041 "Restimulation" is the term used to describe the process in which an individual finds the current situation similar enough to a past distressing situation that it "brings back" the feelings, the "pseudo-thinking," and sometimes the actions of the past distress. This leads the individual to act out the distress recording as if he or she were actually in the past situation. This process often takes place unawarely without the individual realizing that he or she has been restimulated.

Restimulation is also the result of an individual seeking, through introspection, to find an explanation for some intuitively-felt limitation on the individual's own clarity or functioning and bringing the pattern into operation by, with the most hopeful of intentions, putting too much attention to it in conditions where there is not enough contradiction present to produce discharge.

3.042 All old undischarged patterns can be restimulated. These include physical symptoms, even including pain and illness, as well as feelings of greater or lesser degrees of discomfort and numbness, and the "acting out" of old behavior.

3.043 Restimulation, once thought to be *involuntary*, is more helpfully viewed as a *decision*, first made for understandable reasons in an attempt to get rid of the pattern, but becoming rigid and compulsive with repeated unsuccessful repetitions. The decision becomes part of the pattern, but one is still capable of *deciding against it* by sheer determination.

3.044 A decision against restimulation is a contradiction to the distress and when followed up and intensified with other contradictions can lead to discharge of the distress pattern.

3.045 We have used the term "habit pattern" to describe the repetitive submission to restimulation and the unaware cooperation with such restimulation. (An example of such a "habit pattern" is the keeping of one's attention on one's distress habitually.) We have proposed a "reiterative decision" (a decision which is made over and over again) as a useful contradiction to such "habit patterns," which will lead to discharge and the elimination of the pattern or the "habit pattern."

3.046 At least part of every distress pattern operates below awareness. Restimulation can access an unaware trigger that replays the pattern. It may be helpful to think of changing the response to that trigger by *decision*. This can have the effect of "installing new software." Because many of the intuitive functions of our mind are non-verbal, effective change may need to include changes of more than the words involved. Words may be only a small part of the "trigger."

"acting out" distress patterns

3.047 People tend to "act out" or "rehearse" their patterns to others. In the beginning they may do this in an intuitive attempt to secure the attention of another person and achieve discharge as a means of re-emergence from the pattern. As a result of disappointment and other acquired distress when these attempts fail to work (as they usually *do* fail to work), people tend to become "locked into" acting out their patterns compulsively with resulting proliferation of distress for the individual (and for the society).

3.048 In acting out their patterns, people are pulled to try to do so in a "more comfortable" role in the re-enactment than their original role, and they thus impose distress on other persons whom they try to force into *their* own original role. This is the principal channel for the development of distress patterns by "contagion." Such "contagion" is one of the three principal sources of distress patterns—along with *accidents* and *social oppression*.

varieties, similarities, of distress patterns

3.049 The distress patterns of different persons may *appear* to be alike and may even *be* somewhat similar, but each one is completely unique in that it is the recording of the particular distress experience which that person endured, which is different than any distress experience endured by any other person. This is one reason why the "categorizing" of human distresses by the so-called "mental health" system is so damaging and unworkable. "Diagnosing" and trying to deal with distress patterns on the basis of their similarity to other patterns prevents dealing with the specific distress pattern which the victim ("client," "patient") is ready to describe and deal with if offered rational counseling.

3.050 No distress pattern is "worse" or "more repulsive" than another one. They're all just rigid, inflexible, non-thinking recordings. It is misleading to "rank" people on the basis of one's own response to the distress recordings attached to them.

3.051 There are some patterns that interfere with a human's functioning more than others. There are some patterns that have terrible effects on other people, for example, patterns involving rape or murder. Actions may have to be taken by individuals or society to contain such patterns and protect other people from being damaged by them. Such actions and activities must not interfere with or prevent the counseling of the people with such destructive patterns since, long-range, the only effective solution is the dismantling of the patterns themselves, and this can only take place through discharge, re-evaluation, and re-emergence.

3.052 Many "kinds of" patterns have a "history" of their own, having been installed by ancient oppressive conditions and passed on from generation to generation by "contagion" for hundreds of years.

3.053 Some similarities of distress patterns are common worldwide (for example, *powerlessness*). Other similarities of distress patterns are common in certain cultures and/or groups of people (for example, patterns of never being on time). In detail, of course, every distress pattern is absolutely unique to the individual because no one else ever had exactly that distress experience.

3.054 It is very common for people to have patterns which contain powerlessness, invalidation, self-invalidation, preoccupation with one's distress, inhibitions attached to the discharge processes, etc.

3.055 The oppressive society considers some patterns which fit its rigidities as "normal" and "the way to be." Other patterns will be considered by the society to be "weird" and unacceptable. All patterns are equally irrational and ultimately non-survival.

3.056 Some chronic patterns may be socially approved of and rewarded in particular oppressive societies. Others are punished. Both sorts of responses by other people (including loved ones and authority figures) fail to distinguish the human being from the pattern and thus add further hurts. These further distress recordings become linked with the original one, which is simultaneously reinforced.

dealing with distress patterns

3.057 If a distress pattern attacks you (and nothing else ever does), help is always close at hand. This help is the human being inside the distress pattern, the pattern's first victim and your natural ally against it. Reached in the ways you know or can learn, the human being will emerge to your support and the two of you will celebrate a cooperative, human triumph over distress and unreason.

3.058 In any apparent conflict between individual humans, beginning to find a solution to the conflict requires only that *one* person act outside of the distress in order to *begin* to resolve and eventually to *resolve* the conflict.

3.059 It is useless to try to "reason with" a pattern. Dealing with a *pattern* requires a completely different set of tools than dealing with a *person*. Never forget, however, that a person exists "inside the pattern" who can be reached and who can eventually become cooperative with you.

3.060 There are many ways of "handling" someone else's pattern besides counseling the person with the pattern. Even counter-violence may sometimes become necessary. Separating oneself from the patterned person may be a justifiable recourse. "Manipulation" of a pattern to good purposes may be legitimate. One is not obligated to anybody to deal with their patterns nor free them from their patterns. If possible, the person trapped in a pattern should be encouraged to seek help and be given access to a source of information that can lead him or her to use the processes of contradiction, discharge, and re-evaluation. The only permanent solution to a distressing situation caused by a distress pattern is the discharge of the distress pattern.

distress patterns are addictive

3.061 Distress patterns tend to be "addictive," as well as being the basis for all other addictions. Distress patterns tend to compel their "victims" to re-enact, as far as possible, everything that occurred in the original distress experience.

3.062 Addictive patterns that are connected to basic instinctive survival drives such as eating food (a drive at all ages) or acting sexually (an instinctive drive after adolescence) may seem, and be, difficult to discharge. This is apparently because such basic instinctive survival drives as to eat to survive or to reproduce for the survival of the species will "seem" to loan strength to the addictive distresses that become attached to them.

3.063 What are usually called "addictions," that is, the ingestion of some chemicals (drugs or alcohol or tobacco) or excessive food, are just one aspect of a pattern. *All* patterns are addictive in their effects upon the individual victim.

3.064 *Feelings* are unreliable as a guide to intelligent action. Only logical thinking is a dependable basis for action. People often "feel good" at times when hurting themselves or others and may "feel bad" when acting well as a result of contradicting distress (and therefore feeling the distress as it approaches discharge).

rational needs and "frozen" needs

3.065 There are many rational needs which a human being senses and acts to fill—air, water, food, light, exercise, information, companionship, touching, interaction with other human minds, goals, the opportunity to rest, the opportunity to sleep, safety from attack. Some of our rational needs change in the course of our development. Certain needs which are rational for an infant are not any longer rational needs for an adult.

When a person is feeling a rational need and the need is not met, the situation is distressing and can lay in a recording. Or it is possible that a recorded need is being felt and other accompanying distress has added to it the feeling of neediness. We have found it convenient in Re-evaluation Counseling to refer to these recorded feelings, and oftentimes "beliefs," of "needing" something as *"frozen needs."* These recorded "frozen needs," when restimulated, will be projected on a given situation and be felt as (and assumed to be) real needs. A common example is the individual who needed warm, reassuring parental care when very young but failed to receive it. A distressed, recorded "frozen need" for such parenting can be laid in and when later restimulated can be projected at lovers, spouses, bosses, and people in many other kinds of relationships.

The key principle in dealing with such "frozen needs" is that the "frozen need" cannot rationally be met, that attempts to "meet it" will always be doomed to failure. The "frozen need" can only be discharged. To furnish the contradiction to the "frozen need" that allows the discharge to take place can become complicated and confusing. Oftentimes, to begin with, the offer to "over-fulfill" the "frozen need" brings voluminous discharge. However, continued counseling in this way usually leads to a more demanding attitude on the part of the client (the client "raises the ante"), and the counseling relationship becomes less and less effective. Whatever way discharge is started, it is important early on in the counseling on "frozen needs" that the client be encouraged and assisted to say "good-bye to any hope" of filling the "frozen need."

3.066 Humans often feel "frozen needs" which are recorded sensations of needing and desiring that originate in past distress experiences. It is possible to make the distinction between such "frozen needs" and rational needs, possible to contradict the "frozen needs" and discharge them, and possible to meet the rational needs well. Frozen needs are often needs that were rational for us at an earlier stage but no longer are—or not in the same form or to the same extent.

3.067 It is not possible to meet frozen needs. They can only be discharged. What we did not get when we were little (e.g., parental care, full "doting" attention of others, etc.), we will never receive in those forms. We can only mourn and discharge the loss. This discharge can be completed. Rewarding experiences compatible with our present states will then be completely satisfying.

4. THE DISCHARGE PROCESS

the eliminating-distress process

4.001 Certain physical processes, used originally in our earlier evolutionary stages for other functions, have been enlisted by us in our development to accompany, support, and, in part, carry on the intellectual processes of dissolving distress recordings and re-evaluating and making usefully available the information previously present in a static form within these recordings. We have labeled this set of processes and the physical manifestations of their taking place with the collective title "discharge."

4.002 Among the physical manifestations of the discharge process are *crying* (the shedding of tears, sobbing, and grieving noises if accompanied by tears), *trembling* or *shaking* of any degree of gentleness or violence with perspiration from a cool skin (sometimes but not always accompanied by very active kidney function), *laughter* with perspiration from a cool skin, *angry words or sounds* if accompanied by perspiration from a warm skin and violent or abrupt physical movement, *laughter* accompanied by a warm skin, *reluctant talk, eager talk, relaxed laughter, yawning* (of any degree of depth or intensity), *relaxed stretching* and sometimes *scratching*.

4.003 Discharge is the process of freeing a human being of the distress recording left by hurt that has already occurred. The discharge is *not* the hurt itself.

4.004 Any distress pattern exposed to a *contradiction* tends to dissolve into discharge.

Any distress can be discharged if contradicted sufficiently, skillfully, and persistently enough.

4.005 We define *"contradiction"* as anything that allows the bearer or victim of a pattern to see the pattern as *not present-time reality.*

4.006 Any distress pattern can be eliminated completely if discharge is pursued thoroughly enough.

4.007 Even a previously unhurt person tends to not discharge a distress recording completely by himself or herself because the persistence to complete the discharge usually requires very special circumstances or motivations or must come from the insistence of a second person.

re-evaluation/re-emergence

4.008 By *"re-evaluating"* we mean the intellectual processing of the information being freed from a distress recording to be used in the same way as information is used by the mind when it appears without any distress associated with it. Re-evaluation automatically and spontaneously follows discharge as far as the discharge has freed the information in the recording to be available.

4.009 *"Re-evaluation"* is the word that we have chosen or coined to describe the process of thinking through material (in the ordinary way in which information is evaluated by human intelligence) which has previously been inaccessible because it has been part of a distress recording. The final result of re-evaluation is the same as, or at least very similar to, the evaluation of any information received without distress, i.e., the information becomes available to the intelligence bit by bit or in any quantity or combination desired. The distress content of the recording has been dissipated during the discharge process. Whatever portion of the circuitry of the central nervous system has been tied up by the distress recording is free to function again in its normal, inherent way. This re-evaluation process seems to proceed automatically, both above and below awareness, just as far as the previously-inhibiting distress has been discharged. Questioning of previously held rigidities can seem to assist in the re-evaluation of such rigidities, but the general impression of experienced counselors is that the complete re-evaluation will eventually take place spontaneously, even without any intervention by a counselor's questions.

4.010 Thinking and re-evaluation spontaneously take place as far as the discharge process has freed the previously-rigid information for available attention.

4.011 What we call *"re-emergence"* is the process of clearing the rigid distress patterns from the thinking of the client and allowing the resumption of fully rational behavior.

4.012 The process of re-emergence is ongoing. What we mean by "re-emergence" is the elimination of patterns by discharge and the recovery of the rational abilities which have been obscured or distorted by the patterns and thus re-emergence into our inherent flexible, highly-intelligent, natural functioning.

4.013 Among the characteristics of being re-emerged are: 1) being very relaxed and at ease with oneself and the environment, 2) being in benign mastery of the environment, 3) being very knowledgeable and continually learning new data, 4) being in close communicating contact with numbers of other people, 5) enjoying one's job of being benign caretaker of the earth and all its organisms, 6) being in excellent health, 7) being able to quickly discharge and recover from any new hurts which occur, 8) being in complete charge of oneself, of every situation, of all one's relationships, and 9) being able to think flexibly and rationally in all situations.

4.014 Humans, free of distress, would automatically care deeply about the universe around them and seek to work on behalf of building a just society, cleaning up the environment, and all other desirable goals.

4.015 Part of our re-emergence, "healing," and "liberation" will include elements of re-connecting with ourselves, connecting with each other, and being at ease on our planet Earth.

4.016 Buddha's "enlightenment" under the Bo tree was (necessarily) a realization by him that he was "all right."

4.017 There are some indications that if one of us reached the stage of "complete appreciation of oneself without any reservations" that person would be very close to final emergence from all patterns.

4.018 One is totally responsible for one's own re-emergence.

order of/indications of/kinds of discharge

4.019 Dependable outward indications of discharge are: 1) crying with tears, 2) shaking with cold perspiration (perspiration from a cool skin), 3) laughter with cold perspiration, 4) raging (violent physical movement, indignant noises or words, and perspiration from a warm skin), 5) laughter with perspiration from a warm skin, 6) reluctant, non-repetitive talk, 7) eager, non-repetitive talk, and 8) yawning, often accompanied by stretching and sometimes by scratching.

4.020 The various kinds of discharge *tend* to occur in a certain order.

The heaviest *emotional* hurts (approaching or approximating *a complete sense of loss*) discharge with tears (crying, sobbing). If the distress being discharged was this "deep," the discharge will begin with tears (unless a special inhibiting distress such as *fear of being ridiculed for crying* is present). After tears are completely discharged, the trembling kind of discharge ensues (with a cold skin and perspiration), then laughter (cold skin and perspiration), then raging (violent physical movement; loud, angry noises; warm perspiration), then once again laughter will occur (this time with warm perspiration), then reluctant talking, followed by eager talking, followed by a small amount of relaxed laughter, and, finally, the fading of the perception of the memory *as a distress experience*. Yawning discharge interrupts the *emotional* discharges whenever the physical distress present in the recording (which seems to act as a kind of a "core" to the recording around which the emotional distress is "wrapped") becomes available. Yawning is the dependable indication of a release of *physical* distress (pain, illness, anesthesia, fever, acute discomfort, fatigue).

4.021 "Crying from happiness" or "tears of joy" are very real phenomena. These happen when old griefs are contradicted by new safeties or new gains and can then be cried away.

4.022 Interested, non-repetitive talk is a dependable indication of discharge, even if no other indications are present.

4.023 Laughter is always discharge. It occurs at three places in the series of emotional discharges. In most cultures it is not as fiercely inhibited and disapproved of as are the other indications of discharge and is participated in in a mass way by members of the audiences of comedians and comedies. Laughter is an excellent process and certainly one to be enjoyed. Laughter does not, however, indicate a state of "happiness." If you are serene, peaceful, and relaxed, you will not laugh.

4.024 Recordings of distress experiences which have a physical hurt as a major component will eventually require a great deal of yawning discharge to completely erase, but almost always emotional discharge will need to come first to "unwrap" the physical distress and make it available for yawning. The yawning will begin spontaneously whenever it becomes possible.

4.025 Screaming by the client is not in itself a dependable indication of discharge. Caught in a heavy fear pattern, the client may scream repetitively over and over and over again with no indication that actual discharge or re-evaluation is taking place. However, the screaming or attempt to scream apparently was initiated in an effort by the client to rouse himself or herself from the fear enough to begin discharge. So, in some cases, to be allowed to scream or encouraged to scream enhances the shaking, perspiration, and laughter that are the dependable indications of actual discharge and *therefore should be encouraged*. The effect of the screaming on the environment, however, including neighbors, passing police cars, and other clients in a counseling center, needs to be taken into account. The client for whom the screaming turns out to be necessary or helpful can have sessions on a remote mountain top or deserted seashore or in a heavily sound-proofed room, or in the deepest, densest sub-basement available. (Screaming into a pillow can be a partial solution.)

4.026 Many counselors, because of their fear, will take any violent, noisy, or threatening angry sounds to be a discharge of anger. Such sounds are usually actually the *rehearsal* of a pattern, the real content of which is fear or grief, and *are not* discharge.

4.027 DISCHARGE INDICATIONS AND SEQUENCE CHART

"Kind" of Painful Emotion Tension	Manifestation During Discharge
ZEST (absence of Painful Emotion)	Happy relaxation, turning of attention away from experience of hurt.
BOREDOM	Laughter Animated Talking Reluctant Talking
LIGHT ANGERS	Laughter, warm perspiration
HEAVY ANGERS	Angry noises, violent movements, warm perspiration
LIGHT FEARS (Embarrassments)	Laughter, cold perspiration
HEAVY FEARS	Trembling, shivering, cold perspiration, active kidneys
GRIEFS	Tears, sobbing
PHYSICAL PAINS AND TENSIONS	Yawns, stretching, scratching.

The client will begin substantial discharge as close to the bottom of the painful-emotion part of this chart as the tensions exist in that particular pattern and/or as she or he is able to discharge, and will then tend to move upward on the chart as regularly as his or her particular discharge-inhibiting patterns permit.

goal of discharge process

4.028 The *goal* of the discharge process is not feeling "good" (or "comfortable") although at turning points in our re-emergence we will often feel zestfully elegant as we enjoy the gains we have accomplished. The *goal* of our counseling is the recovery of our thinking, functioning, and power. For extended periods of time, as we work through heavy distress which has previously been kept numb or occluded, we may feel acutely uncomfortable, but generally there will be a satisfying feeling of *progress* accompanying the discomfort.

discharge spontaneous, eagerly sought, often inhibited

4.029 The tendency to use our discharge processes is "built in" and spontaneous.

4.030 Discharge is always being sought in some intuitive, persistent way by every human, awarely or unawarely.

4.031 Clients are always eager to discharge whether they are aware of their eagerness or not.

The inhibition on the use of the discharge processes has been conditioned on all of the adult populations. When someone breaks through these inhibitions and begins to discharge, the example is "contagious," and the *pull to discharge* affects all listeners. The resulting discomfort often leads to the attempt by the uncomfortable people to interfere with and suppress the actions of the person doing the discharging.

4.032 Discharge is interfered with by the distress recordings themselves, by cultural conditioning, and by disapproval and interference by the societies and their cultures.

4.033 There is intense pressure in most cultures of the world at the present time to inhibit the discharge processes by semi-deliberate operations of the oppressive society. These pressures tend to keep the individual distressed and therefore conditioned to accept the oppression and the oppressed role assigned to the person in the society. The most blatant examples are the "big boys don't cry" and "don't cry" that are pounded into young males in Western cultures. All this inhibition of discharge is imposed from outside.

These incidents of being forced to not cry, not shake, not laugh, not rage, not yawn are distress experiences in themselves, and often one's re-emergence and productivity as a client can be enhanced by some sessions devoted to locating, reviewing, and discharging these particular discharge-inhibiting patterns.

4.034 The processes of discharge are themselves interfered with by distress recordings, and different people will take different lengths of time to re-establish their use. However, the patterned inhibitions will always eventually succumb to the intuitive determination of the client to reclaim the discharge process for himself or herself, and increasingly uninhibited discharge will follow.

4.035 Societies and cultures have developed patterns of suppressing discharge with the intention and effect of keeping the person conditioned and therefore conforming to the society's patterns.

4.036 The discharge processes are the crucial steps involved in the healing of hurts. The societies often treat the discharge process as if it were the hurt itself and with that excuse attempt to prevent it or cut it off in the name of "stopping the hurt."

4.037 Many patterned blocks on discharge have been installed with some kind of a "keep quiet" or "don't make noise" component. For the counselor to encourage the client to make noise by encouraging or modeling expressive noises *for* the client is often helpful *to* the client.

4.038 "Mental health" system oppression is a major vehicle for interfering with discharge. People who are the agents of this oppression frequently tell each other about the "danger" of discharge or the "danger" of "untrained people" dealing with "strong emotions." Listening to other human beings is a natural human response when not inhibited by societal conditioning. "Long-term clinical training" is not required for a person to be a good listener and to assist another human to discharge.

4.039 Mind-altering drugs (including alcohol, nicotine, caffeine, "street drugs," and medications) interfere with thinking and add new distresses. They also tend to block the effectiveness of discharge toward the healing of old hurts.

4.040 We live in an oppressive society which begins to interfere with our use of the healing/recovery/discharge process very early. As we reclaim our humanness we are going to "feel" much of the distress with which we have been numb. This means that we will not feel "comfortable" much of the time during our re-emergence—but our lives will be fuller, richer, and more expansive.

4.041 The discharge process is facilitated by the individual repeatedly making decisions that contradict her or his "patterns."

"storage" of patterns

4.042 The way in which the rigid distress patterns connect to each other and are "stored" within the mind of the client can be usefully described in several ways. In one way, it's like a completely interconnected hydraulic system. The draining of distress by discharge in one portion of the stored distress is likely to have significant effects in other portions. Certain distresses will stop operating or lose their chronic character without having awarely been worked on or discharged.

In another way, the storage of patterns behaves as if it were a great tangled "brushpile." It's very difficult to get at and remove some particular distresses promptly because they are tied into, interfered with, and protected by other distresses. Sometimes it is impossible to find a workable contradiction to an obvious distress until several distress patterns are discharged first that have been tying into and "holding down" the pattern which was the desired target of the counseling.

Many other kinds of "descriptions" will prove valuable in thinking about the total accumulation of distress.

interaction between "deciding" and discharge

4.043 The interaction between acting on the basis of thinking that has been already freed from distress by discharge, and acting on the basis of choosing and deciding to act *against* distress which has not yet been discharged but is still present, is not yet completely understood and is still being explored in the development of Co-Counseling everywhere. How much is it possible to act on decision alone, regardless of the remaining distress? How exhaustive and complete is it necessary for discharge to be before the new course of action can be effective and permanent? Much remains to be understood in this area. What seems certain is that the interaction between choosing and deciding *against* the pattern and the permanent removal of the pattern through exhaustive discharge are both re-emergent processes, that they support each other, and that neither process must be postponed for or "wait for" the other.

5. HOW TO COUNSEL

the large context

5.001 Re-evaluation Counseling is a completely natural process—it's more a question of getting rid of the blocks against it which we have had installed on us rather than having to train ourselves for an unusual activity.

5.002 We have defined *"Co-Counseling"* to mean the exchange of informed, attentive listening and assistance between two or more people. We have defined *"re-emergence"* to mean the recovery of one's occluded intelligence and of one's completely benign and powerful human nature.

5.003 The purpose of the counseling "session" is to permit and enhance discharge in order for the client to recover and, eventually, to *fully* recover, his or her flexible intelligence and all inherent human characteristics.

5.004 Everyone in the world is, almost all the time, *trying* to assume the role of client in order to re-emerge from his or her distress and regain his or her humanness. All our observations indicate that people are spontaneously deeply motivated to make the discharge-re-evaluation-re-emergence process work for themselves. People observably try to claim the role of client for themselves many times a day and in most situations. Even with all the conditioning that has usually been installed against this process and the interfering factors in people's usual functioning, the process has nevertheless worked to some extent or people would be in far worse shape even than they are. In one sense, the essence of everything we know or have learned that we call Re-evaluation Counseling is the simple notion of taking turns, of two people not trying to be clients at the same time but postponing their turn as client while they give someone else undivided attention to have a full and complete turn in that role. In a sense, everyone knows how to Co-Counsel already. The crucial additional insight is just to *take turns doing it.*

5.005 A great deal of discharge is accomplished in ordinary conversation between human beings. Even though they usually do not pay attention well or listen well to each other, the person who is talking "assumes" or pretends that the other person is listening enough so that the talker is able to process a considerable amount of the patterned rigidity into flexibility even though little or no real attention is being paid by the other person.

In other words, everyone is attempting to Co-Counsel with another person almost all the time whenever two or more individuals are together.

Put still another way, Co-Counseling is not "strange" or "new" to anyone's experience even though results are dramatically better when the listener understands the counseling process and is awarely *trying* to listen and pay attention, and when the person talking is awarely using the counseling process for re-emergence.

5.006 Since, in general, most people have a great pent-up need to be listened to well because it has happened so seldom and so inadequately in their lives, it will in general be a safe attitude to take toward other people to be interested in them, to pay respectful attention to them, to listen well and deeply, and to ask questions of them which indicate your interest in them and what they say rather than questions that express your "curiosity" about them.

To go beyond such respectful interest to being an active, directive counselor for anyone else should in general not be attempted without the informed agreement of the person whom you intend to counsel. In some emergency situations, it will certainly be justifiable to manipulate the person's patterns to help her or him assume the role of client when you are overwhelmingly certain that this is what he or she would desire and would cooperate with if she or he could. To be a "compulsive" counselor, however, and thrust oneself into the role of counselor without any request by the person viewed as client indicating his or her wish to be in that role, or without his or her understanding (at least intuitively) what you are doing, is a patterned mistake on the part of the would-be counselor.

To advance from simply paying attention and listening, to an *organized* session, should either take place spontaneously with obvious enjoyment and cooperation from the person you are considering to be a client, or it should be formalized by a simple question such as, "May I listen to you for a while?"

5.007 The rewards of *receiving* good counseling are obvious. The rewards of *giving* good counseling are at least as great and possibly greater.

5.008 For any individual to adopt and hold the attitude of being a "non-client" and, possibly, a counselor to every other person in any given situation is a useful and possible attitude to hold. The other people in a situation will either act and respond rationally, which can be met by a rational attitude on the part of the first individual, or they may act and respond irrationally, in which case they are only holding out their distresses in an effort to receive help with them. The first person then may decide to adopt the role of counselor, and if he or she does, then has only the task of being a good enough counselor to handle the situation. This decision to be counselor is completely independent on the part of the person making the decision and does not require any "agreement" on the part of anyone else. Such a decision leads to the person making the decision to be in charge of the situation. The first person may, of course, decide *not* to be counselor and tactfully withdraw from the situation but should do so without becoming "client."

5.009 Whenever you find yourself in any kind of a difficult interaction in your life in the wide world, it will be useful for you to deliberately adopt the viewpoint of a *"non-client,"* and, possibly, a *counselor*. This will tend to help you think about the situation better, encourage you to take charge, and tend to interrupt any unaware pull on yourself to try to claim someone else's attention and become a "client" in the situation.

5.010 The basic elements of Re-evaluation Counseling are present or latent in almost every relationship between humans and every conversation between them. In all these situations, regardless of appearances, there is always one human mind attempting to communicate with another human mind. In any relationship there is likely to be present a spontaneous urge to be listened to on the part of one or more people, and sometimes at least grudging acceptance of the role of *listener* by one or more persons.

5.011 The process of re-emergence is always being attempted in ordinary living although people are not usually aware that this is what they are doing. They spontaneously seek contradictions which will bring discharge by telling jokes to each other, by seeking out entertainment which allows them to laugh or cry, by going to sports events to rage and shake and cheer and laugh, etc.

5.012 It is possible to think of the counseling process as "two intelligences applying themselves to one person's re-emergence."

5.013 *Counseling* (in the sense that we will be using it in this book) consists of *two or more* intelligences focusing on *one* person and, if necessary, *one person's distress*. *Co-Counseling* consists of two intelligences taking turns as counselor and client.

5.014 Everyone wants attention. There's only sufficient attention to go around when *people take turns*.

5.015 We are peers. We each inherently have the capability to counsel each other well.

5.016 Individual thinking is greatly enhanced by attentive, non-responsive listening by another person.

5.017 It is not the client's "fault" that she or he has distress. She or he never "chose" to be hurt.

5.018 One important aspect of counseling knowledge is that it can be viewed as a *tool*. It is a tool primarily to be used by the client.

It is a reasonable expectation that an individual client will take the tool of counseling as it is offered and teach other people to be his or her Co-Counselors, teaching them to be good counselors for herself or himself, and teaching them to receive and use counseling for themselves.

Immediately, counseling is a tool to be fully used to help others to re-emerge. In teaching the others to be counselors to you yourself (it is often important that the first session consist of the new person counseling the experienced person instead of vice-versa), it will be a tool for building a cooperative relationship with all the people in your environment.

The experienced person should have the highest expectation about his or her use of the process and its effectiveness for the people around him or around her. However, *unreasonable* expectations should not be placed by yourself as a client on other Co-Counselors who are already supposed to be knowledgeable about counseling, nor placed on any particular Community of Co-Counselors. Such unrealistic expectations lead to disappointment and confusion. Any disappointment which has become attached to existing Co-Counselors or Communities should be recognized as necessarily consisting of distress, and discharged fully.

5.019 The society's "mental health" systems describe people as "mentally ill." Re-evaluation Counseling regards such people as *hurting*, not "ill." People labeled by the society as having "mental illness" simply are carrying particular distresses that the particular society refuses to tolerate. These aren't "worse" distresses than other distresses.

5.020 Terms such as "mental health," "mental illness," "normal," or "abnormal" are completely misleading. These terms were attempts to describe either the unwillingness of an individual to submit to, or function according to, an externally-imposed standard or model from other people or from a culture or a society, *or* the effects of distress patterns on an individual's functioning. If you will picture how a perfectly functioning individual would be without any distresses at all, your client is potentially exactly like that at the present. Except for the interference of the distress patterns, she or he is already functioning excellently and waits only for assistance to contradict, discharge, and be free from the patterns.

5.021 No Co-Counselor is under any inherent *obligation* to help solve the problems of another person by counseling him or her in order to help him or her re-emerge from his or her distresses. However, it is inherently pro-survival for humans to care about and assist in the functioning and improvement in functioning of other humans. The better that all of us think about and take action towards enhancing the survival of all others, the more effective we will be and the more we will improve the lives of all humans. Optimally, however, this should be a voluntary decision on each person's part, not an action taken through feelings of obligation.

Given the present conditions in the world, it is correct not to include in the Re-evaluation Counseling Community people who are unable to contribute effectively *to the Community* as well as *take from it*. While this is true, it is nevertheless important that we do not buy into any discriminatory attitude about *the worth of any human beings* because of the degree to which they are involved with distress patterns or the *kind* of distress patterns with which they are involved. If we ourselves as counselors were free enough of our distresses, any client's distresses would be easily handled by us. The judgmental description of "too deeply-distressed" clients is really a projection on the clients of the distress of too-inflexible, too-timid ("too deeply-distressed"?) counselors.

5.022 Part of the art of being a Co-Counselor includes training a new person to be one's excellent counselor by allowing that person to counsel one *first* so as to avoid "imprinting" the new person with the role of client in his or her first experience. It includes continuing to train the person to be exactly the right counselor for oneself. It includes "counseling the counselor" regularly and in short intervals, which can be interspersed in the time of one's own session, if the counselor at any moment becomes so confused as to need a temporary exchange of the roles.

5.023 It is possible to counsel and to be counseled even if the client and the counselor do not speak a common language. Language is only one of many communication channels which people have with each other. Being listened to with attention and concern enhances the ability of the client to think about what she or he is saying, even if the person listening has little or no understanding of the details of what is being said.

5.024 The skills of being a client and being a counselor can be learned in many different ways. To participate in a counseling *class*, however, seems to be very effective for most people. To be present in a group observing a demonstration in which another human being is discharging and re-evaluating tends to "cut through" the observers' patterns and allow them to grasp the reality of the process. The message that the patterns are not "reality" seems to reach people in a class in an effective way.

5.025 People coming into Co-Counseling with backgrounds in various "therapies" (either as the "therapists" or objects of the "therapy") frequently feel "positive" about certain rigidities that they have experienced in these other "therapies" because they have achieved some discharge while using them and *do* recognize the beneficial effects of the discharge. Any "mixing in" of these ideas will slow down the people's understanding of Re-evaluation Counseling, however, and will eventually cause conflicts and difficulties in their re-emergence.

It is true that there are certain common patterns in the culture, so common that a direction against them can be used by many different people. But the process of using such "set exercises" or following directions slavishly will tend to seal off the person's mastery and understanding of the Co-Counseling process and the operation of the intelligence itself. So, in general, it is best to resist the well-intentioned and "sincere" use of such rigidities or set exercises within the Co-Counseling context or in the Re-evaluation Counseling Community.

5.026 We sometimes make a distinction between "elementary counseling" and "advanced counseling." These terms undoubtedly have slightly different meanings for each person who uses them. Perhaps a useful meaning for the phrase "advanced counseling" is the aware taking of responsibility for the integration of Re-evaluation Counseling insights into one's life. This can mean taking full responsibility for applying these insights' both when one is client and when one is counselor and awarely claiming as one's goal to have a successful life in all aspects.

beginning/ending sessions

5.027 Many sessions, both between Co-Counselors and in ordinary living with non-Co-Counselors, begin spontaneously, without planning or formal protocol. The client makes contact with the counselor and, eager or desperate to discharge, begins to do so. If the counselor pays attention and permits the client to continue to discharge, the counselor *has made an informal agreement* for the session to take place. In times of emergency this is undoubtedly correct and praiseworthy, but it is *not* optimum and, used as a model, can lead to abuse of the counselor. It is much better to make firm, two-way agreements and conduct sessions with care for and courtesy toward both parties. Below are some of the factors to be kept in mind when beginning a session:

Exchange "news and goods." This is a recital of anything positive about recent occurrences or thinking.

It will improve a session if the client has reminded himself or herself of his or her power and independence, has outlined his or her goals, and has been listened to on any immediate, current distress.

When you are counselor, it is sometimes useful to start a session by calling the client's attention *to you*. For instance, greet him or her in a way that he or she can respond to. It may be useful to direct his or her attention also to the *present environment*.

Often it is useful to begin a session by interrupting any isolation that may be present for the client. This can be done in some way acceptable in the culture, for example, to shake hands, to bow, to hold one or both hands, to sit close, or to hug.

5.028 To end a session well, the client may find it useful to review his or her perspective for future counseling and review the concluded session in terms of what worked well and what did not work well. In a good counseling relationship, the counselor will be thinking about the future of the client and will help the client voice some kind of clear attitude toward what directions and policies he or she will hold between sessions until the next session, and what steps can be taken to use the new insights of the concluded session.

5.029 If for any reason the client's attention has become heavily involved in distress *during* the session (this can happen through receiving "bad news," through restimulations, or through injuries or accidents), the counselor should take responsibility for seeing that the client's attention is, as much as possible, directed away from the distress, that he or she is helped to an "awareness of present time" and to preparing to cope with whatever situation he or she faces following the session.

The counselor should never pronounce a negative judgement or a negative interpretation about the session to the client. This includes not being negative about the counselor's *own* role. Let the client make her or his own judgement about that. Otherwise, it may be just the counselor rehearsing his or her own distress. Any session will always turn out to have been of some benefit to the client.

phenomena during sessions

who's in charge of the session?

5.030 Arguments and discussions which occasionally have arisen about who is "in charge of the session," the client or the counselor, are quite misleading. The client and the counselor have two completely separate roles in the session, and each of them is "completely in charge" of his or her separate role.

5.031 Basically, the client needs to be free to decide what she or he wishes to counsel on. It is a disservice for the counselor to try to make this choice for the client unless the client asks the counselor for a suggestion. This guideline is also modified by agreements and commitments between the client and the counselor, where the client has asked to be reminded, urged, or even required to address certain distress which the client otherwise finds it very difficult to face.

This can also be modified in the case of a client who compulsively brings up distress which the client does not have enough aware attention to handle, or for which the counseling pair have not found adequate contradiction in their past attempts. In such a case, the counselor can properly insist on the client working only on material on which she or he can discharge. Alternatively, the counselor can insist that the client work with attention-*gaining* techniques, in preparation for tackling the heavy distress later.

safety/confidentiality

5.032 In order to counsel the client well it is often necessary to establish the reality of "safety" by having the client counsel on the safe factors in the session. The more "unsafe" the client *feels*, however, if he or she *is* safe, the more likely it is that the actual safety occurring in the present is "melting the frozen fear," and the numbness is lifting in preparation for the discharge (which will be indicated by shaking, laughter, and perspiration) of the heavy fear. The counselor, in such a case, will encourage the client to "act cheerful," physically cling to the counselor, "threaten the counselor," or use any other of the proven techniques for helping start the fear to discharge.

5.033 One characteristic which is crucial for the Co-Counseling relationship is that the relationship *be* safe. A good Co-Counseling relationship is of enormous benefit to both partners. These benefits must not be compromised by any attitudes or activities that lower the safety of the relationship for either the counselor or the client.

The *actual* safety of the relationship needs to be distinguished from *feelings of safety or lack of safety* which can vary greatly depending on the material which the client is engaged in processing. Such feelings of lack of safety are often an indication of actual great safety and trust which has contradicted old fears and distrusts enough that they are being felt as they discharge or prepare to be discharged. Actual safety is separate from the issue of restimulated feelings or contradicted feelings which are being discharged, and this actual safety needs to be thought about, guarded, and treated as of the greatest importance.

The "confidentiality rule" is **sacred** and of the utmost importance. This rule is that nothing which the client reveals in a session, or in his or her turn in a class, a support group, or a workshop, is to be repeated to anyone—not to anyone outside of the Community, not to anyone in the Community who is not present, not to anyone who is or was present at the client's turn, not to the client himself or herself. (The sometimes-heard excuse that "I was so upset by what the client said, I have to tell you to get over my feelings" is purely a patterned excuse to rehearse a compulsion to gossip. The "upset" person can discharge without repeating what the client had said, or without identifying the client at all.)

Beyond this, it is important that the client be viewed as fully peer and as a marvelously valuable human being, who deserves complete respect at all times regardless of what weight of patterned distress he or she carries or how addicted he or she is to acting the distress out.

no "bad" feelings

5.034 In the cultures in which we live, certain feelings are often labelled "bad," as if their existence should be denied, as if one should be ashamed of having them, and as if to feel them is something to be avoided. Actually there are no "bad" feelings; there are just the *natural* feelings of a well-functioning self and *distress* feelings, which are signals to remove or avoid the cause of the distress, or that discharge is needed, or that there is some confusion needing to be resolved in the case of the pseudo-attractive feelings attached to yielding to an addiction.

Condemning feelings, suppressing feelings, being ashamed of feelings, is irrational. Feelings are to be treated as signals—enjoyed if they are pleasant and rational, discharged on if they are not from present time, and questioned and dealt with if they are related to an addiction. However, feelings are *not* suitable guides to action. Only logical thinking should guide one's actions.

5.035 No matter how unreasonable or even "unbelievable" a client's feelings or patterned behavior may seem, there is always a reason behind the feelings or behavior which, when asked for, elicited, and contradicted, will "make sense" of what has been going on and can be completely discharged and "cleaned up" with resulting freedom from the behavior and feelings.

apparent non-cooperation

5.036 Whenever a counselor cannot understand the distresses of a particular client, or the client "appears" as if he or she "doesn't want" to be a "good" (cooperative) client, it usually means that there are still unrecognized distresses gripping the client. In such a case of a "very difficult client" much of the significant material that needs to be discharged has usually become occluded. Such a tangle can often require a great deal of patience and persistence on the part of the counselor.

identifications

5.037 Because of the tendency of patterned distress to link up rigidly with other distress patterns, "identifications" tend to become rigidly attached to factors in the counseling situation. The counseling situation itself may become identified with incidents of being "grilled" in the past. The counselor may become identified with persons in the client's past (of the same gender, the same size, the same skin color, or any other possible similarity).

These identifications need to be processed and removed or they will interfere with the success of the counseling session and hinder re-evaluation. Positive identifications, that is, identifications of the counselor with someone who was an ally or supporter in the past, may bring enthusiasm from the client and tempt the counselor to "bask" in the warm approval of the client, but such positive identifications interfere with the effectiveness of counseling just as do the negative ones.

Such positive identifications can be effectively used for discharge. For the counselor to use the identification in this way for the client's benefit is acceptable. However, in such a case, it will be best if the counselor asks the client to specifically contradict the identification, perhaps by saying to the counselor statements such as, "You are not the most wonderful person in the world," "You are actually very different than my father who died when I was a child," or "I trust that you are a good counselor but would be a very poor lover."

5.038 The counselor needs to check regularly for any identifications that have taken place: "Whom do I remind you of?" "How am I like him or her?" "How else am I like him or her?" "How else?" "How else?" "How else?" "How am I different from him or her?" "How else?" "How else?" "How else?"

5.039 The discovered identification may lead to valuable discharge. "If I were him, what would you like to say to him right now?" "Say it again." "Say it again." "Say it again."

"dramatizing"/"rehearsing"

5.040 Any apparent thinking or feeling or speaking or acting in the direction of supporting or rehearsing any part of the content of a distress recording can safely be assumed to be itself part of the distress recording—not the thinking of the client. (To display the distress pattern by acting it out in a session *can* become a contradiction.)

5.041 We have used the phrases "dramatizing a pattern" or "rehearsing a pattern" to indicate the useless acting out or verbal replaying of the content of a distress pattern without any discharge or re-evaluation occurring. Co-Counselors have sometimes mistakenly used these phrases in a pejorative, invalidating way, a way of *reproaching* the client. This is not helpful.

It is true that simply acting out a pattern repeatedly tends to reinforce it rather than dissolve it, if no discharge occurs. Yet there is an advantage often in the counseling process of hearing and seeing the pattern clearly in order to understand it and prepare effective contradictions against it. ("Every pattern deserves one free trip across the chopping block so one can determine where to accurately bring the cleaver down on its later passages.") It is also true that, in a sense, the pattern is being recapitulated as it discharges, and this is thoroughly desirable. So, it is probably useful to restrict our use of the words "dramatizing" and "rehearsing" when applied to patterns, to the unprofitable, useless re-enacting of the patterns that adds a thin layer of reinforcement and produces no benefit.

The most primitive counseling can still sometimes "work." In the very beginnings of Re-evaluation Counseling we often did not know what to do except encourage the client to repeat a rehearsal of the distress pattern over and over. It's still possible to find oneself with a client who is blocked on doing anything but repeating the distress. A confident counselor can relaxedly insist that such a client repeat the distress so many times in the face of the counselor's relaxed encouragement that a kind of boredom intervenes and the client, willy-nilly, notices the senselessness of what he or she has been repeating and begins to discharge. This is the antithesis of "skilled" counseling, but it can still work.

5.042 It is, in general, a very valid and important assumption for every counselor to make that the client is *always* doing the very best he or she can do at any particular moment. This may seem a strange assumption when the client is obviously rehearsing a pattern and it seems "obvious" to the counselor that it would be possible for the client to contradict the pattern instead of rehearsing it. But it will be true that at that moment rehearsing that pattern is the very best that that client can do without some kind of an intervention from outside.

In the tangle of patterns which the client is trying to thread her way through, the best solution that has been so far calculated by her is to rehearse the pattern in the hopes that it will gain the attention of someone (the counselor) who will then *furnish* a contradiction. This is one possible thing that the counselor is thus being invited to do. If the counselor assumes that the client is doing "the best she can," it means that if the situation is to be improved (as the counselor obviously desires and can assume that the client also desires) then the change in the situation that is needed *can* come from the counselor.

For the counselor to slip into feeling critical or impatient with the client at that point is intruding the counselor's distress into the client's session. For the counselor instead to think what contradictions *the counselor* can come up with to help turn the rehearsed pattern into discharge is, on the contrary, very helpful. Whenever a client is "stuck," or appears to be "stuck," the first guess of the counselor should probably be that some "word from outside," probably from the counselor, is necessary.

re-evaluation

5.043 The re-evaluation process is the freeing up of the abilities to think, the releasing of the information (that was stuck in the pattern) to become useful, flexibly available information, and the re-calculation of the past conclusions which had been reached with the patterned material as a limiting factor on the thinking. Re-evaluation takes place spontaneously as far as the discharge process has reached to make it possible. Sometimes the re-evaluation will not be noticed for a long time, until the different attitude toward and the different handling of the environment comes to one's attention.

Sometimes the process is very rapid and very aware. After a major turning point in the discharge of a chronic pattern, clients will report that they're aware of a tremendous amount of computation taking place, no matter what else they are doing, and even in their sleep. They will say that they can "feel the wheels whir" in their thinking and that the process is very exciting, encouraging, and restful as it takes place.

For the client to be listened to in her or his excited reports of the re-evaluation that's taking place seems to expedite the process. It tends also to be very encouraging to the counselor and others who hear the reports. This process will go on spontaneously, is encouraged by conscious recognition and listening, but should never be "forced" because of some eagerness or anxiety on the part of the counselor. The client does not need interference at that point. It's best to just sit back and enjoy what's going on.

physical distress/yawns

5.044 Past physical injuries, illnesses, allergic conditions, etc., have left distress recordings on the client wherever they have not been discharged. Almost all distress recordings contain some physical distress as part of the past recorded situation. Some recordings are dominated by their content of physical distress. Such recordings, when restimulated enough to become chronic, present chronic pain, discomfort, or physical malfunction. These can be discharged, and where the permanent injury is not too severe, recovered from *completely*.

What is crucial for good counseling on such distresses is that the client be helped not to rehearse the distress, not to put attention into feeling it and suffering from it, but that the client's attention be placed strictly on information or directions that are *contradictory* to the physical distress. The person in chronic physical distress restimulation is urged and helped to put his or her attention on incidents of *well-being*, of comfort, of easy, relaxed enjoyment of physical functioning.

The emotional content of the distress recording will usually tend to be discharged first. (The pattern behaves as if the physical distress had become the *core* of the recording and the emotional distress had become wound around it and covering it like the successive wrappings on the interior of a golf ball.)

The appearance of yawns is a signal that the physical distress itself is beginning to discharge. Their appearance should be greeted with encouragement and enthusiasm by the counselor, and the client should be asked to repeat whatever phrases or actions preceded the yawns. A drowsy, relaxed tone of voice adopted by the counselor and yawning noises or actual yawns made by the counselor will tend to encourage continued yawning by the client. A difficulty which the counselor should be aware of is that yawns usually tend to feel "unimportant" to the client. Such yawns will tend to feel "less exciting" than the emotional discharge which the client has been experiencing up until that point. Reassurance by the counselor that important work is being done can prove useful or even necessary for the client to keep on with this important discharge (which will eventually erase the physical distress and/or malfunctions).

first thoughts/"flash answers"

5.045 When asking questions of the client, the counselor will find it useful to repeatedly ask the client for his or her "first thought" immediately after asking any other question. Such a request for the "first thought" helps the client get his or her spontaneous thinking expressed against the suppressing effect of censoring patterns that have commonly been installed on individuals in our cultures.

5.046 Re-evaluation Counselors have learned the importance of a client's *first* thoughts. The intelligence of the client in terms of hearing a question, searching the client's memory for useful or significant answers, and replying, is extremely fast. It often takes only a fraction of a second for this enormously complex process or series of processes to take place. The client on some level understands the question to mean, "What thought in this situation will bring discharge or allow you to discharge?" So the quickly-computed answer that the client comes up with at once is likely to be very, very effective if uttered, repeated, and discharged with. However, almost all clients have had a series of painful experiences which have left them "doubting" their first thoughts, not "noticing" their first thoughts, feeling too doubtful of their own thinking or too embarrassed by old feelings that they will be laughed at or ridiculed, to dare to respond with their actual first thought. "Patterned" circuits tend to operate very quickly to occlude the first image or first thought that the client's mind furnished. The client is likely to feel that he or she must present an "acceptable" first thought or a rationalized explanation of the whole situation.

A skilful counselor will pay prompt, rapid, "demanding" attention to the first sound, the first words, the first expressions on the client's face, and seek to have the client repeat them until the client himself or herself cannot help but notice the significance. Often the client has a first thought that is expressed only with a grunt, but tends to follow it with a detailed analysis of the situation which expresses in some form or other the pattern itself. If, instead of cooperating with this analysis, the eager counselor asks for the repetition of the grunt and appears more and more delighted the more times the client furnishes it, the doors can be opened for very heavy discharge.

5.047 The human mind does not operate at the same speed as electronic computers. Communication between neurons depends on certain chemical compounds which must move between the separate cells. This is very fast compared to physical movements of our bodies, for example, but it's very slow compared to the speed-of-light transmission of electronic signals in electronic computers. The human mind, however, operates by *parallel processing*, which computer science is only currently beginning to explore. With the use of these parallel channels the human mind is extremely efficient and fast.

This means that the "intuitive" thinking, which can be tapped in the counseling process, is often very rapid. We have assumed for a long while in Re-evaluation Counseling that human intuitive thinking is rational and operates on the same basis as the carefully reasoned out, carefully checked thinking that we use in logic or mathematics. Because patterns parasitize on the functioning of our minds, we use logical rigor to confirm our intuitive results and eliminate any patterned inaccuracies that could have crept in. Another set of patterns, however, infest the process for most of us, which are the patterns of *doubting* the accuracy of our own thinking and especially doubting and discrediting the answers that come rapidly.

To contradict these patterns by trusting in the "flash answers" that the client comes up with during the counseling process improves the effectiveness of counseling greatly. One can, over and over again, ask the client for occluded information and then insistently and confidently insist on him or her telling his or her first thought. With such a "first thought" elicited and repeated, very valuable information about the client, leading to voluminous and important discharge, will be forthcoming.

To confidently insist that the client give her or his "first thoughts" can be assisted by the counselor's assurance, "It doesn't have to make sense, just what was the thought?" Material can be brought out of occlusion this way. The amazing accuracy of the client's mind can be demonstrated, and whole areas of the client's expertise can be brought into regular daily functioning. It is a dramatic way of getting the client "in touch with himself or herself" and expediting the re-emergence process.

5.048 In securing flash answers it will often help to get the client's agreement ahead of time not to censor or withhold any "flash thoughts."

inhibition of discharge/"control patterns"

5.049 Incidents of being forced to not cry, not shake, not laugh, not rage, not yawn are distress experiences in themselves, and often one's re-emergence and productivity as a client can be enhanced by some sessions devoted to locating, reviewing, and discharging these particular discharge-inhibiting patterns.

5.050 Because the spontaneous attempts by the client to discharge have been suppressed or discouraged by other individuals and by the society, some distress recordings have become attached to other distress recordings which act to inhibit the discharge process itself. These can be general in their effect, that is, "Don't be upset!" or specific: "Don't cry," "There's nothing to be afraid of" (with the meanings, "Don't shake," "Don't laugh,"), "Control your temper," or "Cover your mouth when you yawn."

These peripheral anti-discharge patterns have been called "control patterns" by Co-Counselors in the past, and sometimes considerable effort has been put into trying to contradict them (and, alas, into criticizing the clients for having them) in an effort to make the general process of discharge less inhibited and easier. This may sometimes (rarely) be useful and necessary, but experience to date has been that it's better to pay attention to furnishing contradictions to the pattern over-all (at least, usually) rather than "sharp-shooting" at the so-called control patterns separately.

"protection of patterns by patterns"

5.051 It can happen that a particular distress pattern which has been targeted by the client and the counselor to be discharged will be "defended" or "held in place" by another pattern which is interfering with the discharge of the one targeted. For example, a pattern of "mistrust" may interfere with the client's accepting the counselor's help on the targeted pattern, and at least part of the "mistrust" pattern will have to be discharged first before the targeted pattern can be dealt with. This interlocking of patterns and "protection of patterns by patterns" can become quite complicated and can occur in series. To untangle this may try the patience of both client and counselor but if the patterns are interlocked in this way will turn out to be necessary. A simple example of this is a pattern which has the client avoiding looking at the counselor because to do so brings tears.

Becoming over-preoccupied with such "control patterns," however, can result in the client feeling harassed or criticized by the counselor and usually needs to be replaced by a broader approach.

"cafeteria-tray-dispenser syndrome"

5.052 As long as there is any distress remaining, part of a client's intelligence and will is always operating, often below awareness, as long as there seems to be any hope of discharge, to keep the discharge and re-emergence process in operation(*So far* no adult has had any experience with being completely free of *all* distress.) This will often have the effect of what we sometimes have called the "cafeteria-tray-dispenser syndrome." As soon as one distress has been dealt with, the client's mind, usually without any *aware* decision, finds itself involved with the next layer of distress. When this operates on a major scale it has been described as an action by "the little girl downstairs" or "the little boy downstairs," who is glad that the part of the person functioning in present time is enjoying the success and freedom from the hurts that have been discharged but who is, personally, still "hanging by her or his thumbs from the dungeon wall" and is able to force the next load of distress on the attention of the present-time part of the person as a way of demanding relief.

5.053 As client, you can "make a deal" with the "little girl downstairs" to discharge on the next load of a specific distress *in sessions* in exchange for her letting you have the present-time use of your free attention *between sessions*.

challenges to the client

5.054 No challenge should be deemed too difficult or too imposing for a client to tackle. Yet if a client chooses to work on making a commitment to getting his socks on straight, the counselor should not reject or scorn the proposal. The client's vast intelligence may very well have chosen this as a place to start work that will have the most profound consequences.

On the other hand, a client can have very productive sessions on such themes as: "I, personally, will see to it that the danger of nuclear war or nuclear explosions or nuclear holocaust will forever be eliminated." The counselor should not conclude that a commitment of this scope is only pretense and bombast on the part of the client. It may start out as such, but it can develop into a serious proposal and project. The capacity and power of any human mind is inherently much greater than the might of a billion nuclear bombs.

exhaustion

5.055 Exhaustion is a form of distress, and an experience of exhaustion will tend to leave a distress recording with a content of exhausted feelings. Additional experiences of exhaustion can restimulate and add to the existing recording and also add an additional amount of fatigue. A person for whom such distress recordings accumulate can eventually become chronically in a fatigued state, or the recording may be so close to chronic that even a small amount of additional overexertion can bring feelings of exhaustion, at least temporarily. Such a person may seem "unable to rest" or unable to "recover from fatigue." In such a case, discharge, often a considerable amount of discharge, is needed before the client can "rest." What kind of discharge is needed will be impossible to predict ahead of time, but almost always there will be some anxious "being on guard" attitudes involved that will have prevented the person from relaxing.

What has worked well is for the counselor to announce to the client that for a specific period of time (one minute, five minutes, one hour, eight hours), the counselor will "stand guard" and see that nothing that the client could possibly be responsible for "goes wrong" in that period. In making such a statement the counselor must be believable, must mean the commitment, must intend to keep the commitment, and must be able to carry it out. The counselor may have the client lie down, may sit beside the client and hold the client's hands, or the counselor may take the client on his or her lap, sing lullabies, recite restful poetry, or repeat the counselor's commitment to the client over and over again.

Sometimes the client, on finding the counselor's commitment believable, bursts into wild sobbing immediately. Sometimes the client begins to yawn and yawn. Sometimes the client immediately falls asleep, even standing up. Even if the promised time is no longer than one minute, the ensuing discharge often has profound effects on the client and allows him or her to rest in ways he or she had not previously been able to. The discharge of the anxiety and recorded exhaustion needs eventually, of course, to be carried through to completion.

5.056 There is a recent phenomenon of chronic exhaustion which has shown up in the wide world and inside the Community of Re-evaluation Counselors. Some medical people are convinced that there is a particular virus or perhaps a group of viruses involved. Others feel that it is "psychological," which is as close as they can come in their language to suspecting that a distress pattern is involved.

At the same time, it has become plain in counseling that fatigue *is* a distress, that it can be recorded, and, when restimulated enough additional times by new fatigue, can become a monstrous pattern, easily restimulated into an enormous sensation of fatigue by even a little additional fatigue. These patterns of fatigue are not eliminated by rest alone. The existence of undischarged anxiety seems to make it impossible for the person to rest enough. The technique in Re-evaluation Counseling called "standing guard" (see 5.055 above) has the counselor assuming total responsibility for everything that the client feels needs to be done, that the client feels any responsibility for, or anxiety about.

The counselor announces that he or she will "stand guard" to see that nothing happens or goes wrong that the client could possibly prevent if she or he stayed alert and aware, and therefore the client is free to rest and give up all responsibility. If the counselor's offer is believable, the typical response on the part of the client is enormous discharge, sometimes violent crying, sometimes heavy shaking, sometimes prodigious yawns. Sometimes the client, even while standing up, simply leans on the counselor and goes to sleep. A substantial amount of discharge achieved while a counselor is "standing guard" seems to allow the client to become free from the pattern of exhaustion to a great degree and then to rest. There are those who suspect that this is the workable remedy, where it can be offered, for the widely discussed "chronic fatigue syndrome," and that the viruses, although they may be present, are not by any means the decisive cause of the fatigue. Certainly, in any case, the use of the "standing guard" technique is indicated for anyone who is suffering from chronic fatigue. It will be helpful to whatever extent it is used, even if it does not turn out to be the complete solution of the chronic fatigue syndromes.

dreams (This section is the same as 13.010.)

5.057 The client's dreams can be used very effectively in counseling. This has been guessed at or intuited in many past philosophies, religions, and therapies. Various ways to use the dreams to the dreamer's benefit have been attempted. It is our experience in Re-evaluation Counseling that having anyone else "interpret" the dreamer's dream to the dreamer is unlikely to be helpful, is almost certain to create confusion, and may even be harmful.

To understand the nature of sleep and the nature of dreaming will be helpful. Sleep is *not* unconsciousness. When it is functioning well, the human's mind is always active—awake or asleep. Sleep is a state or a time of cutting down on the input of new information (by closing the eyes, avoiding noise, or arranging that any noise is at least repetitive, and arranging tactile comfort and a comfortable temperature) in order to "catch up" on one's evaluation of the information that has been received and accumulated during the waking hours.

This evaluation tends to proceed in two manners. The routine information that does not have tension or distress attached to it is simply, easily, and rapidly reviewed in "non-dreaming" sleep. The sleeper lies relaxed and is at least largely unaware of the process taking place.

When this non-dreaming sleep has been completed, a kind of re-evaluation is attempted. The sleeper's attention turns to the accumulated information received during the day or prior times *that has tension or restimulation of some sort attached to it*. During this "dreaming sleep" the sleeper is much more active, is likely to move in his or her sleep, and, particularly, rapid eye movements are noticeably taking place behind the sleeper's closed eyelids. The more critical levels of the sleeper's mind seem to become engaged at this point, and, the more tense the material being addressed, the closer it is pushed to the aware thinking levels of the sleeper. (We have reason to think that certain levels of one's rational mind that characteristically operate closer to awareness are more effective in the solving of difficult problems.) This manner of reviewing tense information from the past involves dreaming, and the more tense the material, the more vivid the dream is likely to seem.

The often-chaotic, surprising relationships expressed in the dream reflect the chaotic, random connections made during restimulation. This is probably true of our waking restimulations as well, but under waking conditions we tend to censor the randomness in order to make it appear to ourselves and others that there is some point and purpose to the restimulation. The more tense the material being addressed in dreaming sleep, the more vivid the dream becomes, and if the tension reaches a certain point the sleeper is wakened from sleep by his or her intelligence in order to secure more reassurance from the current environment of the existence of actual reality in contrast to the pseudo-reality of the dream.

The process of dreaming seems to be *similar* to the process of re-evaluation to some extent, and of course re-evaluation can take place during dreams as well, but it is not usually a complete re-evaluation that is achieved. Instead the results seem to be something like "knocking off the sharpest corners" of the tense material so that the tense material can be restored to the usual "brushpile" type of storage of distress for address at a later time when there will be (perhaps) more resource or more contradiction available.

This means that the dream that is remembered or can be remembered is an important clue to distress that needs discharge and re-evaluation. (Unfortunately, it does *not* follow that the dream that cannot be remembered has necessarily been re-evaluated well and needs no more attention. This is because there are many "forgetter" distress patterns involved for many people that interfere with their remembering of their dreams.)

It follows that every sleeper, optimally, should have the opportunity to tell her or his dreams to an interested audience early in the morning (perhaps at the breakfast table). Everyone's days will go better if dreams can be exchanged and listened to in the morning.

When counseling a client about a dream, the overall technique is quite straightforward. The counselor has the client narrate the dream repeatedly, over and over and over many times. If time is short, the counselor may even "crowd" the process by asking the client for the "significance" which the client assigns to the dream. When enough time is available, the client will spontaneously make these evaluations and will share them with the counselor if it appears safe and useful to do so.

A child awakened from sleep by a "bad dream" and seeking company and reassurance from parents or other adults should be encouraged to tell the dream many times before going back to sleep, and discharge should be encouraged and persisted with. If the child is allowed to resist telling the dream and goes to sleep immediately, the opportunity to unload the distress will have been missed, and the distress will go back into occlusion again.

The repetitive dream is almost certain to be an occluded distress incident trying to force its way to the client's awareness. Again, simply repeating the dream many times, with the addition of any contradictions to the distress which the counselor and the client together can evolve, will lead to discharge and the lifting of the occlusion.

(The currently-occurring revelations of the widespread sexual abuse of children have made the concentration on the repetitive nightmare an important and principal channel for this liberating process of freeing the victim from the terrified occlusion of these distresses.)

Counseling on dreams is an extremely useful channel in the general process of discharge and re-evaluation. The fact that the client has been having the dream is one indication that the client has made some kind of judgment that the material is ready to be addressed and discharged.

"getting lost" in distress

5.058 Rarely, a misjudgment of available counseling resource is made by a client (by a client's pattern), causing a "spiraling down" into preoccupation with distress. If this happens, actions found useful in the past, and therefore recommended, are: 1) encouraging the client to sleep, 2) insisting on the client returning at once to "on the job," ordinary work, and 3) refusing to allow counselors to "counsel" the person (i.e., to reinforce the client's preoccupation with the distress) and instead have counselors insist on the client's attention being pulled to present-time activity. If the "mental health" system becomes involved, counselors should, in most cases, cooperate while shielding the person from the "mental health" system's abuses.

It can sometimes happen at an RC workshop that a person who has been functioning as well as the other people will suddenly "flip out," will begin to rehearse his or her distress incessantly, and will become more and more preoccupied with it the more attention is given to him or her. This seems usually or often to be caused by an unaware and unannounced decision on the part of the person that, since there are large numbers of people who seem able to pay attention surrounding one at the workshop, it is a tempting opportunity to bring up *all* one's distress, rehearse it at the workshop, and hopefully force everyone at the workshop, including the leadership, to concentrate their attention on the dramatizing person so that she or he can discharge "all her or his distresses at once." Needless to say, this is not a workable program. It is a way of becoming "swallowed up" by one's recordings, including helplessness recordings, and violates some of the well-known necessities for good Co-Counseling and re-emergence.

The most serious difficulty is caused by the naive attitude of other people at the workshop that "this person is 'upset' and needs attention; therefore I will be a 'good counselor' and pay him or her lots of attention." This simply reinforces the patterned error into which the "flipped out" one has drifted and encourages him or her further and further into his or her lost preoccupation with distress.

The leader of the workshop must be very firm that people are *not* to pay attention to the dramatizer, that the dramatizer *is* to engage in useful activity and, if necessary, leave the workshop and get back to work on a regular job.

A person who has fallen into this "flip out" state will have a tendency, of course, to repeat the difficulty in similar circumstances, but the situation is not hopeless. It's necessary to have a clear theoretical discussion with the person and to obtain commitments from him or her once his or her attention is in present time again. Later this should be followed by a very cautious exploration of the distress that lies behind this desperate "blackmailing" of the person's associates in an attempt to secure assistance that is neither realistic nor available.

understanding being a counselor/attitudes/actions

5.059 Ninety-eight percent of all counseling could be considered to be "helping the client discharge." The client's problems are not solved unless they are solved by him or by her. The job of the counselor is not to think out solutions for the client, but to help the client discharge so that the client's own intelligence can deal with the problem. The most a counselor can do beyond helping the client to discharge is to offer a new viewpoint on an issue (which, if it expedites the discharge, will generally be because it offers a viewpoint contradictory to the pattern) *or* to furnish information that the client may be lacking (*or* show a client where such information can be obtained, *or* encourage the client to get more information).

5.060 *Aware listening* can be considered to be ninety percent of effective Co-Counseling, even for advanced Co-Counseling. People often need to be listened to for a long time *before* being given any direction (or even offered a verbal contradiction).

Many people's first few sessions (or even first hundred sessions) will include talking, laughing, and yawning, but no other discharge. This is fine. The counselor cannot know if the client is moving forward decisively or not and can only make educated guesses. An interpretation of "moving forward" depends on the client's goals and the client's own clear thinking. The counselor who feels impatience with the client's rate of "progress" should arrange to discharge this impatience in the counselor's own sessions when client.

5.061 It will be helpful to the counselor at the beginning of the counseling session to review in her or his mind (or, if necessary, aloud), four steps of preparation for beginning the session.

In Step 0, the counselor reviews his or her own goal of seeing to it that the client re-emerges decisively. In the process he or she reminds himself or herself that the client is inherently a person of great intelligence, value, decisiveness, and power, as well as a person needing assistance with emergence from distress. In particular, the counselor notices and remembers where this particular client is capable, treasurable, and already functioning, or close to functioning, elegantly and well. In Step 1, the counselor pays enough attention to the client *to see clearly what the distress consists of*. In Step 2, the counselor *thinks of all possible ways* to contradict the client's distress. In Step 3, *the counselor contradicts the client's distress <u>sufficiently</u>*. The client will always discharge.

5.062 A counselor trying to think of what attitudes and expressions should be consistently turned to the client in all or nearly all conditions, may be helped by the analogy of the use of the drone pipes by a bagpipe player. The bagpipes, or the Scottish version of the bagpipes, have several "drone" pipes that sound the same note all the time, while the "chanter" pipe plays a melody. The counselor will offer specific contradictions, specific directions, encouragements, etc., as the flexible, continually-creative "melody" toward the client that she or he "plays on her or his chanter," but there are several consistent attitudes that she or he can undertake to train herself or himself and remind herself or himself to turn to the client under all or nearly all conditions. These "drone pipe" attitudes would include *respect for the client, approval of the client, delight in the client, love to the client, confidence in the client, confidence <u>for</u> the client, and relaxed, high expectations of the client.*

5.063 The counselor does better by thinking of herself or himself as a "journeyman" doing well-understood work, rather than as a "professional" or "expert." This means accepting the understanding that the "genius" work that is taking place is necessarily done by the *client*.

5.064 The counselor's job is to move around the blocks on the client's intelligence and assist the client's intelligence to think where the client's intelligence, because of patterns, finds it difficult to do so alone.

5.065 Always respect the person, no matter how patterned the person's behavior.

5.066 For the counselor to act on the reality of the goodness of every human being will tend to contradict the counselor's own distress. There are no "hopeless" human beings. No human has ever "completely given up."

When counselor, it is important for you, as counselor, to remember that it is the client's enormously effective and powerful intelligence that has the power, strength, and the necessary information that allows the discharge process to take place.

5.067 When counselor, it is important for you to remember that the client's mind is eager and motivated to think, speak, and act to contradict the distress recordings' content and allow discharge and the resulting re-evaluation to take place. Any apparently different attitude than this *is itself a recording*.

5.068 Permissive counseling consists of paying warm, interested attention to the client and allowing the client to direct herself or himself. There is a great deal of variation in how much attention a would-be counselor *can* pay or how *well* the would-be counselor pays attention, and this variation will be noted, taken into account, and calculated on in the client's response to that particular counseling. If the counselor could actually pay *complete* attention and be *completely* rational, *completely* human in his or her attitude to the client, and the communication of this attitude was not interfered with, inhibited, or occluded by any manifestations of the counselor's chronic patterns in facial expressions, tone of voice, or less-than-relaxed availability of the counselor's gaze, a very, very large portion of the client's distresses would be able to be discharged in this mode. A relaxed counselor trusts the client to seek re-emergence and views everything the client does as an attempt to do so.

5.069 Awarely adopting the role of counselor or client is helpful in organizing oneself, but you will be your own unique self in either role. It may help to remind yourself of this. You are "alright," and "where you are at" in the process is "alright" at each moment. (And you are always free to improve things as you go.)

5.070 Rather than be irritated with, condemn, or reject a person whom you perceive as "clienting all the time," it will be helpful if you realize that you, yourself, are focusing exclusively on that person's distress patterns. If you will make the decision to *be counselor*, and find a way to relate to the person and establish communication with the person (the person inside these patterns and rehearsing these patterns), you will untangle yourself from the dramatization and the personal discomfort that you have slipped into unawarely. You can then enjoy the challenge of making contact with the person and helping that person begin to re-emerge.

5.071 When you are the counselor, you, yourself, are your best tool and the biggest resource available in the counseling situation. You, yourself, can be the biggest contradiction to the distresses of the client. You can arrange and improve the environment in many ways, you can organize the client to contradict the distress, remind the client to keep contradicting it, and furnish the persistence that the client needs to play his or her part. In your own role, you have great capacity and great resource to add to the contradiction of the client's distress. You can play exactly the role that is needed, and you can keep improving that role as information from the session enables you to see what is needed more exactly. Your unshakeable confidence that the process *will* work will often be what makes it work.

5.072 Until actual counseling begins, the thinking of the client in proposing what is to be worked on is free and dependable. Once the work begins, the counselor needs to assume the role of organizer or manager of the client since at this point the central nervous system of the client becomes vulnerable to the distresses which are being worked on, and the distress will tend to take over unless the counselor plays a good role as "manager."

5.073 When you are counselor, you will do well to remind yourself that you are exactly *the* counselor the person needs, and that you are *enough*. You can claim the confidence and authority you actually do possess as a loving, rational human being. Unless you act *confidently*, you will not be able to contradict any hopelessness of the client well.

5.074 Do not adopt a critical attitude toward yourself as counselor during the session. You, as counselor, cannot "heal" anyone. It is not your job to be the motive power or "driving force" for discharge and re-evaluation. You can only help a client find contradictions to the distress sufficient for discharge to occur.

5.075 If the counselor is not really "present" with the client and truly caring about the client, the counseling is not likely to be very effective. "Set exercises" are not very useful.

5.076 The counselor's only goal in the session should be the re-emergence of the client. Any other goal or attitude than this in the session itself should be viewed with suspicion as probably a distress recording of the counselor's. (A slight exception to this is for a counselor leading a workshop and doing a demonstration as a teaching tool for the audience to learn how to counsel. This does not usually create any difficulty. The person filling the role of client in the demonstration seems able to function as client and discharge well and still have at least some awareness of being able to be a member of the "audience" or "student body" of the workshop at the same time. The counselor is often playing the role of counselor and teacher without any difficulty.)

5.077 Any particular beginning counselor is likely to come to the session with a number of patterned "goals" still attached to himself or herself which tend to persist while operating in the role of counselor. These can be as varied as: "having an interesting experience," "winning the goodwill (or the 'gratitude') of the client," "satisfying one's curiosity about people or about this particular person," "finding a way to feel close to another person in spite of one's embarrassment or isolation patterns," etc., etc. Many such patterned or partially-patterned goals have served beginning Co-Counselors in the past to get them started in the process of Co-Counseling and re-emergence, and it is well that they have so served toward the beginnings of Co-Counseling.

It is important, however, that as the process continues the Co-Counselors take some time to review their goals and discharge on any irrational components. The basic benefit to any counselor in counseling another person is to assist the person into pro-human attitudes which the counselor is seeking for himself or herself, which redound to the well-being of the counselor. This means that the counselor's goal for clients is to assist them in every way to re-emerge, that is, to regain their full humanness, to operate under their own full intelligence, and to be free from patterned attitudes and behaviors. This is the only satisfactory kind of goal for the counselor to have and, of course, is of optimum value to both the client and the counselor.

5.078 No point of theory should ever be witheld from the client. The client and the counselor are full partners in the application of Co-Counseling. There should never be any hint in the relationship of there being a lower, less-informed status for the client than for the counselor.

5.079 Throughout the process of counseling, the counselor and the client should work to be in clear communication with each other about the process and about what's going on. Neither should have secrets from the other. The client should be in possession of all the theory that the counselor knows, and although the counselor will often attempt to "trick" *the pattern*, it should always be obvious to the client herself or himself what is going on, and the client should never be intentionally deceived.

5.080 When counselor, the Co-Counselor can take the direction at the beginning of each client's session, "It must be logically possible to put my attention completely away from my own distress. I hereby decide to do this."

5.081 It is possible and desirable for the counselor to decide to *love* the client—even if the client has patterns that the counselor tends to find "unlovable."

5.082 It is possible and important in the very first moments of a session with a new Co-Counselor to communicate that you *like* her or *like* him. The lack of such communication will have the effect of a distress upon that person and will have to be discharged in some way in order for the relationship to work as well as it can.

5.083 In many counseling situations, the counselor will do better to pay attention to the distresses and feelings of the client rather than to any rationalizations which the client is rehearsing and offering as a substitute for his or her real thinking. In such cases, a counselor's concern is not necessarily, "What is the issue?" but should be, at least in part, "What is the distress being rehearsed at me here which I may be able to help contradict?" *Don't* try to help your clients "solve their problems." *Do* help them to contradict and discharge their distress. Be relaxed when the client pauses. Allow the client time to think and feel. Don't say too much. It's usually better to listen longer and to hear more.

5.084 Persistence, once the distress is contradicted, lies largely in the hands of the counselor. The client may be able to persist *in bringing the distress up* over and over again, but once discharge has begun, or once the distress is *close* to discharge, the client's avoidance feelings will often take over and the client will *seem* to be resisting and will depend on the counselor's insistent persistence in order to keep going.

5.085 Try to stay relaxed, confident, light, and positive most of the time when you are in the role of counselor. The exceptions would be when you express concern or indignation at the way the client has been treated in the past and when you express determination that the client *will* emerge from the distress. If the counselor obviously *does not get upset*, it makes it safer for the client to bring his or her distresses up and work on them.

5.086 Many inexperienced counselors will feel uncomfortable at the amount of confidence and trust (and high expectations) which the client will tend to project on him or her. It will seem totally unjustified to many counselors because of the invalidation of their own chronic patterns within which they operate and which they have gotten "accustomed to." This discomfort is worth enduring and should be handled, not by the counselor deprecating himself or herself, but by actually living up to the high expectations of the client. In the relationship between Co-Counselors we must play this role for each other as part of our responsibility.

5.087 Ideally, the person in the counselor role will always remain rational and never be upset by anything that goes on in the session, or by any of the client's distresses. *In actual practice,* counselors can and do become restimulated and become "shut down," unable to think, confused, and argumentative. If and when this happens, many kinds of emergency measures can be taken. Either the counselor or the client can suggest a "break," a walk around the block, an exchange of the roles with the upset counselor becoming client for a while, the pair taking turns exchanging random pleasant memories, an appeal over the telephone to a more experienced counselor for help, etc. Such a pause will interrupt the client's session, but much better sessions will ensue, and the counselor will do a better job afterwards. This is one of the "workable" things about Re-evaluation Counseling, that the process can be applied to the process itself.

5.088 Some of the things we have learned that the counselor should *not* do with her or his client include not giving the client advice or in any other way attempting to do the client's thinking for him or for her, not interrupting the client's discharge, not acting as client oneself when one is supposed to be the counselor, not expressing feelings or opinions to the client except when they are clearly intended to contradict the distress which the client is grappling with.

5.089 There are certain common patterned attitudes in our cultures that spoil or damage or degrade the Co-Counseling relationship and "almost" justify the general warning to would-be counselors to "never" allow these things to happen.

One of these is being inattentive to the client. (Even the most desperate client can only pretend to a limited degree that you as counselor are paying attention when you are not.)

Another is "giving advice." (It is crucial that the client does her or his own thinking. Your well-meant "advice" can only constitute a block in the way of his or her own thinking. You may helpfully furnish information that the client is lacking, but you must take the greatest care that the client actually needs and wants the information and that your "offering" it is not to cover up what is actually your compulsive advice-giving.)

Any disrespect is a terrible reinforcement of the distress that you're supposed to be helping the client become free from. So is any breach of confidentiality, any referring to the material expressed by the client in a session *to anyone at any time*, including to the client himself or herself, unless the client has specifically asked to discuss it with you. A breach of confidentiality is enormously damaging and can easily spoil an entire relationship.

5.090 Don't offer your own (counselor's) insights. Your thinking will interfere with the client's thinking. Offering it can feel like attacks or criticism to the client, and it *isn't necessary*.

5.091 As counselor, do not "interpret" the client's words or actions except with the purpose of sharpening the contradiction and accelerating the client's discharge, and in this case, do it very carefully. The client does not need the counselor's interpretation of his or her thinking. She or he needs his or her *own* thinking.

5.092 The counselor should never be negative about the session or the situation. The client has enough hopelessness and powerlessness in his or her background distress without it being added to by the counselor's dramatization.

Don't give advice. Don't ask questions of the client with the purpose of satisfying your curiosity. Don't "worry" about the client in the client's hearing or in your facial expression or attitude. Don't "turn client" and tell your own story.

5.093 When counselor, do not offer "comfort" to the client as a substitute for help in discharging. (Comfort should be offered only when it is a direct contradiction to such distresses as, "No one ever comforted me," or "I am tired, fatigued, and miserable.") Do not sympathize with the client as a substitute for help in discharging (offer sympathy only when it is a contradiction to the particular distress being confronted, such as, "No one ever cared how miserable I was," "It would be nice to have an encouraging word.")

5.094 Do not, when you are counselor, lose sight of the immense importance and value and complexity of your client. Remind the client (and yourself) often of his or her goodness, intelligence, freedom, and power. Remember, every client has been invalidated *billions* of times in the past. (There is no such thing as a "bad client.")

5.095 For a client to see a distress pattern as "not present-time reality" is the essence of the situation that makes discharge possible. However, labeling the pattern as a "pattern," or pointing out its patterned nature condescendingly, is not likely to be helpful. Such activity on the part of the counselor will be quickly recognized by the client as part of the counselor's patterns, and the client's attention will be in that direction rather than in seeing the "pointed out" pattern as *not* reality.

5.096 When it seems appropriate, don't hesitate to ask the client questions. You will seem to ask for "information," and actually some of the answers will be useful to you in guiding you as counselor, but your primary purpose is to encourage the client to "think out loud." Ask what he or she *wants*. Ask what his or her "first thought" is. Notice the expressions on the client's face and how these expressions change. Notice the client's posture and how it changes. You can ask such questions as, "What does that remind you of?" "Who does she remind you of?" "What are you thinking?" "What might happen?" "Where does it hurt?" "What else . . .?" "When was the last time . . .?" "How old were you?" "Can you remember a particular time when . . .?" "What did you like about your father?" "What did you want that you didn't get?"

5.097 All clients will have an enormous accumulation of invalidations of themselves from the past, since all current cultures impose these systematically. This almost guarantees that the counselor can offer validations, approval, congratulations, positive tones of voice, beaming facial expressions, and verbal approval to the client in any situation and to any degree without much risk of mistake. (Bursts of discharge and words of reproach and unbelief will often be turned to the counselor, but these, of course, are simply beginnings of the discharge process.)

5.098 The great majority of people in this society have been invalidated profoundly in a great variety of ways. A common form of the invalidation is to be treated by others as if not much was expected of the person. To counter this, it is almost always useful for the counselor to turn an attitude of *high expectations* upon the client. The expectations need to be relaxed and confident, however, or they will tend to reinforce the anxiety and the criticism to which the client has been exposed before from parents, teachers, and older children. High expectations, yes, but *relaxed, confident high expectations*.

5.099 For the counselor to extend and project eager expectations about the client's progress and future to the client can be very helpful. Such confident expectations are an effective contradiction to the myriads of discouraging experiences and disappointments which almost every client can be expected to have had. Here, as in most counseling, the tone of voice, the facial expression, the unworried confidence can be very effective. It is important that the expectations be based on the *client's* desires and goals, not something projected on the client by the counselor, and it is important that the counselor never, never, never be disappointed in any slowness or confusion in which the client may temporarily become bogged.

5.100 The effect of a pattern on a client will often have been to "freeze" the client to a particular viewpoint towards the subject of the pattern's distress. It is legitimate and will often be helpful for the counselor to offer another possible viewpoint from which the client can consider the subject, or even a series of different possible viewpoints. These should never be enforced upon the client, but only offered.

5.101 Re-evaluation by a client is sometimes inhibited by a lack of particular information, since people growing up in the oppressive societies are often limited to, and have enforced upon them, much false or misleading information as the "truth." It is permissible, and may sometimes be necessary, for the counselor to offer different information or more accurate information. This should not usually be presented in any authoritative way, but as a "possibly different interpretation of the situation," or "what someone else thought," or, again, as "an interesting viewpoint."

5.102 When a counseling relationship is working well, and discharge is taking place, it is quite all right and useful for the counselor to think of additional contradictions that he or she can furnish to enhance the rate of discharge. There is also merit, however, in the counselor relaxing and just "letting the client discharge." The continued success of the discharge in itself will tend to deepen the process, and the many patterns that surround every client from past interference with the discharge process will tend to get worn out and eliminated as the discharge process, with its obvious benefits, continues on over a long period of time. There are times when it is very good to "just let the client discharge."

Many of the previously-installed patterns which tend to inhibit the client's discharge will have an element of "don't make noise," or "be quiet," or "shhh, shhh," in them, which, though not expressed, will be acting to inhibit and interrupt the client's discharge. If the counselor makes a loud, plaintive, or "painful" noise reminiscent of a cry of pain each time the client's discharge tends to taper off, the persistence of the client's discharge can often be extended several times as long as it would persist without this "reminder" or "support" from the counselor.

5.103 It is a contradiction to most clients' distress to offer them a kind of reassurance that their *distress* is not an accurate representation of present reality. The counselor can, at least, speaking confidently for himself or herself, say that he or she does not "believe" or "accept" the negative opinions which the client heard in the past and which had become recorded in the distress pattern. The very best reassurance to the client is to offer an accurate picture of reality, and the tone-of-voice of the counselor needs to accurately express confidence in this reality.

5.104 The use of reassurance by the counselor to the client must be carefully understood and carried out in order to be helpful. "Reassuring" words from the counselor that seem to deny the existence of the distress or the reality of the hurts or the mistreatment which created the distress in the first place, are not helpful to the client. "You're not really too heavy; lots of people are heavier than you are," is no help to the client who is trying to gather courage to move against an addiction to overeating. The reassurance should always be directed to the "all-rightness" of the client, not to the acceptance of the pattern. "In the past you've always done the best you could," needs to be followed with, "The future can be as good as you want to make it."

The "Great Insight" of Re-evaluation Counseling can be your guide in reassuring the client and not supporting the pattern. This is, "*Every single human being, at every moment of the past, if the entire situation is taken into account, has always done the very best that she or he could do, and so deserves neither blame nor reproach from anyone, including self. This, in particular, is true of you.*" This deals with the past. "In the present and future, you have a completely free choice to make your future develop in any way that you are determined to have it develop." This deals with the future.

5.105 If you are paying close attention when you are in the counselor role, you will notice that the facial expressions, the tones of voice, or the mannerisms with which the client speaks or acts are clues to distress patterns or distress recordings. Counseling an adult client is really no different than counseling an infant or young person in that you need not have a lot of information about the client's distresses in order to contradict them well enough to get the discharge started. All you need to do is look and listen closely; the client will give you hints to almost all characteristics of the distress right from the beginning of the first session.

5.106 Sometimes a client is caught in a particular feeling, which she or he hints at or partially expresses, with no discharge. It is often possible to have him or her express the feeling clearly to you, saying it to you as counselor, and saying it over and over and over, and thus begin to hear that it is an echo of the past and begin to discharge.

5.107 Any feelings of impatience on the part of the counselor that the client is "uncooperative," "too timid," etc., are unjustified. The reality in every session is that the client will move *if the counselor is furnishing enough safety and contradiction to the distress*, and the client will continue to move and discharge just as long as this continues to be furnished.

5.108 Unless it is a contradiction to a particular distress, it is not "necessary" that the client's eyes meet the counselor's eyes (although this false information has often been "passed around" the Communities as if it were dogma). It *is* usually essential, however, that eye contact with the counselor *be available* to the client whenever the client seeks it. That is, whenever the client looks at the counselor's eyes, he or she should find the counselor's eyes awarely looking back.

5.109 The counselor should plan to give his or her client evidence of being secure. Being reassured of being secure (whether or not able to "feel" secure) is of help to the client in beginning to discharge.

5.110 Remember! *This* particular client may be the one who will eventually lead the entire world to re-emergence!

5.111 One person reclaiming her or his power should be enough to eventually set *everything* right, and it makes sense to assume as counselor that your particular client (in this session) can or will be the one who does take this decisive action.

5.112 In assisting the human to emerge from patterned accretions, one may assume an attitude of toughness or rigor but it must be consistent with holding a perspective of complete respect and appreciation for the human.

5.113 Be prepared to be aware of the *first* sound and *first* other responses made by the client. Often the *first* thing said or done by the client in response to the counselor is a very clear *code message* as to what will bring discharge. If you have asked a probing "intellectual question" and the client simply grunts, have the client repeat *that grunt* immediately, and you are likely to receive voluminous discharge.

5.114 Encourage the client to relate all the thoughts or images that occur as she talks and discharges.

5.115 Touching and physical contact with the counselor should be available to the client who needs it and may serve as an important contradiction to feelings of loneliness, isolation, etc. Touching and physical contact should *never be enforced upon* a client. Always make it clear that making the contact is her or his choice, but that it is available. (Touching and physical contact are *not* the same as being sexual.)

5.116 It will usually be helpful to discuss and plan the client's sessions with the client. "Would you be interested in trying the young person's commitment?" "What is the best thing we've done so far in our sessions?" etc. "Would you be willing to try . . .?"

5.117 Communicate to the client at some point, and preferably early, that there are no feelings that she or he has felt in the past that are not OK to bring up, talk about, and feel again. Remind the client that any particular feeling was either imposed on the client from outside or was completely justified in terms of the mistreatment which the distressing situation had subjected her or him to. "Feel free to talk about the worst feelings you've got; it's OK to tell how you feel." "It's OK to feel whatever feelings you have."

5.118 The counselor can handle errors which he or she has made by recognizing the error, admitting it, apologizing for it thoroughly, listening to discharge (and, possibly, reproaches) from the client, and, finally, proceeding to counsel the client correctly. Once the counselor has made the decision to do this, it will turn out not to be difficult and will be useful for learning to handle other difficulties with people in his or her life. If the counselor persists in the error and fails to apologize for it, it can make counseling seem unworkable to the client.

5.119 Let your Co-Counselor know that you do think and care about him or her between sessions. This should always be done in the counselor mode, not as a client. This contradicts isolation and any feelings that a Re-evaluation Counseling relationship is not "real."

5.120 When client, a Co-Counselor should be in charge of the client's role in the session, but it is possible for isolation patterns to influence one as a client to not accept the counselor's playing the counselor's proper role in the session. In such a case, the client may seem reassuring to the counselor because he or she is discharging but may need assistance from the counselor to achieve contradiction to a deeper distress. Such contradiction may include contradicting the isolation by the counselor and taking the initiative to do so.

5.121 It is possible for two (or more) people to satisfactorily fill the role of counselor and be discharging (and to that extent, play the role of client) at the same time.

5.122 The counselor's attention belongs on the client, on what the client is doing, on what the counselor can do to assist the client to discharge, BUT for the counselor to discharge during the client's session is not necessarily harmful, and may be helpful. The situation may be so contradictory to the client's distress and at the same time to the counselor's distress that both may discharge well at the same time, and their simultaneous discharge may encourage and reinforce the discharge process for both. (This is the phenomenon involved in the successful comedian eliciting discharge from a large audience, or the "storms of discharge" that sometimes occur accidentally in crowd situations and in Co-Counseling classes.) In a successful session based on "exchanging commitments," with the roles being exchanged at short intervals, it is typical for both parties to be discharging all the time as the one in the role of counselor continues discharging even while putting attention on the other person as client.

5.123 To offer the client the counselor's *full* attention, the counselor must be "outside" her or his own distress. To do this, she or he may have to discharge while in the role of counselor, since acting outside of her or his distress contradicts that distress. This is fine as long as she or he keeps her or his *attention* on the client while discharging.

5.124 Playing the role of counselor well is a contradiction to most of the counselor's distress patterns, and incidental discharge should not be controlled or suppressed but allowed to happen as the counselor keeps a confident, positive tone.

5.125 Use of the *Client's and Counselor's Notebooks* after every session can prevent the forgetting of important directions that have brought discharge.

5.126 When you are in the role of counselor, anything that keeps you from thinking well and successfully about the client is a big "neon sign" directing you to work on some distress of your own the next time you are in the client role. You may find it helpful to make notes at the time to refer to when you are next in the role of client.

5.127 Proficiency as counselor improves with one's own re-emergence, that is, with the amount accomplished when client.

5.128 Becoming an effective counselor will help one's thinking about being a more effective client and getting the most out of every session *as client*.

5.129 You may find it helpful to remember that acting rationally will tend to contradict the distresses of those around you and lead them to intuitively hope that they can use your free attention to achieve discharge for themselves. This may motivate them to try to claim sessions with you on their distresses which your actions contradict. Such "upsets" happening around you are not in themselves indications that something is going "wrong" or that you are doing "wrong." It is much more likely that they are intuitive attempts by other people to claim a session, with you being the counselor.

5.130 It is good to warn persons who begin re-emerging well that their increased "slack" (free attention) will be noticed by the people around them. They should be prepared to meet with heavy, compulsive, patterns of trying-to-take-advantage-of-the-slack-sensed-in-the-re-emerging-person's-behavior. Distressed people will do this by holding out all their distresses and "dumping" and rehearsing them at the person. They will even create "crises" as an excuse for imposing their eagerness to be a client upon the re-emerging person. Among the possible solutions for this are: to out-dramatize the dramatizer (with your private tongue privately in your private cheek, of course); to offer him or her counseling only under rigorous conditions where he or she will follow instructions about how to be a successful client; or insist that he or she enroll in a Fundamentals of Co-Counseling class.

client understandings/attitudes/actions

5.131 When client, the Co-Counselor can awarely "decide" at the beginning of the session to do what will bring discharge. This will tend to make the session more productive.

5.132 It is possible for the Co-Counselor, when client, to decide to successfully discharge in the session, no matter who is the counselor or what the counselor is doing. Making this decision can be pivotal. Without the decision, one can be with an excellent counselor and not discharge. By making the decision, one can even be with an unaware counselor and still discharge, solely on the basis of one's own decision. To make this decision will be helpful in every session.

5.133 Logical thinking is the only acceptable guide to our actions. Feelings are not. If the feelings seem pleasant, they can be enjoyed. If the feelings are unpleasant, ways can be found to discharge them. There is always a correct or optimum way to act, regardless of whether the feelings being felt seem to "agree with" or "contradict" the logic. To relapse to *acting* on feelings is to descend to a pre-human, pre-intelligent mode of existence.

5.134 There are acts which require hard physical effort and persistence, and there are acts which require persistent research and brilliant thinking over a series of difficult steps. For these we propose the respectful appellation "hard." For acts that require us to go against our distresses, require us to resist addictions and give up addictions, to give up pseudo-comfortable distractions or "loafing" which shut down our thinking, and instead choose acts that would seem to reward our persistence against the distress only with discharge (including yawning and falling asleep), we have chosen the appellation "ha-a-a-a-ard." Take pride in doing the *hard* things. Organize your sessions and your counselors and your clients to do the "ha-a-a-ard" things so determinedly and well as to bring discharge in a continuing way.

5.135 Life goes better when one decides, acts, and discharges, *in that order*.

5.136 It is possible to train *yourself* to persist with a given direction *when a client*.

5.137 It is understandable that a beginning client will often approach counseling with the goal of "feeling better" or "feeling good." The recorded distresses have been a principal limitation on the person's enjoyment of life, and a person's successful experiences with being a client will often reinforce this notion that the goal of counseling is the improvement of one's feelings. A better understanding than this, however, is necessary for any profound work or long-range gains in counseling because "numbness" is often equated with "feeling better," and it's quite likely that any significant discharge will bring many sensations, at least temporarily, of "feeling bad." Some of these distresses will be felt for the first time during discharge, since the distress when it was laid in was often so severe that the person turned numb or even unconscious while it was being laid in. The counselor can often encourage the client by reassuring him or her frequently that he or she is not hurting *now*, that he or she is just feeling the feelings that were generated by the hurts a long time ago which are now "on their way out."

5.138 We are not aiming for static "perfection" but for continually improving, limitless development.

5.139 Having been client, always thank and appreciate your Co-Counselor for the session.

5.140 Everyone seems to spontaneously and intuitively desire "closeness" with all other people. Babies who have been treated elegantly well, spontaneously "love everybody." To announce one's intention of becoming "completely close" to another person is a useful beginning contradiction to the feelings of isolation and "uncloseness" that for most of us have become attached to most other people by the time we're out of infancy. To announce such an intention is to contradict the distress well enough that one almost immediately has thoughts come up that are ready for discharge if they are contradicted. For the counselor to try to act out being close to the client is likely to shut the client down and interfere with discharge, but for the client *himself or herself* to "threaten" the counselor with closeness, promise closeness, or describe details of future closeness, particularly while meeting the eyes of the "threatened" recipient counselor, is quite likely to be just the right amount of contradiction for the discharge to take place profusely.

5.141 Your Co-Counselor (to date, at least) is necessarily only partially re-emerged, is intelligent but only partially informed, is still operating against, but undoubtedly influenced by, distress patterns left by her or his past. It is unwise and unrealistic to place expectations on your counselor that do not take this into account. Think of her or him as your partner in a difficult, confusing journey where support and clear communication between you is decisive in keeping the relationship effective.

5.142 None of us is to *blame* for our patterns. We need to, however, struggle to be responsible for eliminating them. Some patterns will tend to make the client feel and act irresponsible for his or her own re-emergence and feel as if the counselor has the sole responsibility. Then, even the very best counseling will be somewhat ineffective without the client's participation. The client may need help in finding contradictions to the pattern that keeps him or her from participating.

5.143 Complete self-appreciation will tend to contradict and bring to our aware attention, and eventually lead to the discharge of, many invalidating distresses which we are otherwise likely to continue to take for granted or not notice.

5.144 A favorable environment is (usually) a contradiction to distress.

5.145 Consider renouncing all "frozen needs" as *addictions to the past*. Remember our basic insight that we are blameless, that we have always in the past done our very best with life's interesting challenges. Consider giving up all addictive substances, all addictions to acting on feelings, and all attempts to fill "frozen needs."

5.146 To trust other people is frequently an important contradiction to the distress. Being open about everything is a useful contradiction to a fear of other people and a suspicion of them.

5.147 One way to achieve every goal is to live *every* moment well.

5.148 The possibility of immortality seems to be taken-for-granted by young children, and most cultures' insisted-upon expectation of death seems to come as a hurtful blow to children. Pursuing the possibility of actually achieving immortality or, if one prefers to say, "an indefinitely long life," seems to be not only ultimately desirable but is immediately a course of action with great benefits to us if we pursue it confidently.

5.149 An assumption of immortality can be very useful in revealing and contradicting many past acceptances of defeats or limitations of which we have often become largely unaware.

5.150 To discharge feelings of inevitably dying or to plan on living two or three times the current normal life-span will bring to light many feelings of having surrendered to discouragement in these areas and, I would guess, probably will tend to increase the length of one's life.

5.151 Give up all unreasonable expectations and their probable resulting disappointments.

5.152 If a client acts persistently self-invalidating, it may help to remind the client that other people tend to accept a person's own judgment of himself or herself so that he or she will draw a much better response from others if *he* or she validates himself or herself. If someone thinks well of herself or himself, others tend to be curious and interested in that person.

5.153 It is valuable to *both* Co-Counsel with a variety of different Co-Counselors *and* to develop committed relationships with a smaller number of Co-Counselors who are chosen on the basis of the Co-Counseling relationship working very well *both ways*.

5.154 An inexperienced counselor can sometimes present a valuable, fresh viewpoint. Both experienced and inexperienced counselors can be valuable to you.

5.155 To set a goal of living a thoughtfully-planned, healthy, well-exercised, well-organized life with well-informed nutritional habits tends to pull Co-Counselors against their distress and towards re-emergence.

5.156 Being committed to working for world change does not require us to neglect ourselves in the present. On the contrary, the future needs us well-rested, well-nourished, well-exercised, and well-organized.

5.157 We can find our own intelligent balance between work, recreation, and rest. Habitual overwork is *not* rational.

5.158 All functioning is enhanced when one's body receives enough exercise. We are fundamentally physical creatures whose excellent bodies and structures demand use. In order to contradict distresses of physical abuse, it may be necessary to emphasize and participate in the enjoyment of exercise.

5.159 Unless a particular non-food substance has been specifically researched and designed by competent scientists for cautious intervention into a well-understood malfunctioning of one's body, it should not be ingested.

Nothing should be ingested by a human on the basis of feelings which the human feels from having used it. (Otherwise the "pull" of an addiction can be misunderstood as a "benefit" because succumbing to the addiction "feels good.")

5.160 To hold "directions" or "commitments" against distress patterns works well and brings discharge when a client is in a session. It tends to have even more profound results if it is done in regular living.

5.161 We could theoretically completely re-emerge with only "a fiddler crab and coconut palm for companions" by thinking how we want our life to be, noticing where we act differently from that, setting the direction of acting in the way we want to, and discharging.

5.162 Chronic patterns often seem to be too difficult to completely discharge in counseling sessions alone. They must be "starved" by continual contradictions against them being held as directions and acted upon *in regular living*, if possible *all* the time.

5.163 To re-emerge more rapidly becomes increasingly desirable as one savors the benefits of partial re-emergence. A number of accelerating factors have been identified. Making a correct decision and acting on it without waiting for discharge tends to lead to very rapid re-emergence and, eventually, very effective discharge. "Act against your patterns and discharge as you go." Taking leadership tends to enhance one's rate of re-emergence. Teaching Re-evaluation Counseling greatly accelerates the deep absorption of the theory.

5.164 Optimum functioning apparently will be something like having our full attention in the present and using information from the past without the effort of remembering it as if it were the past. Many people can hear this state described well as "living in the reality of the present."

5.165 The later stages of our re-emergence will probably be characterized by consistent holding of directions against *all* distress, by great awareness of the reality around us, by the use of our complete freedom of decision in all situations, and by acting closer and closer to being totally powerful as an individual. Probably the people who have re-emerged well will tend to take positions of great influence in the society and its structures but possibly *not* positions of *prominence*. As the movement toward re-emergence becomes a wide-world phenomenon, any distinctions between Co-Counselors and wide-world friends will probably tend to become unnoticeable.

modes of counseling

5.166 Modes of counseling *can* be listed in the order of how much free attention needs to be available from the client for them to work effectively. (This list was earlier termed "the spectrum of techniques.") The least demanding modes in this sense are the ones that pull attention away from distress instead of investing any attention in it. There can be many variations on these modes. The following groups of modes are listed roughly in the order of how much free attention the client needs to have available for the mode to work, beginning with the modes that require the least attention. The first is *noticing the counselor*.

5.167 Noticing plain *facts* in the immediate present situation.

5.168 Recalling and recounting plain *facts* from the *past*.

5.169 Recounting pleasant memories. (Beautiful scenes one has enjoyed. Compliments one has been paid. Excellent meals one has eaten. Successes one has achieved. Etc.)

5.170 If the counselor can ask for a great *variety* of *not-unpleasant* or *pleasant* experiences without staying in any *similar* vein, it helps keep the client's attention from falling into any "rut" through the by-now conditioned pressure on the client to hold out distress, and this will add to the client's store of free attention. At a later time, when the client has more free attention, you will deliberately encourage remembering of similar *real but ordinary* experiences, similar *pleasant* experiences, or even similar *distress* experiences. When attention on the part of the client is in short supply, however, it is good to remember the positive effect of continually varying the kind of experience that is asked for.

5.171 The client can be asked to do a rapid review of similar positive experiences and, after first recounting them individually, can run over them in his or her mind silently, informing the counselor each time that he or she is beginning anew with the earliest situation on the list and also each time that he or she has reached "present time" on the list of similar positive experiences. When new positive experiences are remembered and added to the list, the client informs the counselor about each one.

5.172 The client can also attempt (and often work well with) a similar rapid review of *relatively unimportant negative experiences*. There will be a tendency, however, for heavily distressed experiences to appear on the list and, while these can and eventually will be dealt with by the client, a larger amount of free attention will be necessary to handle them, and clients who are deeply in the habit of keeping their attention involved in their distress will not work well at this level until later.

rapid review of related experiences

Counseling as a Tool for Freeing a Person of Particular Physical Distress Symptoms or Particular Kinds of Non-Survival Behavior (reprinted from *A Better World*)

5.173 Often Co-Counselors (or people whom they wish to help) have particular problems that they wish to solve with some urgency. The same kind of pressures can then be turned on their counselors as members of the medical professions often feel are turned on them. The client presents an impassioned demand and expectation of a "cure" of the *particular* problem.

The general effect of discharge and re-evaluation is, of course, to become more rational. This means becoming free of patterned activity which has been dictated by the distress recording. Such patterned activity will have a number of manifestations. It will always embrace at least some *physical malfunctions*, some *non-survival behavior*, some *distressed emotional tone* or other, and some *"pseudo-thinking"* that is less than fully intelligent.

We in Re-evaluation Counseling have in recent years been working more and more at the frontiers of our theory for *general* approaches that will move people dramatically forward in overall ways toward the recovery of their full humanness in all its aspects. Yet, judging by many of the calls for help that I receive, the urgency of becoming free of a particular physical distress or malfunction or a particular behavioral problem still remains of great importance to many Co-Counselors and to the people they are seeking to assist.

No Co-Counselor should "promise" or "guarantee" to be effective in relieving such a symptom of behavioral or physical distress. The process of discharge and re-evaluation is a very complex one, and the basic responsibility for successful help from its use rests with the person who is client. Though we assume that each client is fundamentally eager to recover excellent functioning and full humanness and intelligence, eager to untangle the patterns which have accumulated and overlay the distress, attaining the freedom which is being sought may be a very complicated procedure. It may even turn out to be much more of a job than the client is presently ready to commit himself or herself to. It may take more time and resource than the counselor has to give.

Nevertheless, it is sometimes possible to "zero in" on a particular kind of patterned behavior or physical misfunction, and sometimes one can solve the particular problem quite effectively and expeditiously. In any case, whether the problem can be solved quickly or only after long effort, it is possible to lay out quite clearly the obstacles that must be overcome, the distress that must be discharged, and the patterns that must be re-evaluated in order to achieve the desired result.

To prepare for this thorough-going effort, whether it turns out to be of long duration or brief, will require enlisting the *client's* own full intelligence in the task of *diagnosis*. The counselor's intelligence and the counselor's thinking alone cannot be accurate enough about the client's hurts. In sorting out this information, the counselor is always only the "helper" of the client and plays a limited role. There are certain resources which the client has, however, which are difficult for the client to keep track of or call into play without the assistance of an outside intelligence such as the counselor's.

Sometimes this can be done very quickly and expeditiously by simply asking the client, "What do you need to say to start recovering from this distress?" (or "to start changing this behavior?") and ask for an immediate thought (or "flash answer"). Taking the client's response, the counselor then has the client repeat it, examine it, and, if necessary, furnish contradictions until discharge begins. Then both client and counselor stay with the discharge and the furnishing of contradictions, perhaps for many sessions, until the pattern which has caused the problem, behavioral or physical, is no longer in chronic restimulation.

More reliably, it's possible to call on the client's mind to systematically lay out all the past incidents of distress that are, or may be, contributing to the particular symptomatic behavior or physical malfunctioning. As counselor, one simply asks the client, "What is your earliest memory that is connected with this distress?" and encourages the client to tell the first memory that comes to mind. There will be a tendency sometimes for the client to have difficulty believing that the memory that came to mind is important or relevant, and the counselor will need to encourage or even insist that the memory be recounted. The first memory that comes to mind should be recounted, no matter when, chronologically, this memory occurred in the client's life. The counselor then asks, "Is there an earlier incident connected with this?" and, if so, accepts the earlier incident and asks for a fuller recounting of that. This procedure is repeated as long as the inquiry yields an earlier memory.

When this repeated inquiry fails to elicit an earlier incident (which should be assumed will turn out to be connected to the distress), the counselor then asks the client to recount the earliest memory elicited so far and then, moving later, recount the next later one. That recounted, the counselor asks the client to recount the next later one, then the next later one, the next later one, and so on. This process is carried through until the client's recounting reaches the present moment. (The counselor might well make a note of the different memories as they appear.) A list of memories, sometimes few, sometimes many, will have accumulated.

If discharge begins on any memory, it is encouraged and supported, but when discharge is no longer available, the next later memory connected with the particular distress is again asked for.

Having reviewed the list all the way to the present, the client is then asked by the counselor to return his or her attention once more to the earliest incident on the list and is then again asked, "Is there a still earlier memory available now?" If there is, the earlier incident is recounted and then a still earlier one is asked for. This is done repeatedly as long as an earlier memory is furnished by the client. When no earlier memory is available, the client is again asked to recount the list of memories all the way from the earliest one to the present.

As the list is reviewed and recounted by the client, additional new (not yet recounted) memories will tend to appear on the list. These are recounted by the client and listened to by the counselor. Discharge will appear with some of these memories and with others, remembering and talking about them is all that will need to happen.

When this process, recounting the list of memories that the client's mind has put forward as being connected with this distress, has been repeated many times, some of the incidents will disappear from the list—will not be "remembered." New ones will appear, ones previously recounted will disappear. This is a natural process. The counselor need not remind the client of the incidents to keep them from dropping off the list. When an incident is left off the list by the client it indicates that the client's mind has re-evaluated on that incident's connection to the distress that the pair are working on and no longer views it as pertinent to that distress. The same incident may appear later in the client's counseling, as connected with another symptom or another problem, but if it drops off the list of incidents connected with this particular physical or behavioral problem, it will have been correctly dismissed.

This process of recounting and reviewing the list of incidents can be speeded up somewhat by asking the client to silently "think through" the list of incidents previously recounted. The client is encouraged to proceed to the next later memory and then the next later memory on the list unless a *new* memory appears, in which case *that one* should be orally recounted to the counselor. If discharge appears imminent on such a new memory, the counselor should help the client with contradictions to the distress so discharge can take place. When discharge is no longer available, the review process is resumed.

After reviewing the list many times, most of the memories that were on it to begin with will have "disappeared." Several incidents, however, will seem to have *gained* importance and will loom very large. Sometimes the client cannot even move his or her attention past them to later memories. This is a signal that discharge is needed. The counselor assists the client to discharge as thoroughly as possible on the incident. When discharge is no longer available, the Cc-Counselors return to the reviewing of the list.

This can sometimes take a long time and involve many, many sessions. When such a particular incident has been discharged as much as seems immediately possible, then the review of the remaining incidents on the list is resumed. The same process is carried forward whenever discharge occurs on an incident. The discharging is supported as thoroughly as possible on each of the incidents left on the list.

As this discharge and re-evaluation proceed, there will come a time when the particular symptom—physical or behavioral—will "disappear." The client may inform the counselor that the problem is "solved." The counselor, however, should keep the client discharging and working on the chain of incidents for a substantially longer time. What has happened is that the distress recording has lost its *chronic* status. It is no longer operating in ordinary situations. This does not mean that it could not easily become restimulated and once again loaded up with tension to the point where it again becomes chronic. If this is allowed to happen, the client is likely to feel profoundly discouraged, even to conclude that "counseling doesn't work." The unreasonable expectation that getting the distress recording out of its chronic state had done away with the distress completely will have been disappointed and the client disappointed with it.

Instead of allowing this to happen, the chain of memories connected with the distress should be pursued, contradicted, discharged, and completely cleared up as far as the situation permits. If this is done, the "reform" of a behavioral problem, or the "cure" of a physical symptom will leave a very solid foundation for the further re-emergence of the client. It will also, of course, give considerable confidence to the counselor about the power of his or her skills.

Such "sharp-shooting" to eliminate a particular symptom or problem is not the only or necessarily the best way to work on one's re-emergence, but it is a *possible* way. In response to the many queries I've been receiving about this as wider sections of the population become acquainted with the existence of Re-evaluation Counseling, it seemed to me that it was probably time to restate this portion in succinct form.

(reprinted from *A Better World*, pp. 201-207)

telling the story/early memories

5.174 It is almost always an excellent beginning or continuation of a counseling relationship to ask the client to tell her or his life story.

5.175 It is always useful, and sometimes absolutely necessary, to ask the client to tell a story repeatedly. The actual content of the story will shift with repeated recountings and discharge, and the client will often re-evaluate on small items even when no very large amount of visible discharge is taking place.

5.176 The client *telling* the story of what happened is different than the client *explaining* what happened or *justifying* what happened. If the counselor can direct the client to review just the account, it is likely to bring much more discharge and re-evaluation then explaining or justifying. Explaining or defending is usually a rehearsal of some pattern of the client.

5.177 You can always ask the client to tell an incident again and ask for more detail as the account is repeated.

5.178 The same points, the same actions, the same words in a repeatedly-recounted incident, will produce different kinds of emotional discharge as the client's mind works through the incident.

5.179 "Cleaning up" a particular distress incident or recording is a desirable goal even though considerable time and effort, including many sessions, may have to be involved. Any particular set of distresses can be cleaned up *completely*. The physical or behavioral misfunctions which were based on those distresses can be *completely eliminated*.

5.180 For any major topic in the client's life (family, money, sex, career, etc.), it will work well (usually) to ask the client to tell about his or her earliest memory connected in any way at all with the topic. To approach a chain of distress experiences at or close to the very beginning tends to afford the client some sort of perspective or insight into the total pattern and how it developed.

5.181 It is usually more effective to counsel on the earliest memories connected with a particular hurt rather than the later memories. Discharge on the earlier memories makes it easier to re-evaluate on the later ones connected to them. However, if only the later memories are available at first, that is the place to start.

5.182 It is not always possible to influence the client on what particular batch of distress he or she brings up and tries to work on in the session. Because of the phenomenon of restimulation, present distress patterns tend to be an accumulation of a large number of experiences, each one of which restimulated the earlier experiences on that chain as well as added new distress. The client will often tend to work first on a present-time restimulation or to treat a chronic pattern as if it were happening now, and these *can* be worked with on that basis.

Generally, however, it freshens up the counseling relationship and affords a better grasp of the whole pattern, if one can reach and work on the *earliest* incidents, the times the *foundation* of the particular pattern was laid in. Just to recount what went on long ago is often to make connections with the continuing compulsive behavior of current days in ways that the client has not been able to do by himself or herself or without a listener. In Section 5.173, you will find descriptions of how to review a list of similar distresses from the earliest remembered ones up to present time, over and over and over. The clarifying effect of this repeated review will show up in the counseling sessions in which heavy discharge is needed and available. You will notice that the less charged-up incidents drop off the list by themselves under repeated review. Thus, working early and then earlier and then earlier, as early as the client is able to remember, and from there moving up the chain of similar experiences to present time, is recommended as a general counseling mode.

5.183 As much as possible (as long as discharge is taking place), it is useful to assist a client to work on early distresses instead of putting the attention primarily on present-time difficulties. The present-time difficulties can usually be understood and solved more successfully when the early recordings are discharged and re-evaluated. Spending too much time working on present-time issues, as if they were an accurate picture of reality (instead of old restimulation), can slow down the process of re-emergence.

occluded memories

5.184 Great portions of most clients' intelligences have been locked away, occluded, or "buried" with the content of heavy distress recordings and a kind of frozen numbness entered into in these areas in order to allow the remaining intelligence to be free to handle the person's living situation as best it can.

5.185 Discharge on the emotional content of occluded memories can take place and be effective to a great degree without the client necessarily remembering all the contents of the occluded memory. The counselor can model saying, "Something happened!" for the client in a tone of voice implying great significance. The client's attempt to repeat the phrase the same way can lead to substantial and effective discharge.

5.186 When discharging the content of early and often occluded memories, much of what the client seems to be feeling will be a literal recording of how the client felt at the time of the original hurt. The client can often use a reminder that the feelings in the counseling situation are "on their way out" and what is being felt is the recording of the hurt that he or she was possibly too numb to feel in the original hurt experience and probably has therefore occluded.

5.187 When part of a distress or distress experience is occluded, the client can be assisted in reaching and discharging the distress through the device of "making up a story," that is, creating a *fantasy*. In general it is not useful to suggest to the client that the fantasy must be similar to the suspected memory. Instead, if the client is urged to be completely free in his or her fantasized version, it will furnish safety for the client to approach the content of the distress with considerably more confidence. Such stories can be about the client himself or herself, or about another imaginary person (or about any other creature or entity).

5.188 Success in the earlier stages of counseling will inevitably lead, at a later period, to the heaviest content of the earliest-occurring distress being brought out of occlusion by an aware or unaware decision of the client to not settle for part of the client's intelligence continuing to be tied up in the occluded distress. This can often be frightening and confusing to the client, who may interpret the un-numbed distress as a mystifying "new hurt," and may even conclude that "counseling isn't working any more," when in fact the counseling is actually "working" at an increased level of efficiency, probably because there is contradiction in the fact of the client's having re-emerged to some degree.

When heavy distresses become unoccluded it will sometimes be unavoidable for the client to be feeling intensely and discharging a great deal *between* sessions.

contradictions

5.189 We have re-defined the word "contradiction" in Re-evaluation Counseling to mean any factor in a counseling situation which assists the client to become aware that the distress pattern is *not* present-time reality. In this sense the concept of *contradiction* becomes central to everything that is done to discharge, re-evaluate, and re-emerge. Such a simple act as relating memories of a *past* distress experience can "contradict" the distress and lead to discharge of it because it is viewed *as in the past*.

5.190 It is useful to examine the possible *kinds* of sources of contradictions by thinking of them as: 1) *environmental factors* that contradict the distress; 2) *actions or attitudes of the client*, which the counselor can help the client organize and persist in, which contradict the distress; and 3) *actions or attitudes or behaviors of the counselor* which contradict the client's distress. There are additional situations or factors, not all of which will fit neatly into any of the preceding three categories, such as the effect of group attention on an individual client, or determined action by a client in meeting a crisis situation, which action often contradicts existing chronic patterns and leads to voluminous discharge. It is also possible for the counselor and client to agree to work towards keeping the client's attention completely away from any distress and let the undistressed character of present reality furnish the contradiction. Doing this may require that the counselor be active and persistent in assisting the client in attaining this "attention completely away from distress" attitude, but once it is attained, a client can often persist with this on his or her own decision for a long period of time, with much benefit.

5.191 Certain distress patterns of a client, particularly chronic ones, will require active intervention and contradiction *from the counselor* in order for discharge to take place. Here the counselor actively offers attitudes, opinions, directions, commitments, and activities for the client to try to adopt in order to contradict the distress. The counselor will assert the reality of these "contradictions" (when they *are* real) against the content of the distress recording.

5.192 Both in offering contradictions and in modeling contradictions for the client to say or act upon, the effectiveness of a contradictory (usually *positive*) *tone of voice* and contradictory (usually *positive*) *facial expressions* tend to be greater than the contradictory meaning of the words.

5.193 The presence of the counselor's *thinking* in the environment of the session is a contradiction to any distress because at the time the distress recording was installed such thinking was usually absent in the situation. Quite apart from doing any particular thing, the counselor needs to be thinking and somehow exhibiting the presence of this thinking to the client.

5.194 There are many possible contradictions to any particular client's particular distress which will bring discharge. Any or all of them can be valuable. Different counselors will bring many different attitudes and different viewpoints. There are many "right" ways of counseling. As counselor you can try out many contradictions, whether they involve tone of voice, posture, physical position, or actual directions, without worrying that false starts or mistakes will permanently interfere with the process. Trying out contradictions, and changing the ones that don't work well and improving them, is all part of getting to know the client's distress and what will contradict it.

5.195 Being listened to with attention *is a contradiction* to most distress patterns.

5.196 Being listened to with attention and a warm, approving attitude toward the client is an even greater contradiction to most distress patterns than simply being listened to.

5.197 The best approach to counseling a client on a big distress is always *contradicting it* (formerly sometimes called "putting attention away from it").

5.198 It is possible to counsel effectively and thoroughly with the client's attention *completely* away from the distress (and, therefore, contradicting it).

5.199 Distress recordings always have *physical* components. Such physical components will include body posture, tissue or muscle tension, facial expression, tone of voice, and physical movements. Contradictions to the contents of the distress recording can be devised in any of these areas and will be effective against the entire recording.

5.200 Although discharge tends to occur spontaneously, one can sometimes effectively contradict the existing patterns of "not discharging" either by firm repeated decisions by the client, or by the counselor repeatedly reassuring the client that it is OK to discharge. ("Let it come.") Yawns can be encouraged, for example, by asking the client whether he or she needs to yawn, by starting to yawn oneself or pretending to yawn, and by modeling stretching and making relaxed "ho hum" sounds.

5.201 A client wears his or her chronic distress as a "costume." Often his or her current posture, tone of voice, facial expression, etc., are those that the client assumed while being hurt in the original distress experience long ago. As counselor, one's ability to observe (see and hear), and sometimes mimic, the client's distress can be very helpful.

5.202 All distress recordings will necessarily have a physical component since the person was necessarily in some physical state or other when the recording was made. These can take the form of activity, nervous movements, acting aggressively, etc., but the majority of such distress will tend to be in the direction of passivity, of being "frozen," or of moving "very carefully" if at all.

Whatever the distress, it can be contradicted on the physical level as well as in words, emotional attitudes, facial expressions, tone of voice, etc. Deliberate physical exercise while recounting distress is likely to accelerate the discharge. For many incidents, careful, friendly wrestling or pushing will make a great difference in the rate of discharge. Children often intuitively sense that their parents need the contradiction of physical activity and will try to get their parents to run with them or play active physical games, and will laugh uproariously as long as the parents will participate. Needless to say, it is excellent for the parents to do this, however uncomfortable they may feel to begin with.

5.203 When a client cannot seem to completely contradict a pattern or a negative feeling in a pattern, it will often disarm the pattern's resistance to have the client admit that there is a "small amount" of the feeling present, such as saying, "I'm just a *little bit* scared." If a client cannot believe she or he is a good person, she or he might be able to acknowledge that "not everything about me is completely, terribly bad."

5.204 If a client finds it very difficult to pay attention to or conceive of a wholesale or total contradiction of his or her distress, the counselor can resort to a tiny, partial contradiction. A client caught in a heavy feeling of being totally "bad," for example, can be asked to say, "I've done a few small things in my life that were at least harmless," and have discharge ensue. Here one is taking advantage of the complete rigidity of the distress pattern which cannot bear even the slightest contradiction. If a counselor can remember this rigidity of the pattern, it becomes easy to out-maneuver the pattern and expose its rigid character, which in itself will tend to bring discharge.

5.205 To contradict a pattern in the obvious ways may have been attempted enough that the pattern is "guarded" and "protects itself" with many unexpressed rationalizations, so discharge does not any longer follow easily. In such cases it is possible to "get out of the other side of the bed," that is, to contradict the pattern by exaggerating it, overemphasizing it, over-agreeing with it, and proceed to get discharge started where the usual ways were no longer working. In doing this, you are taking advantage of the rigidity of the pattern. The pattern is exactly what it is; it has *no* flexibility, so if you need to contradict a pattern that insists that things are "bad," you, as counselor, can "solemnly" or "with alarm" insist that they are "worse than that," that they are "terrible" (with great solemnity), and the client will be moved to begin discharging.

5.206 Humor is an endlessly useful contradiction. All humor *consists* of presenting distress patterns and their irrational contents in ways that reveal their irrationality and their irrelevance to the present. This will allow the audience in a meeting or gathering or a workshop or class to join in the discharge and, to some extent, to free themselves from *their* distresses. A great comedian is a master counselor, which is why people are eager for his or her performances. Laughter is the most common discharge evoked, but the great comedians, such as Chaplin, made sure that their audiences cried as well as laughed.

5.207 Insisting upon the client validating and appreciating herself or himself is an especially effective contradiction to the invalidation distress but needs almost always to be accompanied by appreciation *from the counselor.*

5.208 Complete appreciation of oneself is a contradiction to all invalidation patterns and to many other distress patterns. If the counselor adds to and reinforces the client's appreciation of herself or himself, it is an even more effective contradiction.

5.209 *Accurate information* about the nature of human beings, society, and reality is a contradiction to most distress patterns.

5.210 In a counseling session where it seems that a variety of very promising contradictions are available to use, you, as the counselor, are free to experiment with choosing contradictions which will contradict earlier or more basic distress and possibly allow the client to continue to discharge well between sessions as his or her mind sorts through the distresses which have been contradicted in the session.

5.211 It is a contradiction to fears which have had an intimidating effect on the client to "scorn" them, that is, to treat the fear as if it has no possibility of intimidating you or the client, and to ask the client to follow your modeling.

5.212 It can be important for the client and the counselor to agree to have the client try to act outside the conditioned limits of "safe" functioning. This will contradict the recordings to be discharged. (Acting outside patterned behavior can be as simple as moving one's body in a new way or nodding one's head in a positive gesture instead of shaking it from side to side in a negative gesture.)

5.213 Safety (by which we mean not being or expecting to be threatened by any attack, misadventure, or loss) is the *basic* contradiction to fear of any degree.

5.214 The client in the grip of a recording of fear or terror is likely to be acting frozen or rigid. Any movement will tend to be an effective contradiction to this. Consider having the client wave and shout, run in place, or walk about the room. It is often helpful to over-dramatize a fear, such as by looking the way a person passing the peak of a roller coaster ride acts and looks, and encourage the client to copy your expressions and movements.

5.215 To have the client express terror *cheerfully* is amazingly effective as a contradiction.

5.216 Closeness is a basic contradiction to isolation.

5.217 One of the key ways that we are hurt is to be systematically isolated from other people. Closeness can be an effective contradiction to this distress. Such closeness may include aware touching and physical contact, and this should be available to the client at his or her choice.

5.218 Holding hands, sitting close, and other forms of physical closeness with the client can be useful contradictions since there is an inherent need for physical closeness in humans, but the counselor should insist on any of this only when it is plain that there is a fear or other kind of distress about such closeness and that to move toward such closeness slowly and relaxedly will bring discharge.

5.219 "Play" is a contradiction to most distress patterns, especially for young people, but actually for all clients. "Play" for young people is actually intense learning, a practicing of skills, and a discharging experience.

5.220 Sometimes a very young client who has deep, very early fears, will find a way to "struggle" against the counselor physically, pushing at him or her, opposing him or her verbally in every possible way. It is important that such a young client not have to be "careful" of the counselor or explain what he or she is doing at all. Just this activity of "overcoming opposition" can lead to heavy fear discharge with little or no verbalizing or explanation. It is best if the counselor acts delighted with the client during this activity.

5.221 In counseling survivors of incest or other sexual abuse, it is important that *the client be awarely in charge* of using physical closeness to the counselor as a contradiction to the distress. The client may be encouraged to move toward physical closeness with the counselor, but at her or his own speed, and only when coming closer produces discharge. The same thing applies to touching the counselor by the client. It should be at the client's initiative and pursued only as long as it brings discharge.

For the client to be "over-urged" toward closeness and then become "shut down" in the close position is only a *rehearsal* of past distress. A client can be helped to work on his or her physical "space" or distance, which the counselor will respect once it's located and defined, and which will only be crowded (as an aware contradiction to the old fear content) as it will bring discharge.

5.222 Many chronic patterns have the client giving the appearance of "relaxed calmness," which is simply an absence of discharge and really indicates that the client is numb with the distress, that is, not expressing it rather than being free of it. It will be part of the job of the counselor to distinguish such numbness from real calmness and to create and offer the contradictions which will allow the discharge to begin and the "numbness" to break up.

5.223 People caught in patterns of "settling for," being discouraged, being defeated, can be helped to contradict these patterns by using directions of "wishing." A client who cannot repeat a statement such as "I trust you," with any sense of reality, can be asked to say, "*I wish* I could trust you," as an effective contradiction that will bring discharge. After enough discharge on this level of contradiction, such a client can be asked to use phrases such as, "*Someday I'm going to trust you*," and eventually use stronger contradictions such as "I can," and "I will."

5.224 In challenging a discouraged or "defeated" client, it is important to sometimes reduce your expectations down to a *small* change, then praise and encourage and enthuse when the client makes a small change and ask for another small change immediately afterwards.

5.225 Clients sometimes feel that the difficulty of contradicting "hopelessness" is as great as the difficulty of contradicting "powerlessness." Actually, almost everyone has at least some memories available of being hopeful or even confident, while it is usually very difficult for people in our societies to find any memories of being powerful. The person who is "stuck" in a hopelessness pattern, however, has been argued with enough by determined people trying to cheer him or her up that the usual type of contradictions seem of little use at all. If the counselor is flexible enough, however, to "take over" the pattern and act out excessive agreement that the client's situation is "indeed hopeless"—with facial expression, tone of voice, and lugubrious agreement—the client can usually be "forced out" of the pattern enough to begin discharging. The client will then tend to furnish his or her own contradictions by "arguing" with the counselor against the counselor's dramatized "hopeless" role.

5.226 "I can," said as a preface to words describing something one *wishes* to accomplish, can act as a powerful contradiction to powerlessness patterns. The client should be asked to relate the thoughts which the repetition of the statement brings up.

5.227 The use of "I can," can be followed up with the phrase, "I can and I will," which will often have the effect of being even more contradictory to the powerlessness patterns.

5.228 "*I can* think the thoughts that are hard to think. *I can* do the things that are hard to do. *I can* contradict the distresses that are hard to contradict." This phrasing seems to concentrate the client's attention toward the distresses that would otherwise be avoided because they are uncomfortable to try to think about.

Often repetition of these phrases several times allows the client to move against the hopelessness and the feeling of defeat and begin to discharge.

5.229 Excellent living by the Co-Counselor and by her or his associates can be attained in great part by the design of adequate contradictions to the patterns operating in our regular lives and in our wide-world activity. Part of this will be a direction of active involvement with and communication with other people. Interacting well with other human beings is a contradiction to most distress. Good sessions are important, but they should not be a substitute for acting rationally, for acting outside of distress in our regular life. "How to re-emerge rapidly? Simply do *everything* well."

organized contradictions

5.230 The most effective sessions follow when *the environment of the session* contradicts the distress pattern, *and the client* is contradicting the distress pattern, *and the counselor* is contradicting the distress pattern.

The worst environments can be counseled in, but the less distressing the environmental situation is, the easier it will be to secure discharge. Comfort, warmth, privacy, absence of distracting noise, and any other similar factors should be thought about and prepared before the session as much as possible.

The counselor will be contradicting the distress by his or her very *role* of supporting the human client against the pattern. The client can be assumed to be against the pattern, and in approaching it, may often seem very clearly committed and dedicated to contradict it, but, once having tackled the pattern itself, the client's central nervous system is in a sense "at the mercy of" the pattern and will often appear to be dominated by the pattern and cooperating with the pattern.

It is important that the counselor understand this and not become impatient with, or make disappointed noises or facial expressions at the client, but instead realize that the counselor has the extra job, once the client has addressed the pattern and become vulnerable to it, to manage and organize the client's continued contradiction of the pattern. Many of the techniques that have been developed in Re-evaluation Counseling, such as "directions," "commitments," promises, actions, "frameworks," and "synopses," are tools for keeping the client organized and acting against the distress pattern once they have made contact with it.

5.231 A number of helpful forms for the client to use to contradict distress have evolved. These include: "directions," individual "commitments," commitments against "internalized oppression," "frontier" commitments, "synopses," "frameworks," "decisions," and taking action in reality.

directions

5.232 A *direction* is a statement which is in contradiction to the content of the distress pattern. A distress pattern whose content is, "I am incapable," can be contradicted by a direction such as, "I am a very capable person." A distress pattern whose content is, "I don't dare take any action," or, "I will go on tolerating abuse," can be contradicted with directions such as, "I will act at once, and firmly," or, "No more! Anybody that tries to abuse me again will be very sorry."

5.233 The counselor's job includes observing the pattern accurately, then finding or creating an effective direction against the pattern, then modeling the direction and persuading the client to follow the modeling. Then, while the client does that, the counselor can add further contradiction by his or her own facial expression, tone of voice, physical movement, etc.

5.234 In offering directions, appropriate words can sometimes be thought of easily, but a different tone of voice, different facial expression, and different posture than are usual for the client, if used, are likely to be more effective and will bring more discharge than the words alone. This is so because the words of a distress pattern have usually been "argued with" by the client himself or herself or by well-meaning allies until the pattern has grown a protective shield of inattention to resist the effects of the words. However, in our usual cultures, people's chronic facial expressions, tones of voice, and postures are taken for granted or tolerated by others as "part of one's personality" and allowed to become rigid without challenge. So the counselor who will make the effort to break out of his or her own chronic tone of voice, facial expression, and posture, and model this for the client in ways that are different from the client's usual tone of voice, facial expression, and posture, and insist on the client trying to follow the counselor's modeling, will usually elicit gratifyingly huge discharge from the client. All this applies to the other forms of contradicting distress as well as to the use of directions.

5.235 If the client resists a direction, and insists that it is "wrong," ask the client to tell you *why* it is wrong. If it is the pattern that is resisting, the pattern will not be able to give you a thoughtful answer, and the client is likely to notice this and be a *little more cooperative* in attempting the direction.

5.236 A client who has difficulty in agreeing to, repeating, or acting on a direction, can be gotten started by the repeated modeling of the direction by the counselor (including, remember, tone of voice, facial expression, and posture), coupled with the confident, relaxed expectation *each time* that the client will do it "next time."

5.237 The client does not have to repeat the direction, or do what the counselor suggests, as long as the modeling of the direction by the counselor brings discharge. The counselor can repeat the direction over and over again until the discharge slows down, at which point discharge may be increased again when the client is again expected and encouraged to repeat or act on the direction (or a sharper contradiction is created).

5.238 We seek continually in Co-Counseling to find better contradictions to the distress which has been part of our cultures and our lives. Increasingly the contradictions we find tend to become more general. As we integrate them into our usual attitudes, they furnish resistance to the patterned activity which tends to intrude into our lives from habit and restimulation. One such general direction that a number of us have found helpful is to "live every moment well." The "every moment" is inclusive. The "live" is a reminder of our perpetual activity. The "well" is clear in its direction and is general enough to cover everything. "Live every moment well."

planning/keeping notebooks

5.239 Distress patterns may be usefully thought of as having three "pseudo-abilities" (a pattern, of course, has *no* abilities at all, but through its enslavement of and manipulation of the client, it gives the appearance of being "able" to do these things). The first "pseudo-ability" is the ability to *persist*. As long as a pattern exists at all, it functions rigidly in the same old way. Second, the pattern also has the "pseudo-ability" to *confuse* its victim, to proclaim its own rigid content to its victim, and to other people, as "thinking." Third, the pattern has the "pseudo-ability" to make its victim *forget*. Even when the client has at least momentarily grasped the contradiction of reality to the pattern, this insight is likely to be "forgotten" and the client return to the persisting, rigid, unrealistic attitude embodied in the distress pattern.

The keeping of written notebooks is a precise, effective contradiction to all three of these "pseudo-abilities" of the pattern. Any kind of a notebook which is kept and referred to will be of great benefit in these ways. The *Client's Notebook* and the *Counselor's Notebook* are carefully prepared models and organized frameworks to encourage and remind clients and counselors of the use of the written word. The keeping of, and reference to, these notebooks is crucial to most beginning counselors, but experienced counselors who have used them find them the best single tool for the improvement of one's counseling and of one's re-emergence. They are an *organized* contradiction to the influence of patterns of hopelessness and powerlessness on the counseling process.

5.240 One's re-emergence proceeds better if it is planned, and the planning needs to be done both from the counselor's point of view and the client's point of view. Time in session can well be spent on such planning, with the counselor's insistence, persistence, and questioning helping the client to think about what the client wants, what paths the client can take, which difficulty needs to be discharged to free the approach to the other difficulties, and so on.

The counselor's planning for the client will often include keeping (possibly in the *Counselor's Notebook*) memoranda and reminders of what the client's goals have been stated to be, what are the obvious or likely patterned blocks in the way of attaining these goals, and which of the client's blocks are interfering with the excellent functioning of the Co-Counseling itself, and therefore need to be addressed.

Fears and "shut-downs" will often interfere with the client's remembering to tackle important distress. If the client can adopt a general attitude of "welcoming upheaval" with enthusiasm, it will tend to be an effective contradiction against these difficulties. To identify "sag" as the intrusion of the distress into the counseling process and therefore something to be committed against will tend to expedite the progress of the Co-Counseling relationship.

5.241 As a client, it is helpful to take responsibility for and plan one's own re-emergence instead of assuming that someone else will do it for one. This, in a broad sense, will include the finding and training of one's own counselors. In a more specific way, it will include the planning of each individual session ahead of time (with the plans able to be put aside or postponed if one's counselor has been thinking well and comes up with an even more effective plan for the session). In detail, it includes memorizing specific commitments, commitments against internalized oppression, "frontier" commitments, and a litany of self-validations to run through when alone or without attention from others, in order to block the distress of a pattern from invading and taking over one's mind. This sort of in-chargeness can operate both in and out of session. "Holding" or "keeping" directions and commitments between sessions disrupts the chronic hold of patterns on oneself, and taking physical action can often disrupt a pattern when it is difficult to contradict it emotionally or intellectually.

commitments/frameworks/synopses

5.242 An individual commitment is a promise made by the person as client (to the counselor, to "nears and dears," to reality, to "God," etc.) to act contrary to the pattern in every possible way. To repeat these silently may be helpful, to repeat them aloud is generally more helpful. It is also helpful to follow each repetition of the commitment with a further exploration of the meaning of the commitment or its implications, by saying, "And this will mean_____," and fill in the blank.

5.243 There are a great variety of "commitments" that have been created and widely used to help one be an active ally against the oppression of people in another particular group, to interrupt that particular oppression, to speak out against it, and to organize other people to come to the support of the oppressed group against the oppression. [See the updated list of commitments in the Appendix]

5.244 The person, not the distress, can *always* be in charge of the discharge process. It is possible and useful to practice commitments to focus attention off distress when not in session to the point where one can easily decide to "stay in present time" all the time when outside of sessions. One can also arrange one's life to pull one's attention away from distress by activity so that the process of counseling on "heavy" distress becomes enjoyable and does not overwhelm one.

5.245 What we have called the "frontier commitments" are commitments that are so effectively contradictory to widespread hurts commonly installed by this society that these commitments work for almost everybody and tend to open up all the other distresses to become vulnerable to contradiction and discharge. These will include the commitment *against the "ancient habit pattern"*; the commitment *against pretense*; the commitment *to be one's real self*; the commitment *to see that one is totally responsible and that everything works well*; the commitment *against identifying oneself with distress*; the commitment *to inspire, lead, and organize against every form of humans harming humans*; the commitment *against letting past attitudes influence the way one acts*; and the commitment *that one can and will do anything one decides to do*. There's also the social activists' commitment which is to change society but to act rationally and for one's own survival while doing it, that can be considered a frontier commitment, particularly under modern conditions.

5.246 THE FRONTIER COMMITMENTS:

• TO BE YOUR OWN ELEGANT, WISE, AND POWERFUL SELF: "From this moment on, the *real* (your own name)! This will mean_____."

• AGAINST PRETENSE: "I am obviously completely incompetent and completely inadequate to handle the challenges which reality places before me. However, (fortunately or unfortunately), I happen to be the best person available."

• TO RECLAIM POWER: "From now on I will see to it that everything I am in contact with works *well*, and I will not limit or pull back on my contacts. This will mean _____."

• AGAINST IDENTIFYING ONESELF WITH PATTERNS: "Recordings of past distress experiences have no power of their own at all.

They only contrive to give the appearance of power and influence to the extent that I slavishly submit to letting them use *my* power and *my* influence.

(If I think of these recordings of past distress experiences as if they were pieces of recorded tape, they have, at most, a trifling historical significance, *unless* I insert them in the tape recorder that is myself and allow them to play *me*, an action which I am completely free to decide to do or not to do.)

Therefore, I now decide to deny any past distress any credibility in the present, or any influence or operation in my life.

And I will repeat this decision as often as necessary to free my life completely from the influence of past distress."

• TO UNITY OF ALL HUMAN ASPIRATIONS: "From now on I will inspire, lead, and organize all people to eliminate every form of humans' harming humans. This will mean_____."

• TO ELIMINATE THE INFLUENCE OF PAST ATTITUDES: "Since thinking is necessarily *fresh* thinking, I hereby decide that I will never again let anything from the past influence the way I act in the present or future, and I will repeat this decision as many times as necessary to achieve the clear-cut results that I want."

• TO END PREOCCUPATION WITH DISTRESS: "It is logically possible and certainly desirable to end the ancient habit of paying attention to past distress and replace it with a new attitude or posture of paying attention to interesting and rewarding concerns, including the present-time situation, and so I now decide to do this and will repeatedly so decide until the ancient habit is broken."

• TO DO ANYTHING ONE DECIDES: "I can!"

5.247 What we have called a *"framework"* is a short statement of the fundamentally positive nature of the client, a description of the first devastating distress that occurred in the life of the client which laid the foundation for the chronic distress patterns, an admiring description of the way the client resisted the distress, a positive recognition of the client's achievement in functioning so well in spite of the distress, a recognition of the new resources available and being used by the client in the current scene, and a statement of the expected triumph of the client over the distress. This whole statement is repeated by the client over and over with commentary of new thoughts and insights that occur to the client (as well as discharge) and with supportive comments by the counselor.

Examples of frameworks:			
	FRAMEWORK "A"	FRAMEWORK "B"	FRAMEWORK "C"
1. (EARLY HURTS)	(Pre-natal anesthesia)	(Rejection, attack, not being welcome anywhere, hardship)	(Lack of warmth or affection. Being treated like an inhuman object)
2. (CHRONIC DISTRESS)	(Feeling of not being able to think, especially about important matters)	(Inability to feel cared about. Fear of intruding. Vulnerability to unprovoked attacks)	(Difficulty in caring about others or having close relationships)
3. FIRST STATEMENT	"I revived and survived, and today I can think better than almost anybody I meet."	"I survived the hostile attitudes and the harsh conditions of my infancy, childhood, and youth, and the fierce struggles of my adult years."	"There was not much human resource available to me in the beginning. I was lied to and misinformed about many important things; but I've always done the best I could to be a good, caring human being."
4. SUPPORTIVE REALITY	"The best minds I know regard me as a peer."	"I have achieved such a meaningful life that my older brother would be proud of me if he knew. Large numbers of people regard me as a meaningful, benign factor in their lives."	"I've succeeded already in most areas of my life and have strength available for others who need it."
5. SECOND STATEMENT	"I am engaged in the process of realizing how smart I am, especially about the big picture."	"I am engaged in the process of realizing and feeling that many people care about me, not only for what I do, but for what I am, some few of them in a way that would feel like love to a person without my hurts."	"I am in the process of re-emerging from any limitations on my caring or being cared about."
6. THIRD STATEMENT	"I have a responsibility to continue this process, not only for me, but for the Universe."	"I am committed to complete this process, not only for me but to carry out my existing commitment to achieve the complete re-emergence of every human being."	"I have a responsibility to continue with this process, not only for my own blossoming, but for the general good of the world around me."
7. FOURTH STATEMENT	"The Universe needs a C__ who realizes fully how smart she is."	"The upward trend will be enhanced and accelerated by an H__ who feels deeply loved and cared about."	"The big picture needs a glowing, confident, powerful, loving G__ within its frame."

(Reprinted from *The Benign Reality*)

5.248 What we have called a *"synopsis"* in Re-evaluation Counseling is a shorter version of the "framework" statement, summarizing the severity of the early hurts that occurred to the client, denying the validity of any blame or reproach at the client for having been injured, and expressing admiration for the client's persistence and success in spite of the hurt, *and* a statement that in the light of present information the client is easily discernible as an *admirable, positive,* and *successful* person.

Examples of synopses:

	EXAMPLE 1	EXAMPLE 2	EXAMPLE 3	CONTENT
part 1	"I was told vicious lies while I was hurting and scared.	"Very early I was threatened with death, misinformed, invalidated, and misunderstood *while I was hurting and scared.*	"Something devastating and violent happened to me very early.	"FRANK ACKNOWLEDGEMENT, WITH THE COUNSELOR'S ASSISTANCE AND APPROVAL, THAT THE DEVASTATING HURTS DID HAPPEN.
part 2	And anybody would have been left confused by that!	Anybody would have been left cautious and isolated after that.	Anybody would have been left very, very careful about everything after that.	REJECTION OF ANY BLAME TO THE CLIENT FOR HAVING BEEN LEFT WITH PATTERNED ATTITUDES OR BEHAVIOR BY THE HURT. ACKNOWLEDGEMENT THAT THE PATTERN WAS THE BEST RESPONSE THE CLIENT COULD CONTRIVE IN THE MIDDLE OF THE DISASTER.
part 3	BUT NOW! it's at least possible (probably probable and increasingly certain) that I am totally splendid and always have been."	BUT NOW! knowing what I know, having achieved what I have achieved, and being in deep contact with at least one other fine intelligence, it is *at least possible* that I 'have it made' on all fronts and everything is going to get better and better as I reclaim *all* my power."	BUT NOW! with the theory and my already achieved gains to guide me and inspire me, it is at least possible that my boldness and power are intact and useable, and I can dispense with all self-reproaches and timidity."	SEPARATION OF THE PAST FROM THE PRESENT. CELEBRATION OF THE IMMEDIATE POSSIBILITIES OF RE-EMERGENCE. COMPLETE VALIDATION OF THE CLIENT IN THE PRESENT AND THE PAST.

(Reprinted from *The Rest of Our Lives*)

5.249 We have called the rapid, continuing exchange of the counselor and client roles between two Co-Counselors, *"dual commitments,"* or *"the exchange of commitments."* In this mode each of the two Co-Counselors says his or her commitment once and voices the consequences or the implications of it while discharging. After a reasonable amount of discharge, the person who has begun as client nods to the other Co-Counselor, who assumes the role of client immediately, while the other person assumes the role of counselor. In this way the roles of client and counselor are passed back and forth with, usually, not longer than a minute or two or three for each turn. This has been found to be a very powerful counseling tool. When used well it tends to contradict and brush aside much of the isolation that tends to cling to counseling relationships. Using this technique is a highway to achieving a close relationship with one's Co-Counselor. When practiced well, both people tend to discharge *all the time,* even though they are rapidly exchanging roles from client to counselor and counselor to client. The two people involved will show a tendency to spontaneously commit themselves to each others' re-emergence in addition to the other commitments that they are making. When this happens, the discharge tends to occur very rapidly. The intensity of the discharge can even frighten people away from persisting with the exchange. A possible way to resist this is the use of a third strong Co-Counselor as a *mentor*, who will keep urging the full use of the effectiveness of the technique.

5.250 Making any form of a *decision to contradict distress in all phases of one's life* and carrying out such a decision between sessions tends to improve both one's sessions and one's life.

goals

5.251 It can be helpful to think of "maintenance" counseling as distinct from "re-emergent" counseling. The counseling becomes more effective if one thinks about life goals, about patterns getting in the way, about planning to eliminate the patterns, and about working towards life goals. If one makes a commitment and/or decides to act against patterns and towards the goals, if one acts, discharges, and re-evaluates in that order, discharge and re-evaluation will accompany all the above steps. Waiting to act until patterns in the way are discharged can slow down re-emergence considerably.

5.252 A person rarely achieves a goal unless he or she has *set* it. Setting and reviewing goals is an integral part of the re-emergence process.

In the role of client, the Co-Counselor needs to think and make notes of all her or his desired goals, extending from the goals to be realized immediately to goals that will require more preparation and passage of time, over a series of increasing intervals, to goals for one's lifetime and for the entire future. To discuss and review these series of goals with the attention of a counselor will clarify them and allow the client to implement them.

When in the role of counselor, the Co-Counselor should question the client with interest as to what the client's goals are, ranging from *immediate* ones to *ultimate* ones, and ranging from *completely personal goals* to *goals for all the persons and entities with whom one has relationships*, out to *the entire universe*. The counselor should make notes of the client's goals, both for himself or herself as counselor, and for the use of the client. As counselor, the counselor should have *goals to achieve with the client*, ranging all the way from *helping the client achieve immediate discharge* out to *achieving the client's ultimate re-emergence*. These goals will not, in general, be in conflict with the client's own goals, and if they seem to be, a discussion should be entered into to clarify the possible existence of a pattern (on the part of either the counselor or the client) being the source of the apparent conflict.

5.253 The use of the goals chart, found in all editions of *The Fundamentals of Co-Counseling Manual* and in the Appendix to this book, will clarify the setting and attainment of goals greatly.

As a client, the Co-Counselor needs to fill out a copy of the goals chart for himself or herself personally, in the steps of: immediately, to be attained within a week, to be attained within a month, to be attained within a year, to be attained within ten years, to be attained within a lifetime, to be attained ultimately. The same steps should be decided and noted on behalf of goals for one's family and close associates, then on behalf of one's country and more remote associates, then for one's own total species, then for the totality of living things, and then for the universe. These goals charts need to be reviewed periodically and brought up-to-date and in line with the re-evaluation achieved by the client since the last previous update of the chart.

When counselor, the Co-Counselor should gently insist that his or her clients fill out such a goals chart and periodically review it. The counselor may include the particular client's progress on his or her *own* goals chart. Reviewing this periodically will assist one in being more purposeful in counseling that particular client and more effective for that client's re-emergence.

5.254 *Happiness consists of the overcoming of obstacles on the way toward a goal of one's own choosing.*

"techniques"

5.255 "Techniques" in Re-evaluation Counseling are general summaries of what has been found to be helpful or workable in the past experience of other Co-Counselors. At best, they are general indications of workable processes to be used in a session and almost always need modification for the particular situation in a particular session with a particular client.

5.256 A remarkably effective technique is to have the client agree to repetitively ask the counselor, "Why do you love me, (counselor's name)?" When the Co-Counselors are well-acquainted and conditions are positive, this will often lead the clients to discharge voluminously for a long time before they can even ask the question. When the client can ask the question, the counselor (having had plenty of time to frame a good reply), responds with the first of an endless series of "good reasons." The counselor should never push the client to repeat the question quickly, but should let the client return to the thoughts that brought the discharge the first time, over and over again. When the client is no longer discharging, the counselor prompts the client to repeat the question and has an excellent moving answer which he or she has had time to craft to be counter to the particular parts of the client's invalidation distresses which the counselor is aware of. Deep, important sessions often ensue on this simple arrangement.

Apparently the reason why it works so well is because the client's question, "Why do you love me?" (not "Do you love me?" or "Are you going to love me?") puts the client in the position of having to assume by his or her own words that the counselor loves him or her (in the nature of the language), and so the client is already committed against the nearly universal distresses of feeling unloved. Any thoughtful reply which the counselor makes commits the counselor also (and the whole situation) to the contradiction of the pattern. Other words can be substituted for "love," but the word "love" itself is a very powerful contradiction in most cases.

5.257 In many ways a counselor can play the role of a character in some incident of distress in the past or in some fantasy which the client is devising with the counselor's assistance. Sometimes the counselor will play the role of the oppressor or harmer in the past incident with encouragement to the client to rebel against the counselor's role, to act contrary to the way he or she did in the original experience. Sometimes the entire incident or fantasy can be devised to be in contradiction to the content of the earlier distress, with the client and the counselor cooperating to "handle" the one-time difficult or dismaying situation with confidence and aplomb and success.

5.258 To have a person in the client role sincerely ask, "Am I really all right?" can bring significant discharge because to ask the question tends to put the client in touch with the reality that she or he *is* all right (and may also put the client in touch with how deeply she or he doesn't *feel* all right). Most of us have "gone numb" around this, acting rigidly as if we "*know*" we're all right. To alternate this question with another question, "Do you (the counselor) really think I've *always* been completely all right?" can also be effective.

5.259 There will be clients who insist upon their recorded negative attitudes as reality and "argue" with the counselor's efforts to contradict them. In these cases, if the counselor is relaxed and flexible, it is devastatingly effective to "solemnly," "seriously," agree and over-agree with the negative picture insisted upon by the client. This utilizes the general principle that "there is only room for one person in a particular role of a pattern at a time." This is among the most powerful of all techniques available in Co-Counseling, but it is not effective if only done partially or half-heartedly. The counselor must be free enough from embarrassment to accurately copy the pattern literally.

5.260 The "exchange of roles" has proved marvelously effective in situations that have been difficult with other techniques. The counselor asks the client to begin with a statement, "I'm going to hurt you physically, (name of counselor)," and continue with half-sentences, "I'm going to. . . ," filling in the blanks with all possible ways of hurting the counselor physically. What comes out will tend to be more and more an approximation of the way the client had been hurt physically in the past. However, the client should not be directed to limit it to that but urged to threaten every active hurt which the client can think of from any source at all, including the stories the client has heard, books she or he has read, and movies or television shows she or he has seen. Freely expressing any kind of threat of physical hurt is the goal, rather than limiting the threats to the ones experienced by the client in her or his own past.

There will be a spontaneous tendency, however, for the description of the threats to approximate more and more accurately the threatened or enacted physical hurts which the client has suffered in the past. Occluded memories tend to emerge from occlusion with relative ease in this manner, with the threats which describe them being made and repeated many times before the client has the insight that she or he is threatening and describing what actually went on in her or his occluded experiences. The client, being in the role of the threatening aggressor, and the counselor, being made to occupy the role of the object of the threats, usually works out to be a very effective contradiction. All kinds of discharge will tend to take place quickly and effectively. Laughter is often the first, but the shaking and trembling that discharges heavy fear tends to be not far behind and occurs without the inhibition and difficulty that have often attended "getting started" with this sort of discharge with other techniques.

The beginning threat can be, "I'm going to abuse you sexually, (name of counselor)," followed by "I'm going to...," "I'm going to...," with the blanks being filled in with any possible kind of sexual abuse from any source of information that the client can draw on, including stories, books, films, etc. Graphic details of occluded experiences of sexual abuse surface very easily with this technique, and again, the discharge, especially that of shaking with heavy fear, tends to occur much more easily and quickly than has been common with other techniques. The client is likely to give many clues that this is out of occluded experiences of his or her own by "assigning" sexual organs to the threatened counselor that belonged to the other gender and threatening the abusive use of such sexual organs that belong to another gender on his or her part.

On all these different ways of using "exchange of roles," the counselor can add an additional contradiction of cheerfully and relaxedly accepting the threat of the abuse, being "pleased" with the attention, congratulating the threatener's ingenuity, etc. This little extra contradiction from the counselor's "unexpected attitude" often can precipitate the beginning of discharge much earlier than would occur without it.

Other ways of "exchanging roles" can be ingeniously invented to fit the particular distresses of a particular client. The client can be asked, for example, to threaten the counselor with, "I'm going to make you afraid to take any initiative," "I'm going to embarrass you so that you'll feel self-conscious with everybody," etc. These also will tend to reveal the details of the client's own experiences of the distress and enhance the client's ability to discharge them.

5.261 Once we had realized the central importance of the concept of "contradiction," we were able to relate almost all of the succcessful past approaches ("techniques") of counseling to this general concept. Almost all of our previous successful approaches to counseling can now be seen as some form of applying the "contradiction principle" in a session. In discussions about counseling we defined our use of the word *contradiction* to mean anything that allows the client on whom the patterns have been impressed in the past to realize that *the pattern is NOT present-time reality*. When a distress pattern is thus "contradicted," and the contradiction is persisted in, discharge takes place, and the pattern becomes converted to flexibly-available information only.

5.262 The approach to (or technique of) counseling that we have called the "Reality Agreement" makes it possible for the time being spent in session to be almost totally contradictory to the client's distress pattern and almost completely lacking in any "rehearsal" of it. In this kind of counseling the client and the counselor first reach a binding agreement with each other. The two formally agree to keep the irrational, patterned, *pseudo-reality* from being allowed to intrude into their communication or their attentions, and agree that, if it does intrude, it will be rejected and their attentions will be returned to actual reality.

The counselor first seeks and secures the client's agreement that the *actual reality* of the universe is completely distinct from the *pseudo-reality* interpretation of the universe which has been presented to us and continues to be presented to us by misinformation, by the operations of oppression, by the client's patterns, by other people's patterns, and by the oppressive societies in which we live. The pseudo-reality includes a false picture which has been attempted to be imposed upon us as a substitute for actual reality.

With this agreement secured, the counselor proceeds to ask some very simple questions, about which the client has agreed he or she will answer *only from the position of the actual reality of the universe* and the *actual reality of himself or herself*. The client has agreed not to express *any* pseudo-reality.

A beginning question might be, "How *good* are you?" The profundity of the client realizing that he or she is *completely* good, and the efficiency of the discharge process in the conversion of any distress that would try to oppose or interfere with that realization, is very impressive and satisfying. Many distresses that during previous counseling sessions have seemed to be quite intransigent turn to discharge easily (if, sometimes, slowly). There is no remaining "restimulation" or residue of upset after the session because the client's attention has been diverted to, and tends to have been wholly on, reality all the time.

Other questions that have worked well have been, "How *innocent* are you?" "How *pure* are you?" "How *intelligent* are you?" "How *powerful* are you?" "How *free* are you?" etc., etc. All these questions will need eventually to be answered with sentences that mean, "I am *completely* innocent, *completely* intelligent, etc." Each such answer needs to be explored, and the details of the innocence, intelligence, etc., as they are thought about and spoken about will bring persisting discharge. The counselor pays attention and is present (apparently, principally, as a reminder of the agreement's existence) and is relaxed, calm, pleased, and confident. If the client seems at any time to be losing touch with the counselor's expectation that the question be answered or continued to be answered in terms of actual reality, the counselor may repeat the question.

This approach has the possibility of eliminating in practice the spending of time and attention in sessions in description of, rehearsal of, and dramatizations of distress. It seems to be a way in which most clients can make a dependable commitment to deny attention to their distresses and to repeatedly dwell upon and express fundamental contradictions to that distress. It seems to give us dependable access to the tremendous ability of the client's mind to discharge, re-evaluate, and think when that mind is not hobbled by the rehearsal of the distresses which have claimed part of its attention in most past sessions as a client.

5.263 It seems clear that all of us developed an expectation (as we grew pre-natally) that we would enjoy *closeness* with other intelligences as part of the normal living of an entity such as ourselves. (This has certainly been occasionally reinforced by the presence of a twin sharing our pre-natal environment with us.) *This* expectation was cruelly denied by the circumstances attending the usual birth procedures and by the ridiculous, inhuman separation and calloused treatment given us by the people attending our births. Medical examinations, "periodic" feeding, lack of touch, isolation, interference with the crucially-necessary discharge of the hurts incurred during birth, and other factors tended to be the basis for very heavy and rapidly-deepening chronic patterns that have been repeatedly reinforced by later hurts.

To try to regain touch with that occluded concept of universally-available affection, humans have often relied on fantasies, tried "falling in love," used the stirrings of sexual feelings (whether brought on prematurely by sexual abuse when children or by "normal" development during adolescence), read romantic literature, or pursued any other possible source. Many people have become "stuck" in the pursuit of any of these substitute channels that seemed to offer hope of access to the universal affection that we have longed for. The illusions and disappointments that followed have reinforced the barrier.

The next counseling approach consists of having the client say to the counselor, using that counselor's name, "You and me,(counselor's name)," repeating the phrase a number of times and telling the thoughts that have come to mind. Discharge almost always begins at once. Discharge can be encouraged to start where it is slow to begin by asking the client to add the words, "completely close," to the "You and me, Gertrude," and to deepen the discharge after a few minutes by adding the word, "forever," so that the repeated thought (and sometimes repeatedly-voiced phrase) is, "You and me, Hortense, completely close, forever."

The amount and kind of discharge varies from client to client (and from time to time), but it is usually very substantial. It can include heavy sobbing, shaking, laughing, and deep, deep yawns. People often express great relief at the session. They often volunteer that they have "longed" for such a relationship with someone. They describe a feeling of general relaxation, both physical and emotional, taking place. They seem to sense the results of the session as a profound experience.

This counseling approach has an effect upon the counselor, also, which is similar to the effect it has upon the client. Apparently "sharing" and "closeness" *are necessarily* two-way experiences.

There is a *general* desire of *everybody* to be *close to every other human being*. For the counselor to offer this phrase with his or her own name in it, is a reassurance (which he or she can quickly add to) that this closeness is available with this counselor. It seems to be useful to remind the clients that this is the closeness that the counselor wants with *them* and to remind them of the "completely close" and "forever" parts of the phrase (which they sometimes tend to leave off), as well as to offer a formal agreement that the counselor and the client will be completely close in the future.

5.264 Temporarily "standing guard" for someone while he or she rests or even lies in the counselor's arms is an effective contradiction to recordings of exhaustion. The client is likely to cry voluminously, yawn prodigiously, or fall asleep and rest well.

5.265 If a client "attacks" Re-evaluation Counseling or the process of counseling itself, it's often very effective and easily possible to good-humoredly "over-agree." This is another example of "crowding a client out of a pattern," and will lead to discharge and the possibility for him or her to spontaneously come to take a more cooperative attitude.

5.266 The client *never* deserves nor *has deserved* blame or reproach from anybody—not now, not in the past, not in the future, and especially *never* from the counselor. The client can, however, be encouraged to "blame" the counselor (as another example of "exchange of roles") and begin to move out of the internalized recordings of self-blame in the process. The counselor may help by relaxedly and enthusiastically taking the role of agreeing that, "It's all my fault."

5.267 What has been called "Re-evaluation Counseling wrestling" can be useful. In this the roles of counselor and client are clearly designated, and the counselor's role is to help the client struggle hard physically against old powerlessness feelings by pushing against or "wrestling" with the counselor.

counseling on oppressed/oppressor roles (see section 14 for theoretical discussion)

5.268 Counseling a person on the distress he or she has endured in the role of being oppressed is quite straightforward. The attitude of the counselor needs to be plainly against the oppression and not believing any of the oppression that the client has been forced to accept and internalize as justified. Commitments are needed by the client *and the counselor* to end the oppression permanently.

The counselor himself or herself needs to be free from any part of an oppressive attitude. I am impatient with any more contrived approach to being this way than *just simply loving the client*. The client is always lovable. If the counselor really perceives the client, it is the easiest thing in the world to love her or him, to express love and keep expressing it, with words, tone of voice, facial expression, and, where it is helpful, with touch. This will often make the difference between whether the distress laid in by having been a victim of the oppression discharges or not.

Because of the persistent societal denial of the existence of most oppressions, a first contradiction for oppressed people is often to be able to tell the truth about the reality of their oppression and to have it acknowledged by others.

Members of the oppressed group can frequently discharge well (at least to begin with) simply by having their oppression openly recognized as oppression and by the support of the counselor or of the listening groups in committing themselves to resist and eliminate the oppression. To be listened to with respect on the details of the suffering of one's group can have a powerful effect. To actually listen to these stories frequently begins to "reach" the people who have been in the oppressor groups and produces discharge from them as they hear the details as members of the audience. The distrust and insecurity which the members of the oppressed group feel toward people in the oppressor group can be explicitly contradicted by the oppressed person declaring that from now on he or she will "count on" the members of the oppressor group to cease participating in the oppression and actively oppose its functioning. The members of the oppressor group can openly commit themselves to this agreement. Both groups can frequently discharge at once, and the beginnings of real communication between the people in the two roles of being oppressed and being agents of the oppression can be achieved.

In counseling people on the oppression which they have endured, it is useful to remember to insist on them expressing pride in who they are and the groups they belong to and the fact that they have endured the oppression and flourished, to at least some extent, in spite of it. Each person needs to be urged to take a very fundamental stance of self-validation as a "completely good person," as a person "destined to end all oppression."

The client needs help in discharging grief about the early mis-information and invalidations received about himself or herself and his or her group of people.

The person needs to contradict the separations from the other people in his or her group of oppressed, declare his or her solidarity with them, and plan for "all for one and one for all" unity between them.

If the counselor is outside the oppressed group, he or she can be very effective in seeing more clearly to begin with (than members of the oppressed group usually can) the *wrongness* of the oppression and the *excellence* of the people oppressed. Such a person needs to be willing to listen to resentment and blame, which may be turned upon him or upon her by the members of the oppressed group, but needs to remember not to actually accept or internalize any of the blame.

The tendency of an oppressed person to rehearse "blame" of the oppressors (or of anyone else) should be accepted as a starting point, but the client must not be left stuck in endlessly rehearsing the "blame" because this is, in effect, a rehearsal of the powerlessness component of the oppression itself.

5.269 Almost without exception, every person who has lived in our present oppressive societies has distress needing to be discharged from experiences of having been oppressed, *but also from experiences of being in an oppressor role.*

Because of the universal or nearly universal presence of this conditioning, Re-evaluation Counselors were slow to counsel effectively toward the removal of these oppressor attitudes. For a long time there was (and still is) pressure from the patterned culture around us to reproach the person with such attitudes and add to the guilt in an effort to change the behavior. Finally we reached a general understanding that this was simply adding to the oppressive distress by reinforcing the guilt that was a major component of the distress, and that a *contradiction* was needed instead.

What seems to work well, if persisted in intelligently, is to ask the person who has been a member of a group that plays an oppressive role to remember his or her first contact with anyone who is a member of the oppressed group. (In the case of someone needing to discharge white racism, ask this client for the earliest memory he or she has of noticing that there was any color of skin in the world besides "pink.") Around these early memories, the operation of the oppression being expressed and modeled by older people in these memories is likely to reveal itself clearly.

If the client is asked to speak to the person in the memory who is being treated with oppressive racism and apologize on behalf of himself or herself and the older people who were perpetrating and installing the racism, the client is often revealed as a broken-hearted little child who was resisting the anti-human policies of the oppression as determinedly as he or she could. He or she was being forced by the love for and dependence on the *perpetrators* to accept the oppressive attitude with enormous sorrow and guilt *and then occlude it* so that it operated unawarely for the rest of his or her life until that moment.

To pursue the series of memories associated with this early one is to convert the unawarely-racist client into an aware, active, effective ally *against* the oppression and to free large amounts of free attention and power that had unawarely been tied up in the distress.

If occlusions interfere with finding memories for discharge, fantasies can be produced by the client (or suggested by the counselor) in which the client plays an active anti-oppression role as "heroically" as can be fantasized. This can lead to a great deal of discharge because the "heroic resistance" fantasized and reported by the client is actually an expression of the determined resistance of the small child *as far as her or his strength permitted* until it was overpowered by the oppressive attitudes of the adults whom the child loved and was dependent upon.

building and taking care of a Co-Counseling relationship

5.270 A Co-Counseling relationship can be started between any two or more human beings, if they decide to do so, regardless of any differences in their ages, nationalities, races, languages, or any other factor. The Co-Counseling relationship can be kept workable and profitable for both parties as long the persons involved decide to keep it so.

5.271 A working Co-Counseling relationship is certainly one of the fullest and deepest relationships between two intelligences that we have experienced. Two intelligences can interrelate dramatically well when they are both functioning fully and are dealing with rational problems or real data that is in plain sight. This type of interaction will also take place sometimes in a Co-Counseling relationship. The Co-Counseling relationship, however, will also be dealing with "pseudo-reality," which has been projected at the Co-Counselors from the oppressive society and culture. The Co-Counselors will be having to "reach around" the patterns attached to the other person as they interrelate. Each has to help the other person think in the area the other person finds it difficult to think in, and to reach true conclusions in spite of false data and distorted attitudes. This means that both parties must learn to reach for total honesty and rigorous thinking in their interactions.

5.272 To have another person accept the responsibility for being or attempting to be one's "counselor" is a very precious gift. A person willing to learn to play such a role will correctly be cherished and valued highly. All of the usual courtesies and thoughtfulnesses which one should offer to any other human being should be applied with particular care to one's counselor. One should always be on time for one's session. One should try never to rehearse one's distress at the counselor during one's session unless such rehearsal has been specifically discussed with and agreed to by the counselor in advance as a mutual agreed-upon strategy for outwitting, contradicting, and discharging a particular distress. Any suggestions which one makes to one's counselor need to be phrased thoughtfully and carefully to avoid being offensive in any way, and appreciation can never be expressed too often.

Remember, your counselor will be resisting a pull to be client just as you will have to resist such a pull when you are in the role of counselor, and appreciation and praise will make it much easier to resist this pull. When not a client, one can well devote some of one's time and thought to planning the re-emergence of one's counselor during the times one's counselor is in a client role. This can be discussed and planned with one's teacher, workshop leader, or other Co-Counselors of one's counselor.

5.273 Both the person who is client and the person who is counselor will do well to be scrupulously courteous in their attitudes and treatment of each other. This will include timeliness, respect for each other's environments, viewing each other as precious resources, and turn-taking with, at least over the long run, *equal* turns.

5.274 Treating everything that the client says with complete confidentiality is absolutely essential for Co-Counseling, or for that matter, counseling, to work well and persistently. Whatever the client says or expresses in any way is in some form an aspect of the client's thinking, even if it is a rehearsal of distress, which the client's intelligence is rehearsing in an effort to bring it to the counselor's attention. For most of her or his life, the client has been under some form of pressure of being *told* what to think, and this in itself is deeply hurtful to anyone's intelligence. If the client is making an effort to think in some areas where there has been some distress, this thinking needs to be fully respected and encouraged. Any discussion (with anyone except the client) of what the client has said or revealed is a basic invalidation of the client's safety. Even if the client herself or himself demands the opinion of the counselor about something he or she has said or revealed, the counselor will do well to be interested and enthusiastic about the client's *saying it*, but try as far as possible to be completely non-committal as far as making any judgment about what the client has said, even if the client "insists."

Never bring up or share what the client has said in a session (or turn, in a group) outside of the session, or even in the next session, unless, of course, the client requests that you do so and gives permission for you to do so.

The excuse for breaking this confidentiality toward the client when one is oneself the client in a later session, that "the material has been too upsetting and must be talked about," *is just an excuse* being offered by a *gossip pattern* or a *gossip compulsion* of the one who is doing it. Any upsets can be discharged by contradiction, not by rehearsing the material nor by identifying the source.

The only exception to the above is when a team of counselors are working together to counsel the same client and have the permission of the client to consult each other on all details of the counseling.

5.275 Basically, the client needs to be free to decide what she or he wishes to counsel *on*. It is a disservice for the counselor to try to make this choice for the client, unless the client asks the counselor for a suggestion. This can also be modified by agreements and commitments between the client and the counselor, where the client has asked to be reminded, urged, or even *required* to address certain distress, which the client otherwise finds it very difficult to face.

This can also be modified in the case of a client who compulsively brings up distress which the client does not have enough aware attention to handle, or for which the counseling pair have not found adequate contradiction in their past attempts. In such a case, the counselor can properly insist on the client working only on material which she or he can discharge, rather than being "sunk in." Alternatively, the counselor can insist that the client work with attention-*gaining* techniques, in preparation for tackling the heavy distress later.

5.276 Relationships between Co-Counselors will be enhanced if patterned "identifications" are checked for routinely and discharged.

5.277 When counselor, think about your client before proceeding to counsel him or her. Make an aware decision to not let any feelings from the past affect your counseling of that person, your thinking about that person, your caring about that person, your clear motivation to take responsibility that he or she re-emerges.

5.278 Plan on and experiment with taking brief notes during sessions when you are counselor and then refer to the notes and think about the client between sessions. Use of the *Client Notebook* and the *Counselor Notebook* provides a stability and a continuity to the relationship with a particular client. The same sort of effectiveness tends to be achieved when a client keeps a notebook after every session and refers to it thoughtfully before the next session.

5.279 Most of us have been young, or become young adults, or become adults, carrying a pattern of a frozen need for "parenting" because of the difficulties with which our parents had to contend as a result of their distresses and oppression. Thus there will be a pull to identify our counselor in a Co-Counseling relationship *with our parents* and to unwittingly or unawarely project at them our frozen need for parenting, our disappointments with past relationships, and our blame for any difficulty we encounter (which we are likely to perceive as "failures" in the relationship). It is a good idea to check out any possible identifications of our counselor with anyone in our past on a regular basis and to discharge any identifications that are turned up.

5.280 Co-Counselors are required, and expected, to refrain from setting up any additional, non-counseling relationships with a person whom they meet in the context of Co-Counseling or in the Co-Counseling Community. This is because the Co-Counseling relationship, or co-participation in Co-Counseling activities, is such a precious and important relationship that it is crucially important to keep it "clean" and functional. As Co-Counselor, one hopes and expects to be assisted to re-emerge from all distress to one's own inherent, splendid nature and abilities, and one undertakes to assist others to do the same.

This does not mean that Co-Counselors will not become fond of each other nor love each other. (They inevitably do.) It does mean that this precious commitment must not be diluted or contaminated by using the person for some other relationship, the purpose of which will inevitably turn out to be in conflict with the basic commitment towards Co-Counseling and will carry, or soon acquire, some component of satisfying a patterned or "frozen" need.

Because people often begin counseling in a state of relative isolation and loneliness and are starved for affection, and, as a result, have felt incompetent about setting up relationships in the wide world, the presence of a Co-Counselor who is acting interested and validating towards one often seems enormously attractive and inviting. It is easy for the person who is client to project on the counselor the longed-for satisfaction of all one's dreams of companionship, romance, love, business partnership, marriage, or any other close relationships.

It is very easy for people in the grip of such frozen "needs" or "yearnings" to deceive themselves. This phenomenon operates in the wide world ("when your heart's on fire, smoke gets in your eyes"), but people tend to be somewhat on guard in the usual wide-world situation where the very real attractiveness of the Co-Counseling relationship is not present to distort their thinking.

People who do not take the rules and warnings of the Co-Counseling *Guidelines* seriously in this respect are likely to create difficulties for themselves, for each other, and for their Co-Counseling associates in the Co-Counseling Community. It is difficult and confusing enough if only one Co-Counselor gets caught up in such feelings and dramatizations, but when two people turn such patterns on each other, the confusion is multiplied. They are likely to insist that it is their "own business." They will tell other people and Community leaders that as long as they are "two consenting adults" it "must be all right." However, if they do not refrain from these socializing relationships they will almost certainly "blame" Co-Counseling for "having caused the (inevitable) disaster."

This is why the Community makes it a *rule* that Co-Counselors do not "socialize." With progress and re-emergence it comes to be viewed as a necessary *principle* even though their conformity with it is now by informed agreement instead of by enforced requirement from the Community.

(Among the millions of people who have begun Co-Counseling to date, there are a certain number who could not resist their "feelings" and who socialized with, went into business with, romanced, dated, or married Co-Counselors. Suffice it to say that *not one such relationship* has ever worked well no matter how enthusiastically the people's patterns began it nor what effort was expended in an attempt to make it workable. Inevitably the partners came to feel *betrayed* by each other because they had connived with each other's patterns and had abandoned the meaningful commitment that they had begun with of helping each other re-emerge and regain full humanness.)

These feelings which come up (of being so attracted to one's Co-Counselor) are actually brought up by the person's basic intelligence as an opportunity for discharge, and if the person's counselor treats them as such, a great deal of progress can be made very quickly in important areas. It is quite all right to ask the leaders of the Community for help in getting such discharge started.

One hint: if the attracted person will sit about eight feet away from the person she or he is feeling attracted to and vehemently and repetitively voice every possible expression of the listening person's attractiveness in a voice dripping with emotion and yearning, discharge will tend to occur very quickly. If the attraction is mutual, the parties should take turns encouraging each other to great heights of exaggerated sentimentality. A couple of hours of laughter discharge each way is likely to convert the agonized pair into relaxed Co-Counselors vastly relieved to have the air cleared of the frozen needs and the mawkish sentimentality that had threatened their valuable relationship.

Confused people have sometimes complained that a Co-Counseling relationship is not "real" because they are not encouraged to mess it up by adding patterned activities and strong feelings to it. The truth is that the Co-Counseling relationship is very "real." It is useful and rich because it is strongly and clearly defined. Someone has said it has the beauty of a poem or a song that uses a strict poetic form to achieve great complexity and communication.

The Co-Counseling Community and its teachers and leaders make a great effort to warn people of the importance of the no-socializing rule and principle (often called, in slang, the "blue pages" because of the color of paper on which it was originally added to the Co-Counseling *Manuals*). People are warned and are told not to push socializing on other Co-Counselors whom they meet in classes or Community functions. They are not policed or spied upon (it is their "neck" and their happiness that is at risk). People may not, however, become teachers or leaders in the Re-evaluation Counseling Community if they persist in violating this principle that is part of the requirement of being a member.

5.281 Keeping your relationships within the Re-evaluation Counseling Community "clean" (that is, rational) will lead you to discharge all the patterns which have ever given you trouble with any non-Re-evaluation-Counseling and wide-world relationships as well.

People naturally, intuitively, and inherently seek and build excellent relationships with other humans. Where difficulties appear it must necessarily be where patterns, sometimes involving poor communication, have intruded. If the pattern is attached to the other person in the relationship, it becomes an interesting challenge to understand it and help the person discharge it. If the difficulty is more persistent than that, it implies that you, the first person in the relationship, have a pattern intruding from your side into the relationship and causing the difficulty as well. Tackle this possibility as a client in *your* session, and the difficulty will be resolved, often with surprising ease.

5.282 It is misleading and ultimately unworkable for a would-be client to seek out and pursue people who already have the reputation of being "good counselors" to counsel with him or her as a way of securing good counseling for himself or herself. Unless one is equally well-prepared to counsel such a "good counselor" with great skill and effectiveness, the relationship will soon degenerate into the would-be client imposing on and exploiting the "good counselor," and the "good counselor" becoming increasingly uninspired by the process of continuing to give good counseling and receiving poor quality counseling in return. The very best way to secure the very best and most decisive counseling for oneself is to *find* and *teach* and *train* one's counselor from the very beginning of one's participation in Co-Counseling.

Ask the new person to counsel you *first*. Then as client work on material that is ready for discharge, but not so violently ready that your discharge will frighten your beginning counselor. Be very appreciative and validating of the new counselor's work after the session. After each person has had a session, hold a discussion in a class (or by yourselves) and review what was effective and well done on the part of each person and where mistakes were made that can be corrected and learned from. Periodically take time for each member of the Co-Counseling pair to express pride in her or his progress and effectiveness. This process recapitulates the way counseling actually developed in the last forty-six years, but it can be enormously more rapid, taking into account the knowledge the Community as a whole has already acquired and formulated.

improving sessions

5.283 An effective session is a session in which the client discharges some of the distress carried to the session from the past, on at least the level of interested talking and possibly any other additional levels of discharge, and which leaves the client freer from distress and able to think somewhat better than before, at least to some extent. An ineffective session is a session which restimulates and adds to existing distress instead of contradicting it and enabling the discharging of it, at least to some extent.

5.284 Improvement of one's functioning both as client and as counselor can take place by using the tools of counseling on the counseling process itself: reporting on sessions in class is helpful; reviewing each session at the end, first by the client and second by the counselor, with emphasis on what went well or what was positive is helpful; coached counseling or supervised counseling can be used; a third person can, at intervals, counsel both people on their relationship to each other.

5.285 It is helpful to do periodic review sessions with every ongoing Co-Counseling relationship (with or without the assistance of a third person), including checks for any possible "identifications" that have developed.

5.286 Experienced Co-Counseling relationships benefit from both parties having high expectations that the other will be a full ally both as client and as counselor. This does not mean being unrealistic. In the best of relationships it may well be necessary occasionally to stop sessions and "counsel your counselor" or set up sessions where counselors counsel each other just on how to be more effective for each other.

5.287 If a session is not going well, the client is not "lost." There are many ways to correct and improve the session. The client can counsel the counselor. The client can change the material being worked on. If first attempts to improve the session are unsuccessful, the client can end the session and request the counselor to obtain sessions with someone else on where the process became stuck.

5.288 Various devices have been evolved for the systematic improvement of the level of counseling by a group of leaders or teachers.

One of the more cumbersome techniques evolved was called the "Golden Circle." In this, a group of leaders chose a supervising teacher and chose one of their number to be a client throughout the demonstration. The client introduced herself or himself and presented his or her situation and the present state of his or her re-emergence to the group plus any patterns that he or she was desirous of discharging. Then each person in the group of leaders, in turn, attempted to prepare a validation of the client and a way to offer it to the client that would produce discharge because of the accuracy of its contradiction of the client's chronic negative attitude toward himself or herself. After each person had made an attempt to do this, then each person was encouraged to present an insightful, accurate contradiction to the client's chronic patterns as they had been revealed in his or her responses so far.

In the days when this was invented and attempted, this was a very "heavy" experience for the would-be counselors. Without the concept of contradiction being very well understood at that time, most of the leaders who attempted to play counselor failed to be effective, and most of the learning took place from observing other people's failures and from the comments of the person acting as teacher for the group. Participating in the "Golden Circles" often felt like being systematically invalidated, but the results *did* highlight for people the ineffectiveness of much of the counseling at that time. This was later revealed to be the responsibility of the "ancient habit pattern" of the would-be counselors (of paying attention to their own distress rather than paying attention to the client). Historically, these experiences served the Communities well and led to the breakthrough around the concept of "the ancient habit pattern" in October, 1982.

"Supervised counseling" takes many forms. Some counselors tape record the session and go over it with the client afterwards to see what they both can learn from it. Videotapes were used in the first supervised counseling workshop where the "ancient habit pattern" phenomenon was revealed.

What has been called "coached counseling" involves a third party, the "coach," in addition to the client and the counselor. This coach can ask the counselor for permission to make a suggestion, or the counselor can excuse his or her attention from the client and turn to the coach to ask for a conference, for being listened to for a moment, or for suggestions on any issue on which the counselor feels at a loss. The coach does not, in general, intervene or speak up without being asked during the session, but may talk to the counselor on his or her own initiative later. In the session the coach waits for the counselor to take the initiative of asking for help, asking for advice, or asking to be listened to.

5.289 It is possible to teach one's counselor by "coaching" the counselor as the session proceeds. A special session or two or three could be devoted to this. It should not be continued in regular sessions, however, because the would-be counselor is kept out of the fundamental role of counselor while being coached by the client, and it would be very easy for the client to slip into a critical, complaining pattern, which will not be helpful to either the counselor or the client.

Someone who has been an excellent counselor for the client, and who is experienced, is a good choice for any experiments in "coaching" a new counselor for oneself. With such a coach sitting in the session, the counselor assumes the role of responsible counselor fully, but may pause at any point and ask the coach for suggestions, if he or she so desires. The coach should remain silent but attentive, and if the coach feels that it is important to make a suggestion or comment, he or she should make an agreed-upon signal to the counselor to declare a recess in the session, so that both the counselor and the client can pay full attention to what the coach has to say.

Coached counseling should not continue for any long period of time, but may be useful, with lots of praise and reassurance from the coach, at getting a new counselor started correctly and confidently.

group activities/group attention

5.290 Re-evaluation Counseling support groups, conferences, and workshops will tend to accelerate the effectiveness of individual sessions.

5.291 Since being paid attention to is usually a basic contradiction to any distress, it is not surprising that being paid attention to by more than one person can be extraordinarily effective. The whole, growing, spreading movement of *support groups* is built around this. Group attention has the effect of helping the client see the distress pattern as different from present-time reality and as a result enhances discharge.

It is important, however, in support group meetings or similar uses of group attention, that there be only one person who is taking the initiative on being directive in counseling the client. For more than one to make suggestions verbally, with gestures, or with facial expressions, pulls the attention of the client toward having to watch the interactions between the different people in the group and often creates tension around the restimulation that people will unawarely express. A group will work well *if people just pay attention.* It can work very well if all the group there pays attention and *one person acts as the designated counselor in charge.* It can work well and be a learning situation where there is one designated counselor and one person acting as the "coach" to the counselor, relating as coach *to the counselor but not to the client.* What is involved in group work is basically the usual relationships of a session, but the effects are magnified by the additional attention from the group.

6. IDEAS WHICH CAN BE HELPFUL TO ONE'S LIVING RATIONALLY AND RE-EMERGING RAPIDLY AS A CLIENT

some elements of reality

6.001 Reality is always *basically* benign. When this benign-ness seems to be overshadowed by disasters or accidents or the consequences of distressed decisions made in the past, one can restore one's perspective by taking a *broader* view. Always the negative phenomena are over-matched by the positive reality surrounding them.

Be of good cheer! The universe is knowable, to any desired degree. The universe is handleable, to any extent that you wish to make the effort. You do not need any more intelligence than you already have. You do not have a need for any more information than you can acquire. Any appearances to the contrary will yield to the sometimes difficult and uncomfortable, but also possible and workable, processes of discharge and re-evaluation.

6.002 We have called the great accumulation of patterned behavior, patterns, oppression, and nonsense which we have been taught to accept, beginning when we were children, *"pseudo-reality."* Such pseudo-reality can be exposed, can be organized against, can be faced and eliminated.

6.003 The universe "beams approvingly" on all phases of itself and on every living creature of whatever kind. The universe does not discriminate negatively among people as the patterned conditioning we have been subject to tends to have made us do to each other.

If I could have but one wish granted, it would be to live in a universe like this one, at a time like the present, with friends like the ones I have now, and be myself.

6.004 *The ever-moving line of present time completely partitions the past and the future. The past is completely determined, the future is free choice.*

6.005 Each *new* moment continually offers us a *new* opportunity for starting a *new* future, which can be as we choose and which can be different than anything in the past.

6.006 It is useful to remember that each moment is a fresh, new moment. It never happened before and never will again.

6.007 *We have all the time in the world.*

6.008 *Happiness consists of the overcoming of obstacles on the way toward a goal of one's own choosing.*

rational attitude/action

6.009 In any situation the safest attitude to take is a rational attitude. ("Rational" here does not necessarily mean "cautious" or "careful" in the usual sense of implying timidity.)

6.010 By "rational" we mean actions or policies which are intelligent and pro-survival.

6.011 *Any individual or group can act rationally first, without waiting for rational action on the part of someone else, and can usually take charge of the situation by so doing. Any individual can take charge in any relationship. Any human being can make the critical intervention to begin to help free another person from a distress pattern.*

thinking

6.012 There are no limits to the power of the human mind.

6.013 Intelligence is our most valuable resource.

6.014 *Logical thinking* is the only acceptable guide to our actions. *Feelings* are not. If the feelings seem pleasant, they can be enjoyed. If the feelings seem unpleasant, ways can be found to discharge them. There is always at least one correct or optimum way to act, regardless of whether the feelings being felt seem to "agree with" or "contradict" the logic. To relapse to acting on feelings is to descend to a pre-human, pre-intelligent mode of existence.

6.015 At any moment during our re-emergence, it is likely that our logical thinking is contaminated somewhat by still-present chronic patterns that we have not yet targeted, contradicted, and discharged. It will be helpful to remember that our current actions are very possibly contaminated by illogic from some patterns that we are still unaware of, even though we are thinking as logically as we feel able to at that time.

However, it is equally important to remember that the thinking of the other people around us is also almost certainly contaminated by the intrusion of their still-chronic patterns, so that it is crucial that we do *our own* thinking and follow *our own* best thinking rather than the thinking of others. If we make mistakes in following our own best thinking, we are likely to notice the results and try to correct our illogic as a result of observing the poor consequences. If we rely on someone else's thinking, we have, in effect, "turned off" our own thinking, and we become much more likely to persist in mistaken actions.

6.016 To act on one's own thinking tends to be a contradiction to powerlessness patterns. We tend to be unaware of these powerlessness patterns because they were imposed upon us so early in our lives.

6.017 Trust your own thinking. *Trust your own thinking.* TRUST YOUR OWN THINKING.

6.018 It is important to always be as clear as we can be about the assumptions which underlie our thinking about any given situation. To lay bare and state clearly all one's assumptions usually clarifies one's thinking a great deal. In any puzzling situation, adding to one's minimum set of assumptions should be resorted to only when no explanation has been found possible with the previous set of assumptions.

6.019 In any system of thought there are questions that arise within that system of thought, the truth or falsity of which cannot be decided within the boundaries of that system of thought (see the work of Gödel and Church). It is often, and perhaps always, possible, however, to embed the given system of thought in a larger framework of thought and from this larger point of view reach a satisfactory and useful judgment as to the truth or falsehood of the given question.

6.020 Apparent paradoxes (where something seems to be both true and not true at the same time) expose the results of sloppy thinking, either our own, or that of somebody else, or that embalmed in the culture. To examine paradoxes tends to clear up such hidden errors or mistakes and leads to clearer definitions of what we are thinking about.

6.021 No external oppressive force can require your internal surrender. You may have to yield to the *appearance* of conformity to external oppression for your survival in some oppressive situations, but *you do not need, ever, to agree with or conform to the oppression in your own private thinking.*

There is an old German song which expresses this principle:

Die Gedanken sind frei wer kann sie erraten *(Die Gedanken sind frei, my thoughts freely flower)*
Sie fliehen vorbei wie nächtliche Shatten *(Die Gedanken sind frei, my thoughts give me power)*
Kein Mensch kann sie wissen kein Jäger ershiessen *(No scholar can map them, no hunter can trap them)*
Es bleibet dabei: Die Gedanken sind frei. *(No one can deny, Die Gedanken sind frei.)*

(A song from the Peasant Wars of five hundred years ago in Germany.)

6.022 No person, no force, no situation, can make us give up our own free choices. It will almost always be of advantage to us to question our past choices and see if we ourselves want to change them or improve them. We may under certain conditions of oppression have to pretend that we have denied our own choice and have gone against it, but we do not ever have to give up in our own minds.

6.023 Someone has made a humorous and witty remark that "Talking lies between thinking and doing and is often offered as a substitute for both." I cannot remember the author, and it could be taken to devalue the importance of talking. (But it is witty!)

6.024 Pretending is not a substitute for thinking. To be rigorously honest is the essential characteristic of good communication between humans. Pretense often will keep a problem from being solved by keeping it from being addressed.

6.025 When faced with a confusing situation needing a decision, a roughly helpful guide is to remind oneself to "do what makes sense."

6.026 It will often help to find fresh language and new words and new perspectives from which to discuss issues that have been discussed before. To do this will tend to expose the unaware patterned ideas which have become attached to repetitive language.

problem-solving/reaching agreement

6.027 Any phenomenon is best understood if considered from a variety of viewpoints.

6.028 *There is always at least one elegant solution for any real problem.*

6.029 Each human being necessarily builds a unique mental model of the universe. Even when completely logical, such a model will still be unique. The different models, however, can be brought into as close an agreement as desired.

6.030 There are no inherent conflicts between human beings. Cooperation will always serve both parties better than conflict.

6.031 *Any really good solution is a good solution for everyone: there are no rational conflicts between the survivals of different human beings.*

6.032 In any situation where it seems difficult to decide on which is the best solution, it is a useful guide to choose the one that seems to have "the most interesting possibilities."

death

6.033 Death does not appear to be *necessary* for humans but to be a habit from the kind of functioning we developed before we were rational. It should be possible to eliminate it by research and thoughtful guidance of our living. Even the use of present knowledge should tend to extend the typical present lifetimes by a hundred percent.

6.034 The oppressive society and culture encourage the acceptance of death as inevitable. This is in sharp conflict with the observed, inherent attitude of newborn children, who confidently expect to live forever. To agree to the attitude that death is inevitable hinders re-emergence and reinforces patterns.

no obligations or "shoulds"

6.035 You are not *obligated* to *anyone* for *anything*.

6.036 There are no "shoulds," "oughts," "musts," "have-tos," or other "duties" surrounding any human being that that human needs to honor in any way. People may accept or agree to any of these that they decide to, but the decision is really free choice.

freedom to choose viewpoint/freedom of decision

6.037 *We have complete freedom to choose a viewpoint of our own on any question.* We have complete freedom to adopt a new viewpoint regardless of what our past viewpoints have been. If we have entered into an agreement with others based on a past viewpoint of our own, it is humanly *responsible* to notify others of the change in our viewpoint and open with the others the question of possible re-negotiation of our existing agreements.

6.038 *We have complete freedom of decision.* It is reassuring to ourselves and others to explain the reasons for a decision and cite evidence in support of our decision. However, it is not infrequently the case that part of the reasons for our decision are available to us only as intuititive "hunches" that we are not yet able to explain clearly. Such "hunches" can be the result of the operation of certain patterns of our own which we have not yet gotten out of occlusion, and it is always a good idea to review such decisions as a client in a counseling session (when time permits) before acting on them. However, if our best "hunches" are in the same direction after our session as client, it is probably best to follow them, even if we cannot yet explain our reasons to ourselves or others. Our complete freedom of decision includes a complete freedom to decide "in the teeth of the evidence."

6.039 It is always possible to make a rational decision, even against one's own patterns. Re-evaluation Counseling has produced a variety of tools for achieving this (directions, frameworks, synopses, individual commitments, group commitments, and frontier commitments).

6.040 Making a rational, bold decision to *act* outside of a distress pattern is an effective tool towards re-emergence. Opportunity to discharge after the action should be provided for and allowed.

6.041 Life can go well when one decides, acts, and discharges, *in that order.*

6.042 Even a wrong decision can be better than continuing vacillation because the results of acting on it will quickly expose its incorrectness and allow for one to correct it. The vacillation is necessarily a pattern *and wrong*.

human-to-human

6.043 There are no rational conflicts of interest between any two human beings.

6.044 Agreement can be reached between two humans to any degree desired. It is often helpful to pause in the process of reaching complete agreement to "agree to disagree" and respect each other's remaining differences until it becomes useful to address them and sort them out and eliminate them at a later date.

6.045 Similarities between any two human beings outnumber the differences between them in the ratio of "at least a trillion to one."

6.046 Almost all differences which exist in the behaviors and functioning of humans are *cultural,* are learned and acquired characteristics. As a working hypothesis, we assume that any human being, given the opportunity, can acquire and master the same culture and skills which any other human being has been able to do.

6.047 There are tiny individual differences between individual humans, some of which are based on genetic variations (size, blood type, etc.), on differences in nourishment and exercise and educational opportunities at past periods of a person's existence, and on permanent injuries and ill health. Almost all such differences can be compensated for or overcome, and almost all such variations can be made non-handicapping by discharge, education, training, equipment, and encouragement.

6.048 Patterns deserve no respect at all, not one's own patterns nor anyone else's patterns. Not in a session, not in the wide world. (This does not mean that their existence should be ignored or not taken into account.) The human being *always* deserves one's complete respect. Communication that respects a person will be more successful than communication that respects a pattern. To confuse the person and the pattern always creates difficulties.

6.049 It is sensible to be ready always to think as a counselor (that is, always be in charge), unless someone else who knows how to be a counselor has agreed to function as *your* counselor for an agreed-upon period of time.

6.050 It only takes one person deciding to be rational to begin to make a relationship go well. (It does not require that the second person has already made this decision. The first person can take action which will lead to the second person deciding to make the decision.) So, there is no need to "wait" for the other person to be reasonable before the first person decides to "take charge" of the relationship.

6.051 It is rational to expect and require respect for oneself and one's associates from others. It is rational to maintain in one's own thinking a basic attitude of respect toward all others regardless of what their patterns may be doing or forcing them to do at the particular time. This does not mean respecting their irrational attitudes or acts, but it means keeping in one's mind the fundamental assumption that the *person* is worthy of respect. Such an attitude will be advantageous to oneself in the long run. Others will eventually, and to whatever degree they can manage, respond positively to your respect.

6.052 Affection from others is enjoyable and can be achieved by rational means (even though the process may sometimes be long and difficult) since the inherent attitude of others to oneself must necessarily be that of love. Affection should never be sought through sacrifice of principle or through any demeaning of oneself (except as an awarely-done manipulation of the other person's pattern).

There is no situation in which any human being involved in the situation does not deserve another human being's delight (or respect).

6.053 Loneliness can be contradicted in the most difficult situations by deciding to be with other people and being helpful to them. Mutually committed relationships will require more planning, more working through, and more eliminating of patterns, but are always possible of achievement, and each partial step towards such committed relationships is rewarding in itself. Achieved relationships can be preserved and improved as long as both parties wish to do so, or can be resigned from with responsibility and affection.

6.054 It is possible to have real, successful, and effective communication between people, and *consensus* can be achieved in most cases.

6.055 If you ask for help without rehearsing your patterned distress at the person you are asking, almost anyone in the world will be willing to help and interested in helping you. There is a built-in desire to be helpful to others in every person, and such a person will generally be able to help you if you are clear, open, and genuine about needing help with something. He or she will assist you to the extent that he or she can do so at that moment. (Often complete strangers will give you at least new information or a new point of view, and will be happy to have been of use to you, especially if you genuinely thank them.) This is true for both minor and major problems if you can present each such problem as something *you* personally need assistance with.

6.056 Hardly anyone can be *talked into* doing something good or constructive or positive that you want them to do, but almost everyone can be *listened into* doing such good things.

6.057 We can best persuade another person to change his or her opinion and choice to agree with ours by enthusiastically considering his or her position in a positive manner and warmly encouraging his or her criticism of our position. *Telling* people something almost never changes their mind. *Listening* to people well will always tend to help them consider a rational position. "The man convinced against his will is of the same opinion still."

6.058 There is "room at the top" for all of us. It doesn't make sense to hold back so others can get there. Not praising and encouraging one another with vigor and conviction is based on not appreciating *ourselves* fully.

"no ancestors, no descendants"

6.059 The people that you think of as your ancestors or your descendants are not really such. The line of descent is from DNA molecule to DNA molecule. Each human being is a separate branch off that line of descent. So the people you thought of as your ancestors or your descendants are simply adjacent-to-you "branches." The huge mass of "obligations and duties" that have culturally become attached to the notion of "descent from" or "ancestor to" are *all* patterned. These people can be or become good friends and allies but are never really one's *ancestors* or *descendants*.

loving/being loved

6.060 It is usually (perhaps always, given how frequently people carry patterns of rejection distress) useful and desirable to have another person love us or like us. Work to achieve this will often mean facing the necessity for us *to love or like her or him* and to communicate this to her or him in the first place without relating it to our own desire to be loved or liked.

6.061 As distressing as it may seem to not be loved, to feel that you are not loved, or to have a patterned block that makes it difficult or impossible to realize that you *are* loved, it is far more distressing to not be able *to love*, or to not be allowed to love, or to not have your love accepted.

6.062 It is important and satisfying to receive love from others, and failure to receive it is or can be a hurt. Such a failure to *receive* love is much less hurtful, however, than being unable to *give* love, or, to a lesser degree, not having one's love accepted. This is fortunate, in a sense, because one *always* has the freedom to give love *by decision*, while to achieve the receiving of love may require considerable work on others' patterns as well as one's own.

blame

6.063 *Every single human being, at every moment of the past, if the entire situation is taken into account, has always done the very best that he or she could do, and so deserves neither blame nor reproach from anyone, including self. This, in particular, is true of you.*

6.064 We "did the best we could" in the past, but the future is wide open for us to do better.

6.065 "Shame" or "blame" are unworkable, irrational concepts that only arise out of distress recordings which exist either individually or in the culture. Both activities are completely unproductive in any rational sense.

6.066 Punishment or reproach as a response to mistaken, irresponsible, or irrational attitudes or actions is never called for, never justified, *never effective*.

6.067 All forms of criticism, blame, or reproach are expressions of distress patterns and are *never* helpful.

6.068 Whenever we "blame" others we are in fact adopting a *powerless* position ourselves which is damaging to both the blamer and the blamed.

mistakes

6.069 When one is doing something important and therefore going beyond the routines which have already been understood and mastered, when one is working on "frontier" issues, then mistakes will tend to occur much more frequently than in a routine situation. This is fine and an essential part of the learning process. Mistakes can be quickly corrected and any negative results cleaned up if they are acknowledged as mistakes instead of being persisted in and defended.

6.070 Mistakes can be useful. Mistakes can be an indication that we are reaching to function beyond what we already know. Learning and re-emergence can proceed rapidly when the correction of mistakes is preceded by or accompanied by discharge.

6.071 Mistakes are almost certain to be made in almost any activity. We often do not have enough information to be able to be completely sure of not making mistakes *before* we must take action. To risk such mistakes is not "wrong." It is incorrect to blame ourselves for such mistakes. (Often, however, other people can relax and respond better temporarily if we *appear* to "blame" ourselves so the other people do not get upset and defensive for fear that we will be "blaming" them.) It is usually useful to apologize for a mistake of our own. It is important that we ourselves label a mistake as a mistake and not defend it. It is helpful to be "public" about being willing to examine our functioning and to correct mistakes as we make them. Such behavior will tend to greatly increase people's trust in us.

"all for one and one for all"

6.072 "All for one and one for all" is a direction which interests many individuals but which requires a group commitment *to it* for it to become very meaningful or effective. People with working-class or raised-poor backgrounds will intuit the wisdom and desirability of it in a large percentage of cases, apparently out of their practical experiences or observations of how crucially pro-survival it was in past days of group hardship. Middle-class people often have difficulty in seeing the possibility of a number of people making this commitment to each other all at the same time. They often feel willing to join a group already committed to such inter-dependence but have great difficulty in being the *initiator* and *model* for such a group. People who grew up with owning-class conditioning may intellectually appreciate the direction and find it desirable. However, because of the heavy fears installed on them that they will be totally worthless and completely rejected without some wealth, they find it difficult to move in that direction. This, in today's society, would require that they *dispose* of their wealth and their control of wealth. Especially this would require disposing of it to support action and organization to eliminate the class oppression, and to safeguard the survival of the people taking leadership towards that end.

beauty and order

6.073 A favorable environment is a contradiction to almost all distress.

6.074 Respect for, and taking responsibility for, the maintenance of beauty and order in one's surroundings and environment is a contradiction to one's own distress and to that of others.

6.075 We can leave every situation and every place in at least as good order as we found it.

6.076 A cared-for environment is safer than a sloppy one. A cared-for environment is rewarding, supportive, and aesthetically satisfying. A trim, clean, well-ordered, and well-tended environment tells us that we are functioning well. It acts as if it were a mirror. If it reflects thoughtfulness, intelligence, skill, and achievement, then we are continuously validated. We receive a more accurate picture of our real human selves from such an environment.

6.077 To express positive concepts through art can contradict much distress, can assist discharge, re-emergence, and understanding, and can help put one back in touch with the basic benign reality.

6.078 The essence of humanness is creativity, our ability to synthesize new responses. Our environments should always display, in clear view, evidence of human creativity in general and our own creativity in particular.

6.079 "When housework and gardening become social activities; when the end of littering and pollution are triumphant campaigns in which the whole population participates; when the planning and construction of a park becomes a people's project; then we will be close to the functioning of the future. We will be approaching that style of life where each of us enriches and beautifies our surroundings in everything we do."

7. THE MODES OF RE-EVALUATION COUNSELING

processes of freeing intelligence

7.001 For a human intelligence afflicted by a residue of a distress experience (a "distress recording" or a "distress pattern"), the processes of freeing the intelligence from the distress pattern (often called, as a whole, "re-emergence") include the following:

•*establishing communication* of some kind between the intelligence of the client and reality. Reality may be represented by the actual reality of the universe, by the universe as a whole or some portion of it, by some representation of reality in the form of God or gods, or, usually, by the intelligence of the person playing the role of listener or counselor.

•*contradiction* of the distress (by "contradiction" we mean anything which allows or assists the person's intelligence to view the distress recording and its content as *not* present-time reality) by any factor or factors in the environment, by the client, and/or by the counselor.

•*discharge*, in any form.

•*re-evaluation* (re-thinking through all conclusions that had been drawn from, or influenced by, the distress recording and, eventually, erasing or "forgetting" of the distress experience or experiences *as distress experiences* while retaining the *information* from the experience in a useable and useful form).

These processes can take place in a variety of situations or "modes," some of the most common of which will be described in the following text.

the primary modes

7.002 The primary modes of Re-evaluation Counseling include: the divided session; alternated sessions; one-way sessions; mini-sessions; telephone sessions; taking turns thinking, writing, or composing aloud to each other; organized thinking and discharging by oneself; communicating ("praying") with God or a saint or an entity of some sort; counseling with a "dear departed" loved one; writing letters; reading stories, reading Re-evaluation Counseling literature, reading poetry. They include watching television or movies; listening to recorded words or music, and watching videocassettes. All of the above can be contradictions to one's distress that allow discharge.

7.003 A *session* involves two intelligences paying attention to one intelligence and assisting that one intelligence to discharge, re-evaluate, and re-emerge to more rational functioning. The person paid attention to is often called the *client* or the *first person*. The principal person paying attention is often called the *counselor* or the *second person*. The counselor listens, thinks about what the client is saying, looks for ways in which he or she can suggest to the client greater direct contradiction of the distress, encourages the client to continue with discharge once it appears (rather than allow the client to stop the discharge to explain or rehearse the distress), and furnishes support to the client for continuing with the discharge or the activities which seem to be contradicting the distress and producing discharge. The counselor tries not to offer his or her own thinking as a substitute for the thinking that the client is attempting to do.

The client, on his or her part, tries to keep in mind the thought that seemed to precipitate discharge and to return to it again if anything in the session or the client's mind seems to be resisting staying with it.

The most common form of Re-evaluation Counseling, "Co-Counseling," consists of one-way counseling sessions taking place in pairs, with the roles of the counselor and client being exchanged in sessions of roughly equal time, either on the same date or on different days not widely separated. This mode is effective pretty much to the extent that rational etiquette is observed, including courtesy, timeliness, and confidentiality, and to the extent that the confident, long-range perspective of the counselor is being held out to the client through modeling.

"One-way" counseling can also be very effective but is usually available only in deliberately organized "intensives" for a leader in a particular Community or in the one-way counseling offered at Personal Counselors Inc. in Seattle as a resource for accelerating the development of leaders from around the world.

7.004 Being a "one-way" client with another person or persons being one's counselor(s) can be very effective for short periods of time. However, substantial re-emergence or complete re-emergence almost certainly requires the application of Co-Counseling, where one takes turns being client and counselor. Taking turns being counselor and being client affords many insights into the other role for people in both roles. One works hard to keep the roles separate and distinct in one's mind and uncluttered by any pulls to enter into additional relationships with the Co-Counselor which could mask and disguise the penetration of patterns into the two roles. (This is the basis for the "no socializing" rule and principle of the Re-evaluation Counseling Communities.)

7.005 *Mini-sessions* are very short divided sessions, anywhere from one minute to thirty minutes for each person's turn. They are often sandwiched into classes, gather-ins, or other meetings or group activities. Besides their brevity, they are distinguished in that typically the counselors do not retire into places of privacy but simply turn to each other in the midst of the meeting or group and (with amazing success) create their own atmosphere of privacy as the participants concentrate on each other.

Mini-sessions are often used to accelerate thinking or learning on particular topics in a group or class. They are also used to cope with and drain off restimulation during a controversial discussion.

7.006 *Co-Counseling on the telephone* is a skill that many people have mastered or are mastering. Both the client and the counselor seem able to project the presence of the other and the interest, attention, and awareness which they have experienced in person with each other (or others). They seem to build this around the slender thread of sound coming from the telephone receiver and usually or often seem able to have very satisfactory sessions.

7.007 As Co-Counseling has spread widely, an enormous amount of it has come to take place via the telephone. Many sessions can be fitted into the day's schedule with considerable ease, and the general experience is that they make a great deal of difference in the functioning of Co-Counselors. People can phone each other before rising in the morning, before leaving for work, when the children are in school, after work, in the evenings, and just before sleep. It helps to have counseled in person with the individual on the phone, and to renew contacts in person continues to enhance the effectiveness of the relationship. What seems amazing, however, is how much the human mind can communicate and be communicated to simply through tone of voice, inflection, and expression.

As videophones come into use in the future, I question whether they will enhance the Co-Counseling contact much beyond the present level. If the voice is right, the other person seems able to envisage all other attributes of the Co-Counselor well. (Having to watch the counselor's facial expression can make misunderstandings arise more easily.) (Most people who remember radio being a principal entertainment for their families speak of how well their imaginations functioned when they had only the sound of the radio as compared to the rigidities of the current television screens.)

7.008 The presence of an *interested listener* is a very powerful force in assisting someone to *think, write, or compose*. Often discharge occurs in the process. In fact, the best creative work seems to take place when accompanied by discharge. The creative activity needs to be persisted with rather than abandoned for discharge. If this is done, the creative work becomes assisted by the discharge.

Co-Counselors should divide the time equally when working in this mode.

For the listener to be informed or expert in the topics or fields in which the creator is being creative does not hinder, providing he or she remembers to remain a listener only. It is the interest and attention of the listener that is effective, however, and no special knowledge of the field or topic is necessary for the listening to effectively amplify the ability of the creator.

7.009 If one has prepared a program, a direction, or an outline of what one wishes to think through, or if one has a clear statement that is a contradiction to the distress recording one wishes to discharge (a direction or a commitment), *one can continue to discharge and re-evaluate for extended periods by oneself*. (These periods need to be regarded as extensions of a past session with someone else or anticipations of future sessions with someone else, or the patterned illusion can creep in that one can "counsel oneself" in isolation. This is almost certain to become an excuse for the rehearsal of past distress, to become a "substitute" for the re-emergence process, often justified to the lonely would-be client by noises which are copied from the actual sounds of crying or by *forced* shudders or laughter.)

Great "breakthrough" turning points in re-emergence, happening in regular sessions, are sometimes followed by intense re-evaluation going on day and night for a period of several days. These are sometimes described by the participant as "thinking through at enormous speed every thought I have had in my life previously and every conclusion that I reached which included the distress that I have discharged."

When certain counseling techniques have achieved a sharp awareness on the client's part of the phrases or noises which she or he compulsively uses to end laughter discharge, the client will sometimes laugh for many hours, even by herself or himself, until that stock of discharge is exhausted.

More and more experienced counselors are learning to organize and remind themselves of contradictions well enough that the time spent between sessions is spent in continuing to re-emerge rather than (what used to be typical of *beginning* counselors) falling back into cooperating with a pattern and rehearsing it in practice unless a counselor was present to ceaselessly remind them to do otherwise.

using transcendental forces

7.010 For people who can effectively enough *believe* in the existence of a personal God, saint, prophet, or similar "expression of the transcendental forces of the universe" (Yahweh, Jehovah, Buddha, Allah, Siva, Hera, Odin, Thor, etc.), the use of such entities as one's "counselor" can be marvelously effective, at least up to a point. If one is able to assume that such an entity is listening to what one is saying with interest and understanding whenever one chooses to speak to it (aloud or silently), and if one can assume that the entity being addressed is sympathetic to one's rational goals and is possessed of total power (God-like) and total knowledge, one has created at least the outline of a "perfect" counselor. Enormous amounts of at-least-largely-effective discharge can take place within such a framework. Not everyone can achieve such a "belief," and there appears to be a tendency for the belief to weaken or disappear with re-emergence, but in such a case the model can sometimes improve the expectations one projects towards one's human counselors.

7.011 Much information about a loved one tends to become occluded and unavailable after the death of the loved one, being smothered and "concealed" by the grief and its attendant feelings. Recalling *pleasant* memories of the loved one is usually an effective beginning for counseling in such a situation. Difficulties in these cases can be surmounted by taking into account the spontaneous tendency on the part of the client to "deny" the loss, and the common, although not universal, beliefs derived from this spontaneous "denial" by many (although not *all*) organized religions.

For "Christian" clients, one can ask the client to think of (not necessarily believe in) the possibility of the dear-departed being resident in "Heaven," and have the client (or, if necessary, the counselor) ask the convenient St. Peter to call the departed over to the edge of Heaven, ask her or him to fold his or her wings, place the assumed-to-be-present golden harp firmly on the heavenly cloud beside her or beside him, dangle bare feet over the edge of the cloud, and listen with full Heavenly attention to everything the client yearns to say or yearns to have said while the dear-departed was still alive.

It can be helpful to remind the client that no matter how many difficult patterns the dear-departed had while alive, transcendence to Heaven has certainly eliminated them completely (or it would not be "transcendence"). One can suggest that the dear-departed now is eager to listen to hours of mourning, complaining, sharing of fears, and questions which the dear-departed (sometimes using the counselor's own lovely voice) is eager to answer.

The client with a background in Judaism does not have a standard life-after-death tradition to be called into play, but "Elijah" at least "promised" to return, and the dear-departed can often be satisfactorily addressed seated on Elijah's loving lap. Paradise with Allah, the resting stage preparing for the next reincarnation,

Olympus, Valhalla, the halls of Isis, the moon goddess' gardens, or the Happy Hunting Grounds are all possible addresses where communication with the beloved departed can be sought.

writing and using written material

7.012 Writing letters to another person (an *esteemed* other person is best, if possible) has been discovered and resorted to independently by thousands of Co-Counselors. It helps if the person who is written to, or faxed to, responds in a counseling mode, but some clients report that they write hundreds (a few say thousands) of letters for each one they ever actually send. If the client can assume that the addressee will actually think about whatever the client is saying, the effect is very close to that obtained when a counselor is present and listening. If the counselor actually replies to the letter, he or she should stay aware that he or she is expected to remain in the counselor mode (in the replying part of the letter). The other portions of the letter should be clearly marked off as giving information, being a client with the recipient expected to be counselor, or (heaven forbid) giving advice.

7.013 Most experienced clients have acquired a collection of other people's writings (or their own) where the ideas expounded or the stories told contain general or specific contradictions to the distress recordings of the Co-Counselor as client. Written Re-evaluation Counseling theory (if it is written well) is often specifically contradictory to distress patterns. Such material can be read in an ordinary session with profit, but the Co-Counselor can also often achieve substantial discharge even reading it by himself or herself. Not only can discharge be reached by reading, but the discharge can reveal occluded elements in the client's own life and the contradictions to them to be used in other sessions.

Children to whom stories are read will unerringly claim as favorite the story that they can discharge to and will ask for this story to be repeated many, many times.

The Cat Who Went to Heaven, The Little Match Girl, Water Babies, The Ugly Duckling, were favorites in earlier generations.

Poems and songs and instrumental music will be recognized by clients as contradictions they need. These can be collected and used over and over again, privately and in sessions. Almost anything by Mozart is likely to put the distress-bogged client back into touch with reality. The themes of Schubert's *Trout Quintet* and Beethoven's *Ode to Joy* are candidates for useful music. Poems and songs abound. *The Internationale* strikes against basic oppression. Masefield's *West Wind,* Marge Piercy's *To Be of Use* and *The Low Road,* the excerpt "A Day in June" from James Russell Lowell's *Vision of Sir Launfal,* "The First Time Ever I Saw Your Face," are candidates.

movies, etc.

7.014 The "more total" experience furnished by movies, television shows, videocassettes, and other more modern means of recording, when performed by artists of creativity and honesty, can be and are powerful contradictions for the use of the Co-Counseling pair and the individual client seeking to keep re-emerging between sessions.

rational re-emergent activities/the need to client

7.015 Human beings can create, participate in, and enjoy many rational activities in each other's presence. Resting, exercise, learning, practicing skills, singing, dancing, creating art, acting out dramas, and the nearly infinite ways of working together—all are examples of rational activities that can be participated in collectively.

There is an often-unrecognized deep motivation present in every human (in the current stage of human history) toward using the presence of another person or group of people to attempt re-emergence or make progress in re-emergence. This motivation can take the form of, or lead to, re-emergent activity, but it can also lead, and often does, to the *rehearsal* of distress instead of to its effective discharge. This phenomenon, in one sense, is responsible for all the negative, destructive activity of human beings, especially toward each other.

Participation in Re-evaluation Counseling and the use of all the knowledge that we have been able to recover can be summarized, in one sense, as making sure that our activity with each other which is motivated in this way takes the form of *re-emergence* instead of *rehearsal*. This is the reason for the no-socializing rule between people whose first relationship with each other arose through their participation in Co-Counseling. This is the reason for starting meetings with people offering positive attitudes toward their current situations ("news and goods"). This is the reason for the principle in Re-evaluation Counseling discussion groups that no one speaks twice before each person has spoken once, and no one speaks four times before each person has spoken twice.

The motivation to try for re-emergence is present in every person that we contact, whether the person has any awareness of the information contained in Re-evaluation Counseling or not. The person who does have the knowledge of this information and, in any case, the first person singular (yourself) needs to face and accept the responsibility for determining that the interaction with the other person leads to discharge and re-emergence, not to the rehearsal of the distress.

This does not necessarily mean that the first person singular must inevitably accept the role of counselor. It is possible, at least in some circumstances, to claim the role of client, but only if the other person agrees to "listen" and is informed by the first person singular how to play the role of counselor. ("Will you listen to me for five minutes, please? You don't have to say anything, and if I cry or shake or laugh, just let me do it, OK?") If first person singular takes the initiative and becomes agreed-upon client or self-chosen-to-be counselor, he or she is in charge of the situation and can guarantee that re-emergence rather than rehearsal of the distress and the accumulation of more distress takes place.

In meetings of groups of Co-Counselors (classes, support groups, leaders' groups, gather-ins, workshops) planning and organization should be channeled in this direction and should also allow opportunity for the review of previously-learned theory and the updating of new discoveries and new experiences as an extension and growth of the theory.

permissive and directive counseling

7.016 There is a significant difference in the two principal modes of counseling, the *permissive* and the *directive*. In the permissive mode, the second person (the counselor), can seek to make the counseling situation comfortable and safe for the client but restricts himself or herself largely to paying interested, benign attention to the client. Within this restriction there is a great range of possible effectiveness. The tone of one's voice and the expression on one's face can have profound effects. Generally speaking, patterns which have not yet become chronic, or at least have not become deeply reinforced in the chronic mode, can be discharged with only permissive counseling from the counselor (the client has not as yet deeply identified the pattern as reality or the operation of the pattern as his or her own thinking).

The fact that the permissive mode of counseling allows fewer opportunities for the counselor's own patterns to intrude into the counseling process and because the client tends to feel in charge of the process all the time has led a few people with some knowledge of Re-evaluation Counseling to proclaim as a "discovery" the limitation of counseling *only* to the permissive mode, and to attract a certain number of people with timid or middle-class patterns into divisive "movements" based on this limitation. Observation of the introverted, self-aggrandizing activities of these people after they have made such a commitment to this limitation and the almost complete lack of decisive changes in their lives as a result, clearly indicates that this limitation is in itself patterned.

The directive mode of counseling assumes that the client is fundamentally committed to contradiction of the distress pattern and will initiate and support such contradictory activities to the extent that it is possible for the client to think of them or support them. However, it is likely that it will be too difficult for the client alone to create or persist with such contradictions if the pattern is chronic. This is also true if it began very early in the individual's life, if it is reinforced and supported by the cultural patterns of groups to which the person belongs, or if it is intensely identified in the principal distress experiences associated with it as "the way I survived the crisis" or "what kept me alive." Here all the tools of *directions, "frameworks," "synopses," commitments on the personal level, commitments on the group liberation level,* and *"frontier" commitments* can come into full play.

Often in an introduction to a session on a chronic pattern the client will seem to be completely clear about what the pattern is and why it needs to be contradicted. Yet once the counselor asks the client to begin expressing the contradiction, the client will often seem to "forget" what she or he was saying before and will instead rehearse the pattern itself or "explain" to the counselor why the contradiction is "wrong," "too uncomfortable," or why he or she has "changed his or her mind." This seems to be because the client is able to think outside the pattern to some extent during the preparation. However, once the actual work of the session begins, the client has, of necessity, opened his or her full central nervous system to the impact of the pattern and can be taken over by it unless the counselor stands firm, takes initiative, and insists on the client holding to a contradiction.

It is at this point that the importance must be faced of the counselor recognizing and assuming his or her role in *organizing the client's participation* in the session. The intervention and insistence of the counselor that the client participate in, and continue to participate in, the contradiction of the distress can finally be agreed to by the client, persisted in, and improved on, leaving the counselor with some freedom to create and add new contradictions in clever ways that can "surprise" the pattern and produce ongoing discharge with great effectiveness.

strategizing for re-emergence

7.017 A fully effective Co-Counseling relationship will include each person in the role of counselor thinking about the other partner as client in an ongoing manner, occasionally taking some time in his or her own session as a client (with a different Co-Counselor, if possible) to review any difficulties or questions about his or her work as counselor with this client and, in any case, evolving a strategy aimed at the complete re-emergence of the client and tactics to be applied in each stage of this re-emergence.

As counselor, the Co-Counselor needs to have a general plan and the loftiest possible goals for the client. If the Co-Counselor, as counselor, loses sight of his or her goal for the client *to completely re-emerge, to completely recover all of the client's intelligence and ability,* then the effectiveness of the counseling will be diminished.

Discussion and practice of a commitment to the client will tend to produce eagerness and enthusiasm on the part of the counselor for his or her role as counselor comparable to the eagerness which all of us tend to have ready-made for our role as client (at least until the session begins).

teaching Re-evaluation Counseling

7.018 The Re-evaluation Counseling Communities (the group of people who have jointly agreed to assume responsibility for the accurate communication of the insights of Re-evaluation Counseling and the development of new insights consistent with the existing body of knowledge) require that anyone claiming to communicate any of these insights and theory using the name of "Re-evaluation Counseling" needs to be approved by the Community through a procedure established in *The Guidelines* of the Community.

This does not mean that all "approved" teachers will always communicate accurately (all of us still have patterns which will sneak into our teaching and distort the impression we are giving, if only through our modeling), but it makes each such teacher responsible to all other Co-Counselors for the correction of mistakes once they are recognized and challenged, and it raises a barrier against the introduction of *contradictory* ideas into what is offered in the name of Re-evaluation Counseling.

Such care has not, in general, proven necessary in the case of one-to-one teaching of the ideas of Re-evaluation Counseling from one individual to another. Therefore, the Community encourages all Co-Counselors to teach all other people one-to-one as rapidly and expeditiously as they can. The goal here is that each Re-evaluation Counselor will be "teaching" Re-evaluation Counseling in some manner at all times when he or she is in the presence of another person, at least by the ways in which she or he acts and sounds.

It has worked well to encourage students in a regular class to begin teaching someone else in the wide world after the *first* class session. They are likely to teach well when their enthusiasm is fresh and while they are busy evaluating their own new insights. Teaching this way also has a marked effect in improving the learning of the "teacher," in line with the honored maxim of journeymen training apprentices, "You do not really know what you know until you have taught it to someone else."

7.019 The teaching of regular classes has been discussed in detail in early editions of the *Fundamentals of Co-Counseling Manual,* in the pamphlet *A New Kind of Communicator,* which is sent to every new teacher, and in *The Re-evaluation Counseling Teacher,* a journal printed especially for the exchange of information among successful teachers.

7.020 If you are teaching a class, view it as a marvelous opportunity to become an expert communicator, a stellar demonstrator, and an effective ally for every category of person attending the class. Plan on a lifelong relationship with each person in the class. Encourage them to think of themselves as following in your footsteps: becoming an assistant teacher, a teacher, an Area Reference Person, an expert on liberation from all the oppressions that have affected them, the builder of a world community around each one of them where they will train new leaders to build *their* own world communities, and maintaining a sisterly and brotherly relationship between all the members of the present class.

If you are an assistant teacher in a class, plan on becoming an official organizer who sees that all details go smoothly as well as being a support person for the teacher. (Let her review each class with you beforehand and then again after it's over.) Ask for and take on some of the functions of a teacher, and discharge any distresses which are revealed by these initiatives.

If you are a member of a class, try to move against any compulsive patterns of your own as the class progresses. If you have an eager-beaver pattern and always volunteer and always make comments, try to quietly listen at least part of the time and encourage *others* to talk. If you have some shyness, make yourself speak up in class discussions and volunteer for your share of the demonstrations.

Recognize that the teacher is almost certainly not as competent *or as incompetent* as you may feel her to be, but think of her (or him) as someone just like yourself who is daring to take the initiative and responsibility in spite of the feelings that she has probably had put upon her in the past.

demonstrations

7.021 Demonstrations are intended to show that counseling a person on a particular difficulty is *possible* and to some extent to show *a possible way* it might be done. Since the purpose of counseling is to free the client from distress and to help him or her to be fully rational again, the demonstration needs to move the client in a re-emergent direction, at least to some extent, or it will not have fulfilled its purpose as a good demonstration. But the primary purpose of the demonstration is to show the people before whom the demonstration is conducted that such counseling *is possible*, and to show at least one way that it is possible to do it.

wrestling

7.022 Wrestling is something that needs to be handled with great care and with skilled leadership at a workshop. To date, it has primarily been helpful at women's workshops in contradicting the physical inhibitions that have often been placed upon women against using their physical strength to defend themselves, or to shed inhibitions against becoming physically close to other women. A leader who is knowledgeable about wrestling and is careful that participants do not fall into dramatizing distress at each other is crucial. Similar precautions need also be taken about any other forms of challenging "physical powerlessness" in the context of a class or workshop.

"news and goods"

7.023 "News and goods" at the beginning of each group interaction serve the fundamental purpose of pulling the attention of the participants away from any distress which they may temporarily or chronically have their attention involved in. "News and goods" are crucial to allow interactions between the people present a chance to begin on a rational note.

validation circles

7.024 Validation circles, in which each person says something validating about another person (and no one is left out!), are fairly safe "exercises" which can be used to end any group session and leave the chronic invalidation contradicted and the attention of the participants directed away from distress as they resume functioning in the wide world.

casual/committed Co-Counseling relationships

7.025 A casual Co-Counseling relationship can be very enjoyable, and sometimes unexpected gains will develop from even a mini-session at a workshop or conference. A *committed* relationship can be, and most effectively should be, a very *profound* arrangement. The thinking about the partner in the partner's role as client needs to go on in a continuous way, and insights and ideas that appear in the counselor's mind between sessions can often be very important. The use of the counselor's notebook with separate pages for each client is helpful in organizing this process.

The counselor needs to have clear goals in mind for the client (possibly separate from, and in addition to, the client's goals for the client), and the over-all goal should be the client's complete re-emergence to full functioning without distress, to complete freedom of decision and complete power at all times.

With effective counseling, each party to a Co-Counseling relationship will be making and being aware of very solid changes in his or her functioning, and this will be a contradiction to the patterned factors that otherwise can tend to interrupt and shorten a Co-Counseling relationship. If both parties to Co-Counseling are thinking well and powerfully about each other's re-emergence, the Co-Counseling itself will become an exciting area of both parties' lives, even as it becomes surrounded by the visible gains and changes in each person's functioning and each person's relation to, and mastery of, the environment.

discussion groups/topic groups

7.026 We have evolved some crucial rules for a good discussion in a "discussion group" or a "topic group." These include: 1) the topic of the discussion is proposed by someone who is *interested in that topic;* 2) the only people expected to join the group are those who are interested in *that topic;* 3) the proposer of the discussion topic, who should also propose a time and a place for the discussion meeting, becomes the Convenor of the discussion group or the topic group.

The Convenor's job, once the group has convened, is to see that a chairperson is chosen for the discussion meeting (the Convenor may or may not be chosen as the chairperson), and that at least one reporter is chosen to keep notes of the important things said in the discussion and report them to the larger group of which the discussion group is a part. (If possible, a second reporter is chosen who will take notes of what is important in the discussion and send a written report to any newsletters, journals, daily or Sunday papers, or magazines that are connected in any way to the topic of the discussion group.)

The chairperson's job is to see that a *good discussion* takes place. This means that: 1) the *proposed topic is discussed* rather than the personalities or characteristics of the people involved in the discussion; 2) no one *speaks twice* until everyone has spoken *once* no matter what patience or encouragement is required to secure the participation of those who do not speak up easily; 3) no one speaks *four times* before everyone has spoken *twice*.

coming to a decision

7.027 In the *Guidelines* (up to the present) an elaborate procedure is proposed for helping a group come to a decision when it is difficult for a group to agree. This procedure has practically never been used past the first steps, but it is available as a back-up for any difficulty and just by its existence furnishes some safety in thinking about decisions.

reaching others with Re-evaluation Counseling

7.028 It is a justifiable assumption that all the people who, at any point, have not previously heard anything about the insights and knowledge of Re-evaluation Counseling are *potentially* able to become interested in it, learn it, and participate in its use. Everyone in the world is wildly eager to find solutions to certain common problems that can only be solved through the use of the insights of Re-evaluation Counseling. Thus if each Co-Counselor functions and gives the appearance of being rational, and uses the attitudes and tools of Re-evaluation Counseling in relating to each new person he or she contacts, such persons are nearly certain to eventually become interested.

Having observed the way the Re-evaluation Co-Counselor functions, they will at some point become curious and may express that curiosity by asking, "Where did you learn to function the way you do?" or, "How are you able to act the way you do (in this patterned society)?" Each Re-evaluation Co-Counselor will be having *some* kind of relationship with each person that he or she meets, and, however long or short the time spent with this person is, the relationship might as well be a *good* one. Such a good relationship, in its various stages, will tend to make the new person *notice* the Re-evaluation Co-Counselor, become more interested in the Re-evaluation Co-Counselor, and more curious about "what the Re-evaluation Co-Counselor knows." If every person that the Re-evaluation Co-Counselor contacts is moving in this direction, they will almost certainly move at different speeds, but they will tend to become closer to the Re-evaluation Co-Counselor, more willing to participate in activities with her or with him, and more willing to ask questions of and learn from her or him. At some point, through being taught one-to-one, through a class, or through a support group, the new person can become involved in activity and eventually find his or her way to full participation in the Re-evaluation Counseling Community.

support groups

7.029 A simple support group is an easy entrance into the organized activity of Co-Counseling. The group may be formal or informal. It may be a "Re-evaluation Counseling" group identified as such or it may have no identification. The central point of its functioning is that each person in the group has an approximately equal turn at being listened to without interruption. Each person talks about himself or herself and discharges, if discharge occurs. To get started, the person may need a suggestion such as, "What was your childhood like?", "What do you do as a job?", "What do you enjoy?", "What do you find difficult about managing a family or household?" To be listened to without interruption is very effective, and sharing time equally in the group allows the practice of counseling to be illustrated in a simple, democratic way.

workshops

7.030 The first Re-evaluation Counseling workshop (Buck Creek I) was a two-week-long residential workshop in a remote mountain location. The profound effects upon the attenders of this and subsequent workshops have led to thousands of later workshops being held under a great variety of conditions, of a great variety of lengths, and with groups of attenders sometimes limited to particular backgrounds, experiences, professions, oppressions, or length of experience in Re-evaluation Counseling, and at other times having only the commonality of doing Co-Counseling or being interested in learning more about Co-Counseling.

Some workshops are as short as four hours and merge in function with classes. The Community *Guidelines* set a limit for the basic fees charged by workshop leaders, based in part on the degree of leadership they have attained in the Community, in order to prevent financial motivations from tending to distort the function of the leadership. Only one fee is allowed for a leader at a workshop, and assistants (other than the organizer) whom the leader chooses to employ must be paid out of the leader's own fee. Most of the work of organizing the workshop is on a voluntary basis, and only one paid organizer is allowed, whose basic fee is set at one fourth of the fee of the leader.

The price of the workshop is set by consultation between the workshop leader and the local leaders. It is planned so it can contribute to the International Outreach Fund and subsidize the publication of Re-evaluation Counseling literature, as well as contribute to the functioning of the International Community through an assessment of ten percent of the gross cost of the workshop to be paid to the Community Service Fund of Personal Counselors Inc. for the servicing of the International Offices and towards International Outreach.

Workshops for her or his own students can be initiated by any accredited teacher of Re-evaluation Counseling. Workshops which draw from more than one teacher's students must have approval of the Area Reference Person where an Area Reference Person is functioning. Workshops that draw from more than one Area must have approval of the Regional Reference Persons involved (if there is a Regional Reference Person), and any other workshops must have the approval of the International Reference Person. Attendees at workshops beyond the class level should have the approval of their Area Reference Person for attendance or, if from a class outside an organized Area, the approval of the teacher of the class.

Workshops will tend to include lectures on theory by the leader, Co-Counseling sessions, support groups, topic groups, question answering, organized exercise, creativity and performance, and a great variety of demonstrations of counseling practice.

Rules and guidelines for organizing and leading workshops are furnished by the Community to organizers and leaders.

Except for class workshops, the approval of a Reference Person (Area, Regional, International) is needed for a person to attend a Re-evaluation Counseling workshop.

sports at workshops

7.031 At workshops Re-evaluation Counselors have gradually evolved some validating, non-competitive sports. Not everyone can participate in all of them because of the different disabilities, fears, and vulnerabilities which different people have to contend with, but much of the destructive, invalidating, competitive distress usual in competitive sports has been eliminated. This can be illustrated by *Re-evaluation Counseling volleyball,* where no score is kept, the side that *loses* the point wins the serve, and servers can get as close to the net as they wish and can throw the ball over if they would rather not hit it. Every server is permitted, encouraged, and sometimes required to try over and over again until a good serve is achieved. One can reach under the net to help the other side to keep the ball in the air, and sometimes both sides shout triumphantly the total number of times that the ball is hit into the air before it strikes the ground.

song fests at workshops

7.032 "Song fests" were experimented with in early workshops and still take place occasionally. Every person is encouraged and expected to sing to loud applause no matter what the state of their skill or technique. (This also works where everyone is expected to perform a solo dance.)

Because of the time pressure at most workshops, creative singing by the newly-formed support groups on the first night of the workshop has mostly replaced song fests. Here each group is exhorted to create, in a very short time, a new song on the "theme" of their group and perform it, being allowed to fall back on the song sheets in the workshop workbooks if necessary. Tremendous creativity often appears in these ad hoc performances. Also, "singing committees" at most workshops take responsibility to see that morning and evening classes start with a song.

creativity at workshops

7.033 The assumption is made in Re-evaluation Counseling philosophy that every human being is essentially an artist, that the process of being intelligent involves the creation of new concepts. At workshop-type gatherings, art materials and tools can be provided and enthusiastic encouragement given to people to create and have their creations appreciated. Poster paint, paper and brushes, semi-stiff wire and pliers (for wire sculpture), paper and pencil for poems and songs, penny whistles for instrumental music, and a cleared space for dancing can sometimes bring an enormous outburst of excellent art which can go on being created in people's lives after the workshop.

conferences

7.034 "Conferences" may be called whenever there is a need for wider consultation to develop policy or approve of a policy. Over long distances phone conferences (where all people are present on the same circuit) are almost as effective and much cheaper than in-person conferences. Generally decisions are made by the appropriate individual person, and the responsibility for that decision rests with that individual, but conferring widely in advance tends to improve the quality of the decision.

gather-ins

7.035 What has come to be called a "gather-in" in Re-evaluation Counseling has the general content of a brief conference. Conferences on an Area level or Regional level may be called to take organizational initiatives. Often they are combined with a report from a local or visiting leader followed by discussions, mini-sessions, and summaries, such as, "What did you like best about the evening?" in which each individual present is asked to speak.

Community meetings

7.036 Community meetings can take place in any Community or portion of the Community for any constructive purpose. The Community *Guidelines* require the organized Areas to have Community meetings at least twice a year, at one of which the Area Reference Person and Alternate Area Reference Person must perform self-estimation before the meeting and with participation from the other members, and be either confirmed or replaced in their jobs.

think-and-listens

7.037 The "think-and-listen" group is a format that developed within Re-evaluation Counseling workshops. When it is done correctly, it seems to have profound results, but it has not been widely used because of the rigor needed in its operation.

The essential features of the think-and-listen group are: 1) three to six members; 2) the time is divided equally between all participants; 3) alert, aware, interested attention is given to whomever is speaking; 4) finally, and most important, no response to or interaction with the speaker is permitted. Listeners do not indicate by facial expression, sounds, or words their agreement or disagreement with what is said. No listener gives any response except respectful awareness to what the speaker is saying.

This careful restriction includes not responding in your own turn to what a previous speaker has said during that previous speaker's turn, nor *ever* mentioning *ever* afterwards what any other speaker has said *to the speaker or to anyone else!* Each one's spoken thoughts during her or his "think-and-listen" turn are regarded as "sacred," forever free from any threat of interaction. These thoughts are preserved together in the sanctity of "a crystal chalice of *no comment.*"

thinking on a topic

7.038 A "think together on the same topic" discussion can take place in any meeting, any topic group, at any dining table. One person proposes a topic and offers her or his opinions on the topic, and then each of the other persons in turn comments. When all others have spoken, the person who proposed the topic then summarizes what he or she "heard and found interesting." As time permits, the next person then proposes a topic and speaks on it, either in strict rotation around the circle or as people volunteer on topics they wish to have discussed.

written communication between Co-Counselors

7.039 Written communication between Co-Counselors has become important in the development of the Community. This usually begins (and, historically, began) as personal correspondence between individuals, and it continues to develop and emerge on this level. (The current International Reference Person answers nearly every letter received by him and as promptly as possible.) A format of a personal newsletter from the leader of the Community developed out of the similarities that appeared in writing to individual correspondents. This has continued in the form of occasional letters from the International Reference Person to as many as two thousand local leaders, and letters from Regional Reference Persons two or three times a year for general communication to local leaders in the Region.

Because of the specialized nature of their constituencies, *International Liberation Reference Persons* are given support from the Community's International Office in issuing letters to their local leaders, "not longer than four pages, not oftener than every two months."

Area newsletters developed spontaneously, modeled after early issues of *Present Time* and are today published in most Area Communities. It turns out that to use the written word in the form of a newsletter achieves certain results *just because it is in writing.* A small, isolated group of ten members were once questioned as to why they bothered to publish a newsletter, and they convincingly demonstrated that having the communication in writing substantially improved the functioning of their Community.

7.040 *Present Time* was a newsletter at first and consisted, to begin with, of phrase-length excerpts from correspondence that were thus shared with other correspondents. The effect of "being published" was so substantial that people's letters began being quotable in whole sentences, then in whole paragraphs, and finally in long letters which could be excerpted into short articles. (The best articles still tend to arrive in the guise of letters. The effect of being expected or expecting oneself to write "an article" seems to decrease the expressiveness and creativity for many people far below the level that they easily attain in *letters* to one person.) *Present Time* has become a major institution for communication among Re-evaluation Counselors around the world. Other journals have followed in *Present Time's* footsteps, in the first place, *The Re-evaluation Counseling Teacher.* Some journals have (so far) published only one issue, which apparently has satisfied, for a long period, the need for clarification that first brought them into being. Some of these journals have become major organizing tools (for the men's movement, for the women's movement, and so on).

There is sometimes observably a considerable eagerness to "write about," and eagerness to "have published," ideas that are already well-clarified in existing written theory. This seems to express a need for a "written clienting session" or a yearning for "the prestige of seeing your name in print." This phenonemon has turned out to require aware attention from our editors that the Community's publications not be overloaded for reactive, personal, self-serving motives.

audiocassettes and videocassettes

7.041 The use of audiocassettes of particular lectures, talks at workshops, demonstrations at workshops or gatherings, and from other sources played an important role in the beginnings of the Communities. "Affection, Love, and Sex at the University of Maine" was an accidentally-occurring "hit" that led to ten or twelve standard audiocassettes on various topics being copied and distributed over the last twenty years or so. The ones in use have been very effective, but their issuance has not been pursued vigorously. However, there are probably a thousand excellent audiocassettes waiting to be extracted from the vast tape storage of the Communities and made available to Community members and the public.

7.042 Videotaping of demonstrations at workshops and lectures began out of concern that the founder of the Community, who was vastly more experienced than other leaders at that time, might disappear in a plane crash or through illness, and his skills as a counselor and theoretician might be forever lost. This has continued to be a main concern in the videotaping projects, but as a great store of available cassettes has been recorded, edited, and made available, many other skilful counselors and leaders have been recorded in this way. Here, too, the cost and time involved in reproducing has slowed the project. There's much excellent material waiting to be recovered from storage and made into usable videos. The improvement in the recording equipment has made possible much greater ease in accumulating original material to be prepared as videos.

7.043 Videos have proven a boon in the communication of Re-evaluation Counseling into other cultures, even when no language translation is attempted. The visual recording of an effective session communicates a great deal *around* any language barrier.

It also turns out to be quite simple for a pair of speakers of the new language who are bilingual and who have a printed draft in English of the original transcript, to make an audio-translation that follows the video original quite closely in the *new language*. Thus the video can be played for a non-English-speaking group with the audio sound *turned on* and the video sound *turned down*, to give the audience a good approximation of the demonstration or lecture in their own language. (It works at least as well as most translated or sub-titled movies.)

For new, small Communities, particularly in isolated places, the use of Re-evaluation Counseling videocassettes (possibly shown several times) can furnish correct content to Community meetings, especially when followed by mini-sessions and discussions. Such evenings can be a unifying factor and an economical substitute for bringing in speakers or elaborately prepared programs, and can acclimate new people to the practice of Co-Counseling.

7.044 In a vast taping project carried out by a group of Re-evaluation Counselors, almost all the literature published to date has been read onto audiocassettes by volunteers and made available to people who are blind or who have serious vision difficulties. Thus the entire literature is available, at least in English, to unsighted persons. It can be purchased by anybody for $10 a cassette, can be purchased by a person with vision difficulties for the same price as the printed literature, and is furnished free to any unsighted person whose economic situation does not make it possible for them to afford the regular price. (This has been supported by grants from the Re-evaluation Foundation for most of this past period.)

speak-outs about oppression/"panels"

7.045 When an oppression that has not previously been recognized and dealt with is first discussed, it has proven helpful, and sometimes necessary, to have people who belong to the oppressed group simply take turns "speaking out" while all the members of the Community present who are not members of the oppressed group listen with patience and full attention. If a competent leader is present, that leader may helpfully act as a counselor to the members of the oppressed group, not in urging them to contradict their feelings but in assisting them to express their distress and their thinking fully. After members of the oppressed group have spoken exhaustively, it may be possible for the people who have been listening to say briefly what they have learned from listening. They need to be cautioned, however, that this is not an opportunity for them to "be client" or express their feelings or "argue" with members of the oppressed group, but only to say what they have learned and express their appreciation to the members of the oppressed group for speaking out.

7.046 A better-organized and more advanced way of introducing the reality of an oppression and the need to have allies for the members of an oppressed group is what we have called a "panel." In this situation, at a workshop or gather-in or conference, members of the oppressed group are asked to speak out as a panel to all the other people present. (One member of the group is sufficient, if that is all there is present. A larger number of the group, appearing as a panel, gives a much richer notion of the reality of the oppression.) It has proven very useful, when enough time could be taken, to have, for example, *all the men* present at a workshop appear as a panel, even though they may have constituted half of a large workshop. Sometimes speaking out by the panel has gone on to 3:30 AM, with everyone pleased to have heard so much.

The leader of the workshop or conference acts as a counselor, and two types of questions have proven useful. The first is to ask each person in turn, "What is wonderful about being a member of this (oppressed) group?", "What has been hard or difficult about being a member of your group?", "Has Re-evaluation Counseling been useful to you as an individual member of your group, and if so, in what way has it been useful?", and finally, "How does Re-evaluation Counseling, as it is operating among the members of your group and in the Re-evaluation Counseling Communities in general, need to improve in order to be more useful to the members of your group?" This can be accomplished in a reasonable period of time even with a fairly large group.

The second type of question has proven especially valuable for men as a group, with all women listening (and for women as a group with all men listening). Here the questions are organized chronologically. The leader asks each person, "What was life like for you as a newborn? As an infant? As a toddler? As a beginner at school? At different stages in school? At adolescence? As a youth? As a young adult? As a worker at the present?" At each chronological stage, the person is asked, "What was good about life at that stage? What was hard about life at that stage? Where did you turn for comfort at that stage?" After each question the panel member is given sufficient time to answer the question fully, and the leader continues to ask additional questions, if necessary, in order to elicit the content needing to be expressed by each person.

some early unworkable techniques

7.047 At various periods in the development of Re-evaluation Counseling, techniques were tried (in an effort to solve some previously unsolved problems) that did not work well but in their attempted operation provided certain information which led to more workable insights. Two examples that a new Co-Counselor may hear references made to are the "golden circle" and "the open rehearsal of one's own racism" (out of earshot of any people oppressed by racism).

The "golden circle" simply exhibited the poor level of counseling that was being tolerated among Community leaders at that time. The embarrassment of seeing it exhibited motivated the steps that needed to be taken to reveal and correct the counselor's preoccupation with his or her own distress. The "golden circle" is not in itself a workable technique for improving counseling.

The "open rehearsal of one's own racism" was an attempt to break away from the pretended absence of racism which was keeping white Co-Counselors from effectively discharging their distress in this area. It tended to lead to violence and major upsets, but it cut through the pretense enough that it motivated the search for, and the discovery of, workable techniques. It *was not in itself a workable technique* and is not recommended for use.

introductory lectures

7.048 A regular introductory lecture, offered if possible in a consistent location at a consistent and regular time, can become a useful institution. (Seattle has had an introductory lecture on the third Wednesday of each month at 8:00 PM for forty years.) If an excellent speaker and teacher gives the lecture regularly and people are invited to return, it will tend to become an attenuated *class* that people will come to fairly regularly over a period of years and bring their friends and new acquaintances to in order to have them receive an introduction to Re-evaluation Counseling. (We have many examples of people changing their lives dramatically from something they heard in an introductory lecture.)

If the speakers are rotated and teachers who are about to start a new class do the introduction, it can serve as a recruitment for class membership and be valuable practice for the teacher in speaking, answering questions, and doing demonstrations.

Depending on other factors, attendance at such a regular lecture has built up to about a hundred members at times and constitutes a valuable connection to the wide-world community and a useful channel for the spread of Re-evaluation Counseling insights into the general population.

"self-estimation"

7.049 "Self-estimation," as developed within the Re-evaluation Counseling Community, is a process for the improvement of leadership functioning. It needs to be used regularly and can play a very valuable role. At regular or irregular intervals, any person who is playing a leadership role of any kind is invited to meet with the people whom she or he leads, to review her or his effectiveness in the job. The person doing the self-estimation first speaks to how she or he estimates that she or he is doing well, what parts of the job have been well done, which parts have been improved, and which parts need improvement. Then the members of the group give their estimations. Again they speak to *the job*, not to the personal characteristics of the leader. When mentioning any parts that they feel need improvement, they make suggestions that they feel could be helpful to the person or offer counseling or other assistance to the person in any of these places.

It is important that *self-estimation* be distinguished from *validation*. In a validation process, the person may safely risk being inaccurate in a positive direction because to do so would probably still serve to contradict the usual accumulation of invalidations upon the person and so lead to discharge. In self-estimation we are talking about a realistic assessment of *how the work has been done or is being done*, and *objective accuracy* is the goal. The assumption here is that if the person has the resource to perform the job well and wants to perform the job, any discussion and help will enable the person eventually *to do the job* well. The question of validation or invalidation of the person himself or herself should not enter at all.

If, after full discussion, the group is satisfied with the functioning of the leader, formal approval of the leader continuing in leadership can be made. If the situation does not seem satisfactory enough, the person is thanked for his or her service and discussions are held about finding a replacement.

"counseling the leader"

7.050 As the general level of counseling has improved so dramatically, the problem of effectively counseling the leader of a group has lost some of its urgency. It can still happen, however, that leaders are "abandoned" as clients (a very unrewarding aspect of becoming a leader). If any group asks or expects an individual to assume the responsibilities of leadership, this action automatically places a responsibility upon the group to see that the leader's re-emergence is enhanced by taking the job of leader rather than becoming limited by it.

What has worked well is for the group to occasionally call a meeting devoted just to discussion of enhancing the counseling of the leader. At such a meeting the best counselor available can be designated to conduct a demonstration session with the leader as client and to chair the discussion that follows. The leader first reports, as client, on what is going well, where his or her re-emergence is having difficulty or is "stuck," and any recommendations that he or she would make to the group as to how the members of the group could be helpful.

The designated counselor then counsels the leader as well as possible in a demonstration session. Following this, the leader is excused from the meeting (with a companion if he or she requests it), and then the group discusses and comes up with recommendations for what the group thinks needs to be done to responsibly assist the leader's re-emergence. The leader is then called back into the meeting, and the proposals of the group are made, discussed, and accepted or rejected by the leader. At least a principal counselor and a couple of consultants are designated for the leader to turn to in his or her future counseling.

intensive counseling

7.051 The use of intensive counseling was experimented with soon after the beginning of Re-evaluation Counseling. At first, professional clients at Personal Counselors in Seattle would have thirty hours of one-way counseling in one week, all with the same counselor. This often worked spectacularly well for the client but turned out to be overwork for the counselor (especially since the one counselor was, in those days, trying to counsel other people in between the Intensive counseling sessions), and intensive professional counseling was dropped for several years. When it was resumed, it was on the basis of twenty hours in one week, with several different staff counselors sharing the counseling load. These *"Intensives"* also tended to be very successful for the client, but many difficulties had to be faced and surmounted in terms of the coordination of the staff counselors, securing their agreement to a unified strategy, and allowing for the necessary flexibility required by the clients. Clients usually had a markedly different response to the different staff counselors, responding to each of them in a different manner, and in those years, the varying restimulations of the various staff counselors themselves were also a factor.

Over a long period of time a much higher standard of counseling and responsibility was attained. This came partly by improving some personnel and partly by providing the opportunity for the staff to keep learning more about counseling all the time.

At present, Intensive Counseling at Personal Counselors is, in the main, reserved for leaders of the Community or very promising candidates for leadership. The principal obstacle to this use of it is the cost, which is (in 1997) one thousand dollars for a twenty-hours-in-one-week Intensive.

7.052 "Volunteer" intensives have been developed as an institution in several Re-evaluation Counseling Communities. Here a group of Co-Counselors enters into an agreement that each member of the group shall receive a period of intensive counseling furnished by the other members of the group.

One of the members takes primary responsibility for each particular intensive and schedules people to fill in as counselors. Often a solid weekend is filled with intensive counseling for up to eight hours in each day. Each succeeding counselor confers with the preceding one, and where possible they all meet together prior to the intensive, and again following it, to summarize and share what they have learned from the experience.

Re-evaluation Counseling in schools

7.053 Re-evaluation Counseling is often taught in schools. Usually it penetrates first in the way that the work is organized, the way the students relate to each other, and the way the teacher relates to the students. Also, it tends to lead teachers to use team study. As the teacher learns to have the students make deep introductions of themselves, each student will have an extended series of turns being listened to by all the others as the student makes herself or himself well known to the other students. It easily becomes an accepted practice in classrooms for another student to volunteer to go to the cloakroom with a student who needs to discharge.

Individual validations of each student can be easily prepared as posters to be on display at all times in the classroom. Agreements for mutually supportive play when on the playground are easily worked out on the initiative of the teacher and accepted by the students. Techniques for handling, and winning over, students from other classrooms to the atmosphere of mutual support on the playground are easily arrived at with the teacher's encouragement. This has worked well at all levels of education from preschool classes up through graduate schools, with, of course, adjustments for the differing circumstances *but with a consistent content.*

Some special schools for younger children have been established by Re-evaluation Counselors for periods of a few years in Palo Alto, in Philadelphia, in Stockholm, and in other places. These have been mostly in the nature of "pilot plant" experiments where dedicated parents and other adults set out to free up and follow the children's own intelligence as to what the children themselves want to learn and how the children themselves want to handle the learning. The results have been most encouraging and have led to continuing success in the regular schools for the young people who were given this start.

work with families

7.054 Work with families is an important and growing frontier for the Re-evaluation Counseling Communities at the present (in 1997). For Re-evaluation Counseling to function well in a family the basic requirements are: (1) an insistence on complete respect for every person in the family (modeled by the parents in their relationships with the young people and with each other), (2) democracy in the sense that all people's opinions are asked for before decisions are made that affect them, (3) that if the adults, or a particular adult who is charged with a particular responsibility, makes a decision contrary to the wishes of family members, he or she explains in detail the reasons for the decision and apologizes for acting without first reaching a consensus.

Adults will, in general, tend to be chronically acting out the distresses which were acted out at them by their parents, or, in an alternative direction, rigidly acting in an "opposite way" in their efforts to avoid passing on the distresses of their childhood. A crucial effort necessary for effective family work is for the adults to thoroughly discharge on their own childhoods' distresses. An introduction to this can be furnished by participating in "play days" where skilled adults and cooperating parents spend the day playing with the young people in the ways that the young people choose and under the young people's direction. (The tendency of the adults to suggest, dominate, and dictate the ways of playing must be scrupulously resisted.)

Family workshops usually begin with pillow fights in which the young people *always* win and a great deal of discharge takes place. Such family workshops require thoroughly experienced leaders or harm is likely to be done by the patterns of well-meaning adult leaders who have not discharged their own childhoods' distresses sufficiently. A group of experienced International leaders has systematically trained local and Regional groups of adults to lead family workshops. In general, no group of adults should organize a family workshop whose leadership is not approved by these International leaders (Tim Jackins, Patty Wipfler, Gwen Brown, Chuck Esser, etc.) from personal contact and work with them.

7.055 Within a family, all the young people should participate in special times where they "speak out" and the adults *only* listen. The adults are not required to meet the young people's demands but they must listen without arguing.

Each individual child also needs "special time" *with both parents* and *with each parent*. With the pressure which the current irrational society places on parents, it may seem unreasonable or too difficult to take this time, but it will turn out to be much more economical of time than will dealing with the problems which failure to provide such "special times" will almost certainly cause. These special times may take the form of sessions in which the young person is listened to with great attention. They may take the form of playing games together under the direction of the young person. They may take the form of exploring the wide world (visiting the beach, local factories, libraries, or riding on trollies or subways, spending time in museums, art galleries, or whatever the young person chooses).

"relationship sessions"

7.056 An expressed need to have "relationship sessions" between two Co-Counselors surfaces regularly and spontaneously in the Communities.

There is no question that people who are in poor communication with each other can be assisted to begin communicating through the efforts of a counselor who assists each one to talk about any difficulties while the counselor and the other person listen. When each such person of the two or three or more involved in the relationship has spoken, it will be plain to the person serving as the relationship counselor, and sometimes (or often) to all the participants, that patterns are "crying out" to be discharged on the part of at least one (and usually every) person in the relationship. Sometimes brief demonstration sessions for each person lead to a very quick breakthrough to understanding and to agreements between the people in the relationship to continue to Co-Counsel each other effectively in the areas where the problems have developed.

It also tends to happen, however, that a kind of dependency grows out of such an apparently successful "relationship session." The members of the relationship feel better, get along better, and feel close to the relationship counselor and "grateful" to him or her. They are eager for further sessions. The person playing the role of the relationship counselor in this situation is likely to feel "appreciated," effective, successful, and perhaps "on the brink of a brilliant new career as a relationship counselor." *What is happening here is not altogether healthy.* Quite probably a frozen need for "rational parenting" is seeming to be met for the people in the relationship, and a frozen need for "appreciation" on the part of the "relationship counselor" is inadvertently being "met."

In general, outside of preliminary help at getting people back into communication with each other and highlighting the patterns that need to be discharged, real improvement in the relationship involves work that needs to be done by the parties involved. They need to face each other, be honest with each other, and, if necessary, have a fierce argument, a "blow-up," or even a "fight" in order to get back into real contact, real responsibility, and a real relationship.

counseling with a stranger

7.057 The opportunity to be an effective counselor for a stranger should not be declined on the basis that it will only be a one-time session, with the counselor not likely to see the person later. Our experience has been that often the new person will intuit the opportunity that really being listened to well affords him or affords her and can often make a decisive difference in his or her life by discharging and subsequently thinking his or her way out of a place where his or her life had been "stuck" (operating in a patterned way). It is only necessary to pay good attention and show real interest in the person by your facial expression and tone of voice and by the few but interested questions you ask. Allow the discharge to proceed as much as the time permits. Take your lead from your one-time client, with your expression and manner indicating how pleased you are. If you wish to follow it up, you can exchange names and addresses, you can ask your one-time client to "let you know how it turns out," but it is quite all right to leave it as a one-time event. It will give you a glimpse of your own effectiveness when you are fully "a counselor."

the Community Passover Seder

7.058 The basic distress on which institutionalized anti-Semitism relies is the "fear of the unknown" which existing society tends to install on every child that it can. In general, Gentiles in Western and Arab countries "can't imagine what it's like to be Jewish" or have vague feelings of envy towards Jewish people for having been called "the chosen people" or "specially chosen of God." These feelings can tie in with the slanders about all Jews being well-off (the great majority of Jews in any Jewish population are poor and working-class), or all Jews being "intellectually superior" (the great majority of Jews who do well intellectually are driven by unremitting pressure from their families, who in their turn are driven by unremitting terror from past threats to the lives of their families).

One effective tool for piercing this reactive "mystery" about being Jewish and about Judaism (the traditional religion of the Jews) is the Community Passover (or "Pesach") "Seder" or Feast. Here the local Re-evaluation Counseling Community organizes a celebration of this Jewish holiday, with the work carried out by Gentile members guided by Jewish Re-evaluation Counseling members who are knowledgeable about the holiday and the ceremony. Passover is a *good* holiday. The content of it is the celebration of liberation. The ceremonies are no more surrounded by rigidity than are the familiar ceremonies of the Catholic, Protestant, Buddhist, East Indian, or Islamic religions of the population majorities where the Jews have lived as minorities. To participate will increase the respect of Gentiles for the great Jewish traditions and for Judaism and will arm the Gentiles to be effective allies against anti-Semitism and other oppressions. The Seder can be an important outreach function to new-to-RC Gentiles as well as to non-RC Jews who may be invited to participate.

Co-Counselors together at non-Re-evaluation Counseling events

7.059 When several Re-evaluation Counselors happen to be present at a wide-world conference or other non-Re-evaluation Counseling event, they may find it very useful to counsel with each other, organize a support group, or briefly exchange their opinion of issues with each other.

They should not, however, "huddle." What time they spend together should be formally used for a session or a group session. They should reach out to and spend time with and establish communication with the non-RCers at the conference or event.

It is *not correct* for Re-evaluation Counselors in this position to attempt to dominate the policy of the broader event by, for example, "putting over" policies or decisions, on the basis of parliamentary maneuvering, which the majority of the people attending are not yet in agreement with. This "faction" type of organization (often used by leftists in the past) is an expression of despair and of lack of confidence in the majority of the people. It is completely possible for Re-evaluation Counselors to be on opposite sides of certain questions in the wide-world organization as policies are being worked out, and it's crucial that they treat each other with respect and treat the non-Re-evaluation Counselors around them with complete respect also. Co-Counseling, encouraging each other, helping each other prepare to publicly communicate well, yes. Parliamentary maneuvering on a narrow basis as a group, no.

prepared to be counselor

7.060 "Being in each other's lives in a counseling way" has come to mean being prepared to be a counselor at each interaction (at least to begin with) if the other person is caught in distress. It includes never assuming the role of client unless the other person has *agreed* to play the role of counselor and is free to do so, sharing communication and activity in a mutual, agreed-upon way for rational activities, thinking about each other in between interactions, and planning ways to enhance each other's re-emergence.

publications

7.061 Re-evaluation Counseling publications have one principal goal. This is to communicate clearly the insights into the actual nature of reality and of people, and the means of re-emergence which have been successfully employed by one person or one group of people, to all the other people in the world in ways clear enough and encouraging enough that the communicated-to people will try these insights for themselves. The special importance of publications is that they are written and published, and in the process are thought about repetitively. They are edited, re-edited, and re-edited so that much of the distress that would be accompanying the communication in spoken language is "weeded out" and eliminated, and the communication, as a result, tends to be more correct and more understandable.

Some lesser goals of Re-evaluation Counseling publications are to encourage people to master written communication (people tend to be greatly encouraged in their writing by the effect of seeing their name set in printed type as an "author"), and to communicate so well from one culture, language, or country to another culture, language, or country that the communicators and the communicated-to come to understand each other, feel at home with each other, and become allies for each other.

7.062 Our accumulated literature is our basic stock of working capital. Its systematic distribution, spread, study, and use will mean that the ideas contained therein will eventually triumph over the complex of patterns surrounding and infesting the population.

7.063 There has been much nonsense spoken and written about "Re-evaluation Counseling jargon" and this nonsense has been widely repeated. Some of this nonsense says that the language in Re-evaluation Counseling publications is a "special" language, that it's a poor language, and that other people cannot hope to hear it well or understand what is said unless a different language is found and used for communication.

The truth of the matter is that the language in Re-evaluation Counseling publications is the language of the person who wrote or spoke these words to begin with. In general, it communicates well since it has been edited and reviewed several times before it appears in print. It is in one of the several hundred dialects of English that are spoken in the English-speaking world, and although it is not the "received pronunciation" of owning-class Southeast England nor of the Harvard University campus, it is quite understandable.

What people are attempting to object to, and correctly, is the failure of some people who read this literature to translate it into *their own* language before they speak it to others. This failure is intellectual laziness. One should certainly not attempt to communicate any part of Re-evaluation Counseling until one has understood it oneself. Since each person has his or her own language, the ideas should be expressed in the language of the person speaking or writing, not rigidly parroted in the language of the person who originally wrote the Re-evaluation Counseling literature.

7.064 When you communicate Re-evaluation Counseling verbally or in writing to another person, it is good to try to communicate it *not only in your own language* but also *in the language of the person you are addressing*. That may seem difficult, but your attempt to do it will be appreciated by the person whom you are addressing.

translation

7.065 The translation of Re-evaluation Counseling literature is a crucial operation. Whatever has been written in one language that represents a rediscovery of reality in an area where it has been obscured needs effective, skilful translation into all the languages which other Re-evaluation Counselors speak and, eventually, into all the languages of the world. This requires that the translator (or translators) be a skilful speaker and writer of his or her original language (the one into which the translation is being made), have a deep understanding of Re-evaluation Counseling theory and practice itself, and have at least good competence in the second language (the language in which the material was originally written). Most translations to date have been by volunteer translators, done as "labors of love." (It is only very occasionally that the Community has been able to scrape together the funds to pay a professional translator, and the results have not always been satisfactory.)

We have generally appointed a "Translation Coordinator" for each language and have attempted to enlist a corps of volunteers who will work under the Translation Coordinator's direction. The Translation Coordinator must give approval before any translated material goes into official publication.

Anyone may translate Re-evaluation Counseling material for his or her own use. Anyone in good standing with the Community may make ten copies of a translation she or he has made and circulate it to friends or students, providing it carries a notice that it is *not* an official, approved translation, but is a temporary version.

Copyright to all translations remains with Rational Island Publishers. Any translations that are distributed should carry a copyright notice in the proper place.

the "pilot plant" idea

7.066 The idea of a "pilot plant" experiment in setting up various types of Re-evaluation Counseling "institutions" recurs regularly among Re-evaluation Counselors.

Some of these have actually been set up. The Palo Alto Re-evaluation Counseling school, for example, was an experiment by a number of Re-evaluation Counseling leaders and parents in seeing how completely supportive an environment could be created for pre-school children, where they would be supported in working out what they wanted to learn and in cooperating with other children and with adults toward early re-emergence and rational development and maturity.

One such pilot plant project that was eagerly urged on the International leadership by many Re-evaluation Counselors around twenty years ago was a "retreat center for deeply distressed people," where such people could be safe from the mistreatment and oppression by society and be surrounded by top-notch counseling, and which would allow their rapid re-emergence from distress. It was estimated then that a minimum of $300,000 would be necessary to equip and staff even a small retreat such as that. Only a few thousand dollars were actually contributed to the Re-evaluation Foundation for that purpose. Instead, perhaps understandably, large numbers of Re-evaluation Counselors volunteered "deeply distressed" friends and relatives to be client-participants in the project. Since the leadership of Re-evaluation Counseling was convinced (and remains convinced) that only very skilful, very committed counselors could handle such a concentrated project, the project itself eventually died simply from being held in abeyance.

What has actually happened instead, although not sufficiently by far as yet, is that large numbers of workers in the so-called "mental health" system have become involved in Re-evaluation Counseling themselves and for themselves, and through support groups have introduced it to fellow staff members. They have thus begun the tedious realignment of the mis-trained and oppressed workers in the so-called "mental health" system into becoming allies of the rapidly growing movement of survivors (victims!) of the "system." These last are a growing force working to end this oppressive structure (which, among many other evil effects, acts as a "gendarme" against all liberation movements).

8. SPECIALTIES IN COUNSELING

the complexity and variety of distress patterns

8.001 Every distress pattern is unique, which is one reason why the attempts to categorize distresses in the various disciplines of various psychologies have been so unproductive. The distress pattern is the unique recording of the unique distress experience which happened to the victim at that particular time. It never happened to anyone else and never will happen to anyone else in the future. The complexity and variety of distress patterns is, in a sense, infinite. Each one needs to be tackled in a particular way. The client's intelligence, assisted in the particular useful ways which the second person's (the counselor's) intelligence is capable of, can cope with this particular challenge.

The complexity of the distress patterns, although great, is at least one whole order of magnitude less complex than the intelligent *thinking* of a human being. A mathematician might compare this difference roughly to the difference in the first two orders of infinities: one, the relatively simple infinity of the counting numbers (1, 2, 3, . . .) and, two, the much greater complexity of the real numbers or the complex numbers.

With the above in mind, it is useful and helpful to share experiences in discharging and re-evaluating certain similar, or at least superficially similar, patterns that have been discharged by clients in the past.

Keeping in mind that the material in this "Specialties in Counseling" section does not consist of a "formula" but rather, hopefully, accurately useful summaries of other Co-Counselors' experiences, may help the reader approach the subject of being an effective counselor on these various difficulties with more ingenuity and confidence.

distress patterns as addictions/addictions

8.002 All patterns are "addictive" in that they tend to force their victims through repeated re-enactments of the hurtful behavior that first installed them. In this sense, the re-enactment of any pattern is an addiction whether there are hurtful chemicals involved or not. Some familiar *behavior* patterns to which people become addicted are, for example, chronic patterns of blaming someone else for all difficulties which one experiences, patterns of isolating oneself from other people, overwork, over-busyness, and so on. These may appear to be the "free choice" of the victim but are really compulsive patterns which the person is actually eager to be helped with or eager to be required to contradict, discharge, and give up, even though he or she speaks, sounds, and acts as if he or she were "devoted" to continuing in the pattern. If the counselor remembers the distinctions between the person and the pattern, there is no need for him or her to become confused since the rigid, inflexible character of the behavior makes it clear that it is a pattern talking when the person acts and speaks in defense of the addiction.

8.003 All distress recordings or patterns are "addictive" in the sense that every distress pattern tends to force its victim through a re-enactment of the original hurt. (People sometimes speak of being "addicted" to rational, constructive activities as a kind of a jest, but we are here reserving the words "addictive" and "addiction" for acts which are harmful and anti-survival in their effect upon the individual.)

In ordinary usage people use the term "addictive" to refer to substances which are physically ingested into the human body. These are most commonly poisons of some sort, such as alcohol, tobacco, street drugs, prescription drugs that disrupt the body's functioning, etc. To these are sometimes added *over-use* of substances which are not in themselves harmful, or are even nourishing in sensible amounts, or *activities* which are excellent in moderation but harmful when overdone, so that "overindulgence" creates a whole new group of "addictive" behaviors. Overeating, over-preoccupation with sex, overworking *(work is inherently a rational activity)*, and over-preoccupation with money are often conveniently talked of as "addictions."

Observably, addictive patterns related to food, sex, and work have proven difficult for people to discharge and emerge from. My conjecture about this is that the special difficulty arises because these activities, if carried out rationally in ordinary functioning, are so important to survival. When distress becomes attached to them, the resulting pattern is easily confused with and "seems" to acquire the pro-survival roles which rational eating, normal sexuality, and constructive work have carried in the past.

8.004 A basic step in ridding oneself of an addiction is to halt the *practice* of the addiction, since each such rehearsal of the addictive activity reinforces the pattern and leaves it stronger. A decision to end the addiction will be necessary to completely eliminate it, but the period of "withdrawal" and the apparent "suffering" during the withdrawal will perhaps be necessary before the victim is able to make a decision. Much of the "suffering" of withdrawal, which is treated with such respect in the wide-world culture, is, of course, simply discharge of the distress which has been accumulated in the past *practice of the addiction*. As long as discharge is treated as "suffering," this concept will continue to confuse workers in the field in the wide world. No permanent freedom from an addiction is possible without discharge.

8.005 At the end of the period of withdrawal the victim of the addiction is free to decide to give up the addiction, but the decision needs to be explicitly made, committed to, and practiced intensely for the change to be complete. If the whole idea of recovery has been enforced upon the person and the person has been given no companionship nor support during the withdrawal period, resentment against the enforcement is likely to motivate the addiction victim to resume the addiction at the earliest opportunity.

Thus, interrupting the addiction is necessary, but discharge, re-evaluation, and the person's own firm commitment are also necessary to end the addiction permanently. So, there will be a great need for excellent counseling following the withdrawal period. It is generally necessary to assist the former victim in taking pride in himself or herself as a contradiction to the shame and guilt and the feelings of contempt for oneself that participating in the addiction has generally allowed to accumulate upon the victim. It is important to point out to the client and remind the client many times that the notion of participating in the addiction came from outside originally, that the activity was entered into innocently in the first place, and that the client is "too smart" to have ever entered into the addictive activity if he or she had had full knowledge of what was going on.

As the oppressive society collapses, it generates enormous pressure to involve large numbers of people in addictions to "drugs," that is, chemical substances to be ingested by humans that are addictive in their effect on the people taking them. Any substance which numbs the nervous system of a person in some way or other, and may (but does not necessarily) produce sensations of some kind of euphoria, but which leaves acute discomfort on the user once the effect has worn off, is a candidate for the recruitment of addicts to its use. Generally such substances are discovered by accident, are spread by addicts to other people, are often celebrated as "great discoveries" for an extended period before their destructive effects are noticed or clarified, and then become "illegal drugs." Alcohol, tobacco, opium, cocaine, and many other drugs have taken this route and have wound up proclaimed as harmful and/or illegal, but have also wound up being pushed intensively by crime syndicates, profiteers in business, and people addicted to them.

Large numbers of drugs are used in medical practice based on the fundamental mistake accepted by the medical establishments that numbing out the pain or discomfort sensations of a patient is "relieving suffering." All such drugs tend to be addictive, and large numbers of medical personnel who have access to them have tended to become addicts.

Here the fundamental knowledge that we've had to face and understand in Re-evaluation Counseling can come into play. Using a local anesthetic has the advantage of making it possible for the surgeon or other medical person causing pain to the patient to help the patient hold still for the surgery or other procedure. The pain, however, needs to be experienced and will be experienced after the numbing effect of the local anesthetic wears out. If it is not experienced and discharged on fully, it will become a *distress pattern* which will limit the person's future functioning in some way and tie up his or her intelligence at least to a small degree.

If a person has dental work done under the numbing effect of Novocain, the pain and any associated emotional distress will have to be felt after the Novocain wears off to avoid damage from the experience. This, in general, is not understood in medical circles except by doctors who have themselves participated in and thoroughly understood Re-evaluation Counseling.

The lists of "legal," "approved" drugs include a large number of "psychiatric drugs" which are intended to numb the emotional feelings of the psychiatric patient. These all tend to become addictive and by their very effects impose periods of shut-down on the patient. Their use is completely counter to the use and functioning of Re-evaluation Counseling. They impose additional patterns each time they are used, and if a person who is taking them attempts to re-emerge through the use of Re-evaluation Counseling, that person has a great deal of extra work to do to discharge and recover from each time the drug was used.

With the widespread use of these drugs in the collapsing society, many people are attracted to Re-evaluation Counseling who are also taking these drugs. Many of these people want the benefits of discharge and re-evaluation and re-emergence but are pulled to resist giving up their addiction to the drugs. Many Re-evaluation Counseling teachers have not well understood the completely antagonistic role of RC and the "comfort" attained from drugs and mistakenly take these people into their classes and try to Co-Counsel with them without realizing the hopelessness of that activity. Occasionally people discharge enough that they fight their way free of the addiction and become Co-Counselors (but never very good ones), and some RC teachers assert their "independence" (which they have under RC rules) by taking such people into their classes without an agreement that they will quit the drugs.

I would conjecture that it may be useful and workable to have a class composed only of people who have been addicted (something like the support groups of the "Twelve Step Alcoholics Anonymous" type), where all the people in the class agree to work on giving up the drugs and ending the addictions. However, I think that in the present state of Re-evaluation Counseling and of the collapsing society, and in terms of the large numbers of people who are available to take into one's class who are not confused about their addictions, it may be a real waste of the RC teacher's time to try to help people think when they are systematically interfering with their thinking by taking drugs (whether they can realize and admit this or not).

pre-natal distress/birth

8.006 Human beings are vulnerable to the imposition of distress recordings at any time in their existence. If we count conception as the beginning of the life of a particular human (since individual sperm or ova have no chance of continuing to live unless they participate in conception), then it is correct to say that the newly-conceived individual can receive hurt and survive it and be left with distress recordings to deal with from the moment of conception on. (Recordings can be installed on relatively simple one-celled creatures and also on creatures of increasing complexity at every stage of evolution, including such highly-evolved living things as mammals. These recordings do not have *all* the effects which distress recordings have on humans.)

Any distress recordings imposed early in the pre-natal existence of the individual, before the fetus' central nervous system has developed enough to carry out intelligent calculations or to experience emotional feelings, will be recordings on the physical or "cellular" level. When these recordings are restimulated later in the pre-natal individual's life (when the individual's intelligence is beginning to function), they will also be interpreted in various *emotional* ways. Thus, a very early pre-natal recording consisting purely of pain or intense physical discomfort, restimulated later than the sixth month of term when the baby's intelligence is already functioning, will probably be interpreted as a *frightening* experience and will acquire a fear content in addition to the original physical pain content.

Pre-natal distress will be brought up by a client whenever there is slack or resource enough that she or he hopes to be able to discharge and re-evaluate it. It need not matter to the counselor how the client interprets the distress recording (a nightmare, a "vision," a "past life," a bad LSD "trip," a memory of his or her mother's, etc.). The counselor simply helps the client find contradictions that enable discharge to occur and furnishes the persistence necessary to get the distress fully discharged.

It is currently being revealed that medications, street drugs, alcohol, and tobacco create enormous difficulties for the unborn infant's survival, and various interpretations are offered that such an infant will be permanently handicapped as a result. So little work has been done that no one can know for sure (at this point) that this is true. I think Co-Counselors have everything to gain by assuming that, although it is true that the earlier the distress occurs in a person's existence, the more persistence is likely to be necessary to completely discharge and eliminate it, we should hold out the same expectation for people hurt pre-natally as we do for all others—that with enough persistence and intelligence, any distress can be "cleaned up completely."

8.007 Distresses acquired very early in life usually seem to exert far more influence on the person's life than one would expect from the length of the distress experience or the severity of the distress, at least in some cases. A conjecture is that this extraordinary influence arises when the distress is accepted as reality or in some way or other comes to function as if it were a chronic pattern, so that much of the later experience of the person includes an element of the rigidity of this distress, and therefore such early distress warps a person's general picture of what is going on around him or around her.

Some clients have found the motivation to wholeheartedly challenge these early patterned residues (perhaps because of the intense discomfort which they felt when these recordings were playing). It has nevertheless taken prolonged and committed counseling and discharge over a period of months or years to emerge from the chronic state of functioning within these patterns. Observably, as with any pattern which has emerged from chronicity, there is some urgency about continuing to discharge on it lest the chronicity reappear with the accumulation of additional restimulating experiences.

This has so far usually involved long, hard work, but the clients who have done this or are doing this are unanimous in their judgment that these distresses are to be faced and tackled, that the difference between life still influenced by these early distresses and life after the person has re-emerged from them makes the latter worth any effort.

8.008 Most Co-Counselors (in our experience so far) have found as they begin counseling that they have occluded the memories of their own births. Often they have discharged on their births in the first weeks after being born (this is often called "being a colicky baby") and simply have occluded the rest of the distress in order to get on with the business of living and learning.

A birth can apparently be almost totally free from distress. We have witnessed a few of these. However, it is a climactic experience to begin one's *air-breathing* existence. To review it and discharge any distress is extremely helpful to one's general functioning.

To counsel another person on his or her birth you will find it workable to just ask them "what they think happened," "what they imagine happened," or ask them to "tell the story of another little girl or boy being born," just however they imagine it. The story should be told and re-told many, many times. The elements of the client's birth that need to remembered, reviewed, and discharged on will appear out of the occlusion. With support from the counselor and sufficient contradiction, the distress will be discharged.

improving relationships

8.009 Most people at some time or other have difficulties in their relationships with other people, or at least feel that there is distress involved in relationships.

A useful preliminary procedure in improving relationships through counseling is to face and realize that every person has a concept of what a relationship "should be" for themselves and generally unawarely assumes that other people, including the ones they have or seek a relationship with, have the same concept of what a relationship means as they themselves do. *This is almost certain not to be true.* Therefore, it is highly desirable to clarify each person's concept of what they "want" and expect from the other person in the relationship and then communicate this in great detail to the other person.

A possible procedure for this is to have each person *separately* (with a counselor, if the person chooses, but *not* with the other person involved in the desired relationship) draw up a list of everything he or she expects or hopes to receive from the other person in *actions* or in attitudes. Each person, in making the list, should be urged to be completely open and frank about everything they wish, even if the listed desire seems unreasonable even to themselves. When the long, detailed list is as complete as the person (and the counselors) can make it, the parties to the hoped-for relationship should then exchange their lists.

Each person then, separately (with a counselor, if they wish, but *not* with each other), takes the other person's list and separates it into *three* lists. On the A list go the desires of the other person that this person is happy to agree with, looks forward to furnishing or performing, and is delighted that the other person asks or wishes. On the B list go the desires of the other person that the recipient does not necessarily disagree with, but which he or she will find it difficult to meet. On these items the person putting them on the B list indicates that he or she will appreciate it being understood by the other party that these are not easy for the person and that it may take considerable work and help before these items become possible for the person making the B list to do. The requester may even have to counsel the person or help her or him secure good counseling before these will be possible. On the C list go the requests which the person is opposed to furnishing and asks agreement from the requester to never request them from him or her again. ("Not these, buster, not now or ever!")

The two parties then return each other's lists in the divided form (A, B, and C lists), confer with their counselors about them if they wish, have sessions on them, and then meet person-to-person. The first point on the agenda for this meeting is to celebrate their agreement on the A lists and look forward to enjoying these activities with each other. The second point is to express agreement to never request or expect anything on the C list from each other ever again. ("If you still want something like that, don't want it from me, and I don't want to know about it.") The third point is to discuss possible ways to help each other or find sources of help for each other for the points on the B list.

This procedure does not necessarily *solve the problems* in a relationship, but it certainly clarifies enormously *what the problems are* and allows intelligence to be applied more effectively.

8.010 It only takes one person deciding to be rational to make a relationship go well (it does not require the other person to decide to). So there is no need to "wait" for the other person to be "reasonable" for the first person to take charge of a relationship.

8.011 Most people who have any relationship with each other at all tend to develop several relationships between the same two people. (A typical marriage will involve as many as fifty different relationships between the two people, although the culture will tend to regard it as just one relationship and the conditioned participants will be pressured to think of it in the same way. There are several relationships involved in housekeeping, in the shopping for and preparation of food, in child care, in yard work, in intimacy and sex, in participation in the neighborhood, church, school system, etc.).

A fundamental principle is that each relationship must "stand on its own feet" and must be dealt with and thought of individually. When failure to deal with a problem in any one of such relationships is "handled" by expecting that the mistreatment or malfunction will be compensated for by another of the relationships that is working well, eventual disaster is being prepared. Generosity with money will not forever make tolerable a failure to take an interest in the children. Sexual skills in bed will not forever make a dirty kitchen tolerable. All parties to any relationship need to examine each specific relationship and move to improve it until it is fair and rewarding to both parties. Even a compromise, where one party takes over responsibility in one relationship and the other party trades by taking more responsibility in a second relationship, will become tiresome and irritating eventually. Both parties should strive to function optimally in each separate activity, and the appreciation and mutual support will flourish as a result.

learning

8.012 Learning is a completely natural function of the human mind. Any physically undamaged human brain is apparently quite capable of learning anything. Confidence that this is true needs to be expressed to, and shared with, any client who seems to be limited by any kind of a "block" on learning any particular knowledge or skills. The unbounded confidence of the counselor in the client's ability to become free from the block and to learn *anything* is an important overall contradiction to the distress.

When there is a difficulty in learning, there will always turn out to be a particular distress pattern left by one or more particular experiences of distress. Often the client, asked for such incidents, is able to furnish them immediately. When some pattern of occlusion interferes with these incidents' presentation, general statements, modeled in a confident tone by the counselor, can be offered for the client to repeat. ("I can think well about anything." "I'm really an excellent cook." "I'll just put down on paper what I think. I can always re-write it and improve it later or let someone else edit it." "Tensor calculus is just a collection of a number of small ideas. I'll examine them one at a time and take as much time understanding each one as I want to. Of course I'll wind up understanding them all.")

(After each one or two repetitions of such contradictory phrases [contradictory *to* the pattern] furnished by the counselor, the client should be asked for his or her "thoughts" which the repetition of the phrases has evoked. This will ensure that the client's thinking abilities are engaged, or will tend to become engaged, in the evaluation which the contradictory phrases are intended to produce. Otherwise the client can fall into repeating the phrases mechanically and simply add a new layer of shut-down tension to the distress whose discharge is being sought.)

Once either the distress experiences or the patterned attitudes in which they appear in the current functioning of the client are located, effective counseling simply consists of finding, presenting, and encouraging persistent application of contradictions to the distress. The counselor may, as always, have to furnish the contradictions many, many times (particularly in tone of voice and facial expression) while appearing for a long time to confidently expect the client to do it, himself or herself, at the next attempt. But the ensuing discharge will eventually free the client to do the contradictions himself or herself and allow the counselor to create and add other contradictions to the process (including accurately "rehearsing" and therefore "occupying" the client's original role in the recording, which can "crowd" the client out of the patterned role and enhance discharge substantially).

how the learning process operates

8.013

• The learning process operates between the limits of too much new information too fast (confusion, frustration) and too little new information (boredom).

• Learning consists of evaluating new information in relation to information we have previously understood. New information needs to be presented in small, ordered increments for evaluation to take place most easily.

• New information is quickly *compared* with the information we have already on file in what we usually call our memory, the information from past experiences which we have already understood. Similarities between the incoming information and the information on file are noted, as well as the ways in which similar experiences in the past have been met successfully.

• At the same time, this incoming information is *contrasted* with the information already on file, i.e., the differences are noted as well as the similarities. The incoming information is understood in relation to other information, in its similarities and differences to other data, not ever as a "concept by itself." The background context to which the information is expected to be related must be identified and presented first in any teaching situation in order to prepare for the new information to be understood and integrated.

• In most learning situations a certain amount of repetition is necessary and should be furnished. Any communication will tend to become confused, distorted, or misunderstood during the process of communicating. Such confusion arises from all the possibly-interfering factors. These include not only actual noise or static and other mechanical factors which tend to distort the signal, but also, in particular, the reactive recordings which beset both the communicator and the listener. Relaxed repetition of the message several times will tend to overcome these.

• It is difficult to accept important new knowledge *except* from someone one loves.

• It's easier for a learner to receive information from people whom he or she regards as "peers" than it is from a person that he or she regards as "superior" or "an authority."

- Anything which restimulates *any* distress, anything which *tends to be invalidating* of the learner, interferes with or prevents learning.

- Learning is greatly enhanced by the learner being allowed to talk during the process of learning. Most learning is accomplished by one-to-one transfer of information between two persons. To accomplish this efficiently requires that learners teach each other.

- Being liked, receiving lots of approval, having successes, touching other people, playing learning games, and encouraging group laughter and other forms of discharge are some of the factors which tend to accelerate the learning process.

8.014 Certain areas of learning tend to become "turned off" in most modern cultures by the persistent invalidation involved in the school procedures which are commonly used. As a result, a large proportion of clients will come to a counseling situation with blocking patterns already installed on the processes of reading, writing, and speaking to audiences. On handling these, it is well to remember that the job of the counselor is not to "teach" the client to do these things, but *to help the client discharge the blocks* that interfere with his or her learning to do them. Invalidation and self-invalidation are likely to have already been installed heavily in these areas. The usual attempts to "learn to read" in the familiar context are likely to restimulate and reinforce the distress rather than contradict it. The contradictions needed here are praise, approval, and *success*. So it is wise, for example, to begin with reading one word, but to have the client read that one word "successfully" many, many times, while each performance is cheered, appreciated, celebrated. The discharge can drain the tension out of that pattern by success with that one word, whereas allowing attempts to too quickly read more words will tend to restimulate and reinforce the patterned block.

Again, the counselor needs to endlessly proclaim her complete confidence in the client's unlimited ability to "learn anything." A motivation that exists in every person toward learning, and which has almost systematically been turned off and blocked in most school procedures, is an inherent joy of learning or love of learning. The human mind inherently *loves* to learn new things. All that is inherently required for this attitude to operate, for the joy of learning to turn on fully, is some new information to be learned and some existing information already known to which it can be related.

As this inherent enthusiasm for learning emerges with the particular successes in removing particular blocks, the learning skills of the client will begin to operate generally and widely, and the process of removing any *additional* blocks on learning any *particular* kind of knowledge will accelerate with the client's growing eagerness and enthusiasm.

counseling on sexual distress/sexuality/sexual abuse/sexual preference

8.015 The use of Re-evaluation Counseling can be very effective in removing distress associated with sex or sexuality. In most present cultures the society's picture of what is "natural" or "rational" about sex, sexuality, and sexual behavior is largely composed of distress, false information, and socially-enforced oppression patterns.

We have learned that it is usually best to begin counseling on the *earliest reachable* incidents involving distress about sex. The reason for this is at least in part because current or recent experiences are likely to be contaminated with the heavy distress and the oppression of *sexist* practices accumulated from the earlier incidents.

It has been one of the important insights of the Re-evaluation Counseling movement (now being shared extensively in the wide world) that a very, very large proportion of young people have been abused sexually when they were very young. Terror, threats, inattention, and lack of support have often occluded this distress, leaving many people to think of their sexual distress, however private or shamefaced they are about it, as "their own attitudes." Much of this early material is heavily occluded. It is not unusual to eventually recall that death threats were often made by the perpetrator of the abuse (who was acting out the scenario from the abuse that had been put upon him or her when he or she was a child).

Incidents that often appear to be "remembered" of what has been called "ritual abuse" undoubtedly have happened sometime, to someone, somewhere. These stories often seem to be similar to ones that undoubtedly *are* "remembered." It is also becoming plain as we accumulate more experience, however, that many of them are "stories" told by a "narrator" who had very early in his or her own life been terrified *by such stories* being told *to* himself or herself. These "perpetrations by narration" are usually accompanied by threats, the imposition of great terror, and insistence by the narrator that this actually occurred to the listening victim so that the victim comes to *imagine* the narrated scenes of ritual abuse actually taking place in groups of people that he or she later describes. To take these apparent "memories" of ritual (group) abuse and find contradictions which allow them to discharge requires effective counseling. One does not have to attest to or disprove the accuracy of the account (fantasy?) of the recounting client.

(Our early experiences with people who fantasized "past lives" can be of guidance here. We found that a person who is encouraged by the counselor to "believe" the account of her or his "past life" could discharge to some extent but could be easily caught up in the excitement and the drama of the "wonderful fantasy" she or he was creating, and so could continue to spin earlier and earlier versions of her or his past lives and adventures. When, however, the client was required to repeat (with discharge-producing, contradicting intervention by the counselor) and required to stay with the one version of the "past life," it eventually unmasked itself as an incident in the present life which the client had been too terrified to remember or report directly, and the fascination with the endless string of fantasies disappeared.)

8.016 It is a safe assumption that sexuality is an instinctive characteristic of human beings. By the time a person is sexually mature there is a powerful pro-survival drive toward participating in sex. If there were not, the species would not have survived and would not survive. In our present cultures sexuality is often provoked prematurely and the person is involved in it prematurely (before the person is sexually mature). This means that the experience is, of course, hurtful and leaves warping distress characteristics on the person's otherwise normal sexuality. The recorded sexual feelings in the distress pattern will tend to make the rehearsal of the activity called for by the distress pattern seem and feel "desirable" to the victim even though they will appear painful and repulsive to the same victim once discharge has been completed.

Sexuality is a normal and satisfying activity for humans to participate in. It can give adults an extra or deeper dimension to the closeness which is a rational need for humans at all periods of their lives.

No matter how much distress has been placed upon a client's sexuality, no matter how compulsive or abhorrent some of the patterns attached to it are, the person can be freed completely with enough support and resource leading to enough discharge.

8.017 One "easy" access to occluded distress around sex is to have the client recount in great detail, over and over, all the fantasies which the client has used in connection with masturbation or other explorations of sex. This may take some coaxing of the client by the counselor because these fantasies may seem to the client too "shameful" and "too weird to tell," but if they *are* recounted, they will turn out to be almost a literal blueprint of the sexual abuse which the client endured and which has been occluded until now.

8.018 Reminder: In counseling on distress attached to sexuality it is important to begin with the earliest sexual memories that the client can possibly reach. The counselor may have to accept later memories of the client to begin with *because the client will not be able to remember early ones*, but this should be only a temporary expedient. The heavier distresses and, particularly, the intrusion of the oppressive patterns of sexism involved in the later memories are likely to greatly distort the overall picture of the client's sexual history and, in the case of counseling with a person of the opposite gender, are likely to restimulate feelings of being offended by the counselor.

8.019 People who are survivors of incest (or any other early sexual abuse) are likely to need special assistance from the counselor in order to begin and persist in freeing themselves from this batch of distress. This is because the reality of what happened to them was often denied by the refusal of their allies at the time of the abuse to listen to them or take them seriously, or because threats of death or threats of further abuse by the perpetrator were made if the client were ever to tell anybody (or even remember) the abuse.

For the counselor, in a reassuring voice, to repeat a number of times, "It did happen," or, "It really happened," is likely to be helpful to the client in terms of getting started on the recounting.

It is not unusual for the perpetrator of incest to have also been a beloved ally, and for feelings of deep love and sexual excitement to have been recorded with the distress. So at some point a client may very well need to be reminded of the human side of the perpetrator, that the perpetrator was a *good* person, that it's all right to love the perpetrator and feel warmly toward him or her. The client can even be told that it is all right to temporarily re-experience feelings of sexuality toward the perpetrator in the process of cleaning up the rigidity of the distress recording.

It is also worthwhile keeping in mind that, having found safety and reassurance in an "incest survivors" or "early sexual memories" support group and having experienced the relief of openly identifying oneself as an incest survivor, there may be a pull to hold on to the identification and, in a way, rehearse it as an "exciting characteristic" in what might otherwise seem to have been a very dull life. The general rule on such oppressions is to accept and explore the identification, discharge on it thoroughly, and then reject it as not part of one's successful life as a human being.

8.020 People who identify their sexual preference as that of Gay man, Lesbian, or bisexual have been difficult for some Co-Counselors to counsel well. There has been controversy in a number of Communities over liberation policies for Gay people. In the Gay liberation movement outside of Re-evaluation Counseling, stands have been proposed and taken such as "heterosexuality is irrational," "homosexual sexual preferences are genetic in origin," "sex-change operations are rational," etc., etc., and some of these attitudes have been brought into the Re-evaluation Counseling Community.

These attitudes are understandable since, in general, a person with a Gay sexual preference has been oppressed, demeaned, and persecuted in thousands of experiences before coming into contact with Re-evaluation Counseling. An early statement in Re-evaluation Counseling literature that "homosexual practice always arises out of distress" has sometimes seemed oppressive and threatening to Gay people. The statement that could have been made to follow that statement (which we were too naive at the time to add but certainly would add now) would be that any particular heterosexual practice that you happen to choose to examine in the present patterned population will probably have arisen out of distress as well.

Gay people have a hard time finding effective counselors within Re-evaluation Counseling (or anywhere else). This is because the other Gay people who might counsel them with a positive attitude are not likely to easily furnish contradictions to their distress, since they have not been able, in general, to find them for themselves, and the "straight" Co-Counselors from whom they seek to obtain help are likely to, awarely or unawarely, still hold the homophobic (anti-Gay) biased attitudes which have been laid upon them by the conditioning of the society around them.

Under the leadership of "Jeanne d'Arc" and "David Nijinsky," the Gay liberation movement *within* Re-evaluation Counseling has largely reached agreement that what is workable is to face and accept the identity of "Gay" to begin with, then to search out, contradict, and discharge all the memories connected with Gayness in any way at all, reclaim one's thinking in all these areas as the discharge frees it, and then "throw the identity away." This requires excellent, persistent counseling, but it produces individuals who are free to take any attitude that makes sense to them towards the sexuality of any person under any circumstances. Many people relaxedly come to a heterosexual orientation but never buy into the oppressive attitudes of the oppressive, nominally "heterosexual" culture. They never lose sight of the precious insight which their previous functioning as "Gay" individuals incidentally afforded them the opportunity to gain, which is that to love and to be close to *any person* is completely rational and enjoyable.

aging/immortality/death

8.021 It is by no means clear that the process of aging needs to be inevitable for human beings. In fact, most of what is described as aging in the present cultures is the effect of the accumulation of distress patterns, and, entwined with this process, the accumulation of physical damage from poor food, poor air, poor water, overwork, overfatigue, ineffective or misguided exercise or the lack of it, and the oppression and abuse visited on older people by the oppressive societies.

Re-evaluation Counseling has, for many years now, proposed *immortality* as a conjectured possibility, and sections of the scientific world have been moving more slowly in the same direction.

Individuals who have, through good fortune or chance, had a benign and supportive environment in infancy, childhood, and youth, and, through good fortune or their own efforts or both, been treated well in the years past their youths, have shown a dramatically greater persistence in functioning well in their later years.

It was one of the early conclusions in Re-evaluation Counseling that if one could penetrate past the veil of distresses and oppressive attitudes and achieve direct contact with the human side of the client, people of all ages were "contemporaries." It was plain that the three-month-old infant and the ninety-five-year-old "senior" functioned in the same way and on the same wave-length once one got past or took into account the smaller amount of information available to the very young and the restricted amount of free attention immediately available to the elders.

It is certainly already plain that thorough discharge can slow and postpone the effects of aging as it is usually expected to take place, and that accepting aging and the slowing down of function as inevitable is just a distress pattern installed upon us by the culture and society. The possibility of *complete elimination of aging effects* is yet, however, to be demonstrated.

A substantial amount of scientific research is currently underway, the goal of which, for various reasons, is usually described as the "extension of life" or "the improvement of old age," but which, inevitably, has the goal of living forever. Many of the scientists involved privately admit to yearning for immortality and being hopeful of achieving it just as much as we less-well-informed people are yearning and hopeful.

Since single-celled living organisms are already, practically speaking, immortal, there appears to be no built-in impossibility of achieving immortality for our enormously more complex bodies.

8.022 Apparently every human being begins life confidently expecting to live forever. For almost every person the experience of being confronted with the *possibility* (let alone the *inevitability*) of life coming to an end (for one's pet animal, for one's human acquaintances and allies, or for oneself) is a deeply shocking experience. (This spontaneously-arising confident expectation of immortality and the *shocked* rejection of death is one of the elements leading to our conjecture about the possibility of physical immortality for humans.)

A conjecture proposed in the article "Is Death Necessary?" is that deaths of individual living creatures (and the accompanying recycling of the elements to make them available for other lives) was desirable and perhaps even necessary as long as improved functioning could only appear through evolutionary leaps based on mutations. However, once human central nervous systems had reached the capacity for intelligent thinking, such *recycling of individuals* was no longer useful or profitable for the operation and acceleration of the upward trend.

Various schools of belief have pictured death as an "escape" from the strain and conflict of the "usual" life to an imagined existence of rest, peace, and relaxation, or as the beginning of a "new game of life" with a new "hand of cards" dealt in the hereafter, the content of which would be determined by how one had "played the game" in her or his previous "mortal" life, or as passing into a permanent state of reward or punishment depending on how one had behaved in one's mortal life.

I, personally, tend to think of death as being an interruption of a dynamic function, the "blowing out of a flame."

discharging distresses about death

8.023 The fear of one's own death can be *completely discharged*. I have known a number of people who, through facing dangers confidently in experiences in their lives, were free of such fears. Such a fear can be completely discharged through skilful and persistent counseling. (A technique to expedite such discharge is to express the fear repeatedly in words but in a cheerful, confident tone of voice.) Until such effective counseling has been done, however, most people in our culture will have been loaded up with a considerable quantity of fears of death.

In the grip of such fears, or functioning in such fearful cultures as we tend to be surrounded by, there is a tendency towards identifying "fear of death" *with death itself* and to "suffer" fearful feelings whenever one thinks of mortality as an inevitable characteristic of our beings. *Fear of death is not death but purely and simply a fear.* If it is contradicted it will discharge. If it is contradicted skilfully and persistently, it will discharge completely. In many cultures in the wide world people have responsibly modeled the complete discharge of all fear of death. With the tools of Re-evaluation Counseling, to eliminate fear of death completely is quite simple if one contradicts it all the time instead of usually rehearsing it with a fearful, respectful attitude towards it.

8.024 The deep sense of loss which people feel upon the death of someone that they knew and cared about usually has to begin to discharge in tears. Often the client finds it difficult, by himself or herself, to find a contradiction to what feels like an *enormous* sense of loss, and it will be a principal job of the counselor to find and offer such contradictions. One such classic contradiction that the client will tend to find by himself or herself (or accept easily when suggested by the counselor) is the remembering of happy enjoyable times spent together with the departed person. The pull on the client will be to rehearse the fact of the *loss*, and the counselor can be most helpful in directing attention again and again to the positive part of the memories which, because they contradict the feeling of loss, lead to the tears flowing easily.

A very large amount of crying may be necessary to discharge this deep sense of loss. (My own second significant experience as a client in Re-evaluation Counseling was crying heavily for approximately 200 hours remembering the death of my brother when I was seven years old.)

The total distress of such an experience will not be finished with when the tears are exhausted because there will be a large over-burden of other kinds of distress to be tackled as well. This will tend to include fears of one's own death that might have occurred to one when faced with the mortality of one's loved "dear departed." Later discharge will tend to be light fear and embarrassment, indignant anger, and anger discharging through laughter. Finally, in the typical series of discharges, reluctant talk, eager talk, and a little relaxed laughter will lead to the apparent "forgetting" of the loss *as a distress experience*. Discharge by yawning will occur intermittently at various spots in one's progress through the emotional discharges.

Sometimes patterns will appear in the client of denying the loss, refusing to face the actuality of it, and protecting some of the grief from discharge, as if to finish the tears would be to lose the loved one. At such times the counselor may need to furnish firmness on the client's behalf and, for example, insist that the client bid the departed loved one farewell, over and over, many, many times.

The actuality is (and this will eventually be faced by the client) that all the bereaved person ever possessed of the departed person was the calculated perception of the departed which he or she had created from the information supplied to him or her by his or her nervous system in the form of the little blips of electrical charge which enter the client's mind for evaluation from the neurons connecting them to his or her sense organs. In actuality, he or she *will still have* all this valuable treasure of knowledge about the departed loved one, except that it may have become occluded by the undischarged painful emotion and pain of the loss. Discharging *all* the distress removes this occlusion and brings the treasured information and memories of the departed person and the bereaved person's association with him or her back to full recall, usability, and enjoyment.

suicide compulsions

8.025 Our experience in working with many clients whose distress patterns move them toward suicide has clarified a number of issues about the relationship between decision and death.

In the first place, almost every tendency, urge, or pull in the direction of a person taking his or her own life will turn out to be a distress pattern. The gift of life is such a precious possession that it seems incredible that anyone, while being rational, would ever think or consent to giving it up. One of the crucial insights of

Re-evaluation Counseling has been worded as follows: "It is far better to be alive, if only for one instant and that instant spent in agony, than never to be alive at all."

Thus in dealing with apparent "decisions" to take one's own life, it is a reasonable beginning assumption as a counselor that one is dealing with a distress pattern which has the client in its grip. Since such patterns do actually lead to suicide attempts and to the deaths of clients, the counselor is challenged to effectively contradict them, and this will require the usual care of accurately determining what the distress pattern is, finding accurate contradictions to it, and presenting the contradictions in ways that "surprise" the client and avoid reinforcing any of the painful emotional content. It is always correct to take the survival of the client seriously. It is not necessarily correct to take the *threat* of the suicide pattern "seriously, solemnly, or with wild alarm."

In early counseling, when the concept of contradiction was not yet well understood, I found it effective with a number of clients who threatened suicide to simply "nag" them determinedly until they *promised* that they would not commit suicide without "receiving my permission." This was not easy to accomplish, but the promise, when once given, was later credited by a number of them with "saving their lives."

In order to receive the promise, I had to deal with the "possibility" that a decision to commit suicide could be rational. I did this by agreeing that *if* they could make out a good case for suicide, I would give up my opposition to it. Since then I have known and known of individuals who rationally decided to die, and under such circumstances one must come to the basic principle that each person has the "right" to make such a decision himself or herself.

So, as counselor, one starts with the assumption that the intention to commit suicide is irrational and can be discharged, and one does an effective job in that direction. Only when the person can convincingly show you that it is her or his own free decision may one disengage from the process and allow the person to make her or his own decision.

pain/anesthesia/healing

8.026 All or nearly all present cultures are deeply permeated with a "fear" of feeling pain. The culture is also filled with patterned encouragement to use painkillers or "comforters" of any description. These are promoted as being "pro-survival" (compared to actually *feeling* the pain signals). This tends to prevent any recordings of physical pain and discomfort from being discharged and evaluated because the analgesics, sedatives, and anesthetics lock in the sensation of pain as a recording with additional occlusive effects caused by the chemistry of the painkiller or of the "comforting" agent itself.

The electrical signals travelling from the site of the injury to the central nervous system, which are interpreted by the central nervous system as pain, are identical to other signals travelling down other nerves which are interpreted as pleasure or enjoyment. It is the central nervous system's interpretation of the signals that makes one signal be taken to be pain and "suffering" and another be taken to have one of many other meanings.

To actually *feel* the most intense possible pain signals is not very onerous unless the pain signals themselves are magnified by *fears* which have been attached to the notion of pain and which act in the computation of the central nervous system to magnify the "painfulness" of the actual pain greatly. The "unbearable" pain, once it has the fear attached to it discharged from it, becomes quite bearable. Furthermore, without painkillers or anesthetics (feeling the heat of a dentist's drill without Novocain, for example), the pain is finished the moment the drilling stops. With painkillers or anesthetics the pain will have to be felt for hours and perhaps days in the future as it comes out of the occlusion caused by the chemicals. It is best to discharge your fears of pain ahead of time, experience any unavoidable pain fully, complain loudly while it is going on (if you feel like it) with the previously-organized support and permission of an audience if you can arrange for one, and then simply yawn for a while afterwards while reminding yourself that the entire operation is over.

8.027 Any kind of a hurt, physical or emotional, is most easily discharged immediately after the hurt has occurred and as soon as safety has been established. This is true for *emotional* hurts as well, but it is dramatically true and very important for effective handling of *physical* hurts.

Apparently the actual injury to the physical body takes place only during the actual destruction of tissue by the cut, the burn, the strain, the break. Some additional hurt may take place while the wound is being cleansed, the bone set, etc., but essentially the actual injury occurs during a very brief time. The rest of the "pain" and "suffering" seem to be the *playing out of the recording* made during the moment of injury, and as long as this recording is playing it tends to interfere with the healing process. It is as if the body tends to postpone the healing under the influence of the recording's message repeating over and over in effect, "I am being injured," "I am being injured," "I am being injured."

As long as the pain or discomfort recording is still being felt following the injury, it is available for immediate discharge. If the discharge is delayed, this recording will tend to link up with recordings of similar distresses from the past and become somewhat occluded or difficult to discharge (and may at a later date appear in a chronic form and present itself as a chronic pain). Once such an injury has "quit hurting," discharging the recording requires *contradiction*, and the client's attention needs to be directed toward "comfort" and "well-being" in order to *secure discharge*. Emotional discharge always needs to come first in order to make the physical distress available to be discharged.

For the *fresh injury* which is still hurting, it is possible and desirable to encourage the client to *directly* feel the pain as intensely as possible, to "suffer" loudly, to "make as big a fuss as possible." The counselor can be very helpful to the client if the counselor will model for the client exaggerated sounds of complaint and suffering, encourage the client to "transmit his or her AGONY" directly from the client's eyes to the eyes of the counselor, and with other devices contradict the embarrassment which inhibits the expression of pain. The client will often begin to laugh and then without even noticing it begin to shake off the fear which tends to surround any physical injury.

If the counselor continues to concentrate his or her and the client's attention toward the emotional distress surrounding the physical injury, the emotional distress will discharge with crying, laughter, and shaking, and the yawns will eventually appear spontaneously. The counselor-client pair will then (once the yawns are taking place regularly) attempt to help the client refer to the physical distress in an unemotional tone. The use of a bored tone of voice while expressing, "Ho hum," is one way of doing this. As the yawns continue, the physical pain or discomfort will tend to relieve and disappear quite quickly. For example, a burn that was "agonizingly" hurtful will stop hurting. A huge blister that had covered it will spontaneously deflate. The angry color will disappear, and the flesh and skin will resume the same hue as the surrounding skin. The client will report in amazement, "It doesn't hurt anymore!"

A similar development will take place with regards to a wound, a sprain, or even a break. (All injuries, of course, need to be protected from fresh injury.)

Very rapid healing follows. It is as if the great healing capacity of the body is freed from the inhibiting effect of the recording of distress as soon as that recording is discharged, and the healing of the adult proceeds as rapidly as the previously-referred-to rapid healing of infants.

8.028 General anesthesia is a physical distress during which everything experienced by the client (including the sensation of not being able to move, what is being said in the room, etc.) is installed as a recording. Such a recording needs to be discharged thoroughly, not only because of the physical shutdown, pain, etc., that have been recorded, but also because any words and other sounds which have been recorded during the anesthesia can have very compulsive effects on the individual if the recording is allowed to remain in place. The results can be as bizarre and harmful as anything ever demonstrated with "hypnotic" commands.

8.029 Many cultures have discovered and persisted with the use of physical touch as a healing process. Other people have learned to follow the procedures of the "healer," the "layer-on of hands," or the "witch doctor" with significant, unquestionably positive results. The Co-Counselor should understand why these actions are "healing" and with this understanding the Co-Counselor can be very flexible, inventive, and effective.

The *actual* pain or discomfort from an injury *occurs only at the time of injury*, and the apparently remaining persistent pain or discomfort consists of a *recording*. If the person's attention were not trapped inside the recording but could clearly distinguish the "painful," non-injurious recording from the "painful" event which happened and is over, recovery from the effects of the injury could and would be very rapid.

To touch the site of the injury or place where the recording of the old distress is playing (in the case of the pain still seeming to be present even though the healing was apparently over long ago) is to direct the attention of the client to the place with the support of the counselor's attention. The "comforting" touch of the counselor's fingers allows the "non-injury" character of the present to penetrate the awareness of the client and contradict the recording of the distress.

Touch is a very basic method of communication between two minds that we became expert with very early in our lives. It contradicts the feelings of being isolated with the distress, so not only does a "healing touch" exist and not only is it used with great skill by people who have experimented with it in their folk art or non-Western disciplines, but any Co-Counselor is fully equipped with reserves of skill and effectiveness in this area.

disabilities/illness

8.030 Most of us have internalized a great deal of the oppression about disabilities. Therefore, it is important in beginning to counsel on disabilities, both as client and as counselor, that we are clear that in a very real sense *there is no disablement* of any human being in any fundamental way. What is truly wonderful, splendid, and precious beyond evaluation is the ability of a human mind to think, to be intelligent. There are people, of course, who *seem* to be missing this ability, who do not *seem* to be functioning intelligently at all, but unless a person is dead, that ability, however occluded, exists and is the crowning achievement of the dynamic universe, is valuable beyond all else.

We know of people who have not been able to communicate their intelligence because of blocks, for whom modern technical inventions have established communication, and who have been able to reveal themselves as having been thinking brilliantly all the time.

Any failure to appear intelligent, whether caused by an accumulation of patterned behavior and appearance or by communication blocks, is not to be accepted as reality. In this sense, every human being at the present is "somewhat disabled" and can potentially become "enabled."

The disabilities that we notice, deal with, seek to remove, or find technical paths around are always existing on someone who is a completely "able" person, whether that person is oneself as the client or is the client whom we are thinking about in our role as counselor.

Starting with these correct assumptions, our role as counselor is to "pay attention" to the thinking of the client. It is possible that the client will not be able to communicate at all, which does not mean that we cannot pay attention. Our "positive regard" and occasional reassuring word will enable such a severely disabled client to "think through" material that he or she would not otherwise be able to think about. A victim of a severe stroke may be able only to respond to questions by blinking or not blinking eyelids, but the response is real, meaningful, and needs only thoughtful questioning by the counselor to open very powerful channels of communication. Games such as "Twenty Questions" or charades can give such a counselor insights into the effectiveness that is possible.

With all clients, the counselor needs to be effective towards the comfort and convenience of the client, but this can become *critical* for a client with a disability. Two powerful minds, the client and the counselor, are joining together (as should happen in every Co-Counseling session) to think well together, with the counselor taking nearly total responsibility to find ways that the client may comfortably, fully, and clearly think and communicate his or her thinking.

The disability should never be "respected" but rather treated as an interesting part of the situation, a temporary obstacle to be overcome. The counselor should never make any assumption of powerlessness of any kind or degree on the part of the client and should help the client discharge any such assumptions and prevent any others from being accepted.

The disability can well be viewed as a valuable motivation toward exploring the enormous power of the person's mind which might otherwise never be as thoroughly investigated.

8.031 Human beings, as part of the web of life, necessarily participate and have participated all through their existence in the competition between living organisms for nourishment, room, energy sources, etc. We prey upon, feed upon, and use for our convenience many, many other forms of life. Necessarily, many other forms of life have evolved to prey upon us, parasite upon us, and use us for their shelter, nourishment, and convenience. As a result, we are subject to many, many different kinds of illnesses caused by the activities of these other organisms, ranging from lions and tigers and rhinos to sub-microscopic retroviruses.

The cells of our own bodies sometimes mutate and become malignant parasites upon our bodies as a whole.

Our bodies function well only because of the most superb coordination of all the trillions of parts, and this coordination sometimes breaks down, resulting in many kinds of illnesses.

Recordings of experiences of being subject to (many different kinds of) illnesses create illnesses once more when the recordings are restimulated and replace the rational, coordinated functioning of our bodies with repetitive re-enactment of the recorded illness patterns of the past.

The counselor should beware of mentally leaping to a conclusion about a client's illness simply because it resembles or seems to resemble some previous experiences of his or her own or of others with illnesses. The best-trained and most experienced physicians have great trouble making an accurate diagnosis much of the time.

The best available professional help should always be consulted to the extent possible, although their recommendations need to be examined for the possible presence of individual patterns on their part or common patterns in their profession, or for their ignorance about the distress-recording-causation of illness versus the healing effect of discharge. Unless mind-numbing drugs or submission of the patient to not thinking for himself or herself are involved, any treatments by a professional physician will not interfere with the effective counseling of the client nor will the effective counseling interfere with the helpful influences of the physician.

The use of the "Co-Counseling diagnostic tool" (see pp. 201-210, *A Better World*) is a broad approach. Often a recorded and restimulated illness (which a large proportion of illnesses turn out to be) yields very quickly to the ill person simply being listened to and allowed to discharge.

men/women counseling each other

8.032 During most of the history of Re-evaluation Counseling, women have had difficulty being outstanding, effective counselors for men. This has held back the participation of men in Re-evaluation Counseling to some extent and has slowed the development of a men's liberation movement, for both their own liberation and being effective allies to women's liberation.

The fact that men are assigned an oppressive role toward women by the oppressive society has confused the picture that most women have of what men's lives are really like. The use of men's "panels," which consist of having a number of men recount the actuality of their lives at different ages, has led to a great awakening of women about men and needs to be pursued consistently. Most women have assumed that since, in general, they themselves tend to talk to each other and be clients to each other about their difficulties, men do this with each other, too, the women not realizing that men have been conditioned to feel that it is a "shameful" weakness to do anything but endure hardship and distress stoically. A beginning guide for a woman wishing to be a good counselor to a man, even if she has lived with him fifty years prior to this time, is to ask, "What's it been like for you being male? Start when you were a small boy, tell what you can, and I will listen." If the woman then listens patiently, the man will begin to notice the difference and will move to discharge as rapidly as he can.

8.033 Men can be very effective counselors to women in that they will tend to be outside the oppression, outside some of the terror, and outside of the particular kind of low expectations which have been forced upon the women. For the man to wholeheartedly reassure, enthuse, and support a woman client in the direction of "no limits at all" can be very effective. Except in special cases this may not be too difficult for the particular man because some men are used to being expected to achieve high goals and to refuse to accept limits for themselves. This attitude can furnish an effective contradiction for the woman client that she would find it hard to create by herself or with another woman.

8.034 The general concept of "no limits for women" implies the attainment by women of as much physical power as they desire as well as their ability and power in all other fields. During Chinese liberation, groups of young women in the Chinese steel mills set out to become as strong and powerful as any of the men and attained their goals completely. Our cultures are full of subtle invalidations of women and distorted notions that "to be physically strong is unfeminine," that women are "naturally smaller," that "one's beauty is spoiled by muscles," and so on. Most of these ideas simply have to be reviewed against the general concept of "no limits" for discharge to occur and re-evaluation to take place.

What has sometimes been effective has been special workshops where women leaders who are themselves strong and in excellent physical shape push women to wrestle and struggle physically in arduous ways, and thus participate in the reality of overcoming all the inhibitions that have been placed upon them. Many Re-evaluation Counseling women are leaders in various martial arts and self-defense disciplines which equip women to handle all physical crises well and in the process eliminate their fears through discharge.

As the timidity is discharged, women's natural sense of adventure and courage comes permanently to the fore.

different ages/counseling across age barriers

8.035 The oppressive society poses a special oppression on each age group. Infants, prior to, during, and following their birth, are given many hurtful experiences which contradict their inherent feeling of power and of being in charge of the universe. In general, they also tend to be invalidated deeply as the adults around them shut down because of other strains and act out and rehearse in the new role of parents the oppression which they received when *they* were infants or small children.

Toddlers need some cautionary oversight from adults when they are in dangerous situations (unguarded heights, traffic, threatening animals, and so on) but instead are usually given warnings and threats and "promises" of being hurt rather than useful information.

When young people reach school age, they are often exposed to older or more aggressive children who have been badly mistreated and who act out their recorded distresses on the younger ones. If it were not for the distress already having been imposed, children of school age would intuitively make friends with, care for, and enjoy each other. However, given the likelihood of distress already having been loaded on their new friends, the kind, relaxed, but firm intervention of adults demonstrating how children should and can treat each other, and insisting on their doing so, *with much praise and approval for their cooperation*, is almost a necessity.

School experiences should initially concentrate on children learning to relate to each other. Until this ground-work has been laid, it is almost always premature to expect young people to acquire information well in school. Once they are happily relating and the idea of helping each other learn has been established, learning can go enormously faster than people generally expect.

In the early grades children can be re-educated against the sexism, racism, "putting down of younger people." Fear of and failure to appreciate differences from and between other people (which have usually been imposed on the children by this time) can be contradicted, and a basic understanding can be established for the rest of the child's life.

Patterned confusion and misunderstanding about the process of growing up and achieving sexual maturity are the bases for a great deal of oppression imposed on present populations. The insecurity of teenagers, who have brilliant minds, a great deal of information, and mature bodies, but are denied power or participation in planning their lives and their education gives way to a partial freedom for young adults. They are no longer oppressed in the same way as teenagers, but they are still discriminated against on the basis of age and paid less for their work in the present society.

Finally the full-scale adult supposedly is in charge of his or her life (and of the society) but, in an oppression similar to that of men, is crushed with overwork and over-responsibility and is threatened with inadequate income, unemployment, war, and the devastating consequences of the continuing breakdown of society.

Older adults are often treated as nuisances, are often denied contact with younger people and children (which denial is harmful both for them and for the children), are forced into retirement and idleness, and are relegated to meaninglessness and insignificance. The accumulation of illnesses and distress are treated as if they were the inevitable concomitants of age, when actually most of them are the result of poor health care and inadequate health support. From the moment of conception until death every human being should be encouraged and expected to play a useful role and be given much appreciation.

8.036 All adults should play the role of allies to young people against young people's oppression, but young adults (roughly from twenty-one to thirty years of age) are able to be especially effective in this role. They tend to be able to remember the details and reality of young people's oppressed lives, and with a greater initiative available to them in their adult role they can be very effective at allowing young people to develop their own leadership and build a great young people's liberation movement.

8.037 Adults being effective counselors to younger people or to elders, and the counseling of adults *by* young people or *by* elders, present special difficulties. This is only because of the distresses which the counselor is likely to carry in the form of oppressive attitudes toward people of different ages than himself or herself. The fundamental principle here is that we are all *equally* intelligent and able. Differences in age do not mean differences in intelligence. If the person in the role of counselor can view the person in the role of client as his or her respected, treasured peer, the counseling process becomes simple and works well.

The difficulty in an adult being a counselor to a younger person arises from the fact that the adult has many hurts from his or her own young days of being treated condescendingly, without respect, being preached at and "told what to do." This means the adult must make and keep to a firm decision to listen, listen, listen, listen with respect, listen with respect, listen with respect. Do not "advise," "tell," "furnish information." The young client may ask the counselor's opinion because of the effects of previous treatment by adults, but the counselor should respond by asking for the client's opinion many, many times before "offering information."

8.038 Young Co-Counselors, who are re-emerging from smaller backlogs of distress than adults (on the average), need adult counselors who recognize the young person's advanced position and will not get in the way or slow him or her down.

play/work

8.039 As part of the oppression of young people, the word "play" has often been assigned a pejorative flavor. It is treated as if it were unimportant or an escape from responsibility. The activities described as "play" for adults often include harmful activities such as passively being a spectator to uninformative or restimulative television programs or "sports spectacles," drinking alcohol, smoking, intense competition, overeating, gambling, "consumerism," patterned sex, or dangerous, irresponsible behavior for the sake of the "thrill."

This is very misleading, and the confusion that it engenders is used for oppression.

Play, as it spontaneously arises among young people, is a very precious, creative activity whose roots are already present among simpler forms of life. Young mammals almost always engage in it as a highly developed activity.

For human children, play consists primarily of two activities. The first is the *attempting* and then *practicing* of new skills. A very young baby will spend hours with great interest and absorption practicing the movements of her or his hands, and having mastered one movement will proceed to another with tireless enthusiasm. Good games are excellent training for necessary skills and, unless spoiled by the intervention of someone's patterns, are welcomed and pursued with great vigor.

The second function of play is to provide an opportunity for discharge. Frequently parents, learning something of Re-evaluation Counseling, become very concerned that their children shall have a chance to "discharge" or that they, the parents, should "counsel them well." The parents often worry loudly that they are not counseling the children well enough that they get "lots of discharge." Parallel to this, the children, getting a chance to play with other children freely, are discharging wildly in the midst of their play. Any slight injury brings copious tears, which, listened to, clear up with a few shudders and send the discharger back into the play. The laughter and shouting and shaking goes on as a very excited and cooperative part of the play itself.

Most of us adults have been conditioned so thoroughly that we've almost lost the capacity to play in anything but a "grotesque" manner. Yet to restore real communication with our children, the recovery of our ability to play is an ideal channel. At playdays and family workshops, the guiding principle is that parents and children will play together in games which the children themselves propose and devise, following the children's rules. The adults are to be completely cooperative in spite of fatigue and embarrassment and the yearning to stop and indulge in some patterned shutdown—eating, drinking, or other escape. Quite a number of Re-evaluation Counseling adults and parents have even found that they re-acquire the ability to play and enjoy it as wholeheartedly as they did when they were young.

8.040 Work is rationally the central activity of adult humans. Basically work can be defined as improving the environment to make it more supportive to humans and to their allies among other forms of life. Work is essentially very satisfying, very rewarding. If it has distress characteristics attached to it, then the memories of over-exploitation, over-fatigue, disappointment, injury, and bad working conditions should be asked for, recalled, and discharged. One's inherent enjoyment of work and the goodness of the activity will be uncovered with the discharge, and work will again become a part of life that one naturally looks forward to.

8.041 Cooperating with other people in working, playing, enjoying, and being entertained is essentially a very pleasant part of living. Many of us have been oppressed and otherwise treated badly in the past so that, as a result, we find such active relationships with others interfered with by distress patterns, our own and those of other people.

To review all memories in two categories will improve these difficulties quickly. One of these chains of memories should be *all memories of enjoying such interactions with others*, and this series should be reviewed and discharged about thoroughly. The other chain to be tackled should be the chain of memories where such interactions were difficult, unpleasant, disappointing, etc. Needless to say, this second chain will require more initiative from both the client and the counselor to discharge, but the net result of reviewing both topics thoroughly will be the emergence of much greater enjoyment and skill in relating to others in *any* activities.

creativity

8.042 Every human being is inherently creative. To function intelligently is to create a fresh response for each moment of living. Only the installation of distress recordings has interfered with, has suppressed, and has concealed the natural human enjoyment of continually improving everything in one's living and one's environment.

To live creatively is the essence of living for every person. To pursue creativity as a principal occupation through the creation of new art in any medium is closely connected to living creatively but requires decision, persistence, and application and is the basis of the difference between the artistic person and the "full-time artist." We assume that every person has the capacity to be a creative artist if they so decide but recognize that this is not automatic, that it follows only on the person's decision and application.

The blocks to either level of creativity consist only of distress, and to review the experiences of distress and discharge them simply requires persistence and creative counseling.

8.043 The essence of being human is being creative. The person who awarely creates new concepts is an artist. Every human being is potentially an artist. The person who dedicates himself or herself awarely to creating art and taking responsibility for sharing or communicating these creative results to others could be called a "serious artist" or "professional artist" or "artist by vocation." Such a person, who successfully creates new concepts, is the prototype of a human being. In another sense, such a person is the prototype of a working-class person in that the person creates enormous value but traditionally, in this oppressive society, has the value he or she has created appropriated by owning-class purchasers and receives very little of the value herself or himself.

Judgment as to which attempts at creativity are successful art and which have failed to be successful art because of patterns, will be made historically over a long time period. A possibly useful guideline for a person to judge what has been successful art is to think in terms of the categories of "non-art," "bad art," "good art," and "great art."

"Non-art" includes efforts which have failed to be creative, which have only repeated already-existing ideas. "Bad art" is the expression of distress, distress patterns, or the consequences of distress patterns *as if they were manifestations of humanity or of human beings.* "Good art" is creative expression of the distresses attached to human beings and their activities which makes it clear that these distresses are different from the humans themselves or their human natures, which makes it clear that this distress is parasitic upon, and is distinct from, the humans themselves. "Great art" expresses new, fresh, pro-human, upward-trend combinations of ideas that have not existed before and which model and encourage the movement of human beings in this direction.

money

8.044 Money is a useful human invention. The fact that it can be used oppressively and for oppressive purposes only means that distress can attach to the concept of money and make it difficult for people to think about it. A suggestion for helping someone's thinking about money would be to pick up on the earliest incidents connected with money and review similar incidents that occurred later all the way to present time, with the counselor asking at some point in the review of each incident what irrational ideas were attached to money at that point, and what a rational attitude would be.

decision-making

8.045 The mastery of one's environment and one's life requires the making of a multitude of decisions. All creative work involves repeatedly making decisions. In general, individuals become aware of the importance of decision only when they are having difficulty making a decision, when they are having trouble "making up their minds."

One useful device in dealing with such a difficulty is listing all the advantages to each alternative to the decision and, in parallel, listing of all disadvantages involved in each direction. Reviewing these in a session often will clarify the question enough to make a decision easier.

If this is not sufficient then the client should ask for a session and take time announcing in a positive voice that he or she is deciding one certain way, and then review all the results of carrying out that decision. When this has been done thoroughly, the client should then announce that he or she is deciding the other way, and review the results of that. Repeated sessions in this manner usually lead to a clear-cut decision.

If the difficulty persists, eventually a decision should be forced by the expedient of agreeing to accept the "decision" of a coin toss. Often the person's own decision will emerge (when the coin is still in the air) in the form of a fervent wish that the coin should be either heads or tails when it comes to rest.

In most cases (excepting life-and-death or enormously dangerous decisions), the decision should be put into practice. The early results of carrying out the decision will usually clarify whether the decision was correct or a mistake.

Continued vacillation simply means staying in a vacillation recording. Even a wrong decision is (almost always) better than no decision, when a person is caught in such a pattern.

communication/language

8.046 The communication of *important* ideas is likely to require one-to-one communication between individuals. This can be approximated by a relaxed speaker making eye and voice contact with every member of an audience, but where the ideas are fresh and new and important, the situation is likely to require that two individuals communicate person-to-person.

8.047 Good *language* is always creative. The first time one reads an excellent poem, one is having one-to-one communication from the poet, and if one repeats the poem accurately and well to another person one is being a link in a chain of communication between the poet and the listener. Such models of excellent communication can be inspiring and permanently enjoyable, but they cannot replace the creativity of the individual. Each one of us needs to write our own poems, and in a healthy society we would undoubtedly develop a habit of doing so regularly.

When it comes to the spoken or "prose" word, it is crucial that we do not allow our spoken language to become filled with "clichés." The cliché may have been creative when it was first spoken, and our admiration for the wit of its creator is not necessarily misplaced, but in our communication to others it is worth struggling to see that our words and our phrases are fresh. A new idea deserves new expression, or it's likely to be lost and distorted by the humdrum language if such language is settled for and tolerated.

9. ABOUT TEACHING RE-EVALUATION COUNSELING

9.001 The Re-evaluation Counseling Communities (the group of people who have jointly agreed to assume responsibility for the accurate communication of the insights of Re-evaluation Counseling and the development of new insights consistent with the existing body of knowledge) require that anyone claiming to communicate any of these insights and theory using the name of "Re-evaluation Counseling" shall be approved by the Community through a procedure established in *The Guidelines* of the Community

The Community encourages all Co-Counselors to teach all other people one-to-one as rapidly and expeditiously as they can. The goal here is that each Re-evaluation Counselor will be "teaching" Re-evaluation Counseling in some manner at all times when he or she is in the presence of another person, at least by the ways in which she or he acts.

9.002 The teaching of regular classes has been discussed in detail in early editions of the *Fundamentals of Co-Counseling Manual*, and in the pamphlet *A New Kind of Communicator* which is sent to every new teacher, and in the nearly thirty issues of *The Re-evaluation Counseling Teacher*, a journal printed especially for the exchange of information among Re-evaluation Counseling teachers.

how and when to teach Re-evaluation Counseling

9.003 One teaches Re-evaluation Counseling by modeling rational behavior in one's considerate relationships to every person one meets. Sometimes this includes patient, caring, interested listening or other varieties of what we call counseling, but not always. Always, however, it includes liking and caring about the *person* and declining to respond in any patterned way to any *patterns* the person is exhibiting.

Teaching Re-evaluation Counseling is done by communicating information to people as they ask for it, by indicating where more information may be secured, by liking the persons, being their friend, and welcoming their friendship, and by not mis-using the friendships to "recruit" them but letting them become interested and seek Re-evaluation Counseling knowledge for themselves.

9.004 *When* does one teach RC? *All the time*. All the time one is with others. If you are not teaching RC (read "humanness") you are teaching something else, something you would rather not be teaching if you were aware of it. Teach RC sometimes in class, surely, sometimes in spontaneous listening or counseling, but *all the time* in some form or other.

9.005 The progress of the Re-evaluation Counseling teacher's own counseling will be watched carefully by students and would-be-students. "What you do shouts so loudly to me that I cannot hear what you say," might well have been said about the relative importance of the teacher's own Co-Counseling and life-style as compared to his or her lectures. In personal relationships, in financial matters, in community involvement, the Re-evaluation Counseling teacher will be looked to for an example, and the more rational his or her students become through their Co-Counseling, the more they will expect to learn from him or her in these ways.

requirements for teachers

9.006 Individual Co-Counselors who wish to teach *classes* in Re-evaluation Counseling can do so only when their own judgment that they are prepared and competent is checked and supported by that of the Re-evaluation Counseling Community. The first permission to teach is given for the duration of one class series. After a teacher has completed one class series satisfactorily, he or she may apply for a full credential.

9.007 In approving teachers, Reference Persons should take into account competence, maturity, responsibility, relationships with others, and the person's own mastery of the environment. The goal is to have each teacher be free, or at least becoming free, of any pattern that interferes with being an excellent model in the Community.

the relation of the Re-evaluation Counseling Teacher to the Re-evaluation Counseling Community

9.008 The Area Reference Person speaks for the Area Community of Re-evaluation Counseling. Any teacher of a Re-evaluation Counseling class is, however, also, in a more limited way, a spokesperson for both the theory and the Community of Co-Counselors. Most people will secure their first impression and first acquaintance with Re-evaluation Counseling from the teacher of their Fundamentals Class.

9.009 The teacher of a Re-evaluation Counseling class is in a position to be an unrestimulative collector of the necessary funds for the outreach and growth of the Community. He or she is assigned this function by the Community. Class tuitions should be set so as to adequately compensate the teacher for what can be, in some cases, a difficult and challenging job. The class tuitions should be adequate to allow that twenty-five percent of the gross tuition for each class goes immediately into the Area and International Outreach Funds of the Community so that the outreach work of the Community can be carried on.

Qualified teachers of Re-evaluation Counseling classes are encouraged to charge tuition for their classes. They are free to set the amount of the fee according to their own judgement. Teachers are encouraged to offer scholarships (without compensation from Outreach Funds) to as many as three young people and two people oppressed by racism or the oppression of disabled persons who would otherwise find it difficult to take the class.

9.010 The Re-evaluation Counseling teacher is a principal distributor of literature, pamphlets, books, manuals, tapes, audio-cassettes, and video-cassettes for the students and other participants in Co-Counseling.

9.011 Most English-speaking teachers with English-speaking classes set the cost of their classes to include the price of a year's subcription to *Present Time* and will tend to remind students to renew their subscriptions when they have run out. All new literature (journals, pamphlets, books, manuals, etc.) will be mailed to RC teachers in Teachers' Packets from one to three times a year. These are sent for the teacher to display to her students, both current and former students, and to encourage the students to order literature for themselves from Rational Island Publishers. The teacher may purchase the contents of a Teachers' Packet for herself or sell the contents to the students and re-order others for herself. A teacher will urge the establishment of a lending library in the local Community when economic problems make it difficult for her students to purchase the literature individually and will press for the library to order audio- and video-cassettes which she may borrow to show her classes.

9.012 As a Fundamentals of Co-Counseling teacher, one isn't expected necessarily to counsel everyone *well* at every attempt. The teacher's job is only to show the students that Co-Counseling *well* can be done.

10. LEADERSHIP

what leadership is

10.001 Leadership is necessary.

10.002 Humans cannot engage in group activity successfully without leadership. Successful group action always requires leadership and leaders. Someone, at least one person, must think about the effort as a whole and not only about her or his individual role in it in order for the group effort to succeed.

10.003 A group can have more than one leader, but it must have *at least one* to function successfully. At least one person has to view the group as a whole rather than just thinking about his or her individual role in it.

10.004 Leadership is thinking about the well-being of the group as a whole as well as that of the individual group members.

10.005 A leader cannot do the thinking *for* the group but elicits the thinking of all members of the group, fills in any gaps, organizes the thinking into a consistent form, and communicates it well enough back to the group to secure their agreement and, if possible, their commitment to it.

10.006 Leadership is initiating proposals and actions, securing agreement within the acting group, keeping a long-range perspective, noticing the results and implications of present and immediate actions on long-range results and actions, modeling correct attitudes and behavior, and modeling courageous initiative. Correct attitudes especially include a modeling of *integrity*.

10.007 Leadership is an inherent human characteristic. Leadership is natural to us as humans. All of us will come to play the role of leading as we re-emerge.

Such leadership does not necessarily have to be well-publicized or proclaimed. It is possible and sometimes desirable to "lead without being noticed," or to "lead from behind." The central function of leadership, however, which is to organize other intelligences to act jointly with your own for common goals, needs to be released to function for every individual. This can be partly accomplished by challenges, high expectations, and enthusiastic "loaning" of confidence and "cheerleading" for the person whose leadership has been inhibited. It can also require the uncovering of the distresses that were laid in when leadership was frustrated, denied, defeated, or even punished. Supplied with contradictions, these distresses will discharge, and the person will tend spontaneously to move into effective leadership.

10.008 The essential commitment of a leader is to *see to it that everything goes well*.

10.009 Leadership is choosing to act in a way *that will make things go well*.

10.010 A good commitment for a leader is to see that everything one is in contact with *works well* (and to not limit one's contacts).

10.011 Leadership is organizing other human intelligences with one's own, for the purposes of human liberation, social justice, and other concerted activities to make things go well in the world.

10.012 In wide-world activity, rational leadership itself will be a contradiction to the very widespread hopelessness patterns that have been installed on humankind about the history and future of our species.

10.013 One aspect of leadership is being present in people's lives as a reminder of who they are and of what is possible.

everyone can be a leader and, to re-emerge, needs to be a leader

10.014 In a rational society of the future every person will be expected to lead for the good of the society and for the person's own good.

10.015 We assume in Re-evaluation Counseling that leadership is an inherent capacity of every human intelligence, that every person who is not playing the role of a leader in some way is a victim of distress which needs to be discharged, has distress which is inhibiting her or inhibiting him from functioning as a leader.

10.016 Leadership is not a "special" role or activity only for "special" people. The skills of rational, successful leading can be taught, learned, mastered, and practiced.

10.017 All humans are essentially peers. Leadership is a natural human quality, not the special talent of a chosen few.

10.018 Every person is capable of becoming a leader. Any difficulty a person has in becoming a leader comes from lack of information (which can be acquired) or from having distress patterns (which can be discharged).

10.019 People who have been oppressed will find it harder to lead in some ways than people who have been conditioned to be oppressors, but it is directly re-emergent, pro-discharge, and effective for them to do so. Working-class people, women, people of color, and young people, in particular, should be encouraged and counseled into taking leadership always.

10.020 To fully express one's humanness means deciding to develop oneself and act as a leader (in addition to many other things).

10.021 It is not possible to achieve the full flowering of one's intelligence without becoming, in some way, a leader.

10.022 The more one shows one's real self, the more other people will look to one for leadership.

10.023 Leadership can accelerate one's re-emergence. Leadership can be a contradiction to hopelessness and powerlessness. Leadership will push one towards the channel of deciding, acting, and discharging as one goes ahead.

10.024 The Re-evaluation Counseling concept of leadership is different from the concept of leadership in the oppressive society. In the oppressive society leaders are trained and expected to be competitive, and leadership is treated as a limited, scarce resource.

10.025 Part of good leadership is developing *all* people's leadership.

10.026 In order to lead powerfully and broadly, one must create and lead leaders.

10.027 A crucial function of leadership is the development of additional leaders.

10.028 An early job for a leader is to begin training one's own replacement.

10.029 Encourage individual leaders to take initiative. Encouraging individuals to take initiative themselves, to build their own "world-class communities," is more successful than encouraging collective group decision-making.

patterns and leadership

10.030 "Eagerness" to assume a formal leadership role does not necessarily correlate with the likelihood of immediate success.

10.031 Leadership must not necessarily be entrusted to the person who is "eager" to lead. Patterns can be very "eager."

10.032 In general, the people who are available to become leaders are almost certain to have chronic patterns of *being responsible* or chronic patterns of *being irresponsible*. Neither kind of pattern is rational, *but* in general with adults it is very unusual to find somebody who is *rationally, relaxedly responsible*. So, faced with the choice of promoting someone with a *compulsive responsibility pattern* into leadership versus choosing someone with a *compulsive irresponsibility pattern*, one must choose the compulsive responsibility pattern in order to have a situation that is at all workable. Having promoted such a person into leadership, however, one has an obligation to help him or her discharge and become free of the pattern and become *rationally* responsible. It is unfair to exploit people by continuing to use their chronic responsibility patterns without concurrently giving them help to become free of them.

tips about leading

10.033 Modeling is the basic, fundamental way of leading. Other abilities cannot make up for lack of good modeling. "What you do speaks so loudly to me that I cannot hear what you say."

10.034 If one is a good leader in all other respects, having *charisma* is an advantage. It is not a substitute for any other desirable leadership characteristic, but it can be an additional advantage.

10.035 A leader needs always to keep sight of the "big picture."

10.036 In every situation there are many issues that need to be understood and have policies developed about and acted on. There are always so many issues before groups that to try to deal with all of them becomes too confusing and leads to ineffectiveness. A central decision for a leader is to determine what is the *"key issue"* in a given situation. By *"key issue"* we mean the issue which, if raised clearly before the people involved and then acted upon, will force the group to deal with all the other issues as part of the "key issue" being addressed. Choosing and raising such a key issue for the people one is leading is decisive in achieving unity in action and is a requirement for effective work.

10.037 Re-evaluation Counseling leaders are encouraged to lead within the Re-evaluation Counseling Community but at the same time to lead in the wide world. "One foot inside and one foot outside Re-evaluation Counseling." The importance of this is that each area of leadership illuminates and inspires the other area and makes it easy to expedite the promotion of leadership in both groups.

Leading within the Re-evaluation Counseling Community is an excellent way to learn to lead everywhere. The availability of correct theory and the safety and support of the counseling groups and the counseling processes make the atmosphere in the RC Community a good place to learn to lead. However, if one does not also lead in the wide world, one is distorting the function of Re-evaluation Counseling and is modeling and acting out a distorted "timid" version of Re-evaluation Counseling.

10.038 The leader of any group will do well to become acquainted with and learn as much as possible about the individual members of the group. She or he needs to know their pasts, their present situations, and their hoped-for and *probable* futures. The leader also needs to think about the group as a whole in these same ways.

10.039 *Leading well* is easier and less burdensome than *participating* in an activity or group that is poorly led.

assisting leaders to lead well

10.040 Leadership functions better when the leader teaches other leaders to think well about him or about her.

10.041 "Support" to a leader does *not* mean praising the leader, paying the leader compliments, or being "grateful" to the leader, although these are often offered by people's patterns in lieu of real support. *Real support* to a leader consists primarily of assisting the leader by *sharing in the necessary work* and in *counseling the leader well*.

We can support leadership to a lesser extent by expressing appreciation for good work, by communicating our thinking, by awarely interrupting patterns, by discharging on any difficulty of one's own in becoming close to the leader, by staying close once it is possible, and by not initiating or allowing any attacks on the leader.

Every non-temporary group needs *to take charge of the counseling* of its leader. This can be done in several different ways if regular, routine counseling is not enough. "Coached counseling" is helpful. People can have sessions, in or out of the presence of the leader, on *what gets in the way* of counseling the leader. The most important thing is to persist until good counseling is achieved.

10.042 "Support" for a Co-Counseling leader consists of help with the work and excellent counseling of the leader. Compliments, praise, and appreciation may be pleasant to hear, but they are no substitute for help with the work and for good counseling.

10.043 There is a need for support from followers to leaders and support from leaders to followers. There is a need for accountability from followers to leaders and from leaders to followers. One of the mechanisms for achieving this is the periodic use of *self-estimation* by anyone who leads.

10.044 To have the opportunity to do self-estimation is crucial to enable any leader to grow. Remember, self-estimation deals with *how the job is being done*, not with the intrinsic *worth* of the individual. Leaders will find that they greatly appreciate complete honesty on the part of the people supporting their self-estimation. Being told by another person about one's malfunctioning, where one has had difficulty seeing it and thinking about it oneself, can be a very gratifying experience.

10.045 It is crucial that the motivations of a leader in being a leader are "to have things go well for everybody." Leaders should regularly review their motivations. Looking at the motivations of leaders should be part of regular self-estimation.

10.046 Three conditions favorable to the functioning and development of an individual leader are: a) adequate rest, b) committed closeness, c) thinking and leading *decisively*.

10.047 Effective leadership can be supported well by a life balanced with exercise, work, discharge, learning, love, fun, and thinking. Desperation is a distress pattern, and urgency is usually a distress pattern.

mistakes are OK

10.048 Candidates for leadership should indicate their ability to move forward, not any previously-attained perfection.

10.049 It is not necessary for a leader *to not make mistakes*. If one is growing, one is quite likely to be operating beyond his or her frontiers of well-assimilated information and is therefore likely to, occasionally, make mistakes. *This is fine*. Mistakes are to be learned from. What is important for a leader is for the leader to, as far as possible, not repeat the same mistake, nor defend one's mistake as *not being a mistake*. Instead, a person making a mistake needs to admit the mistake openly and apologize for it.

10.050 There needs to be a clear policy on correcting leaders' mistakes and interrupting leaders' distress patterns. This needs to happen whenever a leader is lost in patterns and the patterns are interfering with the leader's leadership. These difficulties need to be understood and handled completely separately from dealing with *attacks*. This kind of difficulty is best handled by prior agreement between Co-Counseling leaders to challenge and interrupt distress patterns and to counsel the person who seems to be in difficulty.

attacks are not OK

10.051 Being attacked is an almost inevitable accompaniment to being a good leader. Such attacks can stem from the efforts of the oppressive society to overcome any threat of resistance to the oppression. Attacks can arise from the inertia of past activities by the society in an irrational direction. Attacks can also be begun as part of a confused, ineffective attempt by the attacker to draw attention to himself or herself and to "extort" some help from the leader with the leader being forced to act as counselor.

Enduring an attack is one of the least successful ways of dealing with it although the "ignoring" of an attack is probably the simplest and most effective response. The best strategy we have so far evolved is to prepare in advance any group whose leader is likely to be attacked. This is done through having all members of the group understand the crucial difference between simply "being a nuisance in the hope of attracting attention" and *appealing to others in an effort to enlist support for one's attacking position.*

Members of the group should be prepared to recognize this second phenomenon as an ATTACK, requiring prompt action. The attacker should be "moved on" by the members, who make it plain that the attacker is regarded as a hostile force to the organization who will be held answerable for the destructive activity. Everyone should be reminded that the issue is NOT any weakness or failing of the leader (the proper way to deal with any such issue is in a session with the leader or in a discussion with the leader's co-leaders), but that this is simply an excuse to mask the real nature of the attack. The attack should be dealt with promptly, and care should be taken not to serve the (not unusual) desire of the attackers for publicity.

10.052 Patterns attacking a leader often take the vulnerabilities of leaders (which every leader has) and try to capitalize on these vulnerabilities in order to add seeming credibility to the attack. Mistakes by, or imperfections of, a leader don't make an attack valid.

Changing her or his behavior on the part of the person attacked doesn't address the separate issue of the attack, nor will it prevent further attacks on the person's leadership.

10.053 People's patterned feelings against parents and other early authority figures often come into play in an attack.

10.054 The principle that "no attacks on leadership will be permitted" will prove to be as useful in the wide world as it has proven to be in the Co-Counseling Community.

10.055 Part of being effective as a Co-Counselor is being prepared to deal immediately and effectively with "attacks," especially attacks on leaders. Permissive attitudes or counseling of the attacker *are not useful* in this situation. The attack must be stopped first.

10.056 Among the ways that a member can mistreat a leader are: attacking, "idolizing," giving up one's own thinking by thoughtlessly accepting the leader's, and rehearsing one's own powerlessness.

10.057 Fear of being attacked or criticized in one's role as leader is not a good enough reason to avoid leadership.

"pseudo-democracy" versus democracy

10.058 The word "democracy" is used with many different meanings. In the oppressive society it is often a pretentious cover-up for the dictating of policies *for everybody* by an oppressive minority. For example, the ruling section of an owning class will claim that the society is being run democratically because people are allowed to vote for one candidate against another in elections, even though the choice of *who are allowed to be the candidates voted upon* is determined by control of money, the media, and the existing array of leaders, and by very private decisions by very small groups of leaders in the organized political parties.

On the other hand, a real leader acting on behalf of an oppressed constituency will often be attacked in the name of democracy *for being willing to be a leader.* Leadership will be called "dictatorship," existing prejudices against oppressors will be turned against a good leader, and claims will be made that the leader is receiving privileges she or he should not have. Leadership is a job, not an exalted state. Often a leader must take a stand against the common patterns of the group he or she leads. A majority decision will in the long view be ultimately correct, but an immediate majority "vote" is not always well-informed, correct, nor the best way to function.

10.059 To have leaders who are publicly designated as leaders is very advantageous where conditions permit this being done. Some social conditions do not permit this. In certain repressive conditions, to publicly designate a leader would make it impossible for the leader to function because arrests, imprisonment, or even assassination might follow. Such conditions do arise, but rarely in most social situations, and fears of leaders or members should not be allowed to project this appearance where actual conditions are quite safe.

to find out more . . .

10.060 All leaders should read the pamphlet *The Enjoyment of Leadership*. It summarizes much of what we had learned about leadership within Re-evaluation Counseling up to the time of its publication.

11. OTHER THEORIES OF HUMAN BEHAVIOR CANNOT, IN GENERAL, BE RECONCILED WITH THE INSIGHTS OF RE-EVALUATION COUNSELING

11.001 Once the principal concepts of Re-evaluation Counseling were advanced (the essentially limitless capacity of human intelligence; the basic fundamental "goodness" [pro-survival] character of the human; the nature of the distress recording as a regression to a primitive kind of functioning similar to that used by other mammals as a crude type of learning; the fundamental and completely restorative effects of discharge in its many forms; the possibility of complete recovery from the effects of any distress or trauma; the nature of intelligence as the ability to create new, successful responses to every new situation; the complete freedom of choice for every human individual; the [conjectured] complete power of any individual to have the environment respond to him or her, given the necessary [and possible] work and planning by the individual, in exactly the way that the individual desires; the ability to completely erase any effects of any past distress through sufficient discharge and the resulting restoration of the individual to full functioning and complete freedom from any of the limiting effects which the distress had imposed before it was completely discharged), *then no theory of human behavior which did not embrace these concepts and present them consistently and in relation to each other could be very useful.* Such past theories can be respected historically as *attempts* by human intelligence to deal with distress and to improve on previous theories, but without all of these principal concepts of Re-evaluation Counseling, they must rationally be considered out-of-date.

11.002 It has been a persistent goal of Re-evaluation Counseling, its leaders, and its Community to achieve and preserve internal consistency of the theory and the practice. Creative additions to the theory are encouraged and welcomed and are proposed frequently (in almost every session). Any such proposal is, as a routine practice, checked that it is not contradictory to, and is consistent with, other parts of the theory and practice. Re-evaluation Counseling teachers, in particular, are reminded and expected to not teach any theories from other sources that could possibly be contradictory to Re-evaluation Counseling. When they are being creative with their classes and their students, they should label any new conjectures as something to be thought about but not taken to be part of the theory simply because the teacher at that moment has had that particular "thought."

11.003 Traditional "therapy" in the oppressive society has as its goal (whether it is announced as such or not) to make or "help" individuals "adjust" to the society *as it is*. Re-evaluation Counseling has as its goal to empower humans so that they will *transform* the society so that it will meet humans' rational needs.

11.004 The insights of Re-evaluation Counseling are part of the "upward trend" in the universe. The insights of previous theories have in the past contributed toward the upward trend. (Examples of this are Freud's notion that the distressed person could be listened to and "interpreted" rather than abused physically as punishment for being distressed; the humanistic psychologists' limited attempts to address distressed people as humans instead of as their problems; the insights of the behaviorists into the psychologies of animals based on their essentially "conditioned" type of learning; and the "unconditional positive regard" of Carl Rogers.) However, they are not a basis upon which to build a better theory, and Re-evaluation Counseling is not based upon them nor should any future improvements be based on them.

11.005 Existing psychologies support the oppressive society and its constituent oppressions and have as their goal the acceptance by the person of, and the adjustment of the person to, the society as it is. A rational, pro-human psychology would, as does Re-evaluation Counseling, move the individual to reject the oppressive society and to take power to establish a new, non-oppressive society.

11.006 "Feminist" therapies, "anti-racist" therapies, and other "radical" therapies do not fully understand the concepts of the distress recording and discharge (though some are reaching for these concepts and, through the influence of Re-evaluation Counseling, are modifying their practices in these directions). To be fully effective, they need to "borrow" or otherwise assimilate the other concepts of Re-evaluation Counseling. They do not, however, share with the "establishment" psychologies and therapies the destructive goal of adjusting the person to all the oppressions of the existing society.

11.007 The psychiatrists, psychologists, therapists, etc., who are working with human beings, or even those who are trying to teach the theories of these disciplines, often entered their fields with the laudable goal and motivation of being helpful to other people in distress. We should regard them as our potential allies regardless of how mistaken they are in their activities or how hostile they may be at first in their responses to Re-evaluation Counseling. They will tend to have at least the average amount of insecurity that other human beings have; the major investment they have made in training in these other disciplines will seem to be threatened by the simplicity of Re-evaluation Counseling and our challenging assumption that "ordinary" people are capable of being far more effective in helping others than the mis-taught professionals. It will require some actual experience as clients and some success in re-emergence on their part to overcome this bias. Patience, friendliness, and confidence on our part will usually overcome such difficulties. Participation in support groups with other comparable staff members of their clinics, universities, or other institutions will often be an acceptable immediate way to enable them to begin to transform their practices in the direction of present and future Re-evaluation Counseling knowledge.

11.008 To try to understand Re-evaluation Counseling from the viewpoint of other theories or attitudes is fruitless and misleading because these other viewpoints and attitudes are not closely enough in touch with reality. To understand other viewpoints, attitudes, and psychologies from the viewpoint of Re-evaluation Counseling is fairly simple and productive. The assumptions of Re-evaluation Counseling are closely enough in touch with reality to make sense of and show up the weaknesses in the other "theories."

12. THEORY AND POLICY

theory

12.001 A crucial decision made in the beginning of Re-evaluation Counseling was to not assume anything to be true simply because it appeared in other existing theories or other people's theories, but to build *our* theory independently, restricting ourselves to the use of the information from the physical sciences generally agreed to by the scientists in these fields and to the information we Re-evaluation Counselors obtained in the field of human behavior *from our own successful experiences.*

12.002 Re-evaluation Counseling theory is a series of summations of information gained from the actual experiences of Re-evaluation Counselors. To this are added the conclusions drawn from such summations. The theory is checked for consistency among the various conclusions and conjectures and for possible implications of the existing conclusions. It is always to be tested in practice. It is always to remain open to being changed by the accumulation of new experiences and information from practice.

12.003 Theory is developed both *inductively*, through the commonalities observed in practical experiences, and *deductively*, through conclusions that follow logically from what we stated in our first set of Postulates or axioms in 1965 and later re-statements of them.

12.004 Theory does not just sum up individual pieces of information. It attempts to relate them to each other in a coherent structure of thought.

12.005 Nothing has been added to the theory and practice of Re-evaluation Counseling that is contradictory to other parts of it. When new conjectures are made, they are examined first for consistency with the presently-accepted Postulates, and if they are not logically consistent with them, the new conjectures are not advocated or propagated.

12.006 The purpose of having a firm, written theory is to be able to relate the details of our continually increasing experiences to what has already been experienced and the conclusions drawn from these earlier experiences. This process will guide the practice of Re-evaluation Counseling, highlighting any contradictions that show up or any new discoveries which may be in the process of being made, and allow our knowledge to grow consistently.

12.007 Re-evaluation Counseling theory continues to grow through communication between Co-Counselors in the many parts of the world where it is practiced, as they share the results of its application in a continually greater variety of situations.

12.008 One good general guide to the attainment of a correct, continually-growing theory and practice is to decide to "*think* about everything, including Re-evaluation Counseling!"

12.009 In one sense, Re-evaluation Counseling theory and practice can be viewed as the uncovering of reality from the confusions which have been placed upon it by misinformation, oppression, and the operation of distress patterns.

12.010 Dissatisfaction is sometimes expressed that "the practice of Re-evaluation Counseling doesn't live up to the theory." This does not mean that the theory should descend to the level of practice that has been achieved at that point. Any live, correct theory raises expectations higher than previous practice has satisfied and should stay ahead of the practice in order to keep the practice continually improving.

policy

12.011 Policy consists of proposals for the application of theory, guidelines drawn up from past experience for such application, and structures for implementing these actions consistently and cooperatively by all the people involved.

12.012 Policies are plans for action. They are guides and agreements on how people in a group such as the Re-evaluation Counseling Community can and will act together in a cooperative, supportive way.

12.013 The steps to working out a policy can be considered to be: 1) examination of the present situation, 2) determining as far as possible why things are the way they are, 3) determining desirable changes to achieve or recommend, 4) proposing actions to achieve the changes.

12.014 Policy needs also to include various means for communication within the group of involved people and with the people outside the group. Communicating policy to people outside the group has the goal of first winning their *tolerance*, then their *interest*, then, hopefully, their *understanding, support, and participation*.

12.015 Draft policies for liberation have already been drawn up within the Re-evaluation Counseling Community for Arabs, artists, people of Asian heritage, people of African heritage, Chicanos/Chicanas, college and university staff workers, college and university faculty persons, disabled people, elders, Gay men, Lesbians, people of Ireland, people of Irish heritage, Jews, men, young people, young adults, "mental health" system survivors, "mental health" workers (psychiatrists, psychologists, therapists), middle-class people, Native people, owning-class people, parents, physicians, poor and raised-poor people, Southern U.S.ers, women, working-class people, educators, and veterans of the armed services.

12.016 Liberation policy statements are always *draft* liberation policy statements. They are always expected to be revised in the light of further information, more persistent thinking, and experiences in their application. No draft policy statement drawn up in the Re-evaluation Counseling Communities is binding on any Re-evaluation Counselor. They are expressions of the thinking of the particular group that drew them up. The Community, under its *Guidelines,* agrees to encourage such statements, to assist in their drafting, to publicize them, and to help organize workshops and conferences to discuss them, but not to make them binding on anyone except through the person's own spontaneous agreement with them. The only required agreement for a member of the Re-evaluation Counseling Communities is to use the practice of Re-evaluation Counseling to recover her or his occluded intelligence and to help others to do the same.

12.017 Thinking flexibly all the time is the best route to one's elegant survival and the satisfactory fulfillment of one's goals. If one is not able to attain this at any particular time, the next best route is the adoption and use of correct policy.

13. PHENOMENA FOR WHICH MOST HUMANS DO NOT HAVE SATISFACTORY EXPLANATIONS AND NEED TO BE OFFERED SUCH EXPLANATIONS

apparent "mystical" and "psychic" experiences

13.001 Most *"mystical" experiences* can be understood in unmystical terms after sufficient discharge and examination of the phenomena from several points of view.

13.002 Many *"psychic" experiences* are sincerely believed in by the person experiencing them but are easily understood in terms of the effect of a pattern on the experiencer. If there is a distress recording operating which tells the person that she or he had the accurate dream about the event before the event happened, the reality, which is usually that the dream followed the event, is necessarily and quite sincerely denied by the person who insists that she or he "knew ahead of time" what would happen. There is also the below-awareness calculation from real data of the likelihood of an event, which likelihood was not faced or paid attention to until the "prediction" was realized. In addition, there are the effects of the "self-fulfilling prophecy" where the person actually brings about, through a series of unaware actions, the event or events which the pattern had predicted.

confusions about sexuality

13.003 *To be sexual* after attaining physical maturity is a built-in instinctive drive in the nature of human beings and is essential for the survival of the species.

In our present cultures almost all individuals compulsively act out distress recordings which have become attached to their instinctive sexualities. This results from distress experiences, from sexual abuse imposed in the past and, to an extent which is being increasingly revealed, through abuse received *when they were young children*. Some of the distress patterns are very non-survival in their actions and prevent or spoil any rational, relaxed participation in sex. Other distress patterns in this area "conform" closely enough to rigid standards of behavior set up by particular cultures that they are "socially approved of." To *identify* oneself as homosexual, Gay, Lesbian, or bisexual is a clear indication of distress needing to be discharged. However, most currently-accepted forms and practices of heterosexuality, including the many varieties and degrees of frigidity and promiscuity, just as clearly indicate distress as do the homosexual labels.

Thus it is not true that "anything" is rational, nor that the "free choice of consenting adults" is an indication of rationality. It is quite unlikely that any individual has a clear picture of her or his own sexuality or rational functioning in this area without review of his or her entire history of experiences connected with sex in any way at all. (See the pamphlet *A Rational Theory of Sexuality*.)

13.004 For many people emotional discharge occurs during sexual activity and especially on attaining a sexual climax. Many people have examined this phenomenon for themselves and concluded that what often motivates them to be involved in sex is exactly the discharge which they achieve. This discharge happens as a result of the usual loneliness and isolation patterns being contradicted effectively by physical closeness and mutual pleasuring of each other during sexual activity.

13.005 Almost everything which we have been told, or have assumed, to be rational about sexuality will turn out to be patterned distress (see *A Rational Theory of Sexuality*). Much of the activity of the current society operates in such a way as to attach distress to people's sexual feelings and then manipulate these feelings, using the combination of distress and sexual feelings for purposes of exploitation of all kinds.

What would natural, unpatterned sexuality be like for human beings? A conjecture would be that the feelings of sexuality would always arise first with a female. They would arise as a result of glandular shifts taking place during ovulation. The relaxed rational human would recognize the onset of sexual feelings as an indication that her body was working well and would make a rational decision to either: a) enjoy the feelings but take no action about them, or b) act on the feelings for the purpose of becoming pregnant and bearing a child, or c) enjoy the sensations of feeling passionate and desired (and desiring) with another person, or d) enjoy the sensations of sex play (including, possibly, intercourse and climax) with another person but making rational use of contraception to avoid unplanned and undesired pregnancies, or possibly infection.

A male would only become interested in and aware of sexual feelings in response to the initiative of a female. Then rational, open agreement would be quickly reached as to the desires of both, and acted upon. The episode would end with the end of ovulation "until the next time." Again, *this is a conjecture*.

other common confusions

13.006 *"Falling in love"* probably has as many different meanings as there have been people who have experienced it. It almost always seems to include the *restimulation* of a past frozen need. It certainly can be useful when one uses it to secure discharge, but in that case one is apparently using the feelings of "falling in love" as a contradiction to rejection and to not being loved *in the past*.

13.007 The long-standing debate as to whether people's adult characteristics and functioning are determined more by their genetic heritage or more by the experiences and conditioning which they have acquired during their lives (*the nature/nurture debate*) is by no means finalized. Nor will it be until we have learned a great deal more about the details of ourselves. The debate may be to a great extent pointless since in a broad sense one's genetic heritage is part of one's nurture (in the sense that our genes are part of what we receive from the environment). What Re-evaluation Counseling can contribute, which has been missing in most such discussions, is the sharp, qualitative distinction between nurture that comes in the process of good, successful experiences and well-absorbed information, and "nurture" which arrives in the form of distress experiences which leave distress recordings upon the individual.

13.008 *Exhaustion* is a form of distress, and a distress recording can be made of the experience. Additional experiences of exhaustion can restimulate and add to the existing recording and also add an additional amount of fatigue. A person for whom such distress recordings accumulate and pile up can become chronically in a fatigued state, or the recording may be so close to chronic that even a small amount of additional over-exertion can bring the feeling of exhaustion. Such a person seems "unable to rest" or to "recover from fatigue." In such a case, discharge, often *a considerable amount of discharge*, is needed before the client can "rest." What kind of discharge is needed it will be impossible to tell ahead of time, but almost always there are some anxious "being on guard" attitudes involved that prevent the person from relaxing.

What has worked well is for the counselor to announce to the client that for a specific period of time (one minute, five minutes, one hour, eight hours), the counselor will "stand guard" and see that nothing that the client could possibly be responsible for "goes wrong" in that period. In making such a statement the counselor must be believable, must mean the commitment, must intend to keep the commitment, and must be able to carry it out. The counselor may have the client lie down, may sit beside the client and hold the client's hands, or may take the client on his or her lap and sing lullabies, recite restful poetry, or repeat the commitment over and over again.

The client, on finding the counselor's commitment believable, sometimes bursts into wild sobbing immediately, sometimes begins to yawn and yawn, sometimes falls immediately to sleep, even standing up. Even if the promised time is no longer than one minute, the ensuing discharge often has profound effects on the client and allows him or her to rest in ways he or she had not previously been able to do. The discharge of the anxiety and recorded exhaustion needs eventually, of course, to be carried through to completion.

13.009 There is a recent phenomenon of chronic exhaustion which has shown up in the wide world and inside Re-evaluation Counseling circles. Some medical people are convinced that there is a particular virus or perhaps a group of viruses involved. Others feel that it is "psychological," which is as close as they can come in their usual language to suspecting that a distress pattern is involved.

At the same time, it has become plain in counseling that fatigue is a distress, that it can be recorded, and that when restimulated enough additional times by new fatigue, it can become a monstrous pattern, easily restimulated into an enormous sensation of fatigue by even a little additional fatigue. These patterns of fatigue are not eliminated by rest alone. The existence of undischarged anxiety seems to make it impossible for the person to rest enough. The technique in Re-evaluation Counseling called "standing guard" has the counselor assume total responsibility for everything that the client feels "needs to be done," that the client feels any responsibility for, or anxiety about.

The counselor announces that he or she will "stand guard" to see that nothing happens or goes wrong that the client could possibly prevent if he or she stayed alert and aware, and therefore the client is free to rest and temporarily give up all responsibility. If the counselor is believable in making the offer, the typical response on the part of the client is enormous discharge, sometimes violent crying, sometimes heavy shaking, sometimes prodigious yawns. Sometimes the client, even standing up, simply leans on the counselor and goes to sleep. A substantial amount of discharge achieved while a counselor is "standing guard" seems to allow the client to become free from the pattern of exhaustion to a great degree and to rest. There are those who suspect that this is the workable remedy, where it can be offered, for the widely discussed "chronic fatigue syndrome," and that the viruses, although they may be present, are not by any means the decisive cause of the fatigue. Certainly, in any case, the use of the standing guard technique is indicated for anyone who is suffering from chronic fatigue. It will be helpful to whatever extent it is used, even if it does not turn out to be the complete solution of the chronic fatigue syndromes.

dreams

13.010 *(This section is the same as section 5.057.)* The use of the client's *dreams* in counseling can be very effective. This has been intuited in many past philosophies, religions, and therapies, and various ways have been attempted to use the dreams to the dreamer's benefit. It is our experience that having anyone else "interpret" the dreamer's dream is not helpful to the dreamer and may even be harmful.

It will help to understand the *nature* of sleep and the *nature* of dreaming. Sleep is *not* unconsciousness. The human's mind is always active, awake or asleep, when it is functioning well. Sleep is a time of cutting down on new information input (by closing the eyes, avoiding noise or at least non-repetitive noise, arranging tactile comfort and a supportive temperature) in order to "catch up" on the re-evaluation of the information that has been received and accumulated during waking hours. This re-evaluation tends to proceed in two manners. The routine information that does not have tension or distress attached to it is simply, easily, and rapidly reviewed in "non-dreaming" sleep. The sleeper lies relaxed and is at least largely unaware of the events taking place.

When this non-dreaming sleep has been completed, the sleeper's attention turns to the unevaluated information received during the waking hours that has tension or restimulation of some sort attached to it. During this "dreaming sleep" the sleeper is much more active, is likely to move in his or her sleep, and, particularly, rapid eye movements behind the sleeper's closed eyelids are noticeable. The more critical levels of the sleeper's mind seem to become engaged at this point, and the more tense the material being addressed, the closer to the aware thinking levels of the sleeper it is pushed. (We have reason to think that certain levels of the rational mind that characteristically operate closer to awareness are more effective in the solving of difficult problems.) This involves dreaming, and the more tense the material, the more vivid the dream is likely to seem.

The often chaotic, surprising relationships expressed in the dream reflect the chaotic, random connections made during restimulation. This is probably true of our waking restimulation as well, but under waking conditions we tend to censor the randomness in order to make it appear to ourselves and others that there is point and purpose to the restimulation. The more tense the material being addressed in dreaming sleep, the more vivid the dream becomes, and if the tension reaches a certain point the sleeper is wakened from sleep by his or her mind in order to secure some reassurance of reality from the current environment.

The process of dreaming seems to be *similar* to the process of re-evaluation to some extent, and of course re-evaluation can take place during dreams as well, but it is not usually a complete re-evaluation that is achieved. Instead the results seem to be something like "knocking the sharpest corners" of the tension off of the material so that the material can be put back in the usual "brushpile" storage of distress for addressing at a later time when there is (perhaps) more resource or more contradiction available.

This means that the dream that is remembered or can be remembered is an important clue to distress that needs discharge and re-evaluation. (Unfortunately, it does *not* follow that the dream that cannot be remembered has necessarily been re-evaluated well and needs no more attention. This is because there are many "forgetter" patterns involved for many people that interfere with their remembering of dreams.)

It follows that every sleeper, optimally, should have the opportunity to tell her or his dreams to an interested audience early in the morning (perhaps at the breakfast table). Everyone's days will go better if dreams can be "exchanged" and listened to in the morning. When counseling a client about a dream, the overall technique is quite simple and straightforward. The counselor has the client repeat the dream over and over and over many times. If time is short, the counselor may even "crowd" the process by asking the client for the significance which the client assigns to the dream or any part of the dream. When enough time is available, the client will spontaneously make these evaluations and will share them with the counselor if it appears safe and useful to do so.

The child awakened from sleep by a "bad dream" and seeking company and reassurance from parents or other adults should be encouraged to tell the dream many times before going back to sleep, and discharge should be encouraged and persisted with. If the child is allowed to resist telling the dream and goes to sleep immediately, the opportunity to unload the distress will have been missed, and the distress will go back into occlusion again.

The dream which is repeated many times is almost certain to be an occluded distress incident trying to force its way to the client's awareness. Again, simply repeating the dream many times with the addition of any contradictions to the distress which the counselor and the client together can evolve, will lead to discharge and the lifting of the occlusion.

(The currently occurring revelations of the widespread sexual abuse of children have made the concentration on the repetitive nightmare an important and principal channel for this liberating process of freeing the victim from the terrified occlusion of these distresses.)

Counseling on dreams is an extremely useful channel in the general process of discharge and re-evaluation. The fact that the client has been having the dream is one indication that the client has made some kind of judgment that the material is ready to be addressed.

talented/untalented

13.011 Present human cultures almost universally regard *some people as being "talented" and others as "untalented."* There is certainly a wide range of effectiveness in engaging in particular activities observable in any present individuals or groups of individuals. It is necessarily a conjecture, but a very strong one, that, given a person's interest being roused toward a particular skill, art, or kind of creativity, that each of us has a limitless capacity to do or achieve anything we want to. We assume, with good reason, that "Nanook of the North" can master the art of violin playing as well as "Paganini" did, and that "Paganini" is quite capable of matching "Nanook" in his ability to take a fragile boat made of skin into the stormy ocean and bring back a whale a thousand times his own size.

the damage of hypnosis

13.012 *Hypnosis* is the installation of an *artificial distress recording*. The person being hypnotized is in some manner or other convinced *to agree to stop thinking* for himself or herself, and with that block in place, everything that goes on during the so-called "trance" stores as a rigid recording exactly parallel with and comparable to the kind of recording made when *distress* has interfered with the person's thinking. Hypnosis is always harmful, always needs to be discharged and re-evaluated in order to recover the portion of one's intelligence that has become trapped in the recording. It is *never* helpful. A person who understood what was going on would never agree to be hypnotized, that is, to stop thinking by decision. Skillful hypnotic operators can secure the agreement of people to become hypnotized against their will by restimulating already-existing distress recordings to the point where the person is already non-thinking and can be convinced to "agree" to becoming vulnerable to the suggestions of the hypnotist or others.

Hypnosis has been both innocently and not-so-innocently advocated on the grounds that a person can have painful acts such as surgery performed and "not feel the pain." What happens in this case is that the pain goes into the recording with a command which is agreed to as a decision by the subject to *not feel the pain*. Pain still takes place *and is recorded*. It still must eventually be felt and gotten rid of by discharge in order for the human to recover his or her freedom in the area of the recording, but it will require skillful counseling since the victim is committed to being accepting and supporting of the commands which were part of the recording made during hypnosis.

Other benefits claimed for hypnosis are the suppression of uncomfortable physical symptoms and/or the suppression of emotional distress. These are both harmful to the person since the uncomfortable physical symptoms and the emotional distress continue to operate but become difficult to discharge with the hypnotic suppression command installed. The person is left with an internal conflict between the need to feel and discharge the distress and the subservience to the hypnotic command to not feel it and not discharge it. This will constitute a continuing source of tension for the victim and will often lead to other distresses being dramatized.

A third benefit claimed for hypnosis is the recovery of information from occlusion. This can be done, just as it can be done with drugs or partial anesthesia, but while the occluded information may be desired by the inquisitional questioner (police or captors), in terms of the person's own survival it should only be unoccluded when he or she has acquired enough resource, support, and contradiction to handle it. Then he or she will spontaneously bring it up, with discharge. (See *Present Time* No. 71, page 81, "The Harm of Hypnosis.")

When you work with someone who has been hypnotized, you treat these experiences as actual distress incidents. They have to be gone over and over, with flash answers, fantasies, or whatever, in order to free the person from the effect of the shutdown.

vocal difficulties

13.013 *Stammering or stuttering* is the behavior that arises out of fear or embarrassment about talking. It would never occur if people were listened to with patience and respect. To try to "train" people not to stammer is to add additional tension, and in the unlikely event that the symptom is suppressed by such "training," the tension is still there, and the difficulty in speaking has simply been submerged into an internal difficulty.

Discharge will always clear up the difficulty and allow the person's mind and speaking abilities to be free. The only difficulty in doing so will arise from any unintended dramatization by a counselor who unawarely acts tense and anxious and communicates to the client that he or she *is* tense and anxious through many physical and facial clues and in that way adds to the problem for the client.

If the counselor instead learns from the client *one word that is never stammered*, and with great warmth and relaxation and enthusiasm encourages the client to repeat just that one word, and then celebrates the client's success repeatedly with great enthusiasm, calls on any other people present to cheer and celebrate the client as well, and has the client repeat *only that one word* many, many times with no diminution of enthusiasm for it, the client will begin to discharge (usually with laughter) and will continue to discharge for a long time, often moving into shaking and crying as well as the laughter.

The counselor must *never* test or check the client "to see if the problem is solved," but only enthuse and never refer to the question of stammering again except in this context. The stammering symptom can disappear quite quickly depending, of course, on how much tension has been loaded onto the client in this area.

attitudes towards "super" entities

13.014 There are useful and to-be-respected tendencies arising in the nature of thinking human beings to look with awe and respect upon the larger nature of reality. This is sometimes observed as projected into a kind of *"worship"* of a God or group of gods or superhuman entities of some sort. For others this great respect is reserved for the physical universe or the "total nature of things," or the sublime nature of human thought and curiosity. Whatever form it takes for any particular human or group of humans, such an attitude of respect or worship should be respected by all the rest of us humans as a spontaneously-evolved direction toward growth and the upward trend. Where patterns are attached to the attitude, they can be discharged on and re-evaluated, but in general this is not assisted by criticism or opposition.

the general natures of change

13.015 In the *dynamic processes of the universe* around us, changes occur at many different rates of speed. Small changes (quantitative changes) may dominate what is happening for long periods of time, but inevitably the accumulation of a certain amount of these small changes leads to a decisive change (a qualitative change), which changes the state of the situation and the direction and function of the succeeding small, quantitative changes.

(Ice warms gradually, changes decisively to liquid water, warms gradually in its new state as liquid water, changes decisively to water vapor or steam, warms gradually in that new state as water vapor, and at a certain higher temperature changes decisively to dissociated molecules.)

In the development of human organization, *family* groups remain family groups over a certain period, but the accumulation of knowledge and the skills of cooperation will at some point give rise to families clustering together as *clans*. A similar kind of process leads to the appearance of confederations of clans that become *tribes*. Tribes merge into *nations*, and so on.

Class societies based on slavery, composed primarily of slaves and slave-owners, eventually, through large numbers of small changes, prepare and accomplish the change to feudal society. The changes in feudal society prepare for the emergence of working-class-owning-class (capitalist) societies.

"sleepiness"

13.016 *"Feeling sleepy"* when one is well-rested is almost certainly a recording. It can be the effect of "command phrases" in a recorded incident of the past which have been restimulated. It can also be a recording of being "shut down" to some degree or other, up to and including complete unconsciousness. The discharge which will eliminate this distress is likely to consist largely of yawning. In practice, however, it has seemed necessary and useful to allow the very sleepy client to sleep when he or she can no longer yawn. After sleeping for a while, the client tends to awaken able to proceed with discharge. *Keeping the client awake* has not proven workable or useful.

inattention

13.017 *"Daydreaming"* is a term often used to describe a person having his or her attention almost completely away from the present. This is always a spontaneous exploration of past distress, sometimes motivated in part by the boring and monotonous characteristics of the situation in which the person finds himself or herself.

Sometimes the person's attention is running through an early distress experience, seeking to reach discharge on it, but, limited by the inability to acquire enough attention from others to discharge, is simply rehearsing the scene over and over. Sometimes the person is creating fantasies in an effort to contradict the distress and operate free from it or secure discharge of it.

discipline

13.018 A useful meaning for *"discipline"* would be a commitment to, and action on behalf of, what is rational. This would include refusing to be distracted by what is "tempting," "patterned," or "addictive." Such "discipline" would necessarily arise from one's own thinking. Any "discipline" imposed from another person's thinking would be suspect of being patterned, reactive, and oppressive. (A possible exception to this, at least in appearance, would be a "direction," which could feel and be interpreted by the recipient as oppressive, but whose actual role is to furnish a firm contradiction to the content of the patterns which have, up to the present, dominated the recipient, and to assist the recipient to discharge.)

memory

13.019 Everything that we have ever experienced is noticed and kept in our *memory* and is available to be remembered unless something happens to interfere with the naturally perfect operation of our memory. Apparently we have various mechanisms and levels of recovery of memories in our central nervous systems. There is a "current" memory, such as we use to remember a phone number long enough to dial it when we don't intend to use the number again. There is a level of just noticing everything that goes on and remembering it later if we need to. There is a level of paying close attention to and *noticing* everything which allows us to remember book-length conversations, literature, and poetry perfectly. All of these kinds of memory tend to operate beautifully, and the information is recoverable even from the most fleeting experience *unless some patterned decision to "forget" has taken place.*

We have perfect memories. We can remember and recall anything easily except what has been interfered with by a patterned decision or command to "not remember." Even such "occluded" memories can be recalled by discharging the blocks which are interfering (or these "memories" can be "remembered" in a damaging, difficult way through the use of drugs or hypnotic reinforcement).

The patterned blocks on memory can sometimes be evaded by simple "trick" questions such as, "What would it be if you could remember it?", by "flash" questions, etc.

In our usual cultures, attempts to improve people's memories usually mistakenly rehearse difficulties in remembering. Instead, the repeated use of a dependable contradiction, such as remembering over and over again something that one "can't possibly forget" (one's home phone number or one's middle name), with celebration and praise *and the ensuing discharge,* can free one's memory to operate well.

(The question of whether the "loss of memory" ensuing after an insufficient supply of oxygen to the brain during surgery is a permanent loss of memory is still an open one. It may simply be a patterned block operating. The information may even be destroyed in one storage place but be filed in several other parts of the brain to be recovered later.)

"painful" emotions

13.020 There are many emotional distresses which afflict humans—jealousy, despair, panic, frustration, boredom, greed. All of them have played bad roles in many individual and social situations. *Greed*, however, occupies a special place in that it has been made the basis of and a fundamental operating principle or requirement *in all oppressive societies*. It has been stressed to the point where, within current societies at least, it takes precedence in practice over most *human* aspirations. The successful fulfillment of goals based on greed is accepted in the current societies as taking precedence over happiness, health, care of the environment, good relationships with others, and the operation of human intelligence.

Very recent developments have seemed to reveal that *preferment* or *being chosen over* or *being not preferred* or *being not chosen* is perhaps a "seed" distress which is installed even earlier than greed in the hierarchies of oppressive painful emotions and has up until now operated with general approval instead of being recognized as a very damaging distress.

Perhaps it is completely rational to prefer a blue color to a red color, to prefer vanilla to chocolate, to prefer being warm and cozy to being out in the fresh cool air, but to prefer one human being over another, to "choose" one human being over another, or to tell any group of people that they are a "chosen" people is an insidious invalidation which can become a rootstock for all kinds of other damaging painful emotions to become attached to. There will be further exploration of and thinking about this insight.

13.021 *The most dangerous, functionally violent human being*, the sort of person who used to be marked for destruction in previous social epochs and is still treated this way in states or countries which use the death penalty, always is curable if sufficient counseling resource can be brought to bear on the person. Inside the distressing and dangerous patterns there is always a completely ordinary, completely wonderful human being who has in all cases been very badly hurt *or he or she would not be acting hurtfully to anyone else.*

13.022 *Cruelty* of one human to another is completely foreign to our human natures. A very young child can be observed spontaneously acting "cruelly" to another young child, but careful observation of these actions leaves only the impression that the child simply has not realized yet that what she or he is doing is hurtful to the other person and is simply experimenting with all different kinds of behavior toward other people (as he or she does to all other things in his or her environment). Once it has been communicated understandably to the young child that his or her actions are hurtful, the apparent cruelty disappears. There does not seem to be any built-in capacity for humans to harm other humans. The enormous number and spread of examples of humans apparently acting cruelly all seem, necessarily, to be the operation of distress patterns *installed by cruelty which the person has previously received* and which then is being acted out in the other role of the recording by being cruel to someone else.

allergies

13.023 All of our experience in counseling would indicate that *allergies* are components of the playing out of distress patterns, the recording of which included the presence of a chemical substance (usually a protein). The presence of the substance itself restimulates the entire recording with whatever physical misfunctioning and emotional distress were included.

Counseling to free a client from allergies can be as simple as giving her or him free attention to talk about the allergy *or* the listing of all memories connected with the distress and the systematic discharge of them. When enough discharge has taken place, the person becomes free from the "allergy."

menstrual cycles

13.024 *Pre-menstrual, menstrual, and post-menstrual malfunctioning* (in at least the great majority of cases) is exactly a recording of distress which was present when the hormone changes took place in an early menstrual experience. The re-occurrence of the hormonal shifts restimulates the entire recording, which may include water retention, "blues" or depression, cramps, headaches, etc. The recording can be discharged. It can be discharged completely. It is good to tackle it, contradict it, and discharge on it when the symptoms are not present. It is much easier to contradict under those conditions. The motivation to do something about it, however, is usually much more present during the distress. Good counseling here consists of simply finding ways to contradict the components of the distress recording (often the emotional moods). This is often the situation where "sympathy" or "comforting" will bring voluminous discharge. Cramps can often be relieved by holding another person close with the client vigorously pushing her abdomen against the other person's abdomen.

tickling

13.025 *Tickling* is an oppressive activity. It is imposing one's will upon another person. It is frightening, particularly when done by a larger or older person or by an adult to a small child. It is strictly a "no-no." The fact that children "seem" to enjoy tickling is a misleading appearance. They hope to be able to laugh enough to get rid of the fear, and they sometimes seek out being tickled with this hope in mind. (It's exactly analogous to the seeking out of horror movies in the hope that one will be able to discharge the fear.)

One can help a child who is in the grip of a "seeking to be tickled compulsion" by pointing a finger in her or his direction and saying "tickle, tickle" while he or she laughs, but never touching or enforcing him or her. It will also work well to have the child threaten to tickle the counselor while the counselor acts out the discomfort. When the child has laughed and shaken enough, he or she will lose interest in tickling and will not tolerate it in the future.

every age is a good age

13.026 Apparently *every age is a good age* to be if the individual is surviving well, is learning new things, and is being treated with respect. All kinds of mistreatment directed toward a person of a certain age is *oppression* and is *non-survival for both the oppressed and the oppressor.*

The physical difficulties which tend to accumulate as an individual becomes older may not be entirely the result of the accumulation of distress recordings but are certainly largely so. If we could rest well, sleep thoroughly; exercise in an all-around way; eat only the necessary amounts of balanced, nutritious, non-fat foods; and clean up completely the recordings of any injuries or illnesses that have impinged upon us, we could probably easily live to 150 years of productive life, even under present conditions. (Possibilities also exist for research on such things as the use of "growth" hormones and the elimination of certain presently common cellular mechanisms that promote aging. Any one of several such developments could open the door to what will be effectively permanent longevity.)

deliberately view any situation from many different viewpoints

13.027 A confusing situation can often begin to be understood by viewing it with a *"dualities" approach* (considering it from at least two different viewpoints). The counselor can ask, "What is negative or threatening about the situation? What is encouraging? What opportunities does the situation offer?" One can ask what one person's kind of involvement in a situation means to that person. What does it mean to other persons involved in another way? To approach any dilemma from fresh and *various* directions will tend to help the client think freshly where thinking has been blocked or in a rut.

14. OPPRESSION

overview

14.001 Oppression is the systematic mistreatment of a group of people by the society and/or by another group of people who serve as agents of the society, with the mistreatment encouraged or enforced by the society and its culture.

14.002 Oppression exists universally in all present societies. Every adult in all present societies has been conditioned through the imposition of distress patterns into functioning in both oppressed and oppressor roles.

14.003 People were hurt before there were oppressive societies. They were hurt by accident and by the acting out of other people's distresses, but they were not *oppressed*. Oppression only began with the emergence of class societies.

Greed patterns and patterns of violence that were already in existence were undoubtedly involved and became part of the foundation of the origin of oppression and of oppressive societies.

Patterns of *favoring* or *preferring* certain people or groups of people may have been an even earlier root than greed for the growth of patterns of oppression. Being "preferred" or "chosen" as an individual or a group of people seems to occur only out of distress, although it is so commonplace in our current societies as to have received general approval and very little suspicion of or recognition of its patterned basis until now.

14.004 Various oppressions have been organized in the oppressive societies as a means of dividing the economically-oppressed people from each other and keeping them from uniting against the economic exploitation. Such particular oppressions are organized against any sub-group in the population which can be distinguished from the other people in the population *in any way*. There are numerous particular oppressions based on economic classes, on differences in age, on gender, on "race" (whatever that means), on skin color, on disability, on languages, on dialects, on education, on occupation, on size, on sexual preference, etc.

14.005 Oppression is reinforced and maintained in various ways: by the army; by the police; by the legal systems; by the courts; by prisons and jails; by propaganda; by false theories; by reactionary religious groups; and by "confused" religious groups.

14.006 In surviving and enduring oppression, the individual needs to distinguish between *actual conformity* to the oppression, which is destructive both to himself or herself and to others, and the *appearance of conformity*, which frequently "satisfies" the patterned demands of the oppressor or the oppressive structure well enough for the individual to "get by" (survive), at least temporarily.

14.007 It makes sense to interrupt abuse at any moment. It makes sense to stop humans from harming humans at every opportunity.

14.008 The *witnessing* of oppression seems inherently hurtful to people.

oppression and distress patterns

14.009 Oppression is *not* inevitable nor inherent in human beings.

14.010 Oppressions can only arise and operate on the basis of distress recordings. No human being would agree to submit to oppression unless a distress recording of such submission had been installed previously while the human being was hurting. No human being would ever agree to, or participate in, oppressing another human being unless a distress recording had previously been installed through the person being hurt and then later manipulated into the "other end" of the pattern, to play the role of the perpetrator of hurt or the role of the oppressor.

14.011 The sources of distress recordings can be grouped into three large categories.

The first category is *accidents*, where hurt that occurs accidentally leaves a distress recording installed on the individual.

The second category might be called *"contagion."* This is the process of a person "acting out" a distress recording attached to him or attached to her in a way that is hurtful to another person or to other persons. This can leave a distress recording upon the person or the persons hurt by the "acting out."

The third category is the *operation of oppression*. In this case, the society or its agents systematically hurt people in order to impose distress recordings upon them that will have the effect of the hurt person conforming to the role assigned to her or to him in the operation of the oppressive society.

14.012 The basic mechanism for keeping any person in an oppressed condition is the installation upon the person of a distress pattern or distress recording by hurting him or her in an oppressive and invalidating way. This leads to one or both of two results when the distress pattern is restimulated.

The first result is to be forced again into the role the person filled in the original hurt experience. In this case the person is pushed to "accept" or "agree" to be oppressed, to accept the invalidating feelings, to be defeated in the attempt to remain human. The slave "agrees" to be a slave, the serf picks up his hoe and bows his head, the wage-worker feels inferior and "lucky to have a job."

The second result occurs when, in an attempt to escape the role described in the first result above, the victim of the restimulation seeks relief by "occupying" a different role in the restimulated distress recording, *the role of the oppressor.* In this case the male victim may turn upon a woman the abuse and invalidation originally turned on him (the basis of sexism), or a white victim may turn the abuse and invalidation originally turned upon him or her upon a black or other non-white person (the basis of racism), etc.

14.013 No one would agree to, or submit to, being oppressed for more than an instant, except for the effect of the installation of distress patterns. The original decision to submit to oppression was because such a decision appeared to be a necessary choice for survival in the context of real or "perceived" danger or threat.

14.014 The basic "bottom layer" of any chronic pattern is likely to be an oppression. Discharging the oppression exposes the roots of the chronic pattern and eliminates it faster than trying to discharge on the "top layers" of the pattern, that is, the current acting out of the pattern and the hurts incurred in the process.

14.015 The operation of oppression is not only *based upon* the installation of distress recordings but is also *the source* of a great many distress recordings produced by it as it operates.

14.016 There is intense pressure in most cultures of the world at the present time to inhibit the discharge processes. This is done by semi-deliberate operations of the oppressive society which tend to keep the individual distressed and therefore conditioned to accept the oppression and the oppressed role assigned to the person in the society. One of the most blatant examples is the "big boys don't cry" cultural tradition and the "don't cry" commands that are pounded into young males in Western cultures. All this inhibition of discharge is imposed from "outside the person" to begin with and reinforced by later restimulations.

the different oppressions

14.017 Eliminating *any* oppression *completely* requires eliminating *all* oppressions.

In an oppressive society, oppression is tightly woven into the fabric of every system.

14.018 No oppression is *unimportant.*

14.019 Each particular oppression has certain features in common with all other oppressions, for example, lack of respect.

14.020 Each particular oppression is also *unique* in some respects, and its unique features need to be understood in order to move effectively to eliminate it.

14.021 Some *particular* oppressions play key roles in the overall structure of the oppressive societies and in their relationship to the other oppressions.

Among these *particular* oppressions are the oppression of *working-class people*, the oppression of *young people*, the oppression of *Jews*, racism based on skin color, "*mental health*" oppression, oppression of *disabled people*, oppression of *women*, oppression of *men*, and oppression of people because of *the particular patterns that have been inflicted upon them*.

Neglected by progressives, and until recently by RCers, has been the oppression of people through being *targeted for destruction by the society because of patterns that have been installed upon them*. This includes people imprisoned as "criminals;" people confined to mental hospitals or forced or misled into taking psychiatric drugs; members of the armed forces forced into mortal combat; people engaged in prostitution (male as well as female); people addicted to mood-altering drugs, street drugs, alcohol, and tobacco; people who are suicidal; and victims of capital punishment.

14.022 The basic oppression in class societies is the economic exploitation of working people, or "classism." In the earliest kind of class societies *slaves* were economically exploited by *slave owners*. When these societies collapsed (because of their internal contradictions), they were succeeded by *baron-serf societies*, or *feudal societies*. In these, the serfs on the land and the handcraft workers were exploited economically by the barons.

All present societies in the world (regardless of how they describe themselves or what their goals were at the time of their founding) are owning-class/working-class societies or "capitalist" societies. Here the working classes who produce the value are exploited by the owning classes who own the means of production and who take most of the value produced, returning only a portion of the value produced to the producers as wages, as salaries, or as "fringe benefits."

14.023 All other oppressions, except *classism*, have been invented, developed, and promoted in order to support the oppression of the working class by dividing the working class against itself in all possible ways to weaken its resistance to the economic exploitation of classism.

The patterns laid in by *the oppression of young people* are used as a foundation for the installation of all the other patterns of oppression.

The oppression of Jews or "anti-Semitism" is deliberately maintained during periods of social calm with an organized structure held in readiness for its intensive use during periods of social upheaval. In periods of social upheaval, it is always attempted to be used as an "opening wedge" and a precedent for the pillaging and destruction of many other groups of the population.

"Mental health" oppression is used as an ever-present threat against *anyone* who resists conformity and as an excuse for the destruction and denial of individual civil liberties.

14.024 Other oppressions were invented and devised to divide the oppressed working classes on the basis of any differences in terms of gender, age, race, skin color, language, education, skills, sexual preference, culture, etc., that could be found to exist or could be developed. Thus the different groups were (and are) made to oppress and be oppressed by each other. With this oppression of each other as a perpetual source of distress, any hostility of the oppressed working classes to the ruling classes (the *slave owners*, the *barons*, or the *owning classes* in present societies) could be diverted against each other and the oppression maintained with relative ease.

Because all these subsidiary oppressions (sexism, racism, oppression of the young, oppression of the disabled, etc.) operate on the basis of distress patterns, the oppressions show some characteristics that would not be expected if one did not understand the *nature* of distress patterns. One of these characteristics is that the patterns will persist beyond the time of their installation and will come to be "taken for granted" in the culture and in the structure of a rigid society. The operation of particular oppressions will become "hallowed" in the cultural and religious practices of the society and will continue to operate long after any apparent reason for their operation.

14.025 Although classism (that is, the economic exploitation of the working classes by the owning class) is the basic oppression, certain other of the invented or subsidiary oppressions play special roles in the operation of the whole oppressive structure.

The oppression of young people serves as a "training ground" to prepare people for all the other oppressions. Because of their smaller size and their lesser physical strength, their relative lack of information as compared to that possessed by older people, and their dependence on older people and the organs of the society for information (which is often furnished to them distorted and full of falsehoods), young people are very vulnerable to the installation of patterns of powerlessness and submission. These patterns, once installed, are used as a foundation to force the young people, as they grow older, to accept the other oppressions, such as sexism, racism, etc., as they become adults.

The oppression of Jews (often called anti-Semitism) in the countries of the West and in the Arab countries (with people from India enduring the same kind of oppression in East and South Africa, and with overseas Chinese enduring the same kind of oppression in the countries of Southeast Asia) means that Jews are kept targeted as *potential scapegoats* to be used to distract any rebelling people from their struggles against oppression during any conditions threatening social upheaval.

In the operation of this oppression, the Jews in exile, with their strong cultural traditions of literacy, learning, and intellectual capability, have traditionally been promised protection by the ruling circles of a particular country in exchange for serving as administrators, technicians, and intellectual apologists for the social oppression as a whole. This has been exacted as the price of their safety and their being tolerated in the conditions of their exile. They have thus been identified as the agents of the oppressors by their roles (and by a well-financed and secretly-supported "underground campaign structure" sponsored by the rulers of the country during times of relative social calm). When social upheaval and revolt have been threatened by the oppressed majority peoples of the country, the scapegoating propaganda has been brought into the open and the resentment of the exploited people has been attempted (often with vicious effectiveness) to be directed against the Jews.

Once any sizeable number of the majority population has been gotten to tolerate or participate in this blaming or these violent attacks upon the Jews, the precedent has been set for each section of the majority to be similarly targeted, group after group, with the precedent of their having tolerated the destruction of the Jews preventing any very effective resistance.

> *"In Germany they first came for the Communists, and I didn't speak up because I wasn't a Communist. Then they came for the Jews, and I didn't speak up because I wasn't a Jew. Then they came for the trade unionists, and I didn't speak up because I wasn't a trade unionist. Then they came for the Catholics, and I didn't speak up because I was a Protestant. Then they came for me—and by that time no one was left to speak up."*
>
> Pastor Martin Niemöller

Thus all groups are oppressed and to some extent destroyed. Hitler's targeting of Jews and communists became an effective precedent for the targeting of trade unionists, Seventh Day Adventists, Gay men and Lesbians, disabled people, mentally distressed people, Gypsies, etc.

> "People who have researched the oppressions of the "mental health" system report that Hitler's extermination policies were based upon previous work by the German psychiatric establishment.
>
> "The fact is that the program and methodologies for 'exterminations' were worked out in the twenties and thirties, before Hitler came to power, by the German psychiatric establishment. By 1938, six killing centers were created, and by 1940 over 100,000 people (mental and physical 'defectives') were gassed and buried in pits by psychiatric euthanasia. The first Jews were murdered through the same system of psychiatric euthanasia, at the same centers and by the same psychiatric technicians, before gas chambers were built at the camps themselves. The pseudo-medical facade continued in the camps. Apparently, 'mental patients' were still being exterminated in individual 'mental hospitals' even after the war and the liberation of the camps.
>
> "None of this changes the essential point being made about the function of anti-Semitism, but one can be left with the impression that Hitler-inspired 'death as a solution' was then incidentally applied to many other groups including, unremarkably, 'mental patients.' The biochemical and genetic theories of 'modern' Western psychiatry are the direct descendants of pre-Nazi German eugenics and euthanasia. The psychiatrists did not read Hitler, Hitler read and followed the psychiatrists, and it is important for understanding 'mental health' oppression not to obscure this."
>
> *Jamie Alexander*

14.026 The "mental health" system functions, not for "mental health," but as an overhanging, overwhelming threat against people who rebel against any oppression. "Mental health" oppression is the "stop sign" for all liberation movements. In every other oppression there is a piece of "mental health" oppression which threatens and enforces people to submit to that particular oppression.

14.027 The "mental health" systems of the world function as reactionary "gendarmes" of the oppressive society, supporting all oppressions.

14.028 The oppression of women and the oppression of men divide the entire population against itself. This is exactly counter to the interests of both groups. Neither group receives any real benefit from the antagonisms. Theory, policy, and techniques have been evolved to enable any woman to overcome the sexist separation from men and to enable any man to overcome the sexist separation from women.

14.029 At present white racism is central to keeping the class society operating for oppression. People of color are the vast majority of the people of the world. The world majority population is exploited by the society using the world's minority of white people as its agents.

The continued functioning of the world-wide capitalist system is highly dependent on racism. Ending all forms of oppression, and classism in particular, requires the participation of the world majority (people of color).

14.030 Oppression based on racism has been used on a world scale to justify oppression of the majority of the population and of the world's largest nations primarily because it was based on an easily-visible characteristic, the color of a person's skin.

14.031 Many groups of people are oppressed for *having patterns*. Destructive, uncomfortable, and anti-survival sexual practices arise only out of distress, and if effective counseling were available people could be easily freed from them. Nearly all "criminal" behavior is the result of previously-installed distress patterns. To interrupt the operation of these patterns may be necessary for the protection of other people, but to punish people for them is pure *oppression* (as well as being *unworkable*).

internalized oppression

14.032 Oppression can be, and routinely is, *internalized*.

Most of the damage done by various oppressions is done by the operation of the oppression's internalized forms.

These various oppressions have their most disastrous effects on the individuals targeted by them in the form of the oppression, which originated from without, becoming "internalized" by the individual victims. The internalized oppression expresses itself in at least three general forms: (1) the individual in the grip of the imposed patterns takes an oppressive attitude toward himself or herself; (2) the individuals who have been oppressed rehearse the oppression that had been directed at them (from the outside to begin with) *at each other* or *at other members of the same group*; or (3) whole groups act oppressively toward each other *as groups* (in the way that they themselves have been oppressed). (For example, a whole group of people who have been oppressed with the excuse of the color of their skin, sometimes rehearse the same activity against another group of a different skin color.)

14.033 The oppression will become internalized on its victims so that they will continue to *oppress themselves*, oppress each other within the group of the oppressed, and, as a group, attempt to oppress other groups and the members of other groups who are oppressed in a similar way to the way the first group is oppressed. (For example, groups of black and Chicano high school students in the United States have often acted with vicious racism toward members of the other group.)

Under modern conditions, at least, the internalized form of an oppression usually creates more distress, and damages the lives of oppressed people more, than the external form does. This is because the internalized distress can be restimulated by any happenings that are similar to the original oppression in any regard, and this is likely to happen much more often than the external oppression is likely to be repeated.

14.034 The development of "commitments" against particular internalized oppressions has been a fruitful organized activity in the Co-Counseling Communities. Such commitments have led to a great deal of excellent discharge, have tended to clarify for victims of an internalized oppression the existence and nature of that oppression, and have provided a basis for uniting the members of the group around discharging the internalized oppression and acting against the oppression in the society.

14.035 A large number of effective commitments against particular oppressions have been formulated, published, and circulated through workshops and publications. The role of such commitments is quite durable, that is, the person can use them to keep the contradiction against the distress in operation between sessions, support groups, classes, and workshops, and can build support groups around the effectiveness of these commitments.

14.036 A person outside a particular oppression can be powerfully effective in helping the victim of the internalized form of the oppression to discharge the oppression and function freely without it. This is an important role of any ally against the oppression.

As counselor, your knowledge or ignorance of a client's multiple oppressions will expand or limit your ability to counsel the client well.

It is human to be curious about each other. We need to learn the history of the various oppressions which groups of people in our world endure. We need to become familiar with the way these oppressions operate and the harm they do. We need to persist against any present lack of information (and the widespread misinformation in our cultures) to become well-informed.

We can *each* take on the exciting challenge of learning about *all* the peoples of the world, both their triumphs and their struggles.

14.037 Pride in oneself and in one's group can be a simple, yet powerful, antidote to internalized oppression.

14.038 People should not be *blamed* for having internalized an oppression. Pressure upon one to internalize an oppression is an inevitable component of the effect of the experiences of being oppressed. It will never seem "obvious" to the victim of the oppression, to begin with, that the internalizing of the oppression is not their "own thinking."

counseling/discharging on the oppressed role

14.039 In discharging and cleaning up the results of oppression, the counselor should keep in mind that each kind of oppression can leave several categories of hurts. In the first category are the hurts from being oppressed, the instances of being victimized by the oppression coming from outside.

In the second category of hurts are those experiences in which the oppression was internalized and acted out at oneself, at another person, at other members of one's group, or at members of another group (the members of which were oppressed in the same way as the victim of the oppression was originally oppressed).

Third is the category of hurts from having been an oppressor and acted oppressively *toward* other people. Close to this are the hurts (the guilt, the shame, etc.) from having *accepted the role of being the oppressor.*

To clean up the effects of the oppression completely, all of these ramifications of the oppression will need to be reviewed and discharged thoroughly.

14.040 Counseling a person on the distress he or she has endured in the role of *being oppressed* is quite straightforward. The attitude of the counselor needs to be plainly against the oppression. The counselor should plainly and clearly not believe in the acceptability of any of the oppression that the client has been forced to accept and internalize. Commitments are needed by the client *and the counselor* to end the oppression completely and permanently.

The counselor himself or herself needs to be free from any part of an oppressive attitude. I am impatient with any more contrived approach to being free this way than *completely respecting and simply loving the client.* The client is always lovable. If the counselor really perceives the client, it is the easiest thing in the world to love her or him, express love, and keep expressing it with words, tone of voice, facial expression, and, where it is helpful, with touch. This will often make the difference between whether the distress over having been a victim of the oppression discharges or not.

14.041 Because of the persistent societal denial of *the existence* of most oppressions, a first contradiction for oppressed people to help them begin to discharge is often to be able to tell the truth about *the reality of their oppression* and to have it acknowledged by others.

14.042 Eliminating the patterns of any oppression will require effective counseling of the members of the *oppressed* group, the members of the *oppressor* group, and the members of any group who are needed to serve as *allies of the oppressed group.*

Members of the oppressed group can frequently discharge well (at least to begin with) simply by having their oppression openly recognized *as oppression* and by the support of the counselor or the listening groups in committing themselves to resist and eliminate the oppression. To be listened to with respect on the details of the suffering of one's group can have a powerful effect. To actually listen to these stories frequently begins to "reach" the people who have been in the oppressor groups and to produce discharge from them in the audience. The distrust and insecurity which the members of the oppressed group feel toward people in the oppressor group can be explicitly contradicted by the oppressed person declaring that from now on he or she will "count on" the members of the oppressor group to cease participating in the oppression and actively oppose its functioning. The members of the oppressor group can openly commit themselves to this agreement. Both groups can frequently discharge at once, and the beginnings of real communication can be achieved.

14.043 In counseling someone on the oppression which he or she has endured, it is useful to remember to insist that he or she express pride in who he or she is and the groups he or she belongs to and the fact that he or she has endured the oppression and has flourished, to at least some extent, in spite of it. The person needs to be urged to take a very fundamental stance of self-validation as a "completely good person," as a person "destined to end all oppression."

The client needs help in discharging grief about the early misinformation and invalidations received about himself or herself and his or her group of people.

The person needs to be assisted to contradict any installed separations from the other people in his or her group of oppressed, to declare his or her solidarity with them, and to plan for "all for one and one for all" unity between them.

If the counselor is outside the oppressed group, he or she can be very effective in seeing more clearly, to begin with, than members of the oppressed group usually can, the wrongness of the oppression and the excellence of the people oppressed. Such a person needs to be willing to listen to resentment and blame, which may be turned upon him or upon her by the members of the oppressed group, but needs to remember not to actually accept or internalize any of such blame.

The tendency of an oppressed person to rehearse "blame" of the oppressors (or of anyone else) may be accepted as a starting point, but the client must not be left stuck in endlessly rehearsing such blame because this is, in effect, a rehearsal of the powerlessness component of the oppression itself.

14.044 Finding ways to achieve discharge by the individuals in oppressed groups is a crucial step in achieving effective unity *between* the individuals in the groups and *between* the various oppressed groups themselves. Communicating correctly and accurately is necessary *but not necessarily sufficient* in most cases. The people or groups that need to achieve cooperation and unity have been divided by the installation and restimulation of distress patterns, which almost always include in their content distrust, suspicion, hostility, antagonism, and sometimes violence toward the other persons or the other group. Any plan for successfully reaching unity must include specific plans for achieving discharge, even though such planning is probably best not publicized until considerable discharge has first taken place. Discharge is the only effective mechanism available to eliminate the blocking distress patterns, and seeking it and planning for it is the most reliable, quickest, and most effective channel to break through the oppressive conditioning which has left the individuals and the groups hostile to each other. The discharge allows each person and each group to see the other persons' and the other group's humanness and identity of interests to their own.

the oppressor role

14.045 Being an oppressor is itself a dehumanizing experience of *hurt*.

14.046 Any person who functions as an oppressor has necessarily and always *first been oppressed* and then *manipulated into* the oppressor role of the pattern of oppression which had been installed upon him or upon her.

14.047 No human being *rationally* wants to be an oppressor. The person acting as an oppressor is in the clutches of a pattern and can be reached, and human contact can be made with that human.

14.048 Almost everyone in class societies will find themselves in both oppressor and victim roles in different situations; i.e., nearly everyone has had experience *in both roles*.

14.049 Almost without exception, every person who has lived in our present oppressive societies has distress needing to be discharged from experiences of having been oppressed, *and also from experiences of having been in an oppressor role*.

We've all been fed a great deal of misinformation about people younger than we are, about people of a different color of skin than our own, about people in the other gender, about people in other classes, about elders, about Jews, about disabled people, about people who were more successful than we were in school, about people who were less successful than we were in school, about people in any group of the population who could in any way be distinguished from people in any group to which we belonged or were told we belonged.

In many cases, people have been persuaded to identify with these oppressive attitudes and proclaim them as their own. In a larger number of cases, the prejudices, biases, and aversions are held below the awareness of the person who holds them. These patterns operate but behind some "veil of occlusion." Our oppressive attitudes are immediately, glaringly obvious to people in the oppressed groups, but we are likely to "sincerely" deny that they exist. Such attitudes of denial are often characterized (with sarcasm) by others as "liberal" attitudes.

Because of the universal or nearly universal presence of this conditioning, Re-evaluation Counselors were slow to counsel effectively toward the removal of these oppressor attitudes in the beginning of their counseling. For a long time there was (and still is) pressure from the patterned culture around us to reproach the person with such attitudes and add to the person's *guilt* in an effort to change the behavior. Finally we achieved a general understanding that this was simply adding to the oppressive distress by reinforcing the guilt that was a major component of that distress, and that a *contradiction* was needed instead.

What seems to work well, if persisted in intelligently, is to ask the person who has been a member of a group that plays an oppressive role to remember his or her first contact with anyone who is a member of the oppressed group. (In the case of someone needing to discharge white racism, ask this client for the earliest memory he or she has available of noticing that there was any color of skin in the world besides "pink.") In dealing with these early memories, the operation of the oppression which was expressed by older people in these memories is likely to reveal itself clearly.

It also works well for the client to "speak to" the person in the memory who was being treated with, for example, racism and in speaking apologize to this person on behalf of himself or herself and the older people who (in the memory) were perpetrating and installing the racism. In doing this, the client is often quickly revealed as a broken-hearted little child who was resisting the anti-human policies of the oppression as determinedly as he or she could. He or she was being forced by the love for, and dependence on, the perpetrators of the racism to accept the oppressive attitude. If he or she accepted it, it was with enormous sorrow and guilt, and as a result the person then occluded the sorrow and guilt so that the distress operated *unawarely* for the rest of his or her life.

To pursue the series of memories associated with this early one is to convert the unawarely-racist client into an aware, active, effective ally *against* the oppression and to free tremendous amounts of free attention and power that had unawarely been tied up in this "cooperation with oppression."

14.050 The person who has been conditioned to act as an oppressor in a particular oppression will work to discharge those patterns, *not primarily for the oppressed person's benefit,* but for the benefit of the oppressor himself or herself.

A primary contradiction to oppressor patterns is the recalling of early life experiences where the hurts related to oppression were installed. This is likely to lead to discharge and the beginning of the re-evaluation of the patterns of accepting or participating in oppression. Until this is begun, every person's actions will seem to him or to her to be motivated by his or her "good intentions" as rationalized by that person through the distortion of the distress pattern in which he or she has been operating.

Counseling of people in the oppressor role can be achieved by finding the earliest memory that they can locate of *being aware of* the people in the oppressed role, followed by apologies on behalf of the usually-present oppressors in that memory. If occlusions interfere with finding memories for discharge, *fantasies* can be produced by the client or suggested by the counselor in which the client plays an active anti-oppression role as "heroically" as can be fantasized. This can lead to a great deal of discharge because the "heroic resistance" fantasized and reported by the client is actually an expression of the determined resistance of the small child, as far as her or his strength permitted, until he or she was overpowered by the oppressive attitudes of the adults whom he or she loved and was dependent upon.

14.051 It is damaging to a person to be oppressed by an oppression and it is damaging to a person who is playing the role of oppressor in the same oppression, *but* the effect of being oppressed and being an oppressor *are not the same!* "Being struck with a stick has different effects on the struck person than on the striker."

14.052 If we can help a person acting out an oppressor-role pattern to discharge that pattern, the person will gladly cease functioning *as an oppressor* and will become an ally *against the oppression.*

14.053 The early decision to collude with oppression (which was rooted in early recordings of powerlessness) involves enormous grief and fear that need to be discharged. There is also a great deal of grief and hurt involved in watching the oppression of others and feeling not powerful enough to stop it. It is helpful, in counseling someone on "oppressor" patterns, to ask the client to think of her or his earliest memories in any way connected with the group that has been oppressed.

14.054 Acting out an oppressor-role pattern is in itself hurtful to the person acting it out. The oppressor role has "apparent" benefits in an oppressive system, but these benefits are only illusory. Oppressors would live better lives in any human sense as cooperators with the people they oppress rather than as their oppressors. Oppressors are actually hurt by the system that uses them as agents of oppression. For example, in oppressing women, men ruin their opportunity for the greatly-longed-for loving and mutually-respecting relationships that they intensely desire to have with women. Owning-class people create lives of loneliness, terror, and guilt for themselves by isolating themselves from the working classes through acting out their oppressive role.

14.055 The use of early memories about people of a different race (plus basic Co-Counseling steps) in discharging white racism is a tool for people in the oppressor role to discharge and become free of the oppressive pattern.

14.056 Racism, in particular, can be discharged by whites through combining (1) making friends with people of color, and (2) discharging the earliest memories of noticing that other skin colors than their own existed.

14.057 It is not appropriate to expect or require a person with whom you have been conditioned to take the role of oppressor to counsel you on your "oppressor material." On the other hand, it can be empowering (and also advantageous and convenient) to the person in the "oppressed" role to adopt *(by his or her own choice)* the role and attitude of counselor in order to free the "oppressor" person from his or her oppressing distresses.

14.058 There must be no obligation or expectation placed on a Co-Counselor from an oppressed group to listen to, or be a counselor to, a member of the oppressor group on distress from that particular oppression. To be expected to do this is a continuation of the old oppressive attitudes where the members of the oppressed group have often been forced, as part of the oppression, to listen to the oppressive material. The member of the oppressed group may, however, decide freely for himself or herself to assume the role of counselor to the member of the oppressor group for his or her own reasons, such as to change the behavior of the member of the oppressor group in other relationships which they have with each other. A wife, for example, is not obligated in any sense to listen to her husband's sexist distresses but *may* decide, due to the lack of anyone else being concerned or capable enough to do it, to become a powerful counselor to her husband and motivate the husband sufficiently to contradict his distress and discharge his sexism. The wife will be taking on the tough job because of the rewards *to her* of the husband being a better person to live with, a better provider, a better father, etc., as a result of being helped *and required* to discharge his sexist distress.

14.059 Any rehearsal of any distress by a human being who is a member of an oppressor group may appear to members of the oppressed group as *oppression directed at them*. For example, if a white individual responds to a person of color with restimulation *of any kind* (even feeling guilty, apologizing, acting submissively weird), that, in effect, *is racism* on the part of the white individual and will be perceived as such by the person of color. Any kind of upset which the person allows to be restimulated by the person in the oppressed group *acts as an oppression*.

14.060 Oppression is built into systems and institutions but is nearly always played out by individuals; therefore, single instances can often be interrupted either by the oppressed person or by the person in the oppressor role (who is then acting as an ally instead).

In any interaction, the person acting in the oppressor role (a man dealing oppressively with a woman, an owning-class person dealing oppressively with a working-class person) *always has available the delightful possibility of being an ally instead.*

modes of tackling oppression

14.061 The principal steps toward liberation for any oppressed group are: 1) accurately perceiving reality, 2) setting a full range of goals, 3) drafting and agreeing on a liberation policy, 4) communicating the policy widely, 5) organizing: organizing leaders for the group, organizing the members of the group, organizing allies for the group, 6) perpetually THINKING, ACTING on the thinking, and DISCHARGING the distress that is contradicted and revealed by the acting and thinking, 7) reclaiming power, and 8) SUCCEEDING.

14.062 In order to have meaningful communication between people in oppressed groups and people assigned by the society to oppressor roles, all conferences and discussions which include both groups should adopt rules and practices that people from oppressed groups speak and are heard *first* and are encouraged to persist in speaking against any difficulties which they have in so doing *before* the members of groups that play any oppressor roles are allowed to speak. That is to say that women speak before men, people of color speak before whites, young people speak before adults, and so on.

14.063 While unity *between groups* is best achieved *by groups*, a key basis for removing the distress patterns installed by oppression is the connection that can be established *between individuals of different groups.* **Friendship** *is a primary contradiction to both oppressor and victim patterns.*

14.064 In seeking unity between oppressed groups, the groups will need to first *caucus separately*, carefully prepare their positions for the other groups' hearing, and then communicate to each other formally group-to-group in order to begin to understand each other. If they try to meet in the same group and communicate *as individuals*, the restimulation will almost certainly prevent their *really* hearing each other and will possibly inflame their antagonisms. To first caucus separately and then communicate group-to-group with respect is the basic rule for moving toward unity between groups.

14.065 In any hoped-for coalition of oppressed groups against oppression, the divisions which have been installed between people by the oppression of the society need to be faced and dealt with without assuming any beginning unity between them. Calling a caucus meeting of "people of color" will not achieve, in general, as much unity against white racist oppression as will calling separate caucuses of African-heritage people, Latin-heritage people, Native-heritage people, Pacific Island-heritage people, and then, after they have separately prepared statements of their positions, calling a caucus where these groups report to each other and prepare a general program on which they can all agree.

Similar separate caucuses for various divisions of the whole working class, to be followed by a general working-class conference, will work similarly, as will the same procedure for other groups.

After such separate caucuses have been held, a general conference of all oppressed groups has the possibility of being successful if each group first presents its position to all the other groups *without discussion, comment, or argument*, and leading individuals from each group are designated as a drafting committee to prepare a statement of the entire assembly's policy.

Speak-outs—in which each member of the oppressed group is asked to speak to a) what is *wonderful* about being a member of that group; b) what has been *hard* about being a member of that group; c) what *support* that group needs from the members of the oppressor group and the listening people in general; and d) what she or he wishes that non-members of her or his group would never say or do again about members of her or his group—can be very effective.

Caucuses will work in which the members of the different groups caucus separately and prepare their program for dealing with a particular oppression and eventually present it formally to the entire body. So will **"Panels"** in which all members or a very representative number of members of the oppressed group are asked to speak in turn to the questions (a) through d) mentioned in the paragraph above.

The *promotion of a person from the oppressed group to leadership of the entire group* will shake up the usual "tolerance" of oppression and lead to discharge from all groups.

Both members of the oppressed group and members of the oppressor group can have good sessions as clients by recalling memories of *standing up against* the oppression, alternating with memories of *submitting to* and *colluding with* the oppression.

14.066 ***Draft policies,*** frequently reviewed and revised as needed, and kept well-publicized, are very useful in organizing.

14.067 In working to eliminate the patterns of oppression, draft policy statements are an important formulation of the way the oppression operates and provide a program for liberation from the oppression. In preparing such a draft policy statement, *allies* can be of great help because they tend to have a sharper view of certain issues through seeing them *from outside the oppression*. It often works well to have a dedicated ally draw up the first draft of the liberation policy statement and then have people from the oppressed group review it, add to it, criticize it, sharpen it, and re-draft it using the assistance of the ally or any other ally who may be skilled with the use of words. The second draft policy should be circulated as widely as possible *to members of the oppressed group*. Their opinions should be sought in person, by mail, in writing, over the telephone, and in group readings of the policy (with following discussion and note-taking) to expand the completeness of the draft policy's coverage and sharpen it in every possible way.

The new draft policy should still be clearly labeled as a *draft* policy. The perspective adopted that *every policy will be a draft policy* is important. Any policy will be a temporary expression of the aims and plans of the liberation movement, to be clarified and improved as the experience of the liberation movement accumulates.

14.068 ***Liberation workshops*** can be organized for particular liberations, that is, against particular oppressions. A first such workshop for a given group of participants is likely to spend much of its time on discharging the distressed feelings of having suffered the oppression. Following work will tend to be mainly against the internalized forms of the oppression. Skilled insistence on contradictions to the acceptance of the oppression will be needed to prevent too much of the time being spent in rehearsing irritation with, and fear of, the group which acts as agents of the oppression.

14.069 As a liberation movement develops, ***conferences of leaders*** should be called. If people actually convene geographically to attend the conference, it works well to have part of the time organized as a workshop so that the conference participants can discharge their distresses connected with the oppression and clarify their thinking.

We are learning that the often-burdensome expense of, and time spent in, travel can be handled by using modern technology, and using ***telephone conferences*** can often substitute for "in person" conferences. With these the telephone company puts all the participants on a "party line" where they can all hear each other even though they may be in completely different parts of the world. There needs to be an agreed-upon chairperson in such a telephone conference and an agreed-upon order of speaking with no interruptions of any speaker permitted. This works well with, and supports, what we've learned in Re-evaluation Counseling about everyone speaking at least once before anyone speaks twice and at least twice before anyone speaks four times. Each person at the telephone conference announces his or her name at the beginning of each participation. The entire conference can be recorded by a tape recorder (with a microphone suction-cupped on to the earpiece of a phone). Each participant can be encouraged to record the entire meeting for himself or herself.

14.070 For any oppression, people not in the oppressed role have difficulty perceiving the reality of the oppression. This is partly because they have often been placed in the oppressor role toward people in this particular oppression. Sometimes this will happen also because they themselves have been oppressed in another way by people who are the *victims* of this particular oppression. (Children may have difficulty in recognizing that their parents are oppressed.)

There were many difficulties in the way of recognizing that men are oppressed, but a principal one is that a majority of the population, the women, found that their view of men as oppressors to them made it very difficult for them to conceive of the reality of men's being oppressed.

A major tool for communication to numbers of people on this sort of issue is what we have called the *"panel."* In this, a number of members of the oppressed group are asked to appear before the general population (the attendees at a workshop, for instance) and are asked for the details of their lives. One useful set of questions has been: 1) What is very *positive* about being a member of the group to which you belong? 2) What has been *hard* about being a member of the group to which you belong? 3) What do you wish people understood about your life as a member of this group? 4) What do you wish people would *never do or say again* to you or any other member of your group?

For a panel of men, it has been very effective to have them tell the details of what life was like for them as male infants, toddlers, school beginners, at various stages of school attendance, at adolescence, on becoming adults, and currently. Typically, women in the audience listening to such a men's panel, who have been living with or are married to members of the panel for many years, have still been astounded at the reality of the men's lives, having never asked them or listened to them in ways to elicit this knowledge before. (They have been blocked, of course, by the threat of male sexist attitudes coming at them from the men.) They are often unaware that the men have been conditioned to never complain or share the difficulties of their lives with anyone, either women or other men.

14.071 One job of a liberation leader is to *eliminate any isolation* of his or her group from the rest of the population.

14.072 We need to prepare a clear-cut plan and structure for how members of an organization can take the initiative and handle the difficulties which ensue when leaders propose and become committed to wrong, patterned policies.

14.073 The role of *"ally"* needs more thoughtful appraisal from Co-counselors than it has gotten so far. It is one of the most basic and finest expressions of our inherent humanness to go to the aid of a person who needs assistance just because it is an intelligent thing to do. It is a window to our inherent natures. Even under the most vicious conditioning, people "want to help," want to go to the assistance of the person in the stalled car, or to the person caught in a dangerous situation, or to help the bewildered individual who needs information.

14.074 People who assist others out of danger, particularly if they endanger themselves in so doing, are hailed as heroes even in the most backward or confused societies. People who "know what to do" to assist someone else's faltering efforts to cope with a difficult situation are esteemed and admired universally, even though the conditioning of the oppression is to not care about others, to view every other human as a competitor, and to adopt a "what's in it for me?" attitude toward cooperation. Almost every human's inherent nature breaks through a hundred times a day.

14.075 Certainly one of the most effective and profound ways of being an ally that we have found is to be a good counselor for another person, to share information about counseling, to assist her or him to begin to use it, to use counseling to assist people to recover their ability to think brilliantly where they have been stupidly repetitive. There are some specific things, however, that are worth mentioning. (1) One of these is encouragement. If the client is making an effort to move or achieve in a particular direction and it is his or her own choice to make that effort, encouragement will have a marked effect on the power of the client's effort. One of the best ways of offering encouragement is (2) loaning confidence: "You can do it," "I know you can," "You're just the man/woman to do the job," all said in a hearty tone. This can positively affect the client's attitude, particularly when said in the right tone of voice and with a confident expression on one's face.

general liberation/wide-world change

the necessity, the possibility, and the possible procedures for transforming the current owning-class-working-class society

14.076 Every class society is replaced eventually because of its unworkability. Since all class societies are based on the oppression of a majority of the population, they have functioned against the interests of most of the population throughout their existence. They have been able to continue to function only because of the accidental or "deliberate" installation of patterns upon the humans who are the members of the society. The patterns force the exploited and oppressed victims of the oppression to act against their own intelligent interests. The early slave-owner-slave societies conditioned the slaves, by cruelty, by religious teachings, and by false information, to give the value produced by their labor, and even their very persons, into the domination and control of the slave-owners.

In the baron-serf societies of feudalism, compulsive, non-thinking patterns were installed upon the serfs and upon the "middle class" of religious leaders, accountants, artists, and military commanders to act against their own interests and allow the value produced by their functioning and labor to be taken from them and appropriated by the baron. This also was accomplished by physical mistreatment, threats, religious injunctions, and misinformation.

In the current owning-class-working-class society, some of the same mechanisms are used for the installation of patterns of submission as were used in the slave-owner-slave societies or the noble-serf societies. The oppressions suffered by the majority of people in countries which are under the imperialist rule of a foreign nation are often practically indistinguishable from the treatment accorded slaves a hundred and fifty years ago or more. This has also continued under the economic imperialism of the post-World War II period. Native agents of the foreign imperialists, often using the revival of very primitive religious cultures which are proclaimed as "liberating nationalism," use armed force, physical punishments, and peremptory executions of rebellious "wrongdoers" to carry out the cruelest and most total of oppressions.

In general, however, since the principle source of wealth in the current society is the high productivity of skilled labor, the continuance of the oppression has come to rely more on deception, mis-education, and the establishment of a version of greed patterns, sometimes called "consumerism."

A greater number of people are promoted to the "middle class" and are encouraged to seek scholarship, academic positions, and success as artists, managers, foremen, "lead men," in order to tie their interests to that of the actual owning class and make them feel "better than" the less skilled workers. Every possible division based on gender, race, ethnicity, religion, or language is used to pit every group of workers against all the other groups, and these "subsidiary oppressions" are used to prevent any very effective unity between the victims of the social oppression against their oppressors.

The news is "managed" to give the appearance of correct information, but it is actually so slanted as to discourage and divide the bulk of the people from each other in every possible way.

School systems, divided as far as possible on class lines, are structures created not basically for education but for conditioning children and young people to submissively accept the inferior status assigned them by the society. This is somewhat concealed, managed, and "justified" by an elaborate system of grades, tests, and examinations.

overview

14.077 Two necessary activities in human liberation are: 1) social action in the wide world, and 2) effective Co-Counseling of the individuals involved. In effect, the wide-world changer must adopt a "two-legged stance," with one leg of leadership firmly planted in social action activities and the other leg of leadership firmly planted in individual re-emergence activities.

14.078 Any individual can start an effective wide-world-changing movement by listening to and communicating with his or her friends.

14.079 The role of Re-evaluation Counseling in wide-world change is to seek out and furnish an accurate picture of reality and assist the people seeking wide-world change to become free of their patterns of confusion, ineffectiveness, and misunderstanding.

14.080 There are many emotional distresses which afflict humans—jealousy, despair, panic, frustration, boredom, greed. All of them have played destructive roles in many individual and social situations. *Greed*, however, occupies a special place in that it has been made the basis and the fundamental operating principle or requirement in all oppressive societies. It has been esteemed to the point where it, in practice, takes precedence over most *human* aspirations. The successful fulfillment of goals based on greed is accepted in all class societies, and in particular in the current societies, as taking precedence over happiness, health, care of the environment, good relationships with others, and the operation of human intelligence.

We have recently begun to understand that probably an even earlier appearance of irrationality into humans' relations with each other, earlier even than greed, is the idea of *preferment* or *choice of one individual over another*. There apparently is nothing necessarily irrational about an individual preferring a warm room to a cold breeze, liking blue color better than red, or choosing vanilla over chocolate, but any choosing or preferring of one human over another in any sense seems to be deeply oppressive and lays in the patterns for a spreading oppression, out of which greed can flourish, wars can rage, and class societies persist.

14.081 The basic elements for a program for wide-world change are proposals to eliminate the exploitation of one group of people by another. Division of labor is an efficient way for people to work together, but all people should share in the value created by everyone. There can be differences in the share received, adjusted for the greater contributions or greater skills (or greater need) of some people, but no one should benefit from another's work at the cost of the person who did the work.

The beginnings of liberation will probably be around the particular issues that affect particular groups. Each group needs to be encouraged to work out a policy for its own liberation, to work out a program of unity around that policy, and to take steps to win allies outside its own group. Basically, each group will act for humanitarian reasons and on the basis of supporting each other's programs, therefore winning more strength *for* each group.

Every group of people can be reached to participate in liberation *if reached for thoughtfully*.

There will be a tendency for each group of oppressed people to first attack the other oppressed groups rather than countering the *source* of their oppression. This is because they can "feel" that they are taking action without contradicting and *feeling* their fears as intensely as if they moved against the actual sources of the oppression, which actual movement would have brought discharge and clearer thinking. If they move into effective struggle against the actual oppression, they will have to feel and discharge their fears. This will always *in the beginning* tend to make "attacking and criticizing" other oppressed groups *feel like* a "safer" alternative. With discussion, discharge, and experience, the members of the oppressed group come to realize that the other oppressed groups are their natural allies and that unity with them makes all the groups more effective.

14.082 The present world-wide owning-class-working-class society is well along in its way to its final collapse. The timing of the climax of this collapse is unpredictable. It could occur within the next two years, or it could be delayed much longer. It has been in accelerating progress since about 1900. The building of a classless society to succeed the present one will require that the entire population of the world begin to re-emerge from the accumulated distress-pattern conditioning of the past. The timing of this re-emergence is unpredictable from our present knowledge, but it will certainly be an accelerating process.

14.083 Revolutions (genuine ones) are always directed against the structure of oppression and the distress patterns which comprise and support it.

In the past, revolutions have been temporarily successful and then have been sapped away by the persistence of patterns that had been installed on the revolutionaries and revolutionary leaders. These individuals may be pulled by their new role of leadership and domination to slide into the other end of the patterns which had been imposed upon them and themselves take on the (usually concealed and unadmitted) roles of oppressors and exploiters.

A *completely effective* revolution will require the elimination of patterns from the revolutionaries, and particularly from the revolutionary leaders.

14.084 Many social action programs of the past have had excellent liberation goals, but because of the distress patterns still carried by their leaders, their programs were too rigid to be followed. All such past liberation theory is useful for information, but for current and future effective liberation activity, *fresh* thinking is necessary.

14.085 Programs for *reform* will not end oppression nor achieve liberation, but the struggle *for* reforms can be used to build one's *revolutionary organization* and educate the organization's membership.

A majority *of any group* of oppressed people, if approached thoughtfully, can be organized for their own liberation and the liberation of all people. It may be difficult, for example, to reach a majority of the owning class and win their support for the ending of the oppressive society before the oppression is completely ended, but to assume it can be done will hearten and embolden all people toward ending the oppression. It is in *everyone's interests* to end all oppression.

14.086 Attempts to end oppression are often or usually directed by the oppressive society and its agents into "reformist" channels, that is, to adopt as a goal to ameliorate or justify the oppressions but *not to eliminate them*. "Reformism" such as this needs to be exposed as a disguised *persistence* of the oppression. *Complete elimination* of oppression is the only adequate goal on such matters.

14.087 PROPOSITIONS ABOUT HUMAN LIBERATION (*Presented to the Liberation Workshops I and II and revised.*)

1. All presently existing human beings are very closely related. All are members, not only of the same species, *Homo Sapiens*, but of the same sub-species, *Homo Sapiens Sapiens*, an even closer relationship.

2. The most important physical variations that do exist among humans, e.g., blood types, body structures, and brain sizes, all vary more widely *within* each ethnic or skin-color group usually described as a *race* than they vary *between* such groups.

3. Each human being whose forebrain has not been grossly damaged begins life with a far greater capacity to be intelligent than the best functioning adult has ever been able to demonstrate.

4. The differences which do exist in the behaviors and functioning of groups of humans are *cultural*, are *learned* and *acquired* characteristics. Any human being, given the opportunity, can acquire and master the same culture and skills which any other human being has been able to do.

5. There is no human culture which is *superior* or *inferior* to any other human culture in any *overall* human sense, though there may be, and are, particular outstanding richnesses in any culture. Some cultures have developed farther *technically* in the mastery of the environment than others, enabling these cultures to be misused to oppress members of other cultures as well as their own people. This does not imply any *human* superiority of such a culture.

6. Class societies evolved as tools to master the environment more effectively (using existing distress patterns—in particular, *greed*) and functioned to that end through allowing some members of the society time and leisure to think, to accumulate knowledge, and to plan the activities of the society.

7. All class societies which we and our ancestors have experienced and participated in to date have been *oppressive* societies, in which the results of the work (the value produced by the work) of most of the people was taken from them by the *ruling class* of people by a kind of "legal" robbery. All such societies to date have operated primarily to organize this exploitation of the majority of the people by a ruling minority.

8. The principal forms of class societies which have existed to date are, in the order of their evolution, and described by their basic relationships:

A. SLAVE SOCIETIES.
In these the ruling slaveowners own the slaves outright and own their production as well (e.g., pre-Civil War Southern United States).

B. FEUDAL SOCIETIES.

In these the barons or landlords own the lands or workshops. The serf is tied to his or her plot of land or to his or her job and receives part of what he or she produces, with the rest going to the baron or landlord (e.g., post-Civil War sharecropping in the Southern United States).

C. CAPITALIST SOCIETIES.

In these societies the capitalist (the owning-class person) owns the factory, railroad, bank, or farm. The wage-worker is "free" to work or starve, but what he or she produces belongs to the capitalist who returns a variable portion of it as wages (present industrial United States).

9. Societies which will be cooperative, and in which no one is exploited or oppressed, have been imagined and described. Some attempts have been made to establish them (the Paris Commune, the Soviet Union in the 1920's and 1930's, and China after Chinese Liberation in 1949 until Mao's death).

10. The oppressive societies of slavery, feudalism, and capitalism each inevitably arose in turn because of a human need for change. Each contained within itself a built-in long-range unworkability, which, in the case of the slave system, eventually led to its collapse and replacement by feudalism. Similarly, feudalism collapsed from internal contradictions and was replaced by capitalism (e.g., the period of the European Renaissance).

11. There are many indications that capitalist society is now in the late stages of collapsing because of its own built-in, long-range unworkability.

12. Slave and feudal societies were able to be overtly oppressive, using naked force openly against the slaves and, somewhat less openly against the serfs. Since wage-workers are more independent and better informed, capitalist societies have had to become more subtle in concealing and enforcing the exploitation and oppression of the wage-workers.

13. One of the principal means used by classist societies to maintain their oppression and exploitation of people has been to secure the cooperation of different groups of people in *oppressing each other*. This has been done by installing and maintaining attitudes of *racism, anti-Semitism, prejudice, discrimination, sexism, oppression of young people, oppression of the disabled*, etc., among the different sections of the oppressed population.

14. The basic mechanism for keeping any person in an oppressed condition is the installation upon the person of a *distress pattern* or *distress recording* by hurting him or her in an oppressive and invalidating way. This leads to one or both of two results when the distress pattern is, later, *restimulated*.

The first result is for the oppressed person to be forced again into the role the person filled in the original hurt experience. In this case the person is pushed to "accept" or "agree" *to be oppressed*, to accept the invalidating feelings, to be defeated in his or her attempt to remain human. The slave "agrees" to be a slave, the serf picks up his hoe and bows his head, the wage-worker feels inferior and "lucky to have a job."

The second result occurs when, in an attempt to escape the role and behavior described in the first result above, the victim of the restimulation seeks relief by "occupying" a different role in the restimulated distress recording, *the role of the oppressor*. In this case the male who was previously victimized and oppressed may turn the abuse and invalidation originally turned on him upon a woman (the basis of sexism), or a white victim may turn it upon a black or other non-white person (the basis of racism), etc., etc.

15. An oppressive society actively reinforces both of the results described above with false "theories," with propaganda, with discriminatory treatment of all kinds, with religious pronouncements, with secret societies, etc., etc. In this way each group's attempts to resist oppression are discouraged and its confidence sapped, and each group is mobilized to cooperate in the invalidation and defeat of every other group of oppressed people.

16. When any oppressed group begins to awarely organize to achieve its liberation, the members of the group will feel reactively attracted towards blaming and attacking the other oppressed groups who have also been mistreated and as a result have exchanged oppression attitudes with their group, fighting with them as if they were the source of oppression and leaving the real (and more threatening) oppressor forces unchallenged. (Thus women will at first be pulled to see "men" as the source of the oppression, black and Chicano high school students will be urged into gang wars against each other, etc.) Needless to say, *this* tendency will be encouraged by the real oppressor groups and the society in every possible way.

17. To attain complete liberation *two* processes are *both* necessary:
one: effective organized social action and struggle
two: discharge and re-evaluation to free each individual from his or her individual distress patterns.

The two processes are complementary, and each enhances the other. To fight intelligently against social oppression is to contradict one's individual distress patterns and expedite discharge and re-evaluation *provided one pursues one's Co-Counseling systematically*.

To emerge from one's individual painful emotion enhances one's effectiveness in social struggle and helps avoid mistaken strategies and tactics based on feelings, *provided that one really engages in activity and doesn't just settle for talking about it.*

18. To be successful, any oppressed group seeking liberation must move in two directions:
one: It must consistently strive for unity within its own group *around a clear-cut program of goals and actions.*
two: It must consistently seek unity and mutual support *with every other oppressed group*, no matter how difficult this task may seem at first.

19. *"Reform"* of an oppressive society cannot bring liberation from oppression. *"Replacement"* is necessary. Since the sole reason for the oppressive society is oppression and exploitation, such oppression and exploitation are bound to be re-introduced (after any reform) in some other form as long as the oppressive society exists.

20. The great liberation theoreticians of the past are useful inspirations and models to liberation workers today in many ways, but their thinking cannot be applied, except in the most general way, to a current situation. Of most use is their method of concretely examining the real situation they were confronting, making sure they had the facts, and then thinking fresh and hard for *new* solutions to that particular situation. All our situations are *new*.

21. It may be true that "right" in a political sense is *irrational*, but it by no means follows that "left" is necessarily *rational*. The numerous movements and theories that call themselves "left" and "revolutionary" abound in rigidities and can by no means be accepted as workable guides. Fresh, intelligent thinking is required.

22. People can only be organized to participate in liberation effectively enough if the organization is done on an *individual* basis. Calling mass meetings, distributing leaflets, and other "mass" activities are an almost complete waste of time *unless* these activities are peripheral to *a systematic making of individual friends*, who will consider accepting a liberation program if *you* offer it because they trust *you*.

23. Every group of oppressed people can be reached to participate in the struggle for liberation if we make a thoughtful enough approach.

The first job in uniting people for liberation is to counter the fears, suspicions, antagonisms, and resentments that have been installed between us. This means taking a sharp, clear (and patient) stand against sexist, racist, condescending, and invalidating statements and language of all kinds.

In reaching for unity we all begin in a state of being "afraid of" each other. We have been conditioned to fear or be suspicious of anyone who is "different." We can learn to love and trust each other, but we must begin with an attitude of *respect*, of complete respect for every human being in the world. The love and trust can come (and will come) later.

24. Every group of people is important to the unity of the liberation forces. Even individuals from the oppressing classes are important and must be made welcome if they really "throw in their lot with the people."

There is one group of oppressed people, however, who overlap and include parts of nearly every other group and who are centrally important to liberation because of their great *power* in relation to the oppressive structure.

This is the group of *wage-workers,* especially the industrial wage-workers, in particular, the wage-workers in the *basic* industries.

The entire social structure of capitalism is dependent on these workers continuing to cooperate in the productive processes. No profits can be produced without their participation. If they refuse to work, the whole capitalist system comes to a grinding halt.

Liberation cannot hope to succeed without them. It certainly can succeed with them.

25. The *labor unions* are and will remain the basic organizations of the wage-workers. To win the labor union members to a liberation policy, to recover the labor union leadership posts from the employers' agents and the criminal elements who have been smuggled into many of them, is, in some ways, the most crucial organizational job facing the liberation forces. There can be no avoidance of, or substitute for, doing this.

26. Farmers are oppressed as a class and are being forced off the farms by the spread of large-scale capitalist production methods into farming. Many of the former farmers become agricultural wage-workers. The preservation of the smaller farms in this period is important, however, because these small farmers possess a vast treasure of knowledge of how to produce food for good nutrition, while the newer, larger, capitalist operations in agriculture tend to operate only on the motives of *profit*.

27. People cannot be organized successfully for liberation around programs of distress or painful emotion. To appeal to their fear, guilt, shame, or even their rage, is to *paralyze them* by restimulation in the long run. They must be organized by appealing to reason, logic, and confidence. All programs and policies should be rational. The tone of communication between liberation workers should always be one of confidence in the inevitability of success.

28. Liberation of any group will only be complete when *all* oppressed groups are liberated.

Rough Notes from Liberation I & II, pages 137-144

effective organizing

14.088 People can only be effectively organized to participate in liberation on an *individual* basis. Calling mass meetings, distributing leaflets, and other "mass" activities are likely to be an almost complete waste of time unless they are peripheral to a systematic making of individual *friends*. Such personal friends are not likely to consider a liberation program and/or liberation activities unless *you* offer it, because they trust *you*.

14.089 People cannot be successfully enough organized for liberation around programs based on distress or painful emotion. To appeal to them on the basis of their fear, guilt, shame, or rage, can sometimes seem a quick way to mobilize people, but the long-range effect of this is to paralyze them by restimulating their distress, especially their fears and their "powerlessness" patterns.

14.090 Oppressed groups will always be tempted to resort to appeals based on painful emotion in order to more quickly arouse support. It will be hard in many situations to argue against people who advocate and use restimulating the indignation of the oppressed and their "hatred" (actually fear) of the oppressor as a motivation for taking action. However, such tempting policies must be opposed to any extent possible because support for them is based upon patterned "feelings." The person's anger can be quite easily converted into fear and withdrawal by a superior show of force, and the dramatizations against the oppressor group tend to unite that oppressor group when it would otherwise be possible to divide it.

The individuals in the oppressor group should always be spoken of and treated as *human beings who are making a mistake*. They should always be appealed to publicly to *correct* their policies, and individuals within their group or allied to their group should always be appealed to for support in *correcting* those policies, which should be referred to as "mistaken" policies.

Wherever possible, the Re-evaluation Counseling attitude toward owning-class individuals should be taken as a model for dealing with oppressors, that is, that they are human beings as good as the people they oppress, who have, through no fault of their own, been placed in an inhuman position, have been badly mistreated in order to install oppressing patterns upon them, and then have been manipulated through their schooling and other conditioning into occupying the roles of oppressors to others.

When challenging specific acts of oppressor groups or individuals, the *acts* should be attacked, *not the individuals*, and the attitude should be extended toward them (however unrealistic it may seem to the oppressed people at that point) that the oppressor groups are *making a mistake*, which you will continue to expect them to correct and will help them to correct. It is often helpful to make special "understanding" appeals to particular groups among the oppressors, such as to owning-class *women* or to *local* officials of a corporation as distinct from the more distant, remote top officials of the corporation who initiated (or one publicly assumes initiated) the oppressive *local* actions.

14.091 Being committed to working for world change does not require us to neglect ourselves in the present. On the contrary, the future needs us well-rested, well-nourished, well-exercised, and well-organized.

14.092 There is *nothing to worry about*, but that does not mean that there is *nothing to do*. Worry and productive work are not the same thing, and the former cannot substitute for the latter.

14.093 There are many unsolved issues in the world that are *urgent*, but the more urgent an issue is, the more it deserves to be addressed (and can be addressed) with completely relaxed confidence.

nuclear war

14.094 In the period 1945 to 1991, the elimination of the danger of deliberate nuclear war became an overriding challenge. The progressive and liberation forces had real reason to emphasize this as the key danger to the entire world of life as well as to the well-being of the human race. They correctly chose it as the broadest possible issue around which to unite the anti-oppression forces at that time. Peace activists in this period often bravely organized and pushed forward even though permeated with despair instilled in them by the propaganda of the imperialist forces and warmongers. Their work was much more effective than they knew, however, and in the surprising collapse of the Cold War activities and mentality, the danger of the systematically-prepared nuclear holocaust was *eliminated*. (Not all peace activists have as yet been able to realize this.)

A danger of *accidental* nuclear disaster still exists, although such a danger is only a minor threat as compared to the previous one of the imperialist forces' *systematic* preparation for nuclear war.

There also still exists some danger of *adventurous* use of nuclear weapons by forces which once began as liberation forces but have been so taken over by the distress patterns as to have lost sight of everything except the possibility of violence continuing, even to the explosion of nuclear bombs. Both the danger of accidental nuclear disaster caused by the continued existence of large stores of nuclear weapons, and the danger posed by groups of people with desperate patterns of adventurism seeking access to these weapons, can and should be organized against. Wide unity of the people's forces can undoubtedly be achieved on these issues.

Such proposals as the complete elimination of every nuclear weapon and the complete cleaning up of all nuclear waste (it can, if treated correctly and refined, be rocketed into the sun, if necessary) can bring great unity among the people's forces. This unity can carry over to other actions for converting the earth into a lovingly-tended "garden of Eden" with a self-limiting population and enthusiastic participation in the full attainment of all the possibilities of our human existence.

pacifism and "non-violence"

14.095 The policies of pacifism and non-violence can seem very attractive to oppressed peoples looking for successful strategies for liberation. The trading of violence for violence in an ongoing fashion is an obvious characteristic of the operation of the oppression itself. For oppressed people to rely on counter-violence as their policy has become a dead-end for many liberation movements whose activities became increasingly channeled to adventurism, armed raids, taking of hostages, robbing of banks, etc. In the process these movements have tended to become increasingly isolated from the bulk of their supporters. As an alternative to this perspective, a consistent policy of rigid "non-violence" can seem very attractive. It will win recruits to the liberation cause more easily. It will tend to arouse sympathy from other sections of the population in the particular country *and in other countries*.

Such a rigid commitment against the use of force by oppressed people, however, can in effect mean submission to the oppressing forces. It can lead to the sacrificing of thousands of lives at the hands of an intransigent, far-right or "fascist-" or "Nazi-" ideology type of oppressor.

If the three key principles for organizing liberation struggles are remembered—that is, *a correct policy*, the *unity of the oppressed forces around this policy*, and *the winning of allies from other oppressed groups*—then the choice between rigid "non-violent" strategies and rigid "non-violent" tactics on the one hand and the thoughtful organization of the strength of the oppressed *in all possible ways*, including armed struggle, becomes a flexible choice, free to be decided upon in the particular circumstances.

the environment

14.096 At present there is growing awareness of the extreme damage being done to environmental systems everywhere in the world. This is caused in part by the unbridled expansion of the human population, and in part by the short-sighted destructiveness of the currently collapsing oppressive societies. This awareness provides an opportunity to inspire, lead, and organize all humans everywhere to eliminate the two phenomena of *humans harming humans* and *humans harming our environment*.

nationalism and patriotism

14.097 Nationalism, patriotism, and the championing of one's own country and nation *against other people* are all semi-deliberately installed conditionings to expedite the oppressions of whole nations by other nations—for the easy maneuvering of whole populations into wars, and the reactive super-enrichment of the dominant groups of owning-class people in particular countries.

14.098 Whole nations are oppressed under the present development of the oppressive owning-class-working-class societies. It is a logical development of each "incipient nation" in such a society to become a "full-fledged" nation. This means that the destiny of the group of people in the nation is decided by the members of that nation, regardless of how oppressive the relationships between them are internally. Every owning class or potential owning class in each such potential nation yearns to be the triumphant ruler and exploiter of all the other classes in such a nation. The owning class is generally able to mobilize the members of all the other classes to support it in its goals under the slogans of "nationhood" and "national liberation."

Patriotism and the most vicious chauvinism are conditioned on the population ("Deutschland über alles!"). Members of all other nations are attacked and denigrated as inferior while the members of one's own nation are extolled as superior in every way. This conditioning is *very* intense and depends on the invalidation of every person *in every other way except her or his nationality*. No man, no woman, no child, no member of any class, no member of any minority is ever allowed or encouraged to feel good about himself or herself except in comparison to members of another group. Thus the only self-validation open to the person in the nation is the patriotic, chauvinist aggrandizement of one's *nationality*.

The purpose of this is to prepare the entire population to support the launching of wars against other nations whenever special opportunities for super-profits or the looting of other countries beckon to the ruling class. Wars are always intensely profitable to the owning classes of countries, even those whose countries supposedly "lose." Wars are always destructive of the resistance movements against exploitation in the countries which go to war.

Countries which are less developed technically, less well-organized in the structure of a capitalist society, become "easy marks" for well-prepared, well-armed invasions by more technically advanced countries. Thus, many countries fail to achieve the flowering of their owning-class-working-class societies and find themselves developing only with difficulties under a super-oppression organized by the owning class of a victor nation. This "super oppression" is called "imperialism." Imperialism oppresses and exploits everyone in the conquered nation but does not prevent the development of the class relationships common in a capitalist nation. It operates simply so that the exploitation of *each* class is enormously heavier in the exploited nation than it is in the imperial nation. The imperial nation dictates the laws, imposes military rule, and extracts huge profits and plunder of resources from the nation in imperial bondage to it.

All the members of such an oppressed nation continue to be conditioned to be patriotic, to accept the proposition that they are a "superior" nationality and that "national liberation" is passionately to be desired because their lives would obviously be much better without the exploitation of the foreign imperialist nation. They are led in this by the members of the oppressed nation's owning class, who yearn "passionately" to have the nation now in bondage to the imperialist nation be "free" to be exploited only by themselves.

This conditioning must be taken into account. National liberation for most people in an oppressed nation only leads to intense exploitation by their "own" owning class, which frequently turns out to be just as greedy and rapacious (even if not quite as powerful) as the owning class of the imperialist nation has been. Yet, because of the conditioning, the achievement of "national liberation" cannot be skipped and must be used *as a goal* to unite all people in the oppressed nation. The owning class will make every effort to lead this battle for national liberation and turn the achievement of national liberation (when it comes) into an opportunity to install an extreme, cruel internal oppression of the working classes. To avoid this eventuality the working class needs to organize and actually take the leadership of the national liberation struggle with prepared plans to move toward class liberation immediately upon the attaining of national liberation.

Ghandi led the Indian people toward a national liberation which placed the overwhelming majority of them (who were in the working classes) under the rule of the Indian owning class, lock, stock, and barrel, and has kept them impoverished ever since. Mao Tse-Tung, on the other hand, clearly called for *national liberation* for China as a step toward *class liberation*, and, until his death, successfully engineered enormous improvements in the living standards, education, and well-being of the Chinese workers and peasants. (Many of these gains have remained, but the reversion to capitalism, under the leaders of the Chinese Communist Party who succeeded Mao, has interrupted the progress to the good, fair life for all Chinese which seemed within sight until Mao's death.)

cultures

14.099 Everyone's own culture is a conglomerate of useful lore, art, and inventions which deserves to be preserved and shared with all people in the world *and* a great accumulation of distress patterns. These distress patterns have been tied to the culture of the group by the hurts of the past which laid them in. These patterns continue to be insisted upon and re-installed over and over again by the oppression. In the case of "national" cultures, these patterns have been labeled as "patriotic" attitudes to take towards the country where they operate. They are offered as something in the country's culture to be proud of.

All groups of oppressed people must examine their own cultures for themselves and reach a decision on each part of the culture as to whether that part is rational and human or whether it is irrational. Each group must *sort out* its own culture, enhancing and cherishing the human (rational) parts and offering them to the world to share. Each group needs to awarely organize to eliminate the destructive portions of the culture.

religion

14.100 The entire population of most societies has been conditioned to treat any expression of religion (especially the religion they grew up with) with unthinking respect. People in the oppressor groups in the society tend to become skeptical of religions in their adult years but will tend to conform outwardly to attitudes of unthinking respect for religious ideas, institutions, and personnel (including re-installing these attitudes on their children). Sometimes, of course, (recognizing the utility of such attitudes for success in their oppressor roles), they will become fanatical "believers."

Religions began as attempts to grasp and understand the complex mysteries of reality and existence (see the pamphlet *Where Did God Come From?*), but have functioned since the beginning of class societies primarily as the political ideologies of the ruling classes. The teachings of Jesus of Nazareth (for example) emboldened the slaves to struggle against the institution of slavery, but, taken over by the emerging oppressive forces of the new *feudal* society, became (with numerous modifications) the ideology and the intellectual structure of feudal oppression.

The owning-class-working-class societies emerged and overthrew feudalism under the slogans of rationality and anti-religion, but, once established, the owning classes found the anti-rational, believe-don't-think residues of religion too tempting not to take advantage of them. The religious establishments have been maintained and supported in great varieties (there are several varieties of Christianity available, for instance, to conform to any set of oppressive patterns, and the same is true of Islam, Buddhism, and the religions of India) to confuse the opposition to, and enhance the operation of, oppression.

non-oppressive societies

14.101 Non-oppressive societies have been dreamed about for a long time. Non-oppressive societies have been attempted on a large scale at least three times: the Paris Commune, the Russian October Revolution, and Chinese Liberation of 1949. Each of these led to great benefits for ordinary people for a while (for a very *short* while in the case of the Paris Commune). The Paris Commune was "drowned in blood," as the French ruling class and the royal court joined with the invading German armies to crush it. The October Revolution and Chinese Liberation eventually became ineffective through the persistence of oppressive patterns from the past society in the minds of the revolutionary-to-begin-with leaders of the new societies. Their basic principles did not *fail* in either case, even though this is widely and publicly proclaimed at the present time by the oppressive society. These principles were *sabotaged from the inside* as the oppressive patterned individuals came to dominate the new society.

14.102 With an adequate and fair distribution system, even with *present* levels of productivity, there would be enough value and goods produced that each person's rational needs for food, shelter, health care, and meaningful work would be easily met. Increased productivity *without damage to the environment* can also easily be provided for.

14.103 Possible general agreements to be reached to form the basis for a future society:

1. Nothing shall be used from the environment without taking complete responsibility to see that it is returned to the environment intact or reintroduced into an operating recovery cycle in ways that will not interfere with the operation of the forms of life involved. This includes air, water, mineral resources, the soil, and the harvesting of all forms of life including forests and sea life.

2. No human being shall be deemed in any way inferior to, or superior to, any other human being.

3. No human being shall be required to conform to any standards *simply for the sake of conformity*. Cooperation shall be secured by *communication,* and *enforcement* shall never be used except as a temporary emergency measure.

4. A minimum standard of living shall be established, and no advances in the level of comfort and support of other people shall take place until everyone has been assisted to function at or above the minimum standard.

This will include the support, special equipment, and dedicated helpers necessary for this minimum functioning of disabled, disadvantaged, and uneducated people.

In a transition period to a classless society, people shall receive income based somewhat on the amount of value their labor produces. As soon as the rational production of value has reached the adequate level, people shall produce according their ability to produce value and shall receive income based on their needs.

Advances in the standard of living shall take place only when they do not threaten the preservation and flourishing of all other forms of life and the long-range thoughtful use of all the resources of the world.

Special recognition and honors may be granted by the society as a whole to the creativity of outstanding individuals. This shall take place only, however, after full publicity and discussion, and after a vote by the entire population has taken place approving such recognition and reward.

5. Over-population shall be prevented by requiring would-be parents to qualify and receive permission to conceive a child after having thoroughly reviewed and discharged on the distresses of their own childhoods. Such permission shall require having worked as helpers in the care and education of children, and having qualified as "assistant parents." Candidates for parenting shall also present a program of pledged contacts with other parents or with qualified candidates for parenting for collective contact between the families to eliminate isolation or loneliness for the children. (The capacity of big families to provide such resource in the past will not be available in the small families of the future. Such small families will be necessary in the future to provide against over-population such as would threaten or extinguish the functioning of other species of life.)

6. Expansion of humanity into the wider universe shall become an accepted goal and shall be planned for and organized. In the near future, the slowing but still surging growth in population can be handled temporarily by the construction of great floating continents in the climatically favorable portions of the Pacific Ocean, or by the "earthification" of the moon, followed by similar treatment of Mars and Venus, and, eventually, the development of successful technology for reaching and colonizing other star systems.

7. Aquifers shall be tunneled several hundred feet under the surface of all inhabited continents to make a dependable supply of fresh water available in a network everywhere upon land. These aquifers shall be supplied with fresh water from that stored in the icecaps of Greenland and Antarctica. This water can be used for the intelligent modification of climate, growth, vegetation, etc. wherever desired and *carefully planned for*.

8. The surface of, and the upper levels of, the earth can become largely reserved for the support of living things among whom humans will be respectful cohabitants (and visitors). Human dwellings, transportation routes, and manufacturing activities can be constructed underground, located deeply enough not to interfere with the activities of other forms of life in relation to the surface of the earth.

9. All previously extinguished forms of life, whenever possible, shall be reconstituted through the careful application of genetic engineering. All presently surviving and reconstituted forms of life shall be deemed

"sacred" and preserved whenever possible at all. Forms of life harmful to, parasitic upon, or predatory toward human beings (smallpox virus, HIV, etc.) shall be restricted and removed from the general environment, and shall be kept only in carefully guarded containers in the most responsible laboratory conditions. Most kinds of mosquitoes shall be modified to prevent their harrassing of humans or their playing their previous roles as vectors for the transmission of disease organisms. In all other possible ways humans shall be protected from assault by the naturally competing organisms (or organisms predatory toward humans) but in such ways that no strain of organism shall be "wiped out," but instead shall be maintained and guarded as an incomparably precious resource because of its unique complexity.

15. IT IS POSSIBLE TO BUILD A *FELLOWSHIP, SISTERHOOD,* OR *COMMUNITY* OF THE PEOPLE WHO TAKE RESPONSIBILITY FOR THE USE OF RE-EVALUATION COUNSELING INSIGHTS, WHO ARE CONCERNED FOR THE RE-EMERGENCE OF ALL THE PEOPLES OF THE WORLD, FOR THE LIBERATION OF ALL PEOPLE FROM ALL OPPRESSIONS, AND FOR THE ACHIEVEMENT OF A RATIONAL, COOPERATIVE, PEACEFUL, NON-EXPLOITATIVE SOCIETY.

15.001 Co-Counselors tend to relate to each other out of their common interests and similar activities. Beginning in 1971, they have related to each other in a loose structure called the "Re-evaluation Counseling Communities." These Communities (or this Community) consist of part of the people who Co-Counsel, in particular the Co-Counsels who also take responsibility for communicating Re-evaluation Counseling insights to others, for keeping these insights accurate and undistorted, and for discovering and advancing additional insights as our experiences and our thinking (and our discharge of the previously-existing blocks in our thinking) bring them to light.

The existence of this Community is of importance to the functioning of Co-Counseling, not only to the people presently active in the Community, but to the large numbers of people who have in the past learned to use Re-evaluation Counseling (to at least some extent) and who view the continuing Community as a resource that they will resort to "when they need to." This Community's existence is also of importance to the much larger number of people in the world who have not yet had an opportunity to know of the insights and the practice around which Co-Counseling is built. It is desirable to introduce beginning Co-Counselors to the possibility of Community *membership* early, because participation in the Community activities is in itself a massive contradiction to people's distress patterns.

15.002 The Re-evaluation Counseling Community consists of the human beings who have become acquainted with the insights of Re-evaluation Counseling, who have decided that they are in agreement with them, and who feel that these insights are important to themselves and, eventually, to all other humans. These people have agreed to take some responsibility for the preservation of these insights from distortion, incompleteness, suppression, or misrepresentation. They have agreed to communicate them to other interested people. They have agreed to participate in extending the scope of such insights through their practice of Re-evaluation Counseling and through the communication of any new insights which will arise from this practice. They have agreed that they will participate, to the extent that their circumstances permit, in the operation of a loose Community structure (within the *Guidelines* that are periodically agreed to, extended, reviewed, and modified for the guidance of all such participants).

The Community has so far agreed that it will constitute one International Community, uniting all humans of every race, nationality, gender, age, class, education, state of oppression or liberation, of whatever degree of freedom from distress, as long as the person is committed to *seeking* freedom from the distress.

The ultimate goal of the people in this Community is to be committed "all for one and one for all" to *everyone's* successful functioning, *everyone's* liberation, *everyone's* complete re-emergence. Every Community member is expected to work towards being able to commit himself or herself to the complete elimination of any harming of humans by humans.

The Community agrees to assist the organization of sub-groups within itself on the basis of any differences of any sort, so long as the program of the sub-groups is for the liberation, freedom, and unity of all people.

The *Guidelines* of the Re-evaluation Counseling Community, November 1993 edition, read:

"That the only program of the Re-evaluation Counseling Communities which is binding on all members be: Through Re-evaluation Counseling to seek recovery of one's occluded intelligence and to assist others to do the same,

That all other activities undertaken by the Community be in support of this program and that no agreement beyond consistency with this program be required of members of the Community, and

That, starting with Re-evaluation Counseling theory, all Co-Counselors are encouraged to illuminate, examine, and arrive at correct, intelligent positions on all issues facing humanity, including the most controversial ones. That this process be helped by special conferences, workshops, and publication of statements. None of the positions so emerging will be binding on members of our Community even if everyone is in complete agreement."

15.003 The Re-evaluation Counseling Community is organized both on a geographical basis and on the basis of function. Co-Counselors who live in the same neighborhood (a "neighborhood" may be as small as a city block or as large as a city or a province to begin with), relate to each other in classes, sessions, support groups, and workshops. They can also meet, from the beginning, as a "Wygelian" leaders' group. This consists of all the people who are interested in *building* the Community and who meet to give leadership on this question. A Wygelian leaders' group does not meet *regularly* but only when there is "something to meet about" and follows a typical Wygelian agenda: 1) each person reports on what he or she has done as a leader in the recent past; 2) each person gives his or her opinion and estimate of the situation the group is facing; 3) each announces what she or he intends to do as a leader in the following period; and 4) each person receives a demonstration session from the most experienced counselor available on any difficulties that person is facing in her or his leadership.

When there are about thirty active Co-Counselors, the Wygelian leaders' group calls a meeting of all Co-Counselors, and one person, who is called the Area Reference Person, is chosen for five responsible functions. These five functions, which need not take much time (but call for good judgment) are: 1) to participate with the Regional and International Reference Persons in certifying and de-certifying Re-evaluation Counseling Teachers; 2) to give final approval to the spending of Area Outreach Funds; 3) to give final approval to any material published on the Area level purporting to represent Re-evaluation Counseling; 4) to approve Area level workshops that accept students from classes other than the classes of the leader of the workshop; and 5) when consensus cannot be reached quickly enough, to speak for the Area on *policy*. The Area Reference Person, the Regional Reference Person, or the International Reference Person must endorse applicants to Regional or International workshops.

New Community groups can bud off from this existing Community, and become separate Areas, when they have about thirty active Co-Counselors. When there are several functioning Areas, these Areas can be organized as a Region, and the International Reference Person will choose a Regional Reference Person to function as his or her assistant for that Region.

In organizing by function, people of a particular heritage, culture, language, or oppression are encouraged to organize support groups and Wygelian leaders' groups around *their* commonality. When the number of people with such a commonality becomes substantial, the International Reference Person may appoint an International *Liberation* Reference Person for that commonality, who is then encouraged to choose City-wide Coordinators, where such populations exist, who take initiative in organizing support groups and Wygelian leaders' groups around this commonality. The Liberation Reference Persons function as assistants to the International Reference Person, as do the Regional Reference Persons, and are encouraged to take initiative in the *development* of liberation programs, policy statements, and special workshops, and *supporting* the group's liberation in the wide world.

15.004 The *Guidelines* are intended to promote rational associations *between* Co-Counselors.

15.005 Membership in the Community requires agreement by the member on only one point: the use of Re-evaluation Counseling to regain the person's intelligence and help other people to do the same. Unity is sought between all Community members on a large variety of other issues. In practice, Community members tend to become more and more in agreement as their discharge, re-evaluation, and thinking progress, but agreement on other issues is not *required*. People are not expected to give up either their deeply-held thoughts or their most stubborn prejudices in order to be members of the Community and to participate in its work. *Useful* agreement can only be reached through people's actual discharge and re-evaluation. "The one convinced against his will is of the same opinion still."

In the years from 1946 to about 1990, the threat of nuclear holocaust, arising out of the planning of the leaders of the Soviet and the U.S. military establishments for the escalation of nuclear armaments, seemed such an urgent, threatening possibility that the Community accepted inclusion of the elimination of the nuclear threat as part of the "one-point program." It was assumed that unless resistance to the nuclear holocaust was organized effectively enough, the automatic drift toward war by the patterns of the leaders of the two camps would deprive us of the opportunity to recover our full intelligences.

Now, with the development of events having relegated the threat of *deliberate* nuclear holocaust to a vanishing probability and with the great reduction in the threat of *accidental* nuclear holocaust or the use of nuclear arms by desperate, adventurist-patterned "liberation movements," we can sensibly restore our one-point program to its original form—"to use Re-evaluation Counseling to recover our own occluded intelligences and to help other people to do the same."

Even though Proposition 3 of the Re-evaluation Counseling *Guidelines* requires only agreement with the one-point program for Community membership, Proposition 4 calls on Community members to seek for rational viewpoints on *all* issues facing humanity, including the most controversial. Such rational viewpoints are continually in the process of being reached in classes, conferences, workshops, local and international newsletters, and electronic mail communication. They are also reached through the playing of audio and video tapes, voluminous correspondence, and the drafting, publication, and dissemination of draft policies (and such draft policies' replacement by *improved* draft policies through processes involving all the activities listed in the foregoing). They are reached in the publication of journals on all the issues facing special groups of people and the publication of books endeavoring to give overall leadership on the main issues.

15.006 A new growth of the Re-evaluation Counseling Community begins when two or more people acquire interest in the theory and practice, and either Co-Counsel together or meet together to discuss the theory, and decide that they wish to participate in the activity of Co-Counseling. Sometimes these people have access to some of the literature describing how Co-Counseling can work. Sometimes they have encouragement from someone who has experienced Co-Counseling and encourages them to try it. Sometimes the interested people order an audiocassette or videocassette of some demonstrations or lectures and use it to guide them in their beginning experiences.

If their beginning efforts prove satisfactory, or at least encouraging, the people may write to some leader of the Community and ask for assistance. Such assistance may consist of permission to attend a workshop in an already-functioning Community. Or it may consist of a visit by a qualified teacher of Re-evaluation Counseling from an organized Community to address a meeting of interested people organized by the local would-be Co-Counselors. At such a meeting the visitor may give an introduction to the theory, do some demonstration counseling, answer questions, and, if a number of people express interest, may help them get organized to begin simple Co-Counseling. A small group of *leaders* may be set up, and the special manners in which leadership functions in Re-evaluation Counseling may be explained. Sometimes the person who shows most beginning interest and promise may even be designated as a teacher and given a one-time permission to teach one series of classes. The International Community may, through International Outreach funds, subsidize the attendance of such a beginning teacher at a Teachers' and Leaders' Workshop.

As such a Community begins to grow, assistant teachers are trained by the first teacher and recommended by the teacher and the leaders' group to be given one-class-series trial credentials as teachers. If their first series of classes goes well, their credentials will be given full status.

As the number of Co-Counselors increases, there will come a time when the small Community is functioning well, when there are two or more fully qualified teachers, when there are at least thirty people *active* in Co-Counseling, and when one person is willing and appears able to assume the role of Area Reference Person. If there is a Regional Reference Person functioning in the Region where this Community is growing, the Regional Reference Person and the International Reference Person will jointly agree to the organization of a local Area. They will approve a proposed Area Reference Person (and an Alternate Area Reference Person who functions as a "spare part" and steps into the Reference Person's job under any conditions where the designated Area Reference Person is unable to function).

Where there is no Regional Reference Person, the International Reference Person acts individually to approve this organizational step.

Once such an Area Community is established, smaller groups within the Area are encouraged to begin meeting as leadership groups, either on a *geographical* basis, on an *occupational* basis, or on a *liberation* basis. They will continue to meet occasionally and will constitute the seeds of new Communities that will grow into organized Areas as the numbers of Co-Counselors and their degrees of experience develop.

The International Reference Person is basically responsible for the operation of all Areas. Where an experienced, competent leader is available, such a person may be appointed by the International Reference Person as a Regional Reference Person. This means that she or he serves as an assistant to the International Reference Person in assisting the functioning of organized Areas, teachers outside organized Areas, and beginning groups of Co-Counselors within that Region. The Regional Reference Person actually issues teaching credentials to new teachers, but does so as the deputy of the International Reference Person. Credentials for new teachers must therefore be approved by all of the pertinent Reference Persons, whether such Reference Persons are one, two, or three in number. Teaching credentials of a teacher may by removed by agreement of two out of the three of an Area, a Regional, and an International Reference Person combination; by one of two of a combination either of International Reference Person and Area Reference Person or International Reference Person and Regional Reference Person, where these combinations are functioning; and by the International Reference Person alone where there is no functioning Area or Region.

The International Reference Person may appoint an International *Liberation* Reference Person as his or her deputy in providing leadership for a particular group of the population, such as men; women; young persons; young adults; working-class, middle-class, or owning-class people; people of African descent; Chicanos/as, etc. Such International Liberation Reference Persons are expected to serve as interceders within Re-evaluation Counseling for the interests of their particular groups, to see that their groups receive adequate attention and support for their liberation and re-emergence. These International Liberation Reference Persons also serve as deputies to the International Reference Person in the leadership of such groups. They are expected to take leadership in the drafting of liberation policies and in the organization of support groups, workshops, Wygelian leaders' groups, City-Wide Coordinators, and conferences for members of their constituencies. They are expected to speak out for adequate attention and support for the interests of the people in their constituency, particularly when their organization is in the beginning stages.

Every person in the Re-evaluation Counseling Community is regarded as a peer with every other member and is fully responsible for the functioning of the Community. Many people participate in Co-Counseling who do not qualify as Community members. They may not receive the benefits available to Community members, such as attendance at workshops or conferences, assistance from Outreach Funds, and so on, unless they become members of the Community and assume some responsibility for its functioning.

Everyone in the Community has a job, no matter how small the job may be.

People are expected not to rehearse "disappointment" at the Re-evaluation Counseling Community. The Community is exactly what *each person* makes of it, and any disappointment expressed constitutes a rehearsal of the person's own distress.

15.007 The Communities are the "great sturdy packing cases" that give us our structure. The Areas are the "boxes and crates." The techniques are the "wrapping paper," and the one direction that we think of at the particular moment to assist our client, that works perfectly this one time, is the "curly ribbon" that decorates the package.

15.008 A principal function of the Community is outreach to new sections of the population who, because of language, culture, economics, oppression, or geography, would find it difficult to initiate their own first contacts with the Community and with Re-evaluation Counseling or to have the opportunity to participate in Co-Counseling enough to reach their own informed judgments as to their desire to be involved in Re-evaluation Counseling.

It is the firm, established-from-the-beginning policy of the Re-evaluation Counseling Community to eventually reach out to and involve every single variety of human being that exists upon the surface of our planet. Those who are already participating in, and are committed to the use of, Re-evaluation Counseling contribute financially, organizationally, and, through activity, in reaching to, communicating with, making welcome, and involving every possible kind of individual in the use of Re-evaluation Counseling. The divisions which have been installed between groups of people by their past histories and by the oppressive societies have left many difficulties in the way of reaching across these barriers to people of other groups. One of the difficulties is the financial expense which Re-evaluation Counseling activity will pose to people whose incomes are lower because of the oppression they endure.

The Community attempts to solve or ameliorate these difficulties by what are called "Outreach Funds." Re-evaluation Counseling teachers are free to set the amount of their own fees for the classes they teach. They are encouraged to keep the fees low, however, and to give scholarships to, for example, people of color in a white-majority country. They are further encouraged to give scholarships to young people; to disabled people; to working-class, low-income people; to people unemployed or on welfare; and to other people whose incomes are traditionally low because of the oppressions they endure. One-quarter of each tuition fee paid for a class is reserved for Outreach. Three-fourths of that one-quarter is to be spent locally, and one-fourth of it is to be spent Internationally. Portions of any above-expenses income from Area or local workshops and from Regional or International workshops are designated to go to Local and International Outreach.

One-third of any *net* income from a Regional or International workshop is used as a subsidy for the publication of Re-evaluation Counseling literature at lower prices. Ten percent of the *gross* income of any workshop on any level is contributed to International Outreach and to the cost of servicing the International Community by Personal Counselors, Inc.

15.009 The Community is committed to, and intends to follow, a policy of including members of under-represented groups in the membership of all leadership bodies.

15.010 Outreach Funds, both on a Local and International level, are used to establish Lending Libraries of literature, for scholarships for attending workshops and classes, for transportation costs for attending such workshops and classes, and to pay for translation of literature into new languages when it is not possible to have the translation effort done on a volunteer basis.

15.011 Outreach Funds are also used to help finance or partially finance the visit to new territories or new cultures of effective Re-evaluation Counseling leaders or teachers who are expected to help establish new Co-Counseling Communities with new effective "native" leadership while they are there.

15.012 Each member of the Re-evaluation Counseling Community is *urged*, *encouraged*, and *expected* to start her or his own "World Community," centered upon, modeled for, and led by herself or himself.

This means that people who begin as Co-Counselors will be expected to continue to become support group leaders, assistant teachers, teachers, Area Reference Persons, Regional Reference Persons, International Liberation Reference Persons, International Reference Persons, and organizers of all sorts. Re-evaluation Counseling leaders are expected to lead within the membership of the Re-evaluation Counseling Community, but also expected to lead in the "wide world" of people who are not members of the Re-evaluation Counseling Community but who necessarily share many goals, oppressions, liberation policies, and activities with Re-evaluation Counselors.

Experience has shown that when a person has become effective at leading within the Re-evaluation Counseling Community, she or he finds leading in the wide world to be relatively easy and greatly expedited by her or his Re-evaluation Counseling knowledge and experience. Experience has also shown that any decision to withdraw from Re-evaluation Counseling leadership because "leading in the wide world is so much easier and more productive," is a mistake. The inspiration of the wide-world leader soon "dries up" without continuing contact with the Re-evaluation Counseling Community. The slogan, "A Re-evaluation Counseling leader has one leadership foot in the wide world and one in Re-evaluation Counseling," was coined to signalize this observation.

15.013 Forty-seven years after the discovery of Re-evaluation Counseling, the Re-evaluation Counseling Communities are active, to some extent, in eighty-six countries. There are several hundred leaders of Communities who take individual responsibility and initiative. There are eighty-four Regional Reference People, thirty-six International Liberation Reference People, two hundred and eighty Area Reference People, and the same number of Alternate Area Reference People. There are over five hundred teachers credentialed to *teach* Re-evaluation Counseling outside these organized Areas.

Our publishing firm publishes twenty-seven theoretical journals. *Present Time,* our general journal, has published over one hundred issues. We have published nineteen books and forty-one pamphlets. We've translated important parts of our literature into over thirty languages.

We have substantial beginnings of our Communities in the most populous nations of the world, but we also have meaningful, functioning groups in some of the smallest countries of the world.

We have boldly and intelligently tackled the elimination of the oppressions of women, of men, of children, of young people, of young adults, of elders, of disabled people, of indigenous people; of people who have been victimized by racism, by classism, by anti-Semitism, by anti-Arabism, and by anti-Asian prejudice. Co-Counseling is functioning on every continent with the exception of Antarctica, and it may be functioning there without our knowledge.

15.014 It is *possible* to develop sufficient leadership to meet the needs of any Community.

15.015 It is *possible* to formulate, agree upon, and periodically update effective *Guidelines* for the relations between all the different kinds of people in the Community.

15.016 It is *possible* to establish effective enough communication between such people all over the earth.

15.017 It is *possible* to establish continually flexible, effective, and continually-improving relationships between participants and leaders.

15.018 We have learned some effective ways to structure meetings, to reach agreements, to build alliances. For example: every person speaks once before anyone speaks twice in any meeting; people are listened to without interruption; people speak to issues only, not to personalities.

We draw attention to the points of *agreement* between the people involved in a discussion rather than emphasize *disagreements*. We agree to recognize our disagreements and *respect them* until we find ways to eliminate them.

15.019 One can think of a Re-evaluation Counseling Community as an experimental pilot plant in which people can explore ways in which the future rational *societies* may learn to operate.

16. RECENT DEVELOPMENTS IN COUNSELING

the complete, logical distinction between the past and the future

16.001 The assumption has been made in traditional logic that the past and the future can be dealt with and thought about as if they are similar parts of a unified reality. This is a *fundamental* error. The reason why this error has been made and accepted by so many brilliant logicians and philosophers of the past must lie in the operation of distress patterns attached to the logicians themselves.

16.002 Restimulated recordings of distress experiences that have happened in the past tend to present themselves to our attention *as if they were still present.* This effect has undoubtedly prevented logicians, up until now, from realizing that everything that happened in the past *is completely determined* and cannot be changed, while events in the future, on the other hand, are not yet determined. We can still influence what will happen in the future. This confirms our intuitive feelings that we actually possess free will. We *can* modify expected *future* events up until they have happened and become part of the past.

16.003 Once any event has taken place it is permanently and finally determined. It can only be evaluated and discussed in terms of learning more accurately *what did happen*.

16.004 The present instant (and by "instant" we here mean an infinitesimal period of time comparable in duration to the physical length of a point on a line in geometry) comprises our "now." This continually moving "now" allows us freedom of choice. The entire future is also subject to influence by our present free will and free decision.

16.005 Once any part of the anticipated future has become the past, however, *it is completely determined*.

16.006 The past *was* the way it *was*. It cannot be changed. It is therefore necessarily *completely* acceptable and deserving of no regret, even if undischarged feelings from distress recordings of the past still color our understanding of it until we have discharged them. Since these feelings *can* be discharged, this implies that everything in the past is completely satisfactory. If we understand and make contact with this concept of the completely satisfactory nature of the past, the discharge process will usually accelerate.

16.007 Making and facing the assumption that past reality is necessarily *completely good* can guide us and encourage us to *completely* discharge the distress left by past events and come to a relaxed, rational view of any events which had previously felt distressing. Our entire pasts are *completely* satisfactory, *completely* fine, *completely* enjoyable. Our ever-moving present is filled with complete freedom of choice. Our entire future deserves delighted anticipation.

some universal, or nearly universal, oppressive patterns

16.008 Some false assumptions are so universally (or nearly universally) installed so early in most humans' lives in the current oppressive societies as to obscure any clear glimpse of actual reality in these areas for most human beings.

16.009 Even when parents and other caretakers of small children are knowledgeable and forward-looking, the patterned operations of the culture begin early in the life of almost all young children to enforce the "drying up" of sources of aware attention that should optimally be available to them.

16.010 This early lack or shortage of fully aware, human attention is likely to leave a recorded discouragement on the child to the effect that such attention cannot reasonably be expected to be available or to become available to the child.

16.011 Very young children require freedom to initiate, invent, and explore new ways of responding to the environment. Even when this creative freedom is not denied outright, present cultures tend to hedge it in by the "praise," "rewards," and "approval" given for *conformity* (to the rigidities of other people's patterns and of the environment and to the rigid requirements of the society). Pressure is exerted from many directions for the free-to-begin-with intelligence of the child to "conform," to "learn how," to "be a good boy," or to "be a good girl." "Shells" of conforming patterns tend to accrete onto the child. Rebellions against this process are rarely successful and, when they are attempted, the recriminations imposed on the rebelling one tend to leave different but also harmful rigidities upon him or upon her. These patterns will also often bring down fresh recriminations and enforcements upon the one rebelling.

16.012 This pressure toward conformity comes at the new human through almost every channel of the society. There is pressure to conform at every stage of the child's development—in pre-school, in kindergarten, in elementary grades, in high schools, and in colleges and graduate schools. Conformity is explicitly "required" in the worlds of business and industry (although the richest rewards, even in the oppressive structures, are always reserved for the individuals who *do not conform* in particular ways and who "get away with it." Here *initiative*, which the conformity seems to aim to stamp out, is allowed to intrude into the operation of the oppressive structures [but only in the highest circles]. However, it is violently suppressed where it appears in any questioning of, or innovative proposals for change of, the system itself.) The suppression of initiative is so general and so taken for granted that it is likely to be initially regarded as "normal" by both clients and counselors.

16.013 The denial of our lovability, our "deservedness of being loved," begins very early in most people's lives. Its installation seems to lead to other nearly-universal chronic patterns. The impression of not being loved, not being wanted, not being accepted can apparently arise very early in the existence of the zygote or fertilized human egg as it begins to develop. Almost fatal but recoverable-from damage to the tiny organism by contraceptive materials can apparently leave an impression of rejection on a physical level, the recording of which will be rationalized by the child later, as his or her mental abilities begin to function, into a deep feeling of danger and unlovedness.

The emotional dramatizing of a parent at a child is "understandable" in terms of the desperate "need" of the parent "to be listened to by someone," but it is likely to leave the listening child with an overwhelming impression of herself or himself not being lovable, especially when the dramatizing occurs in the earliest years.

That people *inherently* expect to be loved seems indicated by the powerful effect of the "Why do you love me, counselor?" technique on people of almost every variety of background or culture.

16.014 Chronic patterns of *isolation* are an almost universal part of the accumulated patterns of humans. This is revealed by most clients' deep discharge when they first try to say to a relaxed counselor, "You and me, George, completely close, forever."

16.015 A client's attention can be directed towards certain experiences or distresses by asking the client to repeat a phrase or statement. If a "statement" is crafted in such a way that it clearly does not refer to the client nor to members of the client's family nor to his or her friends, so it does not refer to any particular events but also *does refer* to positive reality, the repetition of this statement often will bring discharge. This approach has had some profound and surprising results.

An example of such a statement is, "It sometimes happens that someone likes somebody." If the client is asked to *repeat* this statement, to *not inhibit any discharge* that seems to be evoked by it, and then to accurately report the thought that occurred to him or her, a process ensues that leads to a great deal of discharge, and ongoing, often profound, re-evaluation. Eventually, the client seems to "take over" the counseling session's direction instead of being dependent, to any great extent, on the counselor's thinking.

Clients' responses to this approach are not at all "standardized." Each client's response will be impressive in its "uniqueness."

At first the client's series of "thoughts" may either appear as confirmations of the statement (or, more correctly, understatement) or, just as commonly, may be listings of various skepticisms or data contrary to the "understatement."

The beginning discharge is also quite unpredictable. Many clients will begin to discharge immediately at hearing the "understatement." The discharge can be crying, laughing, shaking, or deep yawning. As it continues, the kind of discharge will shift spontaneously at the client's own initiative. A client will often comment with surprise at the kind of discharge that is taking place, but just as often will appear not to notice he or she is discharging unless the counselor points it out in an effort to encourage him or her to continue.

Clients find this "understatement" approach easy to use and persist with. Long sessions seem to refresh and revive clients rather than tire them. If the discharge continues for a long time the client will seem to, at some point, exhaust his or her thoughts related to the beginning topic of the understatement, but his or her attention will drift to many other subjects while she or he continues to discharge easily and well. The process gives the appearance of being "taken over" by the basic levels of the client's intelligence (what I have often called "the little boy downstairs" or "the little girl downstairs"). The continued repetition of the original understatement seems to serve the purpose of keeping the client's attention rooted in the positiveness of reality while the client's mind is searching out and bringing up just the "right-sized" portions of distress that the client's mind has judged to be contradictable and dischargeable by the resources of the client *in that situation and at that moment.*

This can take place with different degrees of intensity. An effective technique is to treat the repetition of the understatement casually. The understatement itself should be carefully chosen so that it does not seem to be directed *at* the client or *about* the client in particular. As an example, the statement, "It sometimes happens that someone likes somebody," as it continues to be repeated by a client, may be resisted with suspicion by the tense client for a short while. It may even elicit memories of not being liked or of having his or her liking of someone else rejected, but as the repetition of the statement is continued, the general concept of being liked or of liking someone acquires familiarity and safety enough that the client discharges from a position somewhat like that attained in the operation of the Reality Agreement technique. The client then becomes able to discharge with comfort for a long time while spontaneously reviewing myriads of incidents of distress. These incidents are likely for a while to be connected with the topic of "liking" or "not liking." Such material turns to discharge as it comes up because the client has apparently adopted the implication of the repeated understatement (that people inherently like each other), and this reality persistently contradicts the client's distresses.

Continuing with such a carefully-crafted understatement for a long time seems to tend to release the client's intelligence ("the little girl downstairs" or "the little boy downstairs") to bring up exactly the distress which the client intuitively decides is in his or her best interest to discharge and re-evaluate at that particular time in that particular situation. In this way topics far removed from "liking" or "being liked" will be advanced spontaneously by the client and discharged well even though the repetitive understatement has not changed.

This use of a "generalized understatement" process will work with many carefully-crafted understatements. Some that have been considered and tried include the following:

"Sometimes a person likes to be expected to do her or his best."

"It sometimes happens that a person feels delighted to be alive."

"It *has* happened that a person feels completely powerful and confident."

"It sometimes happens that a woman realizes that she is completely human, without any flaws or limitations. (And she successfully encourages men to join her in this kind of realization about themselves as men.)"

"It sometimes happens that a man realizes that he is completely human, without any flaws or limitations. (And he successfully encourages women to join him in this kind of realization about themselves as women.)"

"It has been known to happen that a black person living in the United States feels happy."

"It sometimes happens that a person finally has everything turn out just exactly the way she (he) wanted it to turn out."

"It has been known to happen that someone completely attained the goals he or she had set."

extended understatements

16.016 Extended understatements, of which the following is an example, have proven successful.

The counselor says to the client, "Please take pencil and paper and write down the following statements. These statements are not about you, but they are about a person I know. They may prove useful for you to say and discharge about. Repeat each phrase that I dictate in the same tone of voice that I say it (or as close to that tone as you can approximate). Then write it down on your paper.

"It has been known to happen that a man (woman) from a country and neighborhood that is similar to the one in which you grew up has been struggling to achieve a rational and intelligent life for himself (herself) against many difficulties. He (she) is well-informed and well-educated, and has lived through a wide range of experiences. He (she) is competent, confident, and POWERFUL, is very attractive physically and underneath a cool exterior appearance is very passionate. This person fi-i-i-nally realizes that everything about him (her) is *just exactly right* (!) and always has been! Not only that, but it is also true that the great, magic, elemental forces of the universe who watch over the humans destined for leadership and triumph always keep their eyes upon her (him) to see that no disaster ever threatens her (his) success. Even when he (she) thinks he (she) is all alone, beneficent forces are looking after and guaranteeing this person's success."

integrity and courage

16.017 In this century there has been a systematic drift away from earlier social encouragement to live up to high standards of integrity and courage. As the owning-class-working-class society has moved away from its evolving and growing stage and its early conflicts with the ideas of the feudal society that it replaced, it has come to systematically encourage dishonesty and timidity. The commercial functions of the society have moved away from invention, improvements in manufacturing and manufacturing efficiency, and from improvements in the liveability of the environment. The existing class societies have become increasingly become oriented more toward *wasteful* consumption, *planned* obsolescence, and *monopolistic* rather than competitive functioning.

Substantial conditioning by the societies of young people using the schools, the armed services, and "media saturation" include "waiting to win the lottery prize," "getting away with something," and "escapism." Much rebellion is produced, but of an unprincipled type done thoughtlessly, unethically, violently, and unsuccessfully.

The simple, human ideas of *courage* and *integrity* are more and more treated as "naive" and "un-cool."

Resisting and recovering from such conditioning is a key task for each of us at this point if we are to regain our effectiveness. Great damages have been and currently are being inflicted on all peoples by the presently collapsing society. It is an important struggle for each of us to commit ourselves to and model complete *integrity* (honesty and doing the right thing regardless of convenience or comfort) and *courage* (doing the right thing regardless of fear, greed, embarrassment, or humiliation).

17. RATIONAL HUMAN HEALTH CARE

our bodies, our intelligences, and our environments

17.001 From the Re-evaluation Counseling point of view, intelligence is a high level "function" of the human *physical* body, and, in particular, of that body's nervous system. Thinking is something that a human "body" does. It is a complex process which is carried out to some extent by the entire body, but the bulk of the activity takes place through its central nervous system and, on its higher levels, through its forebrain.

17.002 What an "ego," or "self," or "soul," or "identity" means, as other people use these terms, is difficult or impossible to determine. If these terms are to have any meaning in our discussions in RC, they will have to be taken to refer to some kind of composite group of *functionings*. These functionings will be composed, at least in part, of *"awareness"* (tentative definition: "thinking about thinking while thinking"), an inherent attitude toward other intelligences which we can properly agree to call *"love,"* and a recognition *of the excellence of the universe and our potential place in it as benign masters and mistresses of it.* It will also include enjoyment of the twin complementary concepts of being *distinct from* the rest of the universe, even distinct from other intelligences, but also uniquely suited to and able to achieve close, thoughtful cooperation with other intelligences.

17.003 All the higher-level functions which we tend to identify as our *humanness* are functions of our physical bodies and do not operate apart from them. We reject completely any abstract notion of the "soul" or "mind" as "inhabiting" a body or being able to depart from or function separately from the body. Ideas which have been produced by human minds may "live on" after the mind and the body which supports that mind cease to function, but the intelligence which produced the ideas does not. This intelligence ceases to function when the physical body ceases to operate, similar to the way the flame of a candle "goes out."

health and well-being are rational concerns

17.004 From such assumptions about this reality it is inevitable that we be concerned with, and attempt to be rational and successful about achieving, the best possible functioning of our physical bodies. The attainment and preservation of physical well-being is an important and immediate concern for each of us.

17.005 If we examine the common attitudes of people in our present society, including the effects of the distress recordings which have been imposed upon us, we find that much of "usual" behavior is distressed. In this oppressive class society the widespread ingestion of poisons of many kinds has systematically been promoted, encouraged, and even enforced as a tool for oppression. The phenomenon of "addiction" serves to keep human beings distressed and vulnerable to further distress. The consumption of tobacco, alcohol, mind-numbing drugs, pain-killers, narcotics, psychedelic drugs, etc., etc., is widespread. Overeating is almost a "national characteristic" in the United States and in a few other "well-to-do" countries. Inhibitions against exercise, although challenged recently by the commercial goals of selling exercise machines or gymnasium memberships, continue to be reinforced by the conditions of living.

17.006 In our present society the attainment of profits is the single overriding motivation of the rulers of the society. As a result, pollution of our air and our water and the contaminating of our food with dangerous, non-nutritious chemicals used as "flavors," "colors," or "preservatives," all for the sake of a larger or quicker profit, threaten the healthy functioning of our bodies in many ways. There are also many problems created by the pressure for attaining quicker profits through intensified yields of food by such methods as the use of artificial hormones in raising "meat animals" and the use of long-lasting poisonous insecticides on plant crops. Tolerating these activities creates persisting, long-range difficulties in the way of our physical survival.

there are positive factors also

17.007 Certain modern developments in food production also, however, tend to create effects on the positive side. Modern farming has the ability to raise *more* food safely so that much larger numbers of people in the world can be well nourished if the food supplies are distributed fairly and reasonably. There have been many very real achievements of modern medical science acting against the destruction of human beings by disease. We are attaining a much greater public awareness of the threats to health through soot, "second-hand smoke," pesticides, fat-laden diets, etc., threats that we tolerated in the past.

17.008 We are also attaining an increasing awareness on the part of much larger numbers of people than formerly that pro-human motives *should* operate in our conduct, in our economy, and in our social processes even though they have not yet been allowed to do so by the exclusively-for-profit orientation of the oppressive society.

Of huge potential advantage to our health are the decisive breakthroughs we have achieved in understanding the phenomenon of human irrationality and some of the means for correcting it, that is, in the discovery and aware use of the processes which we call Re-evaluation Counseling.

the experiences of RC Community members

17.009 When the number of Co-Counselors became large enough that the decision was taken to organize as "Communities," information began to be eagerly shared among the Co-Counselors on proposed "ideas" about health and good health practices. Many individual Co-Counselors tried various programs involving nutrition, fasting, exercise, and adequate rest. Information and "guesses" about these matters were exchanged in RC classes, workshops, and gather-ins, and in the various RC journals. An interest developed in trying to state a tentative, *general* program for an RC position on *physical well-being*.

17.010 What will be the essence of a rational position on physical well-being and health care? Some fundamentals will certainly be: (1) good health will depend on enough, but not too much, good, natural food; a well-balanced diet; absence from our food of any chemicals serving any other purpose than the nourishment of the recipient; (2) good health will certainly be aided by adequate rest for the individual; (3) good health will require a thoughtful program of exercise; (4) good health will include the use of such practices of health care assistance from medicine and surgery that appear rational to us after we have subjected them to critical examination; and (5) good health will be assisted by the complete discharge of past and present hurts.

nutrition

17.011 Trying to evolve a rational policy about nutrition has involved questioning all of the "everybody knows" assumptions from the "advertising statement culture" that tends to surround us all in this society. It has involved questioning the "professional" nutritionists whose jobs and claims to wisdom rest upon the educational systems that bestow their "professional" titles upon them. It has involved questioning our particular individual cultures, where what "seems" to be intuitively true will often contain large amounts of childhood *habituation*, the identification of loving parenting with particular foods or particular methods of preparation of food. It has involved questioning "scientific research" labels that often are attached by publicity and advertising to results based on completely unrigorous procedures for checking out the usefulness of the data.

17.012 The discussions about nutrition among RCers have in the past often reflected heavy patterns of "belief," ridiculous "reasoning," and the presence of unquestioned and unchallenged addictions.

(Once at a workshop an RCer showed me a deadly poisonous hemlock plant [remember Socrates?] which he had identified and pulled up from the vegetation surrounding the workshop. [Obviously the hemlock plant was "natural" in its surroundings.] A few minutes later the same person assured me that "herb" teas "must be good for you because they are 'natural.'" All manner of weird generalities have often been passed hand-to-hand in this way.)

17.013 We need the best and the broadest data that we can collect on nutrition from all sources, but we need to draw conclusions from them and act upon them only after critical and thorough examination of the assumptions that go into our conclusions. We need to consider the rigor and honesty of the original source and of the communicator who is offering the data to us. We need to know all the factors involved in the information and judgment being offered to us before we can make even a rough, tentative generalization as to the data's validity.

medicine and surgery

17.014 We need to be equally rigorous in evaluating medical and surgical practices. When the population of RCers was mostly young middle-class "counter-culturalists" (which was true at one stage of our history), it was popular to belittle the profiteering and drug-pushing aspects of medicine and surgery and then, without any critical judgment, embrace and endorse chiropractic, naturopathy, etc., etc.

17.015 What *is* a sensible attitude to take toward the medical establishment? It seems to me that we must accept the usefulness of medical-surgical skill in many areas. I think there is reason to continue to honor doctors and surgeons for their knowledge and skills without approving of the medical establishment's bloated profiteering position. Much of what doctors know and believe is based on careful research and is generally sound and helpful.

17.016 At the same time, we must take sharp issue with the medical establishment on their general assumption that numbing people with drugs and anesthesia, beyond what is absolutely necessary for the accomplishment of the surgery or the process, can be considered "relieving human suffering" (from the Hippocratic Oath). We must be firm in our knowledge that this is a complete mistake, that for people to recover completely from pain and distress they must *feel* the pain and distress, that no kindness but rather fresh damage is being done by any applications of mind-numbing, painkilling, narcotic, tranquilizing, anesthetizing drugs of any kind. The benefits (such as having the patient passive in the area where surgery is taking place) will outweigh the damage in some cases, and the resulting distress recordings installed *can* be discharged, but the chemicals should not be used to make the installation of a distress recording "comfortable." *Local* anesthesia is always preferable to *general anesthesia*, when possible. (General anesthesia leaves far deeper distress patterns which are more difficult to get rid of.) We need to take a sharp, principled position on the issue and insist that the medical profession come around to our position both as individuals and as an "establishment."

In health care we have an intensified version of our familiar battle to allow and assist people to discharge. The discharge process becomes crucial in assisting people to heal or recover from illness. We must re-establish a principle of opposing the present organized suppression of discharge *and the drugging of people to prevent discharge.*

the cost of "profiteering" hospital care

17.017 It is becoming crucial to assist people to take a stand against the astronomical overcharging for hospital and medical care that has developed and is developing. We need to organize people to insist that this proliferating, bureaucratic structure be re-examined and overhauled.

As part of the unfaced panicky thinking of much of the owning class and their managers during this rapidly-approaching final crisis of the oppressive society, a kind of relentless profiteering has systematically invaded the health care field. It has raised the cost of health care several times more rapidly than has even the very high rate of inflation that besets the other expenses which people must deal with.

The relentless profiteering by health care *corporations* is putting adequate health care beyond the reach of very large sections of the population, including middle-class sections which had received nearly adequate care until very recently. Working-class and poor sections of the population are in the process of losing any possibility of adequate care, even in countries like the United States and England, where popular government programs had been functioning for extended periods. Citizens of the countries of the "Second" and

"Third" Worlds are becoming prey to epidemics that will be fully as destructive as any of the vicious plagues of the past unless reforms are quickly insisted upon.

It well may be that the issues which will galvanize the inevitable coming class struggles will not be wages or "pork chop" issues such as in the past, but rather the struggle for adequate immunization and vaccination protection for all people.

re-examine the assumptions made about health care in the past

17.018 It is time to require all forces in the health care field (and this includes medical doctors, chiropractors, naturopaths, and homeopaths, including the practitioners who are presently involved in RC) to re-examine the "logical" basis of their theories and practices.

It must be possible to agree upon a system of health care that really and truly serves the people rather than the drug manufacturers, hospital administrations, bureaucratic payrolls, and disproportionate incomes of the professional health practitioners.

staying healthy

17.019 A highly important change in the future will be a switch of emphasis from "regaining" health for people who have become ill to "keeping" healthy. Health care practitioners *can* reach people before illness to prevent illness through regular examinations and immunizations and through emotional discharge, exercise, diet, and sanitation. This will be far more effective than the present system of, in effect, pursuing and tolerating disasterous cultures of unhealthy living and then settling for trying to sweep up the failures of the system in the manner that the health care establishments have functioned until now.

no mysticism in the RC attitude

17.020 Earlier there had been a tendency among some Co-Counselors to use the obvious effectiveness of counseling in achieving better health to misinterpret the change as a kind of mystical effect. This has often taken the form of telling anyone with an illness that "all one has to do is counsel on it" or that "thinking will make it so," or, "Think well and you will be well." This is *not* consistent with RC theory at all. We assume that the external world can be modified by our minds in any way that we desire but that this modification will take place only through familiar, understandable, real processes operating in the real environment in understandable ways. We do not think that "thinking that something is so will make it so."

The often startling effectiveness of Re-evaluation Counseling in achieving recovery from ill health seems to operate through one of two related phenomena. First, many illnesses are *recorded* illnesses, distress recordings playing the person through a replay of the original distress. If the original distress experience contained illness or misfunctioning of the body, then the person can become ill or can mis-function in a "recorded" sense. The symptoms of the restimulated recording from the past are indistinguishable, at least to casual examination, from the symptoms the person suffered when the distress recording was first made. To discharge the distress from such a recording frees the person from the miseries enforced by the recording. When she or he has discharged enough of it, it "keys out" or drops out of restimulation.

A similar effect stems from the fact that, although the body has marvelous inherent mechanisms for the combatting of disease and the recovery of health, these are often interfered with by certain distress patterns that keep them from functioning. These distress patterns can interfere with the workings of the immune system in various ways, for example, or they can inhibit the person's digestion, etc., etc. Counseling which discharges the distresses and keeps them from having their effect frees the natural healing abilities of the body. (These are all that ever heal a person anyway. No doctor ever *does* the healing but at best assists the healing capacity of the person to operate.) Once uninhibited, these natural abilities of the body can go to work and accomplish the job for which they have evolved, which leads to recovery from the illness. Recognizing the assistance which discharge and re-evaluation can bring to recovery of health will never mean, in any sense, that "all you have to do is counsel." From the very beginning of Re-evaluation Counseling, we who have developed it have insisted that people with illnesses or injury seek out the most competent medical help available (guarding against being senselessly drugged, etc.), use to the utmost the help these resources can give, and *then add counseling* to free and assist the recovery abilities of the person.

opposing aging and death

17.021 Two "unhealthy" processes have, until now, waited to eventually make victims of us all. These processes are *aging* and *death*. There is no prospect of us finding a way to defeat these processes in the *near* future. It is important, however, in my opinion, that we take the position that since these processes are simply misfunctionings of our physical bodies, the one process leading to the other, that it should be *possible* to correct the misfunctions.

The fact that aging and death are inherited mis-functions, and *may* have served a useful purpose for simpler forms of life, should be no reason for a thoughtful person not to take a firm stand for the possibility of prolonging good health, *vibrant good health*, indefinitely. To do otherwise would be, it seems to me, to distort all our other thinking in the area with heavy discouragement arising from our surrender on this point.

17.022 This does not in any sense mean postponing *getting over* our fear of aging and death. If we have fear of either aging or death (and most people do in our cultures) then we should counsel about that fear and discharge it completely. It will enhance the functioning of everything else we do if we free ourselves from that fear.

When that fear is all gone, it seems clear to me that a rational person would still conclude that aging and dying are not suited to our inherent human nature. It is our human destiny, it seems to me, that we must set our thinking toward *eliminating* aging and death, and our efforts in the usual channels for improving our health and well-being will benefit dramatically from our setting these long-range goals.

18. INFORMATION TO WHICH EVERY YOUNG PERSON SHOULD HAVE ACCESS

adults

18.001 Adults are *not* more intelligent than young people are.

18.002 Adults often have more information about more things than young people do (they've had more time to acquire such information), but much of their information is wrong.

18.003 Your parents and other adults are good people, but they often do not *act* like good people. When they do not act like good people, there is a reason why they do not. This reason can be understood, and often, with information and planning, something can be done to improve the situation.

18.004 The adults around you will often behave in many strange, upsetting, and difficult-to-understand ways. *You* have not caused *any* of this behavior. It is not your fault *at all.*

18.005 All the strange ways that adults and older young people behave (and young people your own age also, for that matter) have an explanation. The real explanation for these strange behaviors is not an explanation that you usually hear from most adults or from reading school books. The explanations that are usually given are more like *excuses* which people think up for acting these ways because they don't know the real explanation. There *is* a real explanation. It is an explanation you can understand. We have been talking about it in this book and will say more about it in this chapter.

existence and the universe

18.006 It is very good to exist. This is a marvelous universe that we are part of.

18.007 It would be good even to exist as a rock or a sunbeam or a cloud in this universe. That would be better than to not exist at all.

18.008 Parts of this universe are always tending to become more and more complex, more complicated, "fancier." When certain of these parts become complicated enough, which in the past has apparently taken very long periods of time, they become *alive.*

18.009 All parts of reality are assumed to be included in what we mean by the "universe." We use the word "universe" to mean everything that we are aware of or will ever become aware of. Of necessity, we are viewing and thinking about this phenomenon (the "universe") from inside the universe itself. Though we will often attempt to establish "artificial" viewpoints outside the universe, we will do well to always keep reminders to ourselves that any conclusions drawn from these artificial viewpoints need to be taken with some reservations because of the nature of the total inclusion assumed for the "universe."

We assume the universe to be everywhere *complex.* We assume that any apparent lack of complexity or any claim to having reached a "complete description" of any part of the universe simply means that, concealed by the apparent completion, a great deal of knowledge, unsuspected as yet, is waiting to be discovered and revealed some time in the future.

We assume the nature of the universe to be everywhere *dynamic* (that is, always and everywhere *changing* in different ways and at different rates), with a vast range of differences in the rates of change for the different parts of the universe or for various appearances of the universe as observed from different viewpoints.

We assume the universe can usefully be viewed as influenced by two major trends at any given moment. One trend, which we have called the "upward trend," is toward more and more and greater and greater *complexity, meaning, significance,* and eventual *usefulness.* The other trend, which we have called the "downward trend," is a trend towards *simplicity,* towards *more uniformity, less contrast, thermodynamic monotony, less meaning, slower change,* or in any way towards *being less "interesting."*

The upward and downward trends operate in continual interaction with each other. They often alternate in which one dominates what we observe in successive chronological periods. This alternation tends to be characterized by a more rapid growth in complexity for periods dominated by the upward trend and an increasing tendency toward simplicity in the relationships between matter, energy, space, and time in the periods dominated by the downward trend.

18.010 A useful perspective for humans is to see themselves and the operations of their intelligence as the "leading edge" of the upward trend toward complexity and meaning. The distress patterns which have infested humans until now can be viewed as intrusions of the downward trend into our "basically upward trend" functioning.

18.011 *Life* is an expression of the upward trend. Rational thought is a "more upward" expression of the upward trend.

18.012 It is *very good to be alive!*

18.013 Anything that is alive can do things that a rock or any other non-living part of the universe can't do. You and I are very special because we are alive. We are lucky to be alive.

18.014 It is very good to exist in this universe. It is very special and especially good to be alive in this universe. It would be very good and very special to exist as a dandelion plant, a worm, or a tiny bacterium. It is very, very good and very, very special to have the ability to think intelligently. It is very, very, very good and very, very, very special to be recovering one's ability to think intelligently by re-emerging from an accumulation of distress patterns and recovering one's full intelligence, full enjoyment of living, and full responsibility for being able to change things to the way one wants them to be.

18.015 Over billions of years, some living things have continued to become more and more complex, more "special," "fancier." Some of these living things have become able to *think intelligently*. Probably all the living things (at least those that we know about) that can think intelligently are human beings like ourselves.

18.016 Anything that is alive is very complex, very special, and at least *somewhat independent* of its surroundings.

18.017 There are two main directions in the various activities in the universe. One direction, which some of us call the "upward trend," is the tendency for more and more complicated relationships to develop. This can begin with a simple mixing of a number of substances together, but the different substances will have a tendency to react with each other in very specific ways. If the reactions become very complex, we usually have special names for them. A mixture of some ingredients into a batter and put into an oven will turn into a cake. Two colorless gases, hydrogen and oxygen, will combine to form a colorless liquid, water. Many, many different kinds of mixtures and compounds will result from things being stirred up in the normal course of events. In certain conditions such as occur some places on our planet, Earth, some of the mixtures and compounds tend to duplicate themselves, attaching simpler compounds to themselves, using themselves as a pattern, and then dividing from the attachments to produce a copy of themselves. In effect these compounds multiply themselves by using part of the environment around them as "food" for the process. We say of compounds that do this that they are "alive," that they are "feeding" on the surroundings and "reproducing" themselves.

Given enough time, these "living" compounds will become more and more complex, more and more able to search out the material they need to reproduce themselves, and will take a great variety of different forms.

Because our planet has been in a relatively stable condition for billions of years, there has been time for tens of millions of different kinds of living things to develop. We think of these living things as being "plants" or "animals" or microscopic forms of life. In the last million years or so, some of the more complex forms of life have attained the ability to handle the environment around them with new, continually changing responses which they produce as the result of what we call "thinking." Our species, human beings, are the best at this "thinking" of any forms of life presently alive, but some other forms of life can do a little bit of it or can do things that give the appearance that they are evolving toward being *able to think*. So far, even human beings don't think all the time and part of the time act unthinkingly, but we show the possibilities of achieving a state of thinking all the time.

18.018 All present forms of life upon the earth *cooperate* in their living in a general kind of way. Some very primitive kinds of life "eat" chemicals and convert them into other kinds of chemicals which other forms of life will use. Green plants and some kinds of bacteria turn the energy of sunlight into the energy of chemical compounds which they can use and which all other living things, such as animals and fungi, can use, either by eating the green plants or using their by-products in some way. Almost all forms of life, except green plants, use other forms of life for food, but even though one form eats another form there is an overall cooperation in the use of the environment that allows the whole complex of life to survive and progress. When one form of life becomes too numerous, there is in most cases an automatic effect of the crowding that brings its numbers back into line and allows room for workable cooperation again. In general, any temporary crisis between different kinds of living things has in the past been solved by the effects of the crisis itself.

As our own species has mastered the environment as a result of the use of our intelligence and the powerful tools that we have created, a *real* crisis has been created for other forms of life and is still being caused by our species' thoughtless and careless use of its powers. Humans are just beginning to think well about this problem and just beginning to plan to change our ways in order to preserve *all* the other forms of life (for our benefit as well as theirs).

human capabilities

18.019 You are a very remarkable being. You are not as big as a mountain or a planet or a star, but you are more complex than any of them. You can handle what goes on around you better than any other kind of being that we have any knowledge of. You can make things around you happen the way you want them to happen. You can remember billions of things from the past. You can think ahead to the things that will probably happen, and you can plan to interrupt them, change them, or prevent them from happening. You have a splendid body which is strong and capable and which will become more strong and more capable as you grow older. There isn't anything in the world you can't do (that you would really want to do). You can enjoy everything you do.

Human beings are essentially very marvelous, very complex. They are a very advanced form of life with splendid bodies, splendid skills, and great capacities for enjoying, handling, and improving their environments.

18.020 **We can think** because we have very complex nervous systems, with thousands of billions of separate nerve cells that communicate with each other in an enormous number of ways. This means that we can do at least four important things that non-thinkers cannot do. **We can be intelligent.** We can meet each new situation with a completely new response that we have created, just that moment, exactly to handle that situation. As what happens brings us new information, we can keep modifying what we are doing and become more and more successful as we continue to operate.

We can be aware. We can notice what's going on while it's going on and continually change our appreciation of, and response to, the situation. We can even notice what we are thinking, while we are thinking it, and can think about making improvements not only to the situation but also improvements in the way we are thinking about it. We can be aware of a large number of different things at the same time. We can repair a delicate piece of machinery or solve a complex mathematical problem while enjoying the sound of music, the smell of flowers in the fresh balmy air that is blowing over our faces, and the comfort of our position. We can take account of and handle an enormous amount of information *below our awareness*, but we can also be aware of at least several different factors at the same time and do not have to restrict our awareness to just one item.

We have complete freedom of decision. We can decide *anything* we want to decide, *anytime* we want to decide it, and we can decide it *any way* that we want to decide it. This freedom leads to us making very good decisions. We have freedom to decide what attitude or viewpoint we will take towards any situation.

We have complete power to have things around us happen the way we want them to happen. A human being is very *powerful* in a different way than we usually have been taught by the society to think of *power*. Our real power is not the power to push other people around, but the power to have things be the way we want them to be.

18.021 Our ability to be intelligent is obscured and "apparently" invalidated by the way the society around us functions. We are trained and conditioned by the patterns involved in the society to tell each other that we are "stupid," that we are not smart, or that other people are smarter than we are. Sometimes, if we are feeling bad enough, we may "believe" this and actually start having difficulty *being intelligent* as well as difficulty in *believing that we are intelligent*. We can recover from this distress and confusion and not only become very intelligent again as we get our intelligence free of the patterns and back to functioning in the way that we can use it, but we can also realize and believe once more how intelligent we are.

18.022 Our awareness can be interfered with, also, in other ways. One of these ways is by our becoming preoccupied with the hurt patterns that have been left upon us while we keep trying to make sense of the patterns to ourselves, and in the process tie up so much of our attention that we stop noticing what's going on around us. This can be corrected, too, as we get rid of all the old recordings of hurt and learn to keep our attention in the present except (sometimes) when we are having a counseling session about the old hurts. Other times we will again clearly notice what is going on around us. If we have lost touch with our inherent freedom of choice it is usually because we have been "bossed around" by someone who was bigger, stronger, louder than we were in the way he or she was acting, and we felt we had to "give in" to him or her. This can have become a patterned habit and led to a belief that we are only free to do what someone else tells us to do. We can get back our confidence in our own judgment and in our freedom to act on our own judgment by having sessions on these old, bad times, and also by experimenting with actually acting boldly on our own judgment and re-discovering in practice that we can "stick by our guns" and make our own choices.

18.023 The same kind of situation will lead us to reclaim our power. This may take considerable determination and persistence because the society has generally caused all the people around us, including our parents, our teachers, our bosses, and all the people that we feel drawn to use as models, to also feel that *they* have no power and to act on these non-powerful feelings all the time. We may find that *we* have to be the model for other people. We may have to insist out of our own bravery, that *we* will be completely powerful and that *we* will encourage other people to learn to do it, too.

18.024 There is much that we do not yet know or understand about our own intelligence. An interesting guess is that as a network of communication grows between the different nerve cells in an animal, new possibilities develop at certain critical stages of complexity. We can speculate that the characteristics of intelligence, awareness, self-determination, and freedom of choice would appear spontaneously in some individuals if there were a large population of creatures with these complexities. The individuals who developed these characteristics would undoubtedly have superior survival powers as a result and would tend to soon become the dominant strain of that line of creatures. This might mean that squids or octopi could, and perhaps will, develop intelligences like ours sometime in the next few million years. It could also mean that a computer network that is *complex enough* will begin to act intelligently.

In any case, whether it was inevitable, accidental, or "planned by some higher power," our species is enormously fortunate to presently have the capacities of intelligence, awareness, freedom of choice, and power, even though they have been mostly obscured for most individuals until now by the heavy accumulation of distress patterns on the world population of humans and the long delay (until very recently) in the discovery or re-discovery and use of the procedures for re-emergence.

nerve cells, nerve systems, quantitative complexity, qualitative changes in functioning

18.025 What is especially remarkable about human beings is our *essential nature* which grows out of our very remarkable central nervous systems. A human's central nervous system has many thousand billion nerve cells in it, and the possible ways they can relate to each other is a very, very large number, a number greater than all the atoms in the known universe. A human possessing such a complex central nervous system has a number of remarkable abilities as a result.

the evolution of our central nervous system

18.026 All living cells that we have any knowledge of have some means of communication between the different parts of the cell. In any living creature composed of more than one cell, the various cells communicate with each other for the effective functioning of the whole organism. Over the long time periods involved in evolution, the group of cells develop increasingly efficient and more dependably pro-survival methods of communication.

As living organisms evolve to a larger size and more complex functioning and interacting with the environment, there is a common tendency to develop and to assign certain cells a specialized function in communication. A common name for these cells would be "nerve cells" or "neurons." Animals, in particular, evolve very complex communication systems or nerve networks for receiving information, communicating information, coordinating activity, and dominating and handling the immediate environment. Receiving information and acting upon it becomes more and more critical for survival of the animal and places a higher and higher priority on the organism evolving faster and better means of communication. Greater information storage and the more quickly and more accurately making of choices between different possible responses to different situations are desirable for the successful functioning of the organism.

At some stage in the evolution of mammals (and possibly in the evolution of some strains of mollusks [octopi and some large squids]) a capacity developed to "learn" from tense situations by making a recording of the tense experience and replacing the inherited rigid pattern of response with a new rigid pattern of response consisting of how the tense experience was handled. This was pro-survival enough of the time that it persisted as the operating characteristic for mammals, and when our mammal ancestors acquired the ability to think intelligently (to create a brand new response for *every* new situation), the old mammalian response continued to operate for our species as a "fail safe" emergency functioning. This apparently is the basis for the installation of rigid distress patterns on humans which reduces our human functioning a whole qualitative step when it takes place, and which is recoverable from only through the complexities of discharge and re-evaluation. These discharge and re-evaluation processes have persisted but have in general not been understood, cherished sufficiently, or deliberately sought out and used in a systematic group way until very recently in our history.

18.027 We may speculate on possible turning points in our past evolution to our present functioning.

First, some complex chemical molecules find ways to duplicate themselves from smaller molecules that surround them in their environment.

Then follows a development of cells, individual clusters of these replicating molecules functioning with each other in a distinct entity which maintains boundaries with the environment upon which it feeds and with which it interacts.

Third, groups of more than one cell begin to function cooperatively. Multicellular organisms exist and begin to evolve.

Next, as the numbers of cells involved becomes larger, the specialization of certain cells for communication begins neural networks.

Next, neural networks themselves begin to specialize (information-gathering, information-transmitting, transmission of commands, signalling for complex operations). Variations in behavior arise through random "mistakes" in duplicating the inherited patterns, with some "mistakes" enhancing survival.

Very complex organisms begin to "learn" by replacing inherited rigid functionings by new "rigid functionings" which arise out of recordings made in tense situations.

Enormously complex intelligences become able to produce fresh thinking instant to instant by comparing and contrasting huge amounts of information from their data banks almost instantaneously and become able to present a brand new response for every brand new situation.

This vastly intelligent functioning suspends under crisis and relapses to the more primitive functioning of making a rigid recording of everything that goes on during the crisis situation. The organism seeks in many ways to bring about discharge and the regaining of its former flexibility, occasionally succeeding but generally not succeeding for the first few million years of functioning in this state.

Some non-survival patterns (greed, domination, competition) become entrenched in human cultures. Accumulation of knowledge and the invention of animal husbandry and agriculture (and certain other cultural acquisitions in specific places) allow the evolution of class societies based on greed and competition.

An "idea" of systematically protecting young people from the acquisition of distress patterns and the "group" pursuit of the elimination of patterns and "re-emergence" of the species into totally intelligent functioning becomes an explicit, more-and-more-clearly-stated goal, attracting wider and wider support.

Every possible patterned objection and destructive attack arises and is organized. They all fail to succeed except where they are handled by responses which are themselves patterns.

A long future is waiting to be faced.

18.028 On the one hand, the human being is very, very intelligent. It is as if each one of us has in our head and bodies a super, super, super computer, a billion times more complex than all the computers presently in the world put together.

interference

18.029 For reasons which I can explain, we have been told thousands of times (by people who often believed what they told us) that we are not intelligent, that we have *no* freedom of choice but that we must do what other people do or what we are *told* to do. We have been told that we have no power, and this has often seemed true because we were being pushed around by other people and made to accept things that we did not like or agree with.

you are all right

18.030 You are *all right*. You are just fine, just the way you are. You are a human being and you are the elegant product of three billion years of evolution and probably nineteen billion years of existence and change in the universe. In spite of any feelings you may have that there's something "wrong" with you, that there's something "unsatisfactory" about you, you are *just fine*. You are *just right*. Any suggestions that you should "feel bad about yourself" are wrong and are false. We can find an explanation for and understand why you may have come to have these feelings, why you may get these other negative signals, but the feelings and the signals are *wrong*. You are just fine, just the way you are.

18.031 Notice *right now* what *you* think you are like *right now*. Have you always felt or acted like you are feeling or acting right now? No? Why? Even at times in the past when you have been feeling badly or uncomfortable physically or emotionally or mentally, you were always *all right*. The negative feelings that you were feeling at "bad" times in the past were not your fault. You were always all right even when you were feeling that you were not all right. You are *still* completely all right.

18.032 Our abilities to be intelligent and aware have many times in the past been interfered with, hidden from us, and their existence and reality denied to us, but we can get these abilities back to functioning, too, to the point where they will be functioning all the time if we're willing to do some work. The information as to how to do this work is now available.

learning, acquiring information

18.033 All young people are busy exploring the situation around them, trying to learn more about it, trying to make sense of it, trying to acquire enough information that they can function well in the situation that they find themselves in. To begin with, young people enjoy being surrounded by a great variety of conditions and objects. Inherently, young people learn to handle these different situations well, be comfortable in them, take advantage of them, use them, and enjoy them.

18.034 Young people begin acquiring information and understanding it long before the time of their birth. Their very complex nervous systems have begun to develop and continue to develop in the womb to a point at which they begin to respond actively to the situation around them. At this point a simple (but imcreasingly complex) kind of thinking begins. As the nervous system becomes more complex, the unborn individual thinks better and better, understands and responds to the environment around him or her in more complicated ways, and "makes sense of" and understands what's going on in a more and more capable manner.

18.035 Basically all human beings begin the thinking process by taking in information from the environment through our many senses. All through our bodies and on the surface of our bodies are nerve endings which sense pressure, movement, temperature, contrast, and constriction, and send this information to the central part of our nervous system (largely our brain) where a tremendous amount of comparing and contrasting takes place at a very fast rate. In all the new situations which we experience, (and in which, after birth, we receive visual and sound information, and perhaps many other forms of information in addition to the tactile and temperature information we received before birth), each situation is compared and contrasted with other situations. We have this other information from situations in the past. We have kept this stored in our memories. We judge the current situation always by how it is *like* and how it is *unlike* other situations which we have experienced in the past.

Our central nervous systems are very complex. We have at least a thousand billion nerve cells all connected to each other in a kind of a message system that's many times bigger than all the communication systems in the external world put together. We continually acquire new information and are able to make a better and better judgement and achieve a better and better understanding of each new situation.

18.036 If this marvelous operation of our central nervous sytems was never interrupted we would not only have been born very alert and eager for new information coming to us through the new channels of direct sight and clear sound available to us, but our learning would be continuous and extremely enjoyable. If nothing had interrupted this process we would have acquired more knowledge and understood the world better by the time we were eight or ten years old than the wisest men and women of the past have ever been able to do.

interruption of thinking

18.037 This marvelous equipment that we have in our central nervous sytems is, however, subject to interruption under certain conditions. To understand and deal with this phenomenon is the most important task facing all human beings even though most human beings up until this date have not understood the problem or been able to cope with it well.

What happens when we have been "hurt" (either physically or emotionally) is that this great computer network of ours is interrupted and stops working. Particularly, the computing function (the comparing and contrasting of as many as eleven trillion items of information a second) stops functioning. Only the information-gathering aspects of our nervous systems continue to operate. We continue to take in all the sights and sounds and tastes and smells and characters and conversations and temperatures and pressures, *but*, with our great computing ability suspended, we relapse to operating on a more primitive kind of functioning. This kind of functioning is much like the kind of functioning that animals such as horses or dogs operate on. In this kind of functioning the information comes in to our nervous sytems as a rigid, simple *recording* of what is going on. Instead of being evaluated through being compared and contrasted to what we already know, the *rigid recording* of the incoming information replaces the *flexible functioning*, for at least a short time.

If the "hurtful" experience stops, and if we have the opportunity and the enccuragement to cry or laugh or shake or yawn about the bad experience, we tend to resume the flexible functioning in which we had operated before the hurtful experience. If we do not have a chance to thus "repair" this rigid memory storage, it remains in place. In deliberating (or inadvertently reaching for) information from this rigid memory storage, we can bring it into operation again. This will once again make us "shut down," once again make us stop thinking flexibly, similarly to the way we did when the original hurt experience happened. Then, although it may seem to people around us that we are still functioning in a human way (since our appearance may not change greatly), we will actually be functioning again in the grip of the inflexible behavior contained in the recording that was made previously.

18.038 These "hurt recordings" or "distress recordings" are responsible for everything that doesn't work well, for everything that isn't "good" about human beings. When these rigid recordings are operating we can function stupidly instead of with our usual intelligence. We can feel "bad" instead of enjoying our usual zest for living. We can say things that do not have meaning in the new situation (because they were recorded in the old hurt experience). We can do things that don't work, we can act cruel and mean and destructive, rather than function within our usual friendly, positive, and supportive nature.

18.039 These hurt recordings can accumulate to the point where they seem to dominate the person and appear to onlookers as if the mess of rigid behaviors were the person herself or himself.

Underneath this false rigid appearance, however, the human being is still intact, still in good shape, just, in effect, tied up and locked away from functioning until the recovery processes can somehow take place.

the recovery process

18.040 The recovery process is quite complex. Viewed from outside, it seems to be (in one way) the "cleaning out" of the rigid patterns. It seems as if the discharge processes (the crying, shaking, perspiring, laughing, raging, yawning, and talking) are allowing the information that was *rigidly* stored before to be thought about and understood in the same way that information from an ordinary experience, in which there is no hurt present, is understood. The discharge processes often feel "uncomfortable" to us because while they are taking place we are more awarely feeling the distress that was recorded during the original hurt experience. There is also conditioning from the culture, which has usually frowned upon crying, shaking, laughing loudly, or even talking as much as we need to.

You will have known how to use these recovery processes all your life. You will have tried to use them spontaneously many thousands of times. It's as if the knowledge of how to recover from the hurts was built into all of us in our original nature, but we have not ever been allowed to use it or assisted to use it thoroughly and completely. In general, you will have been interrupted in the past when you tried to use it *by other people's attitudes.* You have been told *not* to cry when you *need* to cry. You have been told *not* to be afraid when you *need* to feel afraid and need to tremble in order to get over the fear. You have been told to "watch your nasty temper" when you simply needed to express your frustration thoroughly. You have been told to suppress your laughter. You have been told you were "being silly" when you needed to laugh and laugh and laugh to free yourself from the rigidity of the embarrassments which you have been made to feel in the past. You have have been told to "cover your mouth" when you yawn. You have been told that you are "sleepy" when you try to yawn (which is not what yawning is about). In various ways you have been "trained" *not to recover* from these hurts.

18.041 One can speculate that it is probable that the present traditions of interfering with and interrupting the recovery processes could have begun in emergency situations in the past. One possible scenario for a such a beginning would be a small group of people hiding in the bushes to escape discovery from a raiding group of people who had attacked their camp. When an infant began to cry and the caregiver would very tensely whisper to the infant, "Don't cry, don't cry, don't cry," with a hand over the infant's mouth, this could certainly produce a recording of feeling very afraid, with the words "don't cry" being very prominent in the scenario. If the infant survived and in later years became a parent himself or herself, the crying of his or her own infant, even in a relaxed situation, would be enough to restimulate the fear and the words "don't cry" and lead to the suppression of the infant's healing tears. This could easily be transmitted generation to generation and permeate the culture and then be rationalized as an admirable or heroic attitude to take. Similar scenarios are easy to imagine leading to reproaches such as, "Don't be such a scaredy cat," "Here now, get a grip on yourself. Stop shaking!", "Cover your mouth when you yawn," "Don't laugh inappropriately."

18.042 Any incidents with a scenario like the foregoing can be easily imagined to have been copied and "learned from" by other children and other parents.

18.043 As the operation of oppression patterns in social situations arose with the beginnings of class societies, the reinforcement of sexist oppression can easily be imagined to have produced the current denial of recovery to men in the familiar form that "big BOYS don't cry!" Hundreds of similar scenarios for the development of the cultural inhibition of the recovery processes are easy to imagine.

complete recovery from distress is possible

18.044 You *can* recover from these hurts completely, however. A young person can do quite a bit in this direction just by himself or herself by *deciding* not to stay within the hurt patterns. More effectively, an individual child or adult can persuade a friend or a family member to join with her or with him in "taking turns." Any two individuals can help each other by paying attention to each other and encouraging each other to talk about any old hurts, and then cry, yawn, shake, laugh, or rage about them. Any person can get back his or her entire real nature and can become again the tremendous human which he or she had the potential to be to begin with, before the growth of this potential was interrupted by the hurts and the distress recordings which resulted from them.

18.045 You, the individual reader, can still be as great a person as has ever lived. How? By pursuing the picture of reality that we have so far been able to extricate from the confusion and "pseudo-reality" that has been pushed upon us by the oppressive society and its distorted culture. By being intelligent about our goals, and brave about achieving them, and by persistently discharging all the distress which has accumulated from the past, we can "get ourselves back."

it is okay to be curious

18.046 It is okay for you to be curious about everything that goes on in the universe, to want to know everything, to want to understand everything. That's a part of your business in life. In developing into a fully-informed human, you need to know everything.

There is nothing that is not all right for you to be curious about, including all the things that people have told you you shouldn't be curious about. There will be many sources of information that you don't know about at present but that you will find out about and use to become better and better informed. We'll suggest some of these sources of information farther on in this book.

it is okay not to "believe"

18.047 You do not have to "believe" anything that anyone says. You can take what they tell you as a possible tentative explanation of whatever topic they are discussing until you can check it out with other information, but you don't ever have to automatically "believe" it. All around you *are* people, and *will be* people, who have been hurt, and while they were hurting, were made to feel that they must "believe" things that they don't have any real information about. This has happened because someone they loved or someone who was in authority over them told them they *must* believe what they were told. In this kind of a restimulated pattern they will try to make *you* believe things just because they say so.

You do not need to believe anything just because someone says so or because it was written in a book or magazine or newspaper or appeared on television or on the Internet. The safest attitude toward any new information is probably to be at least somewhat skeptical of its accuracy (although not necessarily vocal or open about your skepticism. Some people can get very upset if the things that *they* believe without thinking are challenged by anyone else). In your own mind, however, be skeptical to begin with about everything you are told. Always decide only tentatively that something is conditionally accepted as the "best explanation you have heard so far." Always keep the new information that has tentatively been accepted subject to review in the light of further information.

this society is not good

18.048 The society we presently live in is not a *good* society. It is not a very workable society from an intelligent point of view. It pretends to be a workable and acceptable society, and most people have been "trained" to "agree" (pretend) that it is an acceptable society even though they often grumble about and complain about some of the details, or blame themselves or other people for the ways it does not work. They tend to do this instead of seeing that society is fundamentally unfair and, more and more, unworkable.

18.049 This society *pretends* to be helpful to our work, to our education, to the relationships between us, and to our enjoyment of life.

18.050 This society actually does some things incidentally and accidentally that are useful and helpful in particular cases. A good and skillful and thoughtful person can often modify the way the society works a little to make it work much better than it usually works. The basic purpose of this society, however, is to carry out a kind of *robbery*.

18.051 At some points in the past, in an effort to cooperate better in handling the environment, we humans associated ourselves together in societies which have allowed some people to rob and mistreat and oppress most people for motives of *greed*, in ways that have kept everyone insecure and have kept adding to everyone's hurts in ways that tended to keep us from thinking rationally.

18.052 These societies have divided people into "classes."

18.053 Our present society puts a few people into an *"owning class."* These are people who *own* the things that everyone can work with and use—the land, the forests, the factories, the railroads, the trucks, the banks, the offices, the computers.

18.054 This society puts most people into a *"working class."* These are the people who do not own the things the *owning class* does, or at least do not own enough of them to improve their lives very much or make things secure and comfortable for them. The working-class people in this society have to *work for* the owning-class people. Their work produces all the value and wealth there is in the world, but all this value and wealth is taken by the owning-class people or their agents, and the working-class people are allowed to have only a small part of the value they produce. The rest is kept by the owning-class people and divided up between them as property or money and is managed by their banks and their corporations.

18.055 A small number of the working-class people are encouraged with special jobs and special educations and somewhat larger wages or "salaries" and used to manage the work of other working-class people for the benefit of the owning class. These people are often called *"middle-class"* people. These "middle-class" people are really playing a similar role to that of the working-class people, but they are trained by the society to act and "think" as if they have the same goals as the owning-class people.

past societies have been even worse

18.056 Some living things have been alive on our planet for at least three billion years. Living things which are very similar in many ways to you and me have existed in slowly changing forms for at least a million years. Societies that divided people into classes were started about six thousand years ago. Until now, there have been at least three kinds of such class societies.

18.057 Previous societies were more oppressive and functioned even worse than do the present societies.

18.058 The first class societies placed people in a *slave-owner* class and in a *slave* class. There were a only few slave-owners. Most people were slaves. The slave-owner-slave societies took everything the slave produced and gave it to the slave-owner. The slave-owner gave the slave back only enough of the production to keep him or her barely alive and working. The slave-owner could even take the slave's life away from him or from her.

18.059 The slave-owner-slave societies eventually collapsed and were replaced by what are called "feudal" societies. These societies divided people into a "noble" class and a "serf" class. These societies took almost everything the serf produced and gave it to the noble but did not give the noble the right to take the serf's life or take away everything he produced on his little farm or workshop. It was a little more "fair" than the slave-owner-slave society, but not much.

18.060 The societies that exist in the world at present divide people into an "owning class" and a "working class," with part of the working class being called a "middle class." These societies are not usually as openly cruel and vicious as the slave-owner-slave societies or the feudal societies, but they are still very bad. They treat people unfairly and they create much misery and unhappiness for all people all over the world.

young people are oppressed

18.061 In the present oppressive societies, almost without exception, every young person is oppressed. If this were not happening it seems almost certain that by the time currently-living young people became adults they would be brilliantly able, kind, caring, effective persons comparable to the finest people that have ever lived in the past. The excuses given by the oppressive society and its agents for the oppression of young people are of great variety. One is the young people's relative lack of information about the most complicated characteristics of the world around them. To be uninformed to any relative extent should never justify oppression or mistreatment but should be met with care and protection from dangers not yet understood and with the information which they have not previously had the opportunity to gain.

18.062 Young people are oppressed for their *age* which is equated with *lack of experience* or with *physical weakness*. The patterns of mistreatment thus installed are usually internalized, and a whole system of oppression is installed and activated with the oppression descending age by age by age to each younger group.

18.063 Young people are oppressed by differences in physical strength, with the smaller, weaker young people forced to submit to the older, stronger ones. They are oppressed by size: "I'm taller than you are."

18.064 Young people are oppressed by gender: "Boys are smarter and more valuable and more cherished than girls." (sexism) "Boys are so unmanageable." "I scold him and scold him, but it doesn't do any good." "Snakes and snails and puppy-dog's tails; that's what little boys are made of."

18.065 The oppression of young people comes from outside. It comes from the patterns of parents, teachers, policemen, truant officers, and religions ("Children, obey your parents in the Lord, for this is right"). It comes from older, bigger, stronger, "meaner," gang-included children.

18.066 The oppression of young people is internalized with, very early in most cases, attitudes toward oneself being accepted, such as, "I'm dumb," "I'm stupid," "I can't do that," "I tried it once and it didn't work." These attitudes early in life become a fixed, rigid, structure, blocking and interfering with every attempt of the child's intelligence to appreciate himself or herself, to take pride in himself or herself, or to make a determined effort to succeed and achieve his or her own goals. This internalized mistreatment and oppression tends to lay the basis for all the difficulties and defeats with which the older person has to contend the rest of his or her life.

you have been mistreated

18.067 You have not, in general, been treated intelligently or treated well by other people in your life compared to what would constitute *really* intelligent treatment. This is not your fault. You always have deserved good treatment. In a sense, this is not the fault of the people who treated you badly either. There are several reasons why they did not treat you as excellently as you deserved, but given their lack of knowledge of how to do better and their failure to receive the help which would have helped them do better, the reproaches and blame which a person feels toward these people is not exactly justified.

This mistreatment has made your life difficult in many, many ways. In effect, you have been told many lies about yourself and the world around you. Most of the people who told you these lies did not intend to lie to you. They were simply repeating lies that they had been told and had been forced to believe.

18.068 You have been made to feel "bad" about yourself in many ways at many times. None of this was correct. You are a fine person in every way. You have always done the very best that you could do in the past. You have been made to feel stupid, to feel bad, to feel unworthy, to feel unimportant, to feel ridiculous. None of these feelings was ever justified. You *are* very intelligent. You *are* very good. You *are* very worthy and deserving. You *are* very important. Not for one moment in your life have you ever been ridiculous. You have always been a person of great dignity and self-respect.

18.069 At every moment of your life, you should have been treated with respect.

18.070 If you will look back over your life, you will probably agree that most of the time the people around you seemed to be "unaware," that is, their attention seemed to be on something else or somewhere else than the present situation they were in.

18.071 People around you have often seemed to be very mean, to be cruel, to be unintelligent, to be unloving. I'm sure there have often been times when you felt alone in an uncaring world, and you were torn between blaming yourself and thinking that there must be something wrong with you if people acted as they did toward you, *or* having feelings of intense resentment and anger at what was going on.

People are not really the way they seemed to be at such times, even when they were acting badly. Underneath the bad behavior, people are good, intelligent, and loving, just as you are yourself. There is a reason why people act badly and do not act like themselves, and this reason is understandable and is something that can be changed even though it may be a big job to achieve the change.

18.072 The reasons why people got into these bad states, why they hurt each other, why they don't respect each other, why they lead such unhappy lives, are *understandable*. I will explain them to you. These reasons lie in the past, in the changes that took place as we humans evolved from animals that could not think to become humans who could think. As we tried to cope with the environment around us, which often seemed threatening to us, we acquired much false information and many feelings of loss and terror, of embarrassment and anger.

18.073 Today five and three-quarters billion people lead largely unhappy, insecure, and often desperate lives. New, wonderful human beings are being born all the time but then are misinformed, abused, and denied accurate information in ways that tend to force them to become as unhappy as the previous generation of humans was unhappy.

people are still okay underneath

18.074 Underneath the surface appearance of this terrible functioning, people are still *all right*. With help, they can recover their ability to act like wonderful, natural human beings. Sometime in the future, all young people will be fully respected from the moment they are conceived, and after they are born will be told all through their lives how wonderful they are, how much they are appreciated, how well they can function. They will grow up to be adults who live together in love and cooperation and enjoyment, and who treat the next generation of humans with full, loving respect. To get to that place will be a big job. At many places in this book I have told you or will be telling you how some of us are already working to get to that situation and how we would like you to join in this effort to make the world a fine place for everybody.

18.075 Adults who are around young people really want to love them, be close to them, play with them, but much of the time they don't know how. These adults themselves were not loved, played with, cooperated with when they were young. That kind of mistreatment left hurts upon them that make them act as adults the way that older adults had previously acted toward them. If someone else understands this situation and is patient with these adults who are acting harmfully to young people—if they get these adults to laugh, to make jokes with them, these adults can slowly relearn to treat the young people around them thoughtfully and helpfully. As you become an adult, you can learn to do this for the other adults and can gradually help them to relax and act toward young people in ways that will allow the young people to grow up without being hurt.

how to understand, handle, and help the people around you

18.076 It is possible to understand the behavior of the people around you, to protect yourself, at least to some extent, from the harm that it may tend to cause you, to be helpful to people in a temporary way by directing their attention toward topics that they can handle with more satisfactory results than they have been achieving and by assisting them to get a better grasp of how to handle the situation they're in, *and* on at least some occasions, to assist them to discharge the distress recordings which are creating problems for themselves, for other people in their environment, and, on occasion, for you.

Not every situation permits all these things to be done simultaneously, but often some of these things can be done in ways to improve the situation and in ways that allow more of them to be done.

18.077 People who have reached the age where they are or could be grandparents to young people are likely to have a tendency (not always dependably present in any particular case) to have learned something from their own experience of being parents. Perhaps they have learned by watching their own contemporaries go through the experience of being parents and have observed and regretted some of the mistakes that they carried out in *their role* as parents. This may make it possible for a young person to counsel these older people and help them achieve considerable re-evaluation and improvement of functioning by asking what it was like for them to deal with their children when they were parents. They can be asked what they wished they had done differently than they did when they were parents. They can be asked what do they wish they had explained to their children when their children were young that they now realize that they failed to do. This will achieve considerable re-evaluation on the part of the grandparents, will lead to them being more validating and supportive of their grandchildren, and will make it possible for them to have a warm relationship with their grandchildren to the benefit of both groups. It is also possible to ask people of the age of grandparents what ways they wish they had been treated when they were children and to be reassuring to them, if they become immersed in regrets, by pointing out that you think their children (the grandchildren's parents) turned out well.

18.078 In the case of parents, or people of parental age, young people can be very wise and effective by asking for a meeting of the family once every week or fortnight or so where everyone gets a turn to speak without interruption of what they think is excellent about their family, what they think is functioning well, some excellences about each individual member of the family, and, when everyone has had a turn saying these things, where you then propose that the work and responsibility for family activities be divided with every member of the family having some specific responsibilities which he or she will carry out and will be praised for carrying out whenever he or she does so.

18.079 Big efforts are currently underway to remedy some of the worst abuses in the teaching of young people in schools. These efforts take many forms. Middle-class families in small numbers are beginning to resort to "home schooling," which is a sort of a recognition of how inefficient the teaching process has been in the regular schools and how the development of home study and parental teaching allows much more efficient instruction when the parents are thoughtful about the process. It also tends to have other benefits, such as allowing the young student more initiative in learning and more choice of what or how he or she learns.

There are also "movements" of teachers and educators to examine the actual role of the schools and correct some of the worst abuses.

One of the fundamental contributions that a knowledge of Re-evaluation Counseling can bring to students and teachers is the recognition that the oppressive society does not have as a main goal the child acquiring information and skills, but rather has as its main goal the conditioning of the child to conform to the acceptance of oppression and to submission to an assigned role in the operation of *exploitation*.

This makes it seem likely that any very satisfactory solution to the handling of teachers by young people will eventually require complete change in the nature of the society. It also opens the door to the recognition that informed struggle in this direction can make a profound contribution to the general liberation movement of all people and the replacement of the oppressive society with a rational, cooperative one.

Important additions to a program for educational change would include the complete peerness of teacher, student, and parent; the requirement for complete mutual respect for and from these principal groups; and the central role of *consultation* with the student, which is even more important than the *informing* of the student which has traditionally been given the greater emphasis.

18.080 The relationship between young people of different ages has tended to be spoiled in the past by the insertion of oppression between them. We have already had some examples of such unhappy situations being replaced by the most marvelous mutual respect, cooperation, and affection. This has taken place within families as well as between children of different families. An older child, encouraged to think of himself or herself as a model, an object of admiration by the younger child, can become extremely effective in the informing and maturing of the younger ones, and, if praised and appreciated for this role, will be motivated toward positive achievements of a profound degree.

A younger child, encouraged to express admiration and appreciation, can furnish great encouragement and assistance to the older, and of course the praise, encouragement, and appreciation by the older to the younger will cut through the previously existing attitudes in the culture with profound effect.

Praise and appreciate and look up to the older child. Praise and appreciate and give high, relaxed expectation to the younger one. The relations between the pair will flourish as they are encouraged to take these attitudes toward each other.

18.081 It takes a great deal of mistreatment to change a potentially marvelously functioning newborn human into the distressed, poorly functioning adult which our society typically produces. Much of this mistreatment is done by the individual child himself or herself and done by these children to each other. The phenomenon we have called *internalized oppression* is the basis for this hugely destructive process. Hurts are installed that have the effect of the person continuing to hurt himself or herself, or members of the group continuing to hurt each other. It is as if the scheme had been designed by an "evil genius," although of course there was no intelligence connected with it, it was just the working out of the contagious spread of distress patterns. Given intelligent intervention by an older person, the process can be interrupted dramatically, effectively, and successfully. Examples were visible to some extent in the "socialist" schools established after the October revolution in Russia, in the treatment of very young children after Chinese liberation in the 1950's, and in the relationships between children in the days of the Kibbutzim in early Israel. Modelling of thoughtful, curious behavior to each other and of praise and encouragement being used instead of criticism, allowed the marvelous progress of young people, at least until the impact of the adult society upon them at a later age.

The information that we have winnowed out of our experiences in the Re-evaluation Counseling movement so far tends to approximate the thinking that young people would develop for themselves in a society and culture where hurts were prevented from taking place and quickly discharged upon and re-evaluated when they did occur. This means that people from the time of their birth are ready to accept the information that we have been able to garner about rational human functioning (which we have called "Re-evaluation Counseling"). They would handle relationships with each other undestructively if they had access to this information.

The innate nature of a child is ready to learn and use all the information of Re-evaluation Counseling to begin with. It fits his or her own nature, and access to this information, and encouragement in the use of it, can and will be very effective in practice. *A child of any age is ready to hear, understand, and use RC.*

Even among such "partially re-emerged" RCers as the writer and many of the readers of this book might describe themselves to be, there is still the tendency to think of young people as only "partially human" or "on their way to becoming human," rather than seeing the obvious truth that vast intelligence is with every human at least from their birth on, so we have had the tendency to offer our young people only portions of the "Re-evaluation Counseling" information that we have acquired.

Children are ready to understand all of RC and need to have it all available to them!

Adult intervention into patterned quarrels and difficulties between children may be necessary to begin with, but if the adult not only counsels the children well and encourages and allows sufficient discharge, but also explains the situation in terms of the reality of what is going on and how it can be solved, the children can be encouraged to take turns counseling each other, and in the future can often solve any difficulties that arise by themselves and become a spreading influence with their playmates and associates.

If you are young you are also smart. When someone is acting badly, say something nice to the person, appreciate him or her, like him or her, then ask him or her to help you make everybody feel better. You will handle the situation. He or she will learn from you, and together you can handle later situations with more and more skill and ease.

18.082 The first thing to do with people younger than yourself is to *like* them. The second thing to do is to *let them know* you like them. Smile at them, touch them, tell them you like them. This will make anything you do together after that easier and more fun.

18.083 When you look at a baby, look into the baby's eyes. Let the baby look back into your eyes. Smile relaxedly, easily. Don't make faces or strange noises like adults tend to do. Let the the baby look at you. If the baby makes a noise, make the same noise back once in a calm, relaxed way. If the baby makes a lot of noises at you, smile easily and nod your head, and then make a nice noise back to the baby like he or she is making to you.

18.084 Girls and boys are both very special, but they are not very different from each other. The oppressive society tells them that they are very different and tries to make them believe they are very different, but although they have some small physical differences, they think the same way, they feel the same way, they like other people the same way. Girls and boys like each other a little extra much because they are *a little bit different*, but they also like each other easily and they like each other a lot because they are so very much the same.

18.085 If you are old enough to start working (I had a regular job when I was four years old), it will be good for you to know that work is a lot of fun and one of the most interesting things you will ever do in your life if it isn't spoiled by the society and the way employers and bosses try to "make money" out of your working. If we ever get a good society, work will be one of the nicest things in our lives.

18.086 Policemen and soldiers are told that they must be ready to hurt people and so they get in the habit of acting scary. Their job isn't really to scare people. Treat them respectfully, ask questions of them when you need to, ask them for help if you need help, but do not be afraid of them. They are just people wearing special clothes called "uniforms."

18.087 Doctors are people who have special training to help you stay well and help you feel better if you are sick. Tell them you want to know what they are doing when they do something with you and ask them to tell you why they are doing it. If they don't do this when you ask them, tell your parents after you leave the doctor that you want to go to a different doctor next time, and tell them why.

18.088 There are some people who have been hurt so badly and have so many distress patterns that they can't keep themselves from trying to hurt other people. Stay away from such people as much as you can. Ask someone else to help you if a person like this gives you trouble, but be kind to him or her. It will help him or her to try to be kind to you.

18.089 *Strangers* are just people that you haven't gotten acquainted with yet. Even if they speak a different language, wear different clothes than you are used to seeing people wear, and act differently than you are used to having people act, they are people who will turn out, if you ever get the chance to become acquainted with them, to be very much like yourself and all the other people you know.

in the present oppressive society, learning is not the primary function of the schools

18.090 The present school systems' basic function is to condition people to play their assigned roles in society. Communicating accurate information to students, or "allowing" them or assisting them to learn, is, at best, an incidental or accidental process in these present school systems. Different kinds of education are organized for people who are expected to do heavy, boring, repetitive work as members of the working class, for people who are expected to be skilled workers as members of the working class, for people who are expected to become "middle class," that is, people who are expected to use more or less of their intelligence in the service of the owning-class people, and owning-class people, who are expected to rigidly play the role of enforcing oppression, maintaining the system, and acquiring wealth and power to be used for maintaining the oppressive structure. In schools at the present, the students, the teachers, the administrators, the parents, are basically good human beings, but they have all been conditioned to play certain roles in the class society. The pressure on all sections is to conform and to force the individuals to conform to the existing oppressive and increasingly unworkable society and its economic structure. This all leads to putting a great deal of pressure on the students.

Students are basically very eager to learn, but have already been hurt and made discouraged about themselves in many ways, have been trained to be antagonistic to each other, to compete instead of cooperate, and to treat each other with invalidation and violence.

Teachers have been conditioned to believe that submission, "composure," and "order" are the first requirements for their classrooms. They, in general, will be pulled to "teach" students in the same ways that they were mistaught.

Parents are under such heavy pressure in their lives as to feel required to support the same policies being applied to their children as the ones that interfered with their own learning when they were young.

As a result of all these destructive, patterned policies which are acting on all of the people who are involved in schools, the schools tend to function more and more poorly or desperately, and their misfunctioning is one of the sharpest indications of the imminent collapse of the oppressive society.

(Movements are underway for liberation activities for students, for teachers, for administrators, and for parents, and these movements are playing a very encouraging role in exploring the possibilities of rational functioning of schools. What they are learning will constitute programs and policies for the schools under the non-oppressive societies which inevitably will replace the present poorly functioning structures.)

human beings of any gender are much alike

18.091 Boys and girls are very much like each other. The differences between boys and girls that we seem to observe are not, in the main, differences that are natural but are the result of young people being forced to be certain ways that the oppressive society expects of them. Girls are naturally as strong and as brave and as smart as boys are. Boys are naturally as beautiful, as gentle, and as kind as girls are. Being told that we are different or must be different is a kind of hurtful nonsense that we will eventually interrupt. Both boys and girls are all-round human beings and can do anything, be anything, achieve anything they wish.

it is possible to be your real self

18.092 You do not have to give up on your desire to enjoy life, to have fun, to have a good life. Even if things are very hard for you sometimes (even for long periods of time), it will always be possible eventually to find a way out of difficulties and live a good life. There are other people that you can make contact with who will be eager to join you in cooperating in having a good life. Most people privately still wish for a good life even though they have gotten no further for a long while than just wishing for it.

18.93 There are groups of people (which I can show you how to contact) who are deliberately working out how to attain the good life you want and how to support each other in achieving this. These people are a network (a thin network so far) of people in many countries of the world that are learning how to *listen to each other*. They are learning how to help each other cry and shake and laugh and yawn in order to become free of past hurts. These people will encourage you and support you. There are only a few hundred thousand people in this network as yet. It may not be easy to make contact with it, but it can be done. You'll eventually be able to be in touch. Perhaps very soon.

18.94 It may seem to you that you are so surrounded, and dictated to, by grown-ups who have poor ideas that they were forced to believe when they were young, that there is no help, that you are without resource.

Actually, if you share this information with other young people, some of them will be glad to join with you. Together you can survive well and have a good life even for the remaining time that you will seem to be "under the thumb" of adults and their patterns. Explain this situation to a friend your own age or somewhere near your own age. Work out an agreement that you will take turns listening to each other. Try exchanging the position of listening and being listened to every fifteen minutes, or every half-hour, whichever time you find works out for the two of you. You don't have to be rigid about what you decide. Be flexible about it. Just try to see that your turns of being listened to are roughly the same length for both of you. When this is working well, think of a friend that you both know and invite him or her to be part of the procedure where the three of you take turns. After you have gotten used to doing this, find a fourth person. If you are both boys to start out with, think of inviting a girl to join. If you are all girls up until now, think of inviting a boy to join. When there are four or more of you, you can all meet together part of the time, and part of the time divide into two's and three's so you get longer turns being listened to.

helping people younger than yourself

18.95 You can make very good friends of people younger than yourself by deciding to admire, praise, and be friendly to them. If you've been in a habit of "putting down" or "bossing" the people younger than you, you can just stop doing that. (You learned to do this from the way you were treated by older people.) You can listen with warmth and liking while younger people talk and think, out loud. It will make a big difference in their lives. They will love and admire you very much as a result.

18.96 Something else that will be fun for you to do is to spend time looking pleased with younger young people and let them get over the embarrassment that has been put upon them by others. They will laugh a lot. You will laugh with them. If you listen for a long time (a little at a time), they will work their way through much of their shyness and embarrassment and will appreciate and like you very much.

After you have done this for awhile, it will be alright to say, "Now will you listen to me for a while?" and ask the young person or persons to take a turn *listening*. Once they get used to it, they will enjoy listening as well as being listened to.

18.97 You will find that you can get the grown-ups around you to laugh a lot (and even cry, yawn, and shake) if you say nice things to them and tell them you like them and why you like them. They will feel embarrassed to begin with and are likely to even scold you and tell you "you are silly" or "you're being silly" or "behave yourself" or things like that. If they do, just tell them, thanks, but then go right back to saying nice things to them. You are being very helpful to people when you do this. They will come back for more even though they may still have the habit of reproaching you. When you do this you are being a very skillful "counselor," that is, someone who listens well in a way that helps people.

refuse to accept any oppressions

18.98 Refuse to agree to be oppressed as you grow older. Sometimes it will be smart to pretend to accept the oppression temporarily until you can find a way to get away from it, but don't ever accept it in your own mind. No one deserves to be oppressed, and if you don't let yourself accept it in your own mind, you can always find a way to get rid of it.

don't participate in oppressing anyone else

18.99 At times in the past you may have gotten (or will get in the future) messages from some grown-ups that people around you whom you know are poorer than you or don't have as nice clothes as you or don't live in as nice houses as you do, "are not as good as you are" and "should be looked down upon." You know better than that, but in your efforts to please the grown-ups around you and do what they say or copy the way they act, you may have given in to this a little bit. You may have treated such people poorly or without much consideration. You may even have "thought" that some other people weren't as smart as you because they didn't get good grades in school as easily as you did. All this is terribly wrong nonsense.

18.100 It is also possible that you may have gotten wrong messages that the people with nice, new clothes and better bicycles and up-to-date shoes and who live in nice houses should be envied and "looked up to" on that account. This is also terrible nonsense.

18.102 All people are equal, all people are wonderful, all people should be treated with respect and liking. If you were to give in to this "looking up to some people and looking down at others" it would spoil your life. It could make your life very narrow. It has made their lives narrow for many of the grown-ups you know.

18.103 Remember *everyone* is very good. Everyone is very fine. Basically, people are in every case infinitely precious, and along with being, each one of them, *completely unique*, they also are *fundamentally just alike*. The differences between people are very interesting and make them even more valuable to know. People are never to be envied nor looked down upon for their differences.

18.104 Always support everyone as best you can and model for others and lead others as well as you can whenever you can.

18.105 Trust your own thinking. Other people's thinking can be important *information* for you, but only your own thinking is thinking *for you*.

18.106 Enjoy your life thoroughly.

18.107 Lead the world. It is waiting for your leadership.

19. THE ROLE OF RELIGION IN HUMAN AFFAIRS

there are understandable reasons why people create religions

19.001 As human intelligences developed, they were confronted with great complexities in their environments, not only in terms of the objects that compose their environments and these objects' enormous complexity (which present humans are still exploring in greater and greater detail) but also in the dynamic complexities of the interaction of the surrounding objects and energies and entities with each other.

19.002 These complexities and the processes which they participate in must have been interpreted by early human intelligences as purposeful since the activities of the humans themselves would certainly have seemed to them purposeful. With this in mind it is understandable that the notion of *purpose* would occur to the human intelligences as they observed the operation of the universe around them.

19.003 The observation of *another human's* activities by a person would tend to reinforce the idea of purposefulness. The observation by a *young* human of the apparently greater ability, power, and purposefulness of *adult* humans would almost certainly evolve the concept of "a *greater* purpose" as an explanation for the greater complexity and the wider spread of activity of the larger scene in which the humans lived. Great storms, persistent re-growth in the environment, the dependably benign character of natural food supplies, all must have led inevitably to the concept of a "caretaker" type of entity who supported humans' desires under certain conditions, and brought down calamity upon them in other situations.

painful-emotion recordings enter the picture

19.004 Although it is only very recently that we have had an intelligent and useful understanding of the vulnerability of human intelligences to being interrupted and replaced by rigid, unintelligent distress recordings, this phenomenon must have been operating from the very beginnings of human intelligence. We currently observe all around us the installation of distress recordings on very young children by the actions of their parents and other adults who dominate them, dictate to them, "punish" them, and insist on distressed and distressful explanations of what is taking place, in opposition to the child's still-operating intelligence's more accurate appraisal of situations. It is no great leap from the observation of a dominating adult's enforcement of younger and weaker humans to the invention of super-powerful "mother goddesses" or hierarchical male "gods" who rule the earth and all its events wilfully and without reasonable human motives.

19.005 Although the history of all, or nearly all, religions reveals repeated attempts to introduce humanness, kindness, or even a sense of humor into the concepts of whatever functioning god figures exist in a particular religion, it's fairly plain that painful emotions, including fear, were the functioning basis in all cases and that they have been emphasized and added to almost consistently reinforce the "authority" of all or almost all religions.

19.006 Prior to the development of class societies, the enforcement of others by a dominating religious figure or set of rituals would tend to reach no farther than the limits of a family or small tribe. With the development of classism and the more numerous populations which the enslavement of the majority made possible (because of the improved organization of agriculture and animal husbandry), the religions came to be taken over by the oppressive society and became a principal tool *of the oppression*. To the authority wielded by the whip and the knout, the crucifix and the gallows, was added the authority of the priest and the god or gods. Most religions, most of the time, have served the functioning of economic oppression and exploitation since that day.

19.007 Changes in the economic systems and the increasing domination of the environment by the more numerous and better organized humans have brought about a great series of *modernizations* of religions. Some have disappeared and are cherished only in surviving literature from the ancients. Others have been replaced, reformed, and divided with a particular "wing" of the continuing religion prepared for each class division or political trend within the classes.

19.008 The dominant religions of today—Islam, Buddhism, Judaism, Christianity, Hinduism, Confucianism, and Taoism—have in most cases been built around outstanding figures from the past who were humanist reformers compared to the milieu in which they operated, extolling in some way the goodness of humanity and holding out goals for fulfillment, enjoyment, and love between people—and between people and the environments in which they lived.

Large numbers of people still hold loyalty to their understanding of the principles that these religious figures of the past put forward, but the religions which have been organized around them have been largely taken over by the oppressive society which continues to manipulate them and their relations with their followers in order to try to ensure submission by the people who follow the religion to exploitation by the current society and by the ruling classes of that society. This is carried out through imposing fear and threat of rejection and condemnation by their fellow worshipers, or even by the threat of punishment in a "future life."

ways in which existing religions can be useful to conforming "believers"

19.009 If the postulated "god" is presented as a benign, supportive-of-humans entity, it is possible for the person practicing the religion to "borrow confidence" from the presumed goodwill of the god entity.

19.010 The use of communication through "prayer" to the god entity can afford the believing human access to an ever-available listener who is interested and can be assumed to be benign and whose attention assists the person (who is doing the praying) to discharge and think out problems that would be unsolvable without the god-like "listener" and this listener's presumed goodwill or even this listener's "support" for the prayerful one's desired goals.

19.011 The holding of group "religious services" can be useful as a means of bringing together people of similar upward-trend beliefs or commitments to interact jointly and encourage each other toward their upward-trend goals. Repeating aloud in unison some of the agreed-upon "articles of faith" or the singing together of religious songs whose lyrics reassert some of the upward-trend teachings of the founders of the religion can have the effect on the worshipers of reasserting their confidence in and their commitment to the positive goals of the religion.

19.012 Under conditions of extreme oppression, the holding of group religious services can provide a "cover" for the oppressed people to encourage each other in their resistance to the oppression and communicate to each other in the guise of religious words and songs the goals of liberation, which would be otherwise ruthlessly oppressed by the society. Very earthy and immediate goals can be expressed and understood if cloaked in the guise of "after enlightenment" or "future rewards in paradise (or Heaven)."

19.013 Oppressed people struggling for liberation can reach to other groups and attempt to make allies of them through appealing to commonalities in the religious beliefs (or even to a *formal pretense of commonalities* of religious beliefs) between the two groups.

20. THE PROSPECT OF COMPLETELY IDENTIFYING ONESELF WITH REALITY AND COMPLETELY REJECTING THE PSEUDO-REALITY OF DISTRESS

the complete "all-rightness" of oneself

20.001 General positive statements appeared early in the development of RC. One of the first was the sentence: "All is well." In the development of "Frameworks" and "Synopses" the culmination of the statements of which they consist would be a triumphant validation of the client. For brief periods of time some years ago Co-Counselors experimented with making pronouncements such as, "I am God" or "I am immortal," with interesting and generally positive results in terms of discharge and re-evaluation.

More recently the surprising effects of the "understatement" techniques seem to allow clients to bypass the often thick accumulation of internalized invalidations of themselves that living in this society has placed upon them and allow them to envisage "finally realizing that he (or she) is completely *all right* in every way—and always has been!" This, for many clients, seems to afford an enduring glimpse into the splendid reality of *being an awarely intelligent entity!* At the time of this writing it appears as if this can become an attitude *permanently* possessed by the client who has once grasped it. I anticipate that this will cut through and allow the discharge of the remaining accumulation of distress with greater ease and speed than we have usually attained in the past.

20.002 Gaining such contact with one's own essential, completely positive nature, the creation of which is probably the greatest triumph of the universe in the upward trend direction to date, will certainly be a path that every re-emergent human will attempt to follow.

20.003 Even casual observation of the humans in the present societies makes it plain that they are greatly preoccupied (whenever they have leisure to think about it) with an attempt to establish a similar benign and satisfying view of at least one other person whom the first human can esteem as deeply as he or she has had a glimpse of esteeming himself or herself. Even the thoroughly "messed up" current societies permit and encourage apparently intense pursuits of "love." This seems to be, inherently, an attempt to attain an attitude toward at least one other person similar to the one we have been struggling hard to attain about our first-person selves (and, in my opinion, are presently on the verge of achieving).

"Falling in love" with another person has been commonly confused with an attempt at fulfillment of one's sexual "drives." There is a built-in, inherent drive in humans to participate in sex in order to reproduce our species. This sex "drive" is separate from the loftiest, most exciting, and challenging aspects of "love."

Those of us who have struggled to distinguish the built-in "drive" towards participation in sex from the completely positive interaction of one's intelligence with another intelligence are universally clear that the latter is the most rewarding aspect of our lives, however infrequently it has been achieved to date. Our finest art and literature, poetry and music have been dedicated to this elusive goal. Paraphrasing Robert Frost, the rational attitude of any human is,

> "No one can know how glad I am to find
> In any place the slightest trace of mind."

20.004 My own experiences as a "standard bearer" in the struggle of Re-evaluation Co-Counselors to find our way out of our patterned existences are finally allowing me, after many years of difficulty left by very early chronic rejections, to know that I am deeply cherished by large numbers of people who know me. These people seem to find in me some characteristics which I am not yet able to see clearly but which seem to be related to my confidence about the benign nature of reality and the great satisfaction of relating to other intelligences. This leaves me very pleased with myself, in ways that I was not able to easily accept before, with having "fallen in love" with thousands of people and having tried in numerous ways, some rational and some irrational, to experience and enjoy the resulting closeness.

20.005 At a conference of about a hundred and thirty RC leaders in 1995, the attendees spontaneously, without any planning for it (or even any expectation on my part), expressed their overwhelming delight at simply *being with each other*. To be in each other's presence and enjoy their common dedication to actual reality was obviously refreshing and exciting.

20.006 I think that it is possible that this is one of the most important functions of the Re-evaluation Counseling *Communities*. At least a few hundred thousand people are awarely reaching to realize their goodness, to realize their basic nature of unpatterned intelligence, and to realize their confident destiny as the lucky advanced scouts of the great expedition of humankind into the future of the universe.

20.007 All of existing humanity will, I think, feel like this in the future, as they stream out to the stars and the galaxies, carrying the intelligence that evolved so slowly and has had so many obstacles to overcome on our planet to the far corners of the universe.

21. HOW TO BEGIN RE-EVALUATION COUNSELING IN A NEW LOCATION OR WITH NEW PEOPLE

situation: you have learned Re-evaluation Counseling in an already-organized Community and are familiar with some of the benefits of using it

21.001 Begin by reviewing in your mind the people to whom you will have convenient access, *or* that you "find interesting," *or* that you "wish you knew better." You might also think of significant people that you will have to resist your own chronic patterns in order to establish friendships with. Make a list of as many as fifty such people if you can, or as close to that many as you find possible.

21.002 Make an aware decision to: (1) start with a group that will be relatively easy for you to pursue contact with; or (2) start with a group such that, if they become interested, they will tend to bring large numbers of other people into using Re-evaluation Counseling as they begin to practice it. You can add other groups later, such as the group of people you will feel guilty about if you do not attempt to reach, or any other groups which you have any other motivations for seeking out. Have sessions for yourself as a client about which group would really make the most sense for you to begin to contact. Then choose one group and, having chosen it, stick with it for the first six months of your effort.

21.003 Decide which member of your chosen group you wish to approach first. Make contact with him or her. Arrange to bump into him or her on the street, look for him or her at the ball game, or speak to him or her after church, after first having practiced in front of a mirror at saying to him or to her, "Hi. I've been wanting to get to know you. My name is ————. What's your name? What do you know about this neighborhood that I ought to know?" (It's all right for all of the preceding to occur over several meetings.)

Meanwhile, listen, don't talk fast, look relaxed, look at the person as if you are pleased by his or her existence. If the person begins talking, pay warm attention and don't talk very much yourself. Remain casual and relaxed, at least in appearance. When the person begins to talk—listen, listen, listen.

21.004 After your fourth such contact with each person on your list, say something like, "I am thinking of starting a class about people learning to listen to each other. I was in one where I lived before and I enjoyed it a lot, and the person who taught it has been encouraging me to start teaching one since I moved away from that neighborhood. I'm planning to do an introduction to it at my house (or at the public library or the at the local bank branch community meeting room, or at the local mosque or Methodist church). Do you know some people that might be interested?"

21.005 Write to the International Reference Person of the Re-evaluation Counseling Communities and ask for a one-time teaching credential, or ask who the Regional Reference Person is for your Region and apply to her or him for a teaching credential.

21.006 Do an introductory lecture. Announce the time of the first class. Either tell them the cost that you think will be acceptable to them, or say that you're teaching the first series of classes free and letting the people decide after their first series of classes what you should charge for the second series of classes.

21.007 Hold your first class. Make sure everyone gets to tell about himself or herself through having a turn answering your particular questions. Look at every person in the class as if you like her or like him. Tell them what an interesting group they are (they will be), and at the end of the evening tell them that you'll see them at the next class. Ask a promising person to be your assistant teacher, and give each person in the class assignments to read literature and report on it at following meetings. At each class meeting let each member of the class report on what happened during his or her past week. Have each person who had a session as client report on that experience, followed by a report from the counselor in that session. Be pleased with the meeting. Ask each person at the end of each class to say briefly what he or she liked best about the evening.

21.008 Explain how easily a support group can work. Encourage people to try support group meetings in different corners of the meeting room by answering questions for a men's support group such as, "What was good about being a man this week? What was hard about being a man this week?" and for a woman's support group, similar questions about being a woman. For any other support groups that seem to be called for, use comparable questions. Explain to the class members how easy it is to organize support groups in many different situations. Hold out the perspective that organizing support groups will be a powerful tool for them to use to accomplish their goals in many parts of their lives.

21.009 Enthuse regularly and privately to each assistant teacher about how well he or she has done and is doing. Enthuse to each support group leader about how well her or his support group is functioning.

21.010 Keep expanding your teaching until all the world's people are participating in classes that "caught fire" and spread out across the world from the successful class you taught.

situation: you have heard about Re-evaluation Counseling from a friend or from reading some literature and want to find out how to "get started" and try to use it with your neighbors

21.011 Write to any address that you have available for anybody who is a member of the Re-evaluation Counseling Communities. (An address that is likely to be stable for a long time is The Re-evaluation Counseling Communities, 719 Second Avenue North, Seattle, Washington, 98109, USA. An e-mail address that is likely to be stable for many years to come is <ircc@rc.org>. A telephone number is (U.S.) 206-284-0311. A fax number for Re-evaluation Counseling is (U.S.) 206-284-8429. Send the following message or its equivalent to any of these: "Please send me information as to how to organize participation for myself and/or my friends in the practice of Re-evaluation Counseling and permission to do so to (your name, your address, your e-mail address, or your telephone number, or your fax number).

21.012 Communicate with any knowledgeable Re-evaluation Counseling contact who is furnished to you. Ask for the possibilities for attending classes or support groups or workshops or conferences.

21.013 Ask for and order the introductory books in your own language if they are already translated, in any other language that you know if they are not already available in your own language. (These two books are *The Human Side of Human Beings*, four dollars, an introduction to the theory, and the *Fundamentals of Co-Counseling Manual*, six dollars. If your economic situation makes it very difficult for you to afford these books, ask the Community to furnish them as a gift from the people who are already Co-Counseling.) Ask for a recent issue of *Present Time*, the quarterly magazine of Re-evaluation Counseling, either for three dollars and fifty cents in the U.S., or for four dollars outside the U.S., or as a gift under the second conditions above.

21.014 As you begin to learn to use Re-evaluation Counseling, if it should happen that you run into unanticipated difficulties, ask the experienced Co-Counselors and any leaders of the Communities for assistance. You will have to think and make some efforts to get the benefits of Re-evaluation Counseling, but you deserve assistance with any difficulties from people who have more experience from the past than you have yet attained.

21.015 Write to the Re-evaluation Counseling Communities for catalogs listing the great variety of literature covering the special applications and uses of Re-evaluation Counseling so that you have access to the rapidly growing store of knowledge that is accumulating in this field.

21.016 Plan on becoming an assistant teacher, support group leader, RC teacher, Area Reference Person, Regional Reference Person, International Liberation Reference Person, Information Coordinator, Community librarian, newsletter editor, journal editor, workshop leader, translator, or even International Reference Person, as your skills develop and your mastery of building a rational society develops.

22. COMPLETELY INTELLIGENT FUNCTIONING

22.001 The natural way of functioning for human beings is to *be intelligent* in everything we do. To propose this is not a *new* program. It is not a proposal only for members and leaders of the Re-evaluation Counseling Communities. To be intelligent in everything we do has been the intuitive (though seldom clearly faced or fulfilled) program of *all* human beings for a long time.

Big advances in this direction have already been achieved. The presently existing nearly six billion human beings are all struggling, however unawarely, to achieve this. They are all making some gains in this direction.

The irrational actions persuaded and enforced upon us in the past have gradually been replaced with newer sets of irrational actions, which may incidentally and accidentally have increased some of the survival potential of humans, at least up until the present. These changes and any slight improvement in the society's functioning as a result of them are used by the oppressive society as an argument for support of the oppressive society's activities. As an example, humans for the first hundred thousand years of our species' existence could expect to live to an average of ten to twenty years in their lifetimes. Now most humans currently alive can expect a total lifetime of fifty to eighty years, depending on the intensity of the oppression and exploitation they suffer. Much of this improvement has taken place during the last hundred and fifty years. If our actions were to not just improve somewhat, but become totally rational, much greater improvement in the functioning of human beings would quickly take place.

22.002 These temporary improvements in the functioning of the oppressive class societies have allowed enormous increases in the total number of humans. This increase is threatening to overcrowd the planet. It has also in many other ways made a continuation of the domination of human behavior by irrationalities extremely dangerous, dangerous to human survival and to the health of the planet.

22.003 Re-evaluation Counselors, in their forty-seven-year existence so far as a group, have moved toward agreeing and concurring on a goal that could be stated as "becoming more rational." Attempts to reach this goal have taken many different forms.

Campaigns have been organized to contradict and discharge particular categories of irrational patterns. These campaigns continue to take place. Some of the results have been that we have learned to routinely contradict open invalidations of ourselves and of others (frequently marveling as we did this at the *volume* of invalidations that we came to realize had accumulated in our lives). We have dug away at the *powerlessness* that has seemed to enshroud almost every human's almost every act. We have located and exposed some of the big oppressions (sexism, racism, classism, etc.). We have established good *directions against* these major oppressions. We have made significant progress at lessening the damage caused by these oppressions to at least some of their victims.

22.004 Yet, until now, the idea of achieving a sharp break from *any* insidious domination of our lives by distress patterns (which to an "observer from Mars" might have seemed an obvious and exciting place to begin this work) has hardly even been stated as a goal within the Re-evaluation Counseling Community, let alone made a central activity. Judging by most verbal and written discussions to date, *re-emergence* is still treated as a hopeful but possibly interminable process, devoutly to be wished for, but not yet planned and organized for as an immediate and realizable goal.

22.005 I propose that we as of this moment take up the beginnings of change in this respect. My proposal arises out of certain observations and out of certain theoretical considerations. (One observation is that Re-evaluation Counselors are, in general, still heavily loaded with embarrassment, which they seldom seek to discharge directly and seldom "tackle" in most discharge activities except in the guise of "entertainment" where "someone else's embarrassment" becomes an excuse for discharging one's own.)

22.006 As far as I have contact with the current level of Co-Counseling (through my attendance at and leadership of workshops, through telephone, e-mail, and regular mail communication), habitual making of excuses for one's continuing addictive behavior is widespread. Openly patterned behavior is "tolerated." A client's rationalization of and defense of his or her own poor behavior (often by leaders as well as rank-and-filers) is often "handled" (more correctly "not handled") by "changing the subject."

22.007 Some small challenges to this state of affairs are beginning to take place. I know of a few groups and classes which have begun discussions in which each person takes a turn answering the question, "How do you lie to yourself?"

A few groups of Co-Counselors have actually issued and accepted challenges to and from their fellow group members to jointly examine each person's current functioning. In these discussions, consensus is sought by the group on which parts of a Co-Counselor's current usual behavior are clearly the acting out of patterns. Some groups have pledged each other to eliminate these patterns completely.

22.008 In our lives we have always attempted, in making important decisions, to distinguish between "good" and "bad," between "correct" and "incorrect," between "honorable" and "dishonorable." These and many similar distinctions were attempts to make a *general* distinction. Perhaps the general distinction we have been seeking to make could be well made by calling it the distinction between "an action that is arising out of intelligent thinking" and "an action that is arising out of the influence of distress patterns and misinformation."

Recent discussions in RC about regaining "integrity" and "courage" are probably also attempts to state the same distinction, a distinction between "intelligent" and "unintelligent."

22.009 I think it is time for all Co-Counselors to make a decisive change in our attitude toward distress patterns. I think it is time for a total withdrawal from any toleration of or cooperation with distress-patterned behavior. I think at least some of us Co-Counselors have enough understanding of theory by now, enough clarity, enough experience in overcoming enough chronic patterns of a wide enough variety that we can make a sharp break with our past functioning in this way. I think we can very quickly produce a sizeable number of Co-Counselors who can assume the position of being bold models on this issue for the rest of us.

22.010 Let us move from *"struggling against"* patterns to *eliminating all patterns* from our functioning.

appreciations

The information in "THE LIST" has been created and discovered and tested by tens of thousands of people.

An early decision, agreed to by those of us who were trying to do Re-evaluation Counseling, was that we should not accept any "theory" from someone else's writing or thinking in the fields of psychology, social science, or counseling, that we should add to our growing structure of theory only information that *we* had tested and found dependable in our own work with people.

It was plain, from the first, that any useful knowledge that we evolved must be true of everybody, must work for everybody. Any time our first guesses didn't work, we "guessed again," as many times as necessary, until we had a piece of workable knowledge, at least for that person, in that session, on that day. Only when it worked for many clients on many days, would we cautiously begin to consider it an item of general knowledge, of general workability.

This general attitude has pretty well guided the accumulation of the knowledge in THE LIST. Many thousands of Co-Counselors have counseled hundreds of thousands of clients and have shared their successes, their failures, and their insights widely through all the many publications of RC. Agreement has continued to be reached as the theory has broadened and deepened and reached out to embrace much wider realms of activity.

Not everyone who made contributions to the theory is presently an active participant in Re-evaluation Counseling. I am deeply indebted to possibly two-score people who assisted me in reaching the early generalizations but whom I was not able to keep continued agreement with nor counsel well enough to help them with the difficulties that arose for them. To these men and women who made early contributions to RC, my deepest thanks. The continuing achievements we are making rest, in a very real sense, upon your early contributions. I am grateful to you, and I miss you.

To the large number of Regional Reference Persons, International Liberation Reference Persons, editors of RC journals, Information Coordinators for special subjects, Area Reference Persons, Alternate Area Reference Persons, Re-evaluation Counseling teachers and support group leaders, this is *your* book, the result of *your* work. I know you are grateful to, and appreciative of, each other for this great breakthrough into effective knowledge. I here formally express my thanks to each one of you. If I began mentioning names in this appreciation, a second book would be needed.

One name, however, should be mentioned. The task of assembling this volume had to be tackled at a time when my health was poor and my memory was working badly. I had experienced the deep anesthesia involved in open heart surgery. There had been careless language spoken in the surgery during the anesthesia. It took an extremely competent person, acting with deep commitment and determination, to make it possible to put together the first draft of THE LIST.

Katie Kauffman was the one who stepped into this breach and made it possible for that first, limited-circulation draft of THE LIST to come into existence.

When it came to expanding that first version, which was circulated only among a few top leaders of RC, she persisted with equal determination. This marvelous present volume, which is now in your hands and which I think can be an effective guarantee of the success of your future, is a result of the persistence and skill of Katie Kauffman.

APPENDIX

MY GOALS

	NEXT WEEK	NEXT MONTH	IN A YEAR	FOR 5 YEARS	FOR 20 YEARS	FOR ALWAYS
FOR ME						
FOR MY FAMILY						
FOR MY ALLIES						
FOR HUMANKIND						
FOR ALL LIVING THINGS						
FOR THE UNIVERSE						

COMMITMENTS

TO BE YOUR OWN ELEGANT, WISE, AND POWERFUL SELF

From this moment on, the *real* (your own name)! This will mean _____.

AGAINST PRETENSE

I am obviously completely incompetent and completely inadequate to handle the challenges which reality places before me.

However, (fortunately or unfortunately), I happen to be the best person available.

TO RECLAIM POWER

From now on I will see to it that everything I am in contact with works well, and I will not limit or pull back on my contacts. This will mean _____.

AGAINST IDENTIFYING ONESELF WITH PATTERNS

Recordings of past distress experiences have no power of their own at all.

They only contrive to give the appearance of power and influence to the extent that I slavishly submit to letting them use *my* power and *my* influence.

(If I think of them as pieces of recorded tape, they have, at most, a trifling historical significance, *unless* I insert them in the tape recorder that is myself and allow them to play me, an action which I am completely free to decide to do or not to do.)

Therefore, I now decide to deny any past distress any credibility in the present, or any influence or operation in my life.

And I will repeat this decision as often as necessary to free my life completely from the influence of past distress.

I can.

TO UNITY OF ALL HUMAN ASPIRATIONS

From now on I will inspire, lead, and organize all people to eliminate every form of humans' harming humans. This will mean _____.

TO END PREOCCUPATION WITH DISTRESS

It is logically possible and certainly desirable to end the ancient habit of paying attention to past distress and replace it by a new attitude or posture of paying attention to interesting and rewarding concerns, including the present-time situation, and so I now decide to do this and will repeatedly so decide until the ancient habit is broken.

A PROPOSED NEW FRONTIER COMMITMENT

Since thinking is necessarily fresh thinking, I hereby decide that I will never again let anything from the past influence the way I act in the present or future and I will repeat this decision as many times as necessary to achieve the clear-cut results that I want.

Against Identifying As A Victim

I now know that all my distresses are simply literal recordings from my past of distresses that I was not able to fully process at the time they occurred.

I also know that the information in these recordings, as well as all the information content of all my other experiences, have contributed in essential ways to making me the unique, wonderful, and completely good human being that I am.

I therefore promise that from this moment on I will cherish every moment of my past as being completely good and right. I will never wish that anything happened in any way other than precisely the way it did, and I will never act on the distortions of reality that these distresses imposed on me. Instead, I will discharge them to gain full and flexible access to the valuable and unique information that they contain.

COMMITMENTS, continued

BLACK PERSONS

For the complete liberation of my beautiful, wise, strong, and courageous black people, I solemnly promise I will always remember our/my own goodness and strength. I will fight against every division that tends to separate us from each other and from other people. I will settle for nothing less than complete liberation, complete equality, complete opportunity, and complete respect for everyone.

IRISH

For the long-range encouragement of my brave and noble people, I joyfully promise that, from this moment on, I will never again demean myself, or permit myself to be demeaned, nor permit any Irish person to be demeaned by anyone, including the person herself or himself, but shall stand as a proud example of the beauty, nobility, and wisdom of my wonderful people.

JEWISH

For the long-range survival of my people, I solemnly promise that, from this moment on, I will treat every person I meet as if she or he were eager to be my warm, close, dependable friend and ally, under all conditions. This will mean that _____.

CHICANO/A

In respect for my beautiful land and the enduring and proud people that inhabit it, I promise that I shall cherish my culture and language, unite my people, and, in alliance with all peoples of the world, see that all oppressions are ended.

PILIPINO/A

For the real freedom and unity of my beloved people, I solemnly promise that I will take pride in myself and the Pilipino Nation under all conditions.

I will work to wipe out the last vestiges of colonialism.

I will strengthen the bonds between all Pilipino people of whatever religion, language, or background, including the Philippines' sons and daughters overseas.

FOR A UNITED, FREE PHILIPPINES WITHOUT OPPRESSION.

ISRAELI

From now on I will see to it that everything I am in contact with works well. However, remembering that the person and the pattern are completely different and separate, and that the pattern is reinforced and the person is hurt by criticism, I promise that from now on I will never again speak or act critically to, or about, another person, including myself, but instead in every contact with every person I will find and express some appreciation of that person and of myself.

(in Hebrew)

בזכרי שהאדם והדפוס נפרדים ושונים זה מזה לגמרי,
ושהדפוס מחוזק על ידי ביקורת בעוד האדם נפגע ממנה,
אני מבטיח/ה מעתה ואילך לעולם לא אדבר ולא אפעל
בבקורתיות כלפי או אודות אדם אחר, כולל עצמי.
במקום זאת, בכל מגע עם כל איש ואישה אמצא ואבטא
הערכה כלשהיא לאיש/ה זו ולעצמי.

COMMITMENTS, continued

CANADIAN

I promise to always treasure our beautiful land and waters and our vast spaces and thriving cities, and to love every Canadian, celebrating our diversity, our Native hosts, and our anglophone, francophone, and other guests, and remembering our stamina and boldness now and throughout our history.

The True North, Strong and Free!

ARAB

In total respect for the beauty and wisdom of my people, I cheerfully promise that I will cherish my culture and language, and remember how delightful and important we are to all human beings.

ENGLISH

If the entire situation is taken into account, we English people have always done the very best that we could. And it wasn't all bad. The future, however, is going to be extraordinarily better. England expects every Co-Counselor, led by the working class, to model rapid re-emergence with full respect, equality, and support for every other human being.

NORTH ENGLAND

We northern English were colonised. We have been forced, for our survival, to oppress other folk in the name of English freedom and superiority. We resisted. We kept our pride and identity. Now, led by the working class, we can win the freedom of the North, from which to lead the liberation of all England.

SCOTTISH

I promise always to remember that my ain beautiful Scotland was betrayed, colonised, and impoverished to the present day by England. Partly we endured to stay alive. Partly we were occupied and colonised. Partly we were scattered around the world in order not to die. Now, however, our freedom can be redeemed. With the support of the working classes of the neighbouring countries, Scotland will be free. I promise to think, plan, and work unceasingly to that end. From now on Scotland will have at least one voice: MINE.

SCOTTISH OWNING CLASS

Bribed, bamboozled, moulded, and manipulated, we have remained 100% Scottish (with English accents). Now every privilege and advantage that was pushed on us will be turned to the support of Scotland's freedom. Head on, working class! We will follow! Whae hae!

SOUTH AFRICAN

I promise to remember to be proud of every tribe and race and its contribution to the history of South Africa, our rich and beautiful land, and our brilliant and promising future.

I promise to fight without pause for the elimination of racism, fear, greed, special privilege, and all other oppressive factors from the life of South African peoples and for the achievement of a just South African society based on equality and opportunity, sisterhood and brotherhood of all people living in South Africa.

For a united, peaceful, and prosperous South Africa for everyone! (said in Bushman, Zulu, Xhosa, Sotho, Afrikaans, and English).

COMMITMENTS, continued

JAPANESE-AMERICAN
With all my honor, I solemnly promise that from this moment on I will never again be less than fully visible as a proud, strong, beautiful, and dignified Japanese-American—Hi!

LES QUÉBÉCOIS
Pour moi, pour mon peuple, et pour mon beau pays je permets solennelement de toujours être fier(ère) de ma langue, de ma culture and de mon héritage, et d'exprimer cette fierté en tout temps.

D'éliminer tous les effects de l'oppression intériorisée sur moi-même et sur les autres québécois.

De travailler sans relâche à construire l'unité entre les québécois et à établir le respect et l'amitié entre tous les peuples d'Amérique du Nord. Je me souviens!

Vive le Québec libre!

QUÉBÉCOIS
For my own sake, and for the sake of my beautiful country and people, I solemnly promise that I will forever express pride in my heritage, my language, my culture, and my nation.

I will resist and eliminate all the effects of internalized oppression, upon myself and upon other Quebecois, and shall work unceasingly for unity among us and for respect and friendship between all the peoples of North America. I will remember!

We will be free!

LES ACADIENS
Sous le joug de l'éxil et de l'oppression, avec un coeur plein de confiance, d'espoir and de détermination, je promets de toujours chêrir mon héritage et ma culture. De toujours être fier(ère) d'être acadien(enne) et toujours être de tous les Acadiens où qu'ils soient. D'éxiger le respect pour tous les Acadiens de tous les autres peuples et d'offrir le respect en retour à tous les autres peuples, de favoriser la sororité entre tous les francophones du monde. Pour l'unité entre nous où que nous soyons!

Pour la fin de l'éxil!

Pour une Acadie libre!

ACADIANS
Out of exile and oppression with a heart full of faith, hope, and determination, I promise that I will forever cherish my heritage, my language, and my culture, that I will forever be proud that I am an Acadian and forever be proud of all Acadians everywhere, that I shall require respect for Acadians from all other peoples and shall offer respect to all other peoples in return. That I shall advance the sisterhood and alliance of all French-speaking people in the world.

For unity among us wherever we are!

For an end to exile! For a free Acadie!

PEOPLE OF CHINESE HERITAGE
For the liberation of all Chinese people (and there are a lot of us!), I promise to always be proud of my Chinese heritage, to remember my inherent closeness to my family and to all Chinese people, to openly show my love, and to be visible and proud—(pause)—forget being dignified!

COMMITMENTS, continued

SWEDISH

Som en stolt svensk vägrar jag att acceptera några gränser för min kärlek eller för mitt inflytande på världen. Jag kommer att visa fullständig respekt och förvänta mig allt av mina medmänniskor men aldrig låta snällhet eller omtanke om andra hindra mig från att ta de djärvaste initiativ.

SWEDISH

As a proud Swede I refuse to accept any limit for my love or my influence on the world. I will show complete respect and expect everything of my fellow human beings but never let kindness or caring about others prevent me from taking the boldest initiatives.

SWEDISH

From now on I promise that I, in every situation, will remind myself and others in a bold, self-assured, and enthusiastic way about what a special, unique, and unusual human being I am.

UNITED STATESER

For the survival and cleansing and long-range flourishing of my beloved United States, I promise that, from this moment on, I will speak out and act against every injustice, no matter how long-established. I will insist that the ideals and goals which inspired the founding of our country and for which our people have repeatedly striven and fought and sacrificed, shall be lived up to.

The United States is my country. I shall forever claim her with pride in her every good quality and with determination to correct any of her past, present, or future wrongs. My United States! With freedom and justice for all!

SOUTHERN UNITED STATESER

I sincerely promise that, from this moment on, I will never falter in my pride in being a Southerner, in my love for the beautiful Southern land, for the thoughtful courtesy and caring of its people, for their often-obscured but always-persisting resistance to oppression, for all our proud heritage and our brilliant future. I shall never lose sight of the fact that *all* people of the South are my sisters and brothers, nor allow any slight against any Southern person to go uncorrected, not even if voiced by Southerners themselves. The *real* South will rise again!

U.S. MIDWESTERNER

I promise that from this moment on I will be proud of the strong cities, beautiful corn fields, lakes, and forests which are my home. I will remember that my people are special and worth every effort it takes to reach them. I will boldly lead all humans from the solid center of my country, firmly trusting my thinking and speaking my mind. The world can depend on my power and intelligence for its survival.

NATIVE PEOPLE

I promise never to forget that as a Native person I belong to this earth and my very special gifts are needed here, that all beings in Creation are my relatives and cherish me as I cherish them, that my people have survived and will survive all attempts to exterminate us, that we are strong and wise and loving, and we will show our children and the rest of the world how to live in love and harmony and care for the earth and all creatures without ever losing our sense of humor.

COMMITMENTS, continued

GERMAN-SPEAKING HERITAGE

I am a German-speaking human.

I am inherently fully human in every way.

I denounce every wrong that was done or participated in by German-speaking peoples during the Nazi period as I denounce all other instances of oppression in the world.

I will wage unceasing battle to eliminate every trace of the pernicious effects of Nazism in German-speaking societies, cultures, and in our relations with each other and with all other peoples of the world.

As I carry out this activity, I will be proud. I will be an ally to all peoples of the world. I will be a dependable force to eliminate all oppressions and thus deserve everyone's love, support, and, in particular, my own complete pride in myself.

WELSH

With respect for our proud, courageous, intelligent women and men, and for our beautiful and resourceful country, I promise that from this moment on I will cherish Welsh people in all our diversity of class, colour, language, and dialect.

I am Welsh. I will accept no limits to my power, knowing my leadership and Welsh Liberation are essential to a free and just world.

RAISED-EXPATRIATE

Knowing that we are at the center of all wide-world matters, we will confidently expect to be welcomed and cherished exactly as we are by everyone.

We promise to take pride in the position in which events placed us, the strengths this has given us, and the close ties we have with all people. The world is our home!

POLISH

From this moment on, I will treat all Poles, starting with myself, as intelligent, creative, and loving. I promise to remember that Poland is the center of the European culture, and I will take a significant part in its bright future.

PERSONS OF MIXED HERITAGE

Recognizing that we are the people of the future, and that every one of our cultures and our heritages is valuable and to be respected and appreciated, we proudly proclaim ourselves to be 100% universal humans, and we invite all human beings to join us in this claim.

LESBIANS

Because I am good, and belong, like every other woman, at the center of all matters, I promise never again to accept any limits on my loving, my relationships, or my abilities. I am completely good, I am fully feminine, I am a Lesbian.

GAY MEN

Beloved brothers, because of our supreme importance to the world now and forever, I promise to always remember that my love is good and my manhood is complete and without limits.

COMMITMENTS, continued

"DISPLACED" PERSONS

We have endured loneliness and exile and have survived. We have struggled to keep our roots in the culture of our homeland. We have tried to be excellent guests and win a permanent place in the land of our exile. Now, realizing the common goals and common interests of all humanity, we proclaim ourselves and all other people citizens of our beautiful planet Earth, welcome wherever we abide or travel. The world is our home!

WOMEN

I solemnly (fiercely, cheerfully) promise that, from this moment on, I will never again settle for anything less than absolutely *everything*. This means that _____.

MEN

I promise that, from this moment on, I will be proud to be male, and will seek closeness and brotherhood with every other man of every age, race, nation, and class.

I will permit no slandering or disrespect or blaming of any man for the hurts which have been placed upon him and I will seek to restore safety to all men to discharge these cruel hurts.

I will fight to end and eliminate the burdening of men with over-fatigue, over-responsibility, and coercion into armed service in which we have been brutalized, and forced to kill or be killed.

I will cherish my birthright of being a good, intelligent, courageous, and powerful male human.

DISABLED PERSONS

I cheerfully promise that from now on I will always remember that my body is wonderful and that I am fully human, that I am totally admirable and lovely to be close to, and I will confidently expect to be cherished exactly as I am by all human beings.

YOUNG PEOPLE

I solemnly promise that, from this moment on, I will never again treat any young person, including myself, with anything less than complete respect. This will mean that _____.

YOUNG ADULTS

I joyfully promise, from this moment on, to never give up my dreams and goals. I choose to remember always that the whole world is mine, and I need never be alone in figuring it out and making it just right.

ADOPTEES

From this moment on I will remember that I am completely good and okay and have always been good enough. The universe wanted me and continues to celebrate my existence. I belong everywhere. My birth parents and families always wanted me underneath their distresses and the absence of support from an oppressive society. I have a right to know my origins. I deserve a good, healthy, easy life and can expect loving, healthy, lasting relationships. I am powerful, lovable, and loving. I am not alone. My allies are everywhere. It is safe to connect deeply with other humans.

COMMITMENTS, continued

PARENTS

I am a good parent. I love my child/ren. From this moment on, I will relish my excellence as a mother/father, enjoy my precious, resilient child/ren, and discharge my every regret.

I hold myself and my fellow parents blameless for the struggles we still face due to our heavy oppression. I am proud of the goodness and commitment of all parents, and am proud of the vital work we do. As a mother/father, I will remember that there will be time to pursue every goal that is dear to my heart.

ELDERS

I promise that I will never die, that I will never slow down, and that I will have more fun than ever.

ELDERS

I promise that, from this moment on, I will live my life with unabashed delight and confidence, using my full wisdom, creativity, love, and energy to ensure that the world around me proceeds exactly the way I want it to and envision that it can.

I will do this by inviting and encouraging others to join with me, think with me, and act in all of our best interests.

As a basis for living this fully, I will pay loving and thoughtful attention to the needs of my body, mind, heart and soul, and welcome other people's love and attention when it is freely given.

I will respect and honor other elders and never permit anyone, including myself, to invalidate or stereotype elders again.

PARENTS

I promise to remember always that I am a good parent, that I always have done the best I could, that I have passed on to my child/ren as few of the hurts that I endured as a child as I could possibly manage, and that some day I'll get a little rest.

ALLIES TO ELDERS

I promise that from this moment on I will invite, encourage, and expect elders to live their lives with unabashed delight and confidence, using their full wisdom, creativity, love, and energy to ensure that the world around them proceeds exactly as they want it to and envision that it can.

I will also encourage them to take loving and thoughtful care of themselves and to make and maintain strong relationships with others based on mutual attention, interest, and affection. I will never again permit anyone to invalidate or stereotype elders.

To this end, I will persist in inviting them to notice what is good in the present moment, what their strengths and contributions are, and how deserving they are of my love and attention, as well as the love and attention of others.

To assist them in attaining and maintaining a full and vigorous life, I will listen lovingly, respectfully, and attentively to past and present experiences, triumphs, hurts, and disappointments, encourage them to notice and discharge their feelings, and invite them to think about how the world should proceed, how they can be effective in making the world right, and what help they need from me and others to move things along.

COMMITMENTS, continued

WORKING CLASS

I solemnly promise that, from this moment on, I will take pride in the intelligence, strength, endurance, and goodness of working-class people everywhere.

I will remember to be proud that we do the world's work, that we produce the world's wealth, that we belong to the only class with a future, that our class will end all oppression.

I will unite with all my fellow workers everywhere around the world to lead all people to a rational, peaceful society.

I am a worker, proud to be a worker, and the future is in my hands.

MIDDLE CLASS

I cheerfully promise from now on to stand proudly visible, to be my true self without caution or pretense, to work for the unity and liberation of all working people, and never to be quiet again.

OWNING CLASS

I promise that, from this moment on, I will refuse to feel guilty or accept blame or isolation for the class position in which my birth or other events placed me, but will instead take full pride in my complete humanness. I will recognize and remember my close ties to all other human beings. I will treasure and appreciate the favorable factors in my background which allowed me to keep much of my humanness and abilities intact and functioning. I pledge that this humanness and these abilities and advantages will be used, with zest and joy, for the complete liberation of every human being from every oppression.

OWNING CLASS

I promise always to remember that I and my people are completely good, and I never need pretend again. No matter how frightening it feels I will give up the control of wealth and the justification for it. And I will come home and humbly take my own place with working-class people in setting the world completely to right.

RAISED POOR

I am a bold and brilliant thinker. I can change the world. I refuse to settle for anything less than complete liberation of my mind and the minds of all people from the effects of classism. I will expect and reach for complete respect, complete equality, and complete closeness, and I will take complete responsibility for seeing that all human beings get treated well.

RAISED POOR

I solemnly promise to always remember it was never my/our fault that I/we was/were born into a society which uses poverty to perpetuate the oppression of all people. We are the majority and the natural leaders of the entire world. I promise to remember my/our goodness, strength, and intelligence. I will settle for nothing less than complete respect and complete opportunity for everyone. Furthermore, I will personally see to it.

COMMITMENTS, continued

GEREFORMEERDE BEVRIJDING

Ik geloof oprecht dat ik goed ben geboren en gebleven als mens en als gereformeerde.

Ik ben heel gewoon en evenveel waard als ieder ander.

Ik mag uitrusten zonder dat ik iets heb gepresteerd en tevreden zijn over wat ik doe.

Ik beloof dat ik altijd van mezelf zal houden en dat ik nooit zal vergeten dat mijn leven mijzelf toebehoort en dat ik ervan mag genieten.

Ik ben gereformeerd en geschapen naar Gods beeld en Zhij zag dat het goed was en dat geldt ook voor mij. Dat betekent _____.

CALVINIST LIBERATION

I sincerely believe that I was born and have remained good, as a human and as a Calvinist.

I am just an ordinary person and I am worth just as much as anybody else.

I may rest without having achieved a thing and I may be satisfied with the things I do.

I promise that I will always love myself and that I will never forget that my life belongs to me and that I may enjoy it.

I am a Calvinist, created after the image of God, and S/He saw that it was good and this also applies to me. This will mean _____.

CATHOLIC

I pledge to never again demean or apologize for myself, my family, or my church for being Catholic, but to esteem them all as beloveds of God and all the universe.

AGAINST RACISM

I resent and will fiercely oppose racism's crippling limits to the progress of my beloved human race. Always keeping in mind my proud heritage of fighting oppression, and wanting to enrich my present and future, I will engage and join with others to smash racism so that we all may live in a free world.

AGAINST MONEY DISTRESS

I will do everything necessary to arrange ample funding for all my projects. I will discharge completely any of my patterns that gets in the way, and I will counsel anyone who needs to think differently in order to help me accomplish this.

I promise that I will never again let money stand in the way of accomplishing my goals.

WORLD CHANGERS

I have chosen to change society, but I also choose to be intelligent in the way I go about it.

The future needs me, well-rested, well-nourished, well-exercised, and well-organized.

The past is useful as a source of information, but never as a substitute for my own fresh thinking. Mao (or any more recent leader) respected Marx (or any more previous leader), but did his own fresh thinking. I will respect all past thinkers but my thinking will necessarily be more brilliant than theirs because I stand on their shoulders.

If I am not enjoying what I am doing, then there is something wrong with how I am doing it and I will correct it.

COMMITMENTS, continued

CLASSROOM TEACHERS

As a proud worker in the liberation of all human intelligence, I cheerfully promise that I will always treat every learner and every teacher, including myself, with complete respect.

COLLEAGUES

As a full-fledged human being, I promise to think and to respect thinking, to allow no invalidation of any scholar or teacher, including myself, to refuse to be isolated from my colleagues or to act as an agent of oppression, and to boldly apply my full knowledge and power to the creation of a just world.

ARTISTS

I promise to always remember my power, love, and intelligence as an artist, and the vital role that artists have played in every culture and time. I will never again invalidate any artist, including myself, or any work of art, but rather ally myself with all artists to end our economic oppression, and enthusiastically encourage the creativity of every human.

AGAINST CRITICIZING

From now on I will view each person in the light of his/her value to me, to the RC Community, and to the world. I will under all circumstances *think* no critical thoughts of anyone; and I will under all circumstances notice and comment on the slightest contribution, service, and evidence of growth; because no matter how slight these actions feel to me, they are immense if they lead toward the re-emergence of me and my students. And I will repeat this as often as necessary until the ancient habit pattern of criticizing has been broken.

THERAPISTS

I promise always to remember that I am no more than an assistant to the person I am seeking to help; that nothing I do that strains my survival can be of real, long-range assistance to another; that everything I do will be directed to enhance the power, the independent thinking, and the humanness of the person I am assisting; and that the factor of approval by authority will never sway my judgment in what I do to assist.

INCEST SURVIVOR

Victoriously proclaiming my total innocence and discarding any shame or secrecy for what was done to me, I joyfully and proudly reclaim my tenderest love for my sacred body, my control over my full sexuality, my unconditional love for myself and others, my full trust in myself and ability to rely on others, my connection with humans everywhere, my joy in life, my unbounded intelligence to think about everything, and my complete power and visibility as a human with unlimited choice and impact in the world.

"MENTAL HEALTH" SYSTEM SURVIVOR

I decide that, from now on, I will always be proud of myself and all other "mental health" system survivors.

I will remember that I can choose the viewpoint on my life experiences and current situation which gives me the most satisfaction.

I am the perfect person to lead all people toward liberation.

I can take complete charge of my mind and fulfill my wildest dreams.

COMMITMENTS, continued

CIVIL SERVANTS

From now on I will take complete responsibility for the liberation of Blankville.

With my excellent leadership, Blankville will become a beacon of peace and progress to the rest of Blankland and the world.

RC LEADERS

I promise that, from this moment on, I am in complete charge of *absolutely everything*, including the entire RC Community. Ha! Ha! Ha! Ha! (In tones of triumph, satisfaction, and power.) This means that _____.

HOW TO BEGIN "RE-EVALUATION COUNSELING"

If you have heard of Re-evaluation Counseling and of the advantages of using it in your life, and are eager to try it, the following will help you get started.

In its basic form, the practice of Co-Counseling simply consists of two people taking turns listening to each other. It's like a conversation in some ways, but it's different, too. It's a more careful, effective kind of listening. We are talking about listening and paying attention to what you hear. It is thinking about the person who is saying it, and thinking about what he or she is saying, without interrupting the listening by offering suggestions or comments, but simply listening wholeheartedly.

Take Turns Listening

It's simple to get started. It just takes two people. Find a friend (or co-worker or spouse) who will try it with you. Agree that you will take turns listening to each other without interruption for an equal amount of time, and agree how long that time will be. Then decide who is going to listen first. The other person then talks about whatever he or she wants to talk about. The listener just pays attention and doesn't interrupt to give advice or comment or tell how he or she feels.

After the agreed-upon time, the talker becomes the listener, and the one who listened first now talks about anything he or she wants to talk about.

It's a fair exchange. Neither person owes anything to the other. Afterwards, both people usually feel refreshed and think more easily. It's fun, too.

This is good to do whenever you get a chance. As you listen this way more times, you get to know each other better and like each other more and more.

You also get better at listening. The whole process becomes more effective the more times you use it.

Co-Counseling "turns" or "sessions" can be as long or as short as you have time for. Even a few minutes shared with your Co-Counselor can make a big difference in how you are able to think and function, and two hours shared is that much better.

Getting One's Feelings "Out"

Sometimes the person talking (the "talker" or the "client") may begin to laugh or cry or speak loudly, or sometimes tremble or yawn. This is a fine thing to have happen. It simply means that the person is tense about something, perhaps feeling some embarrassment or grief or fear or physical discomfort, and she or he is releasing the tension this way. She or he is becoming "un-embarrassed," "un-sad," "un-afraid." We sometimes call any release of tension in these ways "discharge." The person listening (the "counselor") can feel pleased and relaxed if this happens, and just continue to pay attention to the client without trying to stop any discharge that is occurring. If the client stops his or her own discharge, the listener can reassure him or her that it is fine to continue.

WHAT DO YOU THINK?

This is the basic idea of Co-Counseling—two people take turns listening to each other. You can make many changes in your life just by knowing and doing this.

If you're reading this with someone, you might want to stop reading at this point and try listening to each other, ten minutes each way. Afterwards, tell each other what your impression was.

Once you have "Co-Counseled" a few times with the same person, take time to talk it over and see what you each think of the experience. How did you like having someone listen to you without interrupting? Did you enjoy it? How did you like listening without interrupting? Would you like to continue trying this? You can read on in this article for more information about how to do this well.

WHAT TO DO IN A SESSION

Time spent listening to each other without interruption is often called a "session." Below are some things that you can experiment with doing in your sessions.

"News and Goods"

You can start your session as client by telling your counselor about "good" things, big or small, that have happened lately. It could be the beautiful sunset you saw last night, or your new job, or a problem you figured out last week. The idea is to give yourself a chance to notice the things that are going well. (This is especially a good idea if you feel discouraged. It helps remind you that maybe things aren't as bad as they feel.) Sometimes people spend whole Co-Counseling sessions just telling "news and goods" and leave feeling much more positive and thinking more clearly.

Recent Upsets

If something has happened recently that you are upset about, a Co-Counseling session is a good place to talk about it. You can tell as much or as little about it as you would like, and you can tell it once or you can tell it over and over. You will probably find that lots of your problems seem to get much smaller if you just get a chance to talk about them without someone trying to give you advice or solve them for you. You will find, more often than not, that you can think of a good solution if you just have someone hear you out and show some confidence in you while you feel upset and talk about the problem.

Troubles from the Past

If you use your turn as client to talk about something that is bothering you, you can sometimes, after you have had a chance to talk about the upset for awhile, ask yourself (or your counselor can ask you), "What does this situation or this feeling remind you of? When have you felt like this before?" You will almost always think of some situation from the past that was hurtful or upsetting in a similar way. It will be plain that old feelings from that time are still lingering in your mind, adding more confusion and bad feelings to the present situation than there would otherwise be. If you can talk about the earlier situation, what happened then, how you felt, and how it affected you, some of those old bad feelings can then be discharged, leaving you with a fresher look at the present difficulty.

Life Stories

If you come to your session as client and there seems to be nothing in your present life that you need to talk about, try telling your life story. Most people have never had a chance to tell the whole story of their life, and everyone needs a chance to do this. As you tell the story of your life, certain incidents will seem more important in their effect on you, good or bad, than others. These incidents are worth coming back to and talking about many times in Co-Counseling sessions. Getting a chance to review them over and over, with someone who is really listening, can make a surprising difference in your thinking. Bad feelings left over from old, hurtful experiences (including experiences that you thought were "behind you") can come to the surface and discharge, leaving you with a lighter step and freer thoughts. Good experiences, when reviewed with the attention of a good listener, can also help bad feelings from old, difficult times to discharge, and this can help you regain a positive outlook.

Self-Appreciation

Most of us have been belittled or mistreated enough that it is now difficult for us to feel good about ourselves. We have been "blamed" for things when we were doing our best. We have been told many untrue things. We have been told that if we like ourselves, we are "conceited" and that we shouldn't feel good about ourselves. This isn't true. People need to feel good about themselves. When we do feel good about ourselves, we treat other people better, not worse.

In a Co-Counseling session when you are client, tell your counselor what you like about yourself. Tell this to him or her in a tone of voice that sounds like you are proud of yourself (not "superior," just proud). Tell your counselor this over and over. You may find it difficult, but stick with it. Don't stop yourself from laughing or crying or any other type of discharge. Try to appreciate everything about yourself (EVERYTHING). When you notice which things feel harder to appreciate (for example, how you look or how smart you are), focus on appreciating those things. You will probably remember incidents from your life of being criticized, blamed, or mistreated. These incidents will be good to look at and talk about in a counseling session when you are client.

Goals

It helps your life go better to set goals for yourself or review your progress towards goals that you have already set. This is a useful thing to do when you are client in a Co-Counseling session. Talk through the different periods of your life, tentatively deciding what you want to accomplish tomorrow, next week, this year, in the next five years, in the next twenty years, in your lifetime. As you talk about each future period, you can think through the steps that you will need to take to reach these goals.

Occasionally reviewing your goals and any apparent obstacles will tend to assist you in achieving them.

Letting Discharge Continue

If you talk about something as client that results in lively talking, laughter, tears, shaking, sweating, or yawning (all forms of discharge), don't rush on to something else. Try repeating what you were saying or doing several times until you are no longer discharging. It's worth doing this over and over for as much time as you can take. The greatest benefits of Co-Counseling come after these releases of tension. They make it possible to think and act in ways that have been inhibited before.

Ending a Session

At the end of a Co-Counseling session, especially if you've been talking about something difficult for you, take a few moments to re-direct your thoughts to something you are looking forward to, or to some simple subject you don't feel tense about, for example, the names of some friends or some favorite foods, or some scenery that you enjoy looking at. This helps make a relaxed change from being a client to becoming a counselor if it is your turn to do this, or to going on to other activities.

For each person to feel safe to talk about whatever he or she needs to, it works best to agree that you won't discuss it with anyone later. Also, keep in mind that alcohol and drugs interfere with the good effects of discharging.

SUPPORT GROUPS

It also works well to get a small group of people together to take turns listening to each other. (In RC we call this a "support group.") Each person gets a roughly equal amount of time to talk while the rest of the group listens.

One person acts as the leader of the group to help the group decide how much time each person will get, who will go first, and so on. When each person has had his or her turn as client, you can end the group meeting with each person getting a chance to say what he or she liked best about being in the group meeting or something he or she is looking forward to.

Support groups can meet as often or as many times as the group members wish. The group can be a group of friends, co-workers, neighbors, or people with a similar background or interest. Sharing something in common with the group often helps people feel safer to talk about things they need to talk about. For example, there have been support groups of women, men, parents, young people, working-class people, people of a certain ethnic group or religion, disabled people, artists, and many others.

Inviting friends to the group is a good way to introduce more people to Co-Counseling. If the group becomes too large, it can be divided and a second group formed with a new leader chosen for the new group. About eight people seems to be the optimum size for a group, but they can function well both smaller and larger.

Support groups are a good structure for people from a similar background or similar situation to use to talk about what they like about being a part of that group and what they are proud of about the people from that group. Support groups are also good for talking about what has been hard, what they wish people understood about their group, what hopes and dreams they have for people from their group, and what they would like to do in relation to that group.

For example, in a women's support group, each woman would get a turn sharing what she likes about being a woman, what has been hard about being a woman, what she would like men to understand about women, how she would like to see women's lives improve, and what ways she would like to reach out to other women.

IF YOU WANT TO LEARN MORE

If you try Co-Counseling and you decide that you'd like to learn more, you may get in touch with the main Re-evaluation Counseling office (look at the end of this article for the address and phone number), and ask that office if there are any Co-Counselors who live near you. You could also order a few introductory publications. Some good readings to start with are:

The Human Side of Human Beings (the theory of RC), $4.00 (US)
The Fundamentals of Co-Counseling Manual (the beginning practice of RC), $6.00 (US)
The Art of Listening (an introductory talk about RC), $2.00 (US)
An Introduction to Co-Counseling (a very short description of RC), $1.00 (US)
The Human Situation (essays on different topics), $6.00 (US)
Present Time (a general journal published four times a year), $4.00 (US)

Videotapes and audiotapes are also available. (They are all in English, but we do have different video formats for different countries as well as typed transcripts for each videotape.) Someone at the main office can tell you which ones might be good for you to start with.

If you can't afford to pay for literature, explain this to the office and ask if it is possible for Outreach Funds to pay for some literature in order for you to get started.

If you are very interested in learning more about RC and know other people who are eager to learn, we may be able to send a teacher to your group or bring one of you to a workshop.

There is an RC Web site on the Internet, <http://www.rc.org/>, with lots of information and articles. If you are in an area which does not yet offer RC classes but you can connect to the Internet, you might find the on-line "class" on this Web site helpful.

People who use Re-evaluation Counseling find that it helps them think better, improve relationships, stand up for the right things, and enjoy life more. Co-Counselors usually get "smarter" as they use RC, and they get better at using it. They teach other people about RC and teach them how to teach other people, so that in some places lots of people are using RC, holding classes and workshops, learning from each other, and supporting and encouraging each other.

We have literature published in about thirty different languages, written by Co-Counselors from all over the world, with stories about using RC and with RC information about people of different ages, backgrounds, and situations.

There are a few ground rules and a set of "Community Guidelines," which help Co-Counselors keep things well organized.

Good luck.

> The International Re-evaluation Counseling Communities
> 719 Second Avenue North
> Seattle, Washington 98109, USA
> Telephone: 206-284-0311
> FAX: 206-284-8429
> E-mail: ircc@rc.org
> Web site: http://www.rc.org/

The previous article is available as a small, sixteen-page booklet (see its first page below). The booklet can be ordered from Rational Island Publishers for $1.00. You may also order, at no charge, a master copy from which you can create booklets yourself to distribute to others. Order from Rational Island Publishers, PO Box 2081, Main Office Station, Seattle, Washington 98111, USA.

How to Begin "Re-evaluation Counseling"

If you have heard of Re-evaluation Counseling and of the advantages of using it in your life, and are eager to try it, the following will help you get started.

In its basic form, the practice of Co-Counseling simply consists of two people taking turns listening to each other. It's like a conversation in some ways, but it's different, too. It's a more careful, effective kind of listening. We are talking about listening and *paying attention to what you hear*. It is thinking about the person who is saying it, and thinking about what he or she is saying, without interrupting the listening by offering suggestions or comments, but simply listening wholeheartedly.

Copyright © 1996 by Rational Island Publishers

THE POSTULATES OF RE-EVALUATION COUNSELING

(The Postulates were first printed in 1973 and were revised in 1990.)

Re-evaluation Counseling is a theory of human behavior and set of procedures for solving human problems. It is a complex theory, still growing, containing a large amount of information in its details and techniques. Its main assumptions can be summarized at present (1990) in the following 28 points.

1. Rational human behavior is qualitatively different from the behavior of other forms of life. (It is not just more complicated.)

2. The essence of rational human behavior consists of responding to each instant of living with a new response, created afresh at that moment to precisely fit and handle the situation of that moment as that situation is defined by the information received through the senses of the person (other living creatures typically respond with pre-set, inherited response patterns—"instincts," or with conditioned, equally-rigid modifications or replacements of the inherited response patterns, acquired through experiences of stress).

3. This ability to create new, exact responses may be defined as human intelligence. It operates by comparing and contrasting new information with that already on file from past experiences and constructing a response based on similarities to past situations but modified to allow for the differences.

4. Each human with a physically undamaged brain has a large inherent capacity for this rational kind of behavior, very large as compared to the best functioning of presently observable adult humans.

5. The complexity of our central nervous systems (now estimated to contain at least one-thousand billion individual neurons and a number of possible states of relationship between these neurons larger than the number of atoms in the known universe) has brought us not only human intelligence of a very, very high level but also has conferred on us the capacity to be aware, to notice what is going on while it is going on, to think about the rational processes while they are taking place. This ability or function of awareness is very hard to define or describe, but humans are completely aware when it is present in another person or not, and enjoy it fully in themselves when it is operating.

6. This complexity of our central nervous systems has also conferred upon us complete freedom of decision. Even though this freedom is denied unendingly and emphatically by the societies in which we live, it still persists and is completely available to us. This complete freedom of decision is not just freedom to make a good decision, to make a rational decision, to make a correct decision. It is an unfettered freedom. We are completely free to make wrong decisions, destructive decisions, irrational decisions as well. Our freedom of choice is unfettered, unlimited.

7. This complexity has also conferred complete power on each individual, if we define power as the ability to have the universe respond to us in the way we rationally wish it to (not in the usual oppressive society's definition of power as "the ability to enforce our will upon other intelligences, other humans").

8. The natural emotional tone of a human being is zestful enjoyment of life. The natural relationship between any two human beings is loving affection, communication, and co-operation.

9. The special human capacity for rational response can be interrupted or suspended by an experience of physical or emotional distress. When this occurs, information input through the senses then stores as an unevaluated and rigid accumulation, exhibiting the characteristics of a very complete, literal recording of all aspects of the incident.

10. Immediately after the distress experience is concluded or at the first opportunity thereafter, the distressed human spontaneously seeks to claim the aware attention of another human. If he or she is successful in claiming and keeping this aware attention of the other person, a profound process of what has been called discharge ensues.

11. Discharge is signalized externally by one or more of a precise set of physical processes. These are: crying or sobbing (with tears), trembling with cold perspiration, laughter, angry shouting and vigorous movement with warm perspiration (tantrum), live, interested talking; and in a slightly different way, yawning, often with scratching and stretching. Discharge requires considerable time for completion.

12. During discharge, the residue of the distress experience or experiences is being recalled and reviewed (not necessarily with awareness).

13. Rational evaluation and understanding of the information received during the distress experience occurs automatically following discharge and only following discharge. It occurs only to the degree that discharge is completed. On completion, the negative and anti-rational effects of the experience are completely eliminated.

14. As a result of long-term conditioning of the entire population, the spontaneous attempt to claim the aware attention of another person and proceed to discharge and evaluation is almost always rebuffed. (Don't cry. Be a big boy. Get a grip on yourself. Don't be afraid. Watch your temper.) Applied to small children, these rebuffs begin and perpetuate the conditioning of the population which prevents discharge.

15. Undischarged and unevaluated recordings of distress experiences become compulsive patterns of behaving, feeling, and verbalizing when restimulated by later experiences which resemble them strongly enough. Under such conditions of restimulation, the rational faculty of the human is again suspended, and the new information of the current experience is added to the rigid distress pattern, making it more far-reaching in its effect and more easily restimulated in the future.

16. We have called the association of distress recordings from the past with the current scene, and the resulting rigid, "inappropriate" responses, "restimulation." This kind of association must have been originally a decision, a decision apparently motivated by the hope that bringing up and "restimulating" the distress recordings would

create a possibility of discharging them (if the attention of another person could be found or some other contradiction to the recordings could be achieved). The repetitive attempts at this kind of decision and the resulting lack of success (since we seldom found the resource of contradiction and resulting discharge we hoped for) tended to make restimulation into a "habit" and a pattern.

It is possible (and profitable) to decide not to be restimulated. Such a decision can be repeated as many times as necessary.

17. The effect of an undischarged distress experience recording in "playing" the bearer through a compulsive, repetitive re-enactment of distress experiences is an adequate explanation for all observable irrational behavior in human beings, of whatever kind or degree.

18. Any human being, and human beings in general, can become free of the restrictions, inhibitions, and aberrations of accumulated distress experience recordings by reinstating a relationship with some other person's or persons' aware attention and allowing the discharge and re-evaluation processes to proceed to completion.

19. Any infant can be allowed to remain free of aberration by protection from distress experiences and by allowing full discharge and re-evaluation on the ones that do occur.

20. Though a greater degree of awareness, rationality, understanding, and skill on the part of the person whose attention is used ("the second person," "the counselor") provides for more rapid and more complete discharge and re-evaluation, the process is workable if even a small degree of awareness is available and if even a roughly correct attitude is maintained by the second person.

21. By "taking turns," i.e., by exchanging the two roles periodically ("Co-Counseling"), two people can become increasingly effective with each other and help free each other from accumulated distress patterns to a profound degree.

22. Distress patterns which have become too reinforced by repeated restimulation can become chronic, i.e., surround and envelop all behavior and activity. To discharge these requires initiative, skill, and resource on the part of the second person and considerable time for handling, but they are not different in origin or effect from lighter distresses, and can also be completely discharged and evaluated.

23. Distress experiences result from any unfavorable aspect of the environment. In our present state of civilization, the bulk of early distress experiences of any child result exactly from the dramatized distress recordings of adults which the adults received from earlier generations when they were children. We have a sort of transmission of aberration by contagion here—well-meaning adults unawarely but systematically infecting each new, healthy-to-begin-with child with their burdening distress patterns.

24. The irrationalities of society (enforcements, punishments, exploitations, prejudices, group conflicts, wars) are reflections of the individual human distress patterns which have become fossilized in the society and often enforced by the rigidities of the society itself.

25. No individual human has an actual rational conflict of interest with another human. No group of humans has an actual, rational conflict of interest with another group of humans. Given rationality, the actual desires of each individual and each group can best be served by mutual co-operation.

26. Nothing prevents communication, agreement, and co-operation between any humans except distress patterns. Given knowledge of their nature, these distress patterns can be coped with, handled, and removed.

27. Any individual or group can act rationally first without waiting for rational action on the part of someone else, and can take control of the situation by so doing.

28. It is always safe to be rational. Knowledge of the above information can be applied to all aspects of living and to all relationships with real profit and success.

Re-evaluation Counseling is a meaningful and useful description of the nature of human beings and the source of their difficulties. It is a rediscovery of the workable means for undoing human distress. It is a system of procedures for expediting this discharge and re-evaluation process. It is a promising and successful alternative to individual and social irrationality and distress.

"Re-evaluation Counseling," as a title, correctly denotes the collection of insights into the actual nature of reality which we have assembled as the result of our practice and thinking, in the areas of human thought and activities where this actual reality has been occluded or undiscovered as a result of lack of information, misinformation, distress patterns, and the operations of the oppressive societies.

RESOURCES

The following resources in publications, videocassettes, and audio cassettes are available from

RATIONAL ISLAND PUBLISHERS

P.O. Box 2081, Main Office Station, Seattle, Washington 98111, USA
Telephone (206) 284-0311   Fax (206) 284-8429
E-mail: ircc@rc.org

BOOKS

The Kind, Friendly Universe

By Harvey Jackins. New Counseling Theory, 1992-1995.
Paper: $13 (ISBN 0-885357-10-9) Hardcover: $16 (ISBN 0-885357-09-5)

A Better World

By Harvey Jackins. Advances in Counseling Theory and Practice, 1989-1992.
Paper: $13 (ISBN 0-913937-64-9) Hard-cover: $16 (ISBN 0-913937-63-0)

Start Over Every Morning

By Harvey Jackins. Advances in Counseling Theory and Practice, 1987-1989.
Paper: $13 (ISBN 0-913937-35-5) Hardcover: $16 (ISBN 0-913937-36-3)

The Longer View

By Harvey Jackins. Advances in Counseling Theory and Practice, 1985-1987.
Paper: $13 (ISBN 0-913937-18-5) Hardcover: $16 (ISBN 0-913937-17-7)

The Rest of Our Lives

By Harvey Jackins. Advances in Counseling Theory and Practice, 1983-1985.
Paper: $13 (ISBN 0-913937-06-1) Hardcover: $16 (ISBN 0-913937-05-3)

The Reclaiming of Power

By Harvey Jackins. Theoretical and organizational advances from 1981 to 1983.
Paper: $13 (ISBN 0-911214-87-9)

The Benign Reality

By Harvey Jackins. Important breakthroughs in human perception of the Universe and the empowerment of the individual against oppression, discouragement, and powerlessness.
Paper: $16 (ISBN 0-911214-77-1) Hardcover: $19 (ISBN 0-911214-76-3)

The Upward Trend

By Harvey Jackins. Collected writings on Re-evaluation Counseling, 1973-1977.
Paper: $10 (ISBN 0-911214-81-X) Hardcover: $13 (ISBN 0-911214-57-7)

The Human Situation

By Harvey Jackins. A collection of writings on Re-evaluation Counseling, revised edition, contains updated chapters: *The Postulates, Multiplied Awareness,* and *Allow Ourselves Time to Grow.* Paper: $7 (ISBN 0-913937-47-9) Hardcover: $9 (ISBN 0-913937-55-X)

Quotes

By Harvey Jackins. Memorable, pungent, pithy comments. Paper: $6 (ISBN 0-913937-75-4)

"The List"

By Harvey Jackins. "Everything I know about Re-evaluation Counseling (and the world) until now." Hardcover only: $50 (no quantity discounts) (ISBN 0-885357-48-6)

The Human Side of Human Beings

The Theory of Re-evaluation Counseling

By Harvey Jackins. An introduction to a completely new theory of human behavior.
Paper: $4 (ISBN 0-911214-60-7) Hardcover: $6 (ISBN 1-885357-09-5)

Fundamentals of Co-Counseling Manual

By Harvey Jackins. For beginning classes in Re-evaluation Counseling.
Paper: $6 (ISBN 0-911214-02-X)

A New Kind of Communicator

By Harvey Jackins and others. Fifth revision. A Re-evaluation Counseling teacher's manual.
Paper: $4 (ISBN 0-911214-20-8)

Rough Notes from Calvinwood I

By Harvey Jackins and others. Transcript of the first Re-evaluation Counseling Classroom Teachers' Workshop. Second revised edition. Paper: $7 (ISBN 0-913937-71-1)

Rough Notes from Buck Creek I

By Harvey Jackins and others. Transcript of the first Re-evaluation Counseling Workshop.
Paper: $15 (ISBN 0-911214-52-6)

Rough Notes from Liberation I & II

By Harvey Jackins and others. Transcript of a workshop for Co-Counselors interested in liberation movements. Paper: $10 (ISBN 0-911214-42-9)
Hardcover: $15 (ISBN 0-911214-46-1)

My Notebook as a Counselor

and

My Notebook as a Client

Pre-fabricated pairs of notebooks with standard outlines for beginning the notebooks, and printed form pages for filling in individual material.
Large/letter size (8 1/2 x 11 inches): $10 per pair (ISBN 0-913937-39-8).
Small/pocket size (4 1/4 x 5 1/2 inches): $10 per pair (ISBN 0-91397-40-1)

Zest Is Best

By Harvey Jackins. Poems. Paper: $5 (ISBN 0-911214-24-0)
Hardcover: $7 (ISBN 0-911214-06-2)

*All prices are in U.S. dollars. We accept checks in most local currencies for literature orders.
Postage and handling to be added.*

PAMPHLETS

The Art of Listening
By Harvey Jackins. A succinct review of the interactions involved in paying attention.

Co-Counseling for Married Couples
By Harvey Jackins. A guide to self-help for marriage problems.

The Communication of Important Ideas
By Harvey Jackins. An essay on interpersonal communication.

The Complete Appreciation of Oneself
By Harvey Jackins. A theoretical guide for advanced students of Re-evaluation Counseling.

The Distinctive Characteristics of Re-evaluation Counseling
By Harvey Jackins. What differentiates Re-evaluation Counseling from humanistic psychologies.

The Enjoyment of Leadership
By Harvey Jackins. Price: $3.00

The Flexible Human in the Rigid Society
By Harvey Jackins. An essay on rational relationships of the individual to society.

The Good and the Great in Art
By Harvey Jackins. Distress, attitudes, and transcendence in art.

How "Re-evaluation Counseling" Began
By Harvey Jackins. The story of how RC started.

Is Death Necessary?
By Harvey Jackins. Conjectures on the possibility of physical immortality.

Letter to a Respected Psychiatrist
By Harvey Jackins.

The Logic of Being Completely Logical
By Harvey Jackins. An essay on being rational.

Logical Thinking About a Future Society
By Harvey Jackins. Proposals for rational attitudes and actions during the collapse of the current society. Price: $3.00

The Nature of the Learning Process
By Harvey Jackins. Guide to the solution of learning difficulties.

The Necessity of Long Range Goals
By Harvey Jackins. The role of farsighted goals in the achievement of immediate ones.

A New Kind of Communicator
By Harvey Jackins and others. A Re-evaluation Counseling teacher's manual. Fifth revision. Price: $4.00

A Rational Theory of Sexuality
By Harvey Jackins. Common sense and good thinking in a turbulent area of human cultures.

The Uses of Beauty and Order
By Harvey Jackins. The importance of upgrading an individual's environment.

Where Did God Come From?
By Harvey Jackins. A seminal essay on rationality and religion.

Who's in Charge?
By Harvey Jackins. An essay on responsibility.

Accommodating Disability
By Marsha Saxton. An essay on meeting the challenges of including disabled people in the RC Communities.

All the Time in the World
By Margery Larrabee. An account of an experience with Re-evaluation Counseling.

Competition—An Inhuman Activity
By Perry Saidman. From a talk on competition.

All prices are $2.00 (U.S.) except where indicated otherwise. Postage and handling will be added.

Counseling on Early Sexual Memories

By Joan Karp. A thorough description of techniques being used to discharge distresses connected to sex in any way at all. Price: $3.00

Guidelines for the Re-evaluation Counseling Communities

How Parents Can Counsel Their Children

By Tim Jackins. Price: $4.00

How to Begin "Re-evaluation Counseling"

A convenient pocket-size booklet with simple instructions. Price: $1.00

How to Give Children an Emotional Head Start

By Marion Riekerk.

Internalized Racism

By Suzanne Lipsky. An essay on the internalization of racist oppression.

Introduction to Co-Counseling

By Dan Nickerson. Price: $1.00

The Liberation of Asians: Thinking About Asian Oppression and Liberation for People of Asian Heritage Living Outside of Asia

By Cheng Imm Tan. Price: $3.00

The Liberation of Men

By John Irwin, Harvey Jackins, and Charlie Kreiner. "The Liberation of Males," "It's Time for Men to Organize," and "Giving Up Sexism." Price: $3.00

Permit Their Flourishing

By the Staff of Palo Alto Pre-School. First year of the preschool. Price: $3.00

The Postulates of Re-evaluation Counseling

The axiomatic foundations of Re-evaluation Counseling theory.

Primer for Clients

By Elton Dunbar. Humor.

Re-evaluation Counseling: A "Culturally Competent" Model for Social Liberation

By Eduardo Aguilar. A Chicano man looks at Re-evaluation Counseling.

The Re-evaluation Counseling Communities

By Carol Carrig. A scholarly survey of the communities developing among Co-Counselors.

Re-evaluation Counseling: Social Implications

By Thomas Scheff. A sociologist looks at Re-evaluation Counseling.

Re-evaluation Therapy: Theoretical Framework

By Bernard Somers. A clinical psychologist looks at Re-evaluation Counseling.

We Who Were Raised Poor: Ending the Oppression of Classism

By Gwen Brown. An essay on the strengths and difficulties of being raised poor and how to fight classism.

What's Wrong with the "Mental Health" System and What Can Be Done About It

A Draft Policy prepared for the Re-evaluation Counseling Communities. Price: $3.00

Women

Summary report of the International Women's Conference of the RC Communities held in The Netherlands, October 12-17, 1984. Price: $3.00

All prices are $2.00 (U.S.) except where indicated otherwise. Postage and handling will be added.

JOURNALS

BLACK RE-EMERGENCE

For people interested in black liberation. Issue No. 1 available, $1.00 each; Issues No. 2, 3, and 4 available, $2.00 each; Issues No. 5, 6, 7, and 8 available, $3.00 each.

THE CARING PARENT

For people interested in parenting. Issues No. 1 and 2 available, $2.00 each; Issues No. 3, 4, 5, and 6 available, $3.00 each.

CLARITY

For people interested in the physical and biological sciences. In preparation.

CLASSROOM

A journal of the theory and practice of learning and educational change. Issues No. 1 and 2 available, $1.00 each; Issues No. 3, 4, and 5 available, $2.00 each; Issues No. 6, 7, 8, and 9 available, $3.00 each.

COLLEAGUE

For communication among college and university faculty and other interested people. Issues No. 1 and 2 available, $1.00 each; Issue No. 3 available, $2.00 each; Issues No. 4 and 5 available, $3.00 each.

COMING HOME

For communication among owning-class people and their allies. Issue No. 1 available, $3.00 each.

COMPLETE ELEGANCE

For communication among disabled people and their allies. Issues No. 1, 2, and 3 available, $.10 each; Issues No. 4 and 5 available, $.50 each; Issues No. 6, 7, 8, and 9 available, $2.00 each.

CREATIVITY

A journal about all kinds of art and artists and Re-evaluation Counseling. Issue No. 1 available, $2.00 each; Issue No. 2 available, $3.00 each.

FOREVER AND EVER

For people interested in exploring the possibility of physical immortality. Issue No. 1 available, $2.00 each.

HERITAGE

For exchange of information on RC in Native American cultures. Issue No. 2 available, $2.00 each; Issue No. 3 available, $3.00 each.

LAWYERS' RC JOURNAL

For communication with and between RC lawyers and others who work in the legal system. In preparation.

MEN

For communication among men and their allies. Issue No. 1 available, $2.00 each; Issue No. 2 available, $3.00 each; Issue No. 3 available, $2.00 each; Issue No. 4 available, $3.00 each.

MIDDLE-CLASS JOURNAL

For communication among middle-class people and their allies. In preparation.

OLDER AND BOLDER

For communication among older people and their allies. (Former titles: *Growing Older* and *The Elders Speak*.) Issue No. 1 available, $1.00 each; Issues No. 3 and 4 available, $2.00 each; Issue No. 5 available, $3.00 each.

OUR ASIAN INHERITANCE

For exchange of information on RC in the Asian and Asian-American cultures. (Former title: *Asian-American Re-evaluation*.) Issue No. 1 available, $.10 each; Issues No. 2 and 3 available, $1.00 each; Issues No. 4 and 5 available, $2.00 each; Issue No. 6 available, $3.00 each.

PEACE

For peace and disarmament activists. Issue No. 1 available, $3.00 each.

PENSAMIENTOS

For exchange of information and ideas among people of Chicano/a ancestry. Issues No. 1, 2, and 3 available, $1.00 each; Issue No. 4 available, $3.00 each.

PRESENT TIME

For everybody; all about Re-evaluation Counseling. Issued quarterly; January 1, April 1, July 1, and October 1. Yearly subscriptions are available. Issues No. 11, 12, 13, 14, 15, 16, 17, 18, 19, 20, 21, 22, 23, 24, 25, 26, 27, 28, 29, and 30 available, $1.00 each; Issues No. 31, 32, 33, 34, 35, 36, 37, 38, 39, 40, 41, 42, 43, 44, 45, 46, 47, 48, 49, 50, 51, 52, 53, 54, 55, 56, 57, 58, 59, 60, and 61 available, $2.00 each; Issues No. 62, 63, 64, 65, 66, 67, 68, 69, 70, 71, 72, 73, 74, 75, 76, 77, 78, 79, 80, 81, 82, 83, 84, 85, 86, 87, 88, 89, 90, 91, 92, 93, 94, 95, 96, 97, 98, and 99 available, $2.50 inside the USA and $3.00 outside the USA, each; Issues No. 100, 101, 102, 103, 104, 105, and 106 available, $3.50 inside the USA and $4.00 outside the USA, each.

Later issues will be available at quarterly intervals.

continued . . .

It is possible to order sets of *Present Time* from No. 11 (April '73) to No. 20 (July '75) at $10.00, from No. 21 (Oct. '75) to No. 30 (Jan. '78) at $15.00, from No. 31 (April '78) to No. 45 (Oct. '81) at $20.00, and from No. 18 (Jan. '75) to No. 58 (Jan. '85) at $50.00. Also available are *PRESENT TIME INDEX Vol. 1* 1977-1986, $3.00, and *INDEX TO PRESENT TIME Vol. 2* January 1977-July 1992 (inclusive), $6.00.

RAISED-POOR JOURNAL

For communication among raised-poor people and their allies. In preparation.

THE RC TEACHER

For people interested in the theory and practice of teaching Re-evaluation Counseling. Issues No. 1, 2, 3, 4, 5, 6, 7, 8, 9, and 10 available, $1.00 each; Issues No. 11, 12, 13, 14, 15, 16, 17, 18, 19, 20, 21, 22, 23, 24 (Index), 25, 26, and 27 available, $2.00 each.

RECOVERY AND RE-EMERGENCE

For "mental health" system survivors and others interested in "mental health" issues. Issues No. 1, 2, and 3 available, $2.00 each; Issues No. 4 & 5 available, $3.00 each.

RUAH HADASHAH

For everyone interested in Jewish liberation. Issues No. 1 and 2 available, $1.00 each; Issues No. 3 and 4 available, $2.00 each; Issues No. 5, 6, 7, 8, and 9 available, $3.00 each.

SEEDS AND CRYSTALS

For poets and poetry lovers. Issues No. 1 and 2 available, $1.00 each; Issues No. 3 and 4 available, $2.00 each.

SHURUK شروق

For everyone interested in Arab liberation. Issue No. 1 available (in Arabic only), $2.00 each.

SIDE BY SIDE

For communication among people interested in Lesbian/Gay liberation. Issue No. 1 available, $2.00 each; Issues No. 2 and 3 available, $3.00 each.

SISTERS

For communication among Co-Counselors who are interested in women's liberation. Issues No. 1, 2, and 3 available, $1.00 each; Issue No. 4 available, $2.00 each; Issues No. 5, 6, 7, 8, 9, and 10 available, $3.00 each.

SONGS ON OUR WAY OUT

Original songs with RC content. Issue No. 1 available, $1.00 each; Issue No. 2 available, $2.00 each.

THERAPIST

For psychiatrists, clinical psychologists, and other professional therapists. In preparation.

TRANSCENDENCE

A journal about all kinds of religions and Re-evaluation Counseling. Issue No. 1 available, $3.00 each.

WELL-BEING

For exchange of information and ideas about health. Issue No. 1 available, $.10 each; Issues No. 2 and 3 available, $1.00 each; Issues No. 4 and 5 available, $3.00 each.

WIDE WORLD CHANGING

For people interested in social change. Issues No. 1, 2, and 3 available, $2.00 each.

WORKING FOR A LIVING

For everyone interested in working-class issues. Issues No. 1 and 2 available, $1.00 each; Issues No. 3, 4, and 5 available, $2.00 each; Issue No. 6 available, $3.00 each.

YOUNG AND POWERFUL

For young people and everyone interested in young people. (Former title: *Upcoming*.) *Upcoming* Issues No. 1 and 2 available, $1.00 each; *Young and Powerful* Issues No. 1, 2, 3, and 4 available, $2.00 each; Issues No. 5 and 6 available, $3.00 each.

LITERATURE IN LANGUAGES OTHER THAN ENGLISH

The following are translations that have been produced up to April, 1997. Additional translations in the languages below and in other languages will be appearing in the future. Our goal is to have at least the principal publications available in every language spoken by more than ten million people.

AMHARIC
The Human Side of Human Beings
Paper: $4   ISBN 1-885357-43-5

ARABIC
Shuruk No. 1
(contains Fundamentals Manual, The Human Side of Human Beings, The Art of Listening, and How to Give Children an Emotional Head Start)
Paper: $3   ISBN 0-913937-83-5

How to Give Children an Emotional Head Start
by Marjon Riekerk
Paper: $2   ISBN 0-913937-67-3

The Postulates of Re-evaluation Counseling
Paper: $2   ISBN 0-913937-21-5

The Human Side of Human Beings
Paper: $4   ISBN 0-913937-77-0

CHINESE
The Human Side of Human Beings and the Fundamentals Manual
Paper: $5   ISBN 0-911214-84-4

The Postulates of Re-evaluation Counseling
Paper: $2   ISBN 0-913937-27-4

The Distinctive Characteristics of Re-evaluation Counseling
Paper: $2   ISBN 0-913937-31-2

How "Re-evaluation Counseling" Began
Paper: $2   ISBN 0-885357-42-7

CROATIAN
The Human Side of Human Beings
Paper: $4   ISBN 0-913937-56-8

Fundamentals Manual
Paper: $6   ISBN 0-913937-57-6

ESPERANTO
La Homa Flanko de Homoj
(The Human Side of Human Beings)
Paper: $4   ISBN 0-911214-32-1

DANISH
Det Menneskelige I Mennesker
(The Human Side of Human Beings)
Paper: $4   ISBN 0-911214-64-X

Handbog Genvurderingsvejledning
(Fundamentals Manual)
Paper: $6   ISBN 0-911214-55-0

DUTCH
Het Menselijke Aan De Mens
(The Human Side of Human Beings)
Paper: $4   ISBN 0-911214-65-8

Handleiding Voor De Beginselen Van Het Co-Counselen, Voor Beginnersklassen in Re-evaluation Counseling
(Fundamentals Manual)
Paper: $6   ISBN 0-911214-31-3

De Situatie Van De Mens
(The Human Situation)
Paper: $7   ISBN 0-911214-88-7

Het Hernemen Van Macht
(The Reclaiming of Power)
Paper: $13   ISBN 0-913937-80-0

Richtlijnen Voor Herwaarderingscounseling Gemeenschappen
(Guidelines)
Paper: $2   ISBN 0-913937-44-4

De Goeden en de Groten in de Kunst
(The Good and the Great in Art)
Paper: $2   ISBN 0-913937-94-0

Een Rationele Theorie Over Seksualiteit
(A Rational Theory of Sexuality)
Paper: $2   ISBN 0-913937-95-9

Doeltreffend cocounselen
(Efficient Co-Counseling)
Paper: $3.25   ISBN 1-885357-30-3

Een moderne filosofie
(A Modern Philosophy)
Paper: $2   ISBN 1-885357-31-1

Client/Counselor Notebooks (large size)
Paper: $10/pair   ISBN 1-885357-39-7

FARSI
The Human Side of Human Beings
Paper: $4   ISBN 0-913937-92-4
Fundamentals Manual
Paper: $6   ISBN 1-885357-18-4
Introduction to Co-Counseling
by Dan Nickerson
Paper: $1   ISBN 1-885357-41-9

FINNISH
Parikeskustelun Perusteet
(Fundamentals Manual)
Paper: $6   ISBN 0-913937-68-1

FRENCH
Le Côté humain des Etres humains
(The Human Side of Human Beings)
Paper: $4   ISBN 0-911214-41-0
Manuel Elementaire pour Co-conseillers
(Fundamentals Manual)
Paper: $6   ISBN 0-911214-40-2
Le Courant Ascendant
(The Upward Trend)
Paper: $10   ISBN 0-911214-78-X
*Comment donner aux Enfants
un bon départ affectif*
(How to Give Children an Emotional Head Start)
par Marjon Riekerk
Paper: $2   ISBN 0-913937-33-9

GERMAN
Die Menschliche Seite der Menschen
(The Human Side of Human Beings)
Paper: $4   ISBN 0-911214-36-4
Handbuch für elementares Counseling
(Fundamentals Manual)
Paper: $6   ISBN 0-911214-39-9
Die Situation des Menschen
(The Human Situation)
Paper: $7   ISBN 0-9111214-75-5
*Richtlinien Für Die Neubewertungs—
Counselgemeinschaften*
(Guidelines)
Paper: $2   ISBN 1-885357-32-X

GREEK
Fundamentals Manual
Paper: $6   ISBN 0-911214-71-2
The Postulates of Re-evaluation Counseling
Paper: $2   ISBN 0-911214-99-2
The Human Side of Human Beings
Paper: $4   ISBN 0-913937-13-4
Introduction to Co-Counseling
by Dan Nickerson
Paper: $1   ISBN 1-885357-39-7

HEBREW
Fundamentals Manual
Paper: $6   ISBN 0-911214-70-4
The Human Side of Human Beings
Paper: $4   ISBN 0-911214-96-8
Clarifying and Summarizing
the Fundamentals of Counseling
Paper: $2   ISBN 0-913937-22-3

HUNGARIAN
Fundamentals Manual
Paper: $6   ISBN 0-913937-87-8
The Human Side of Human Beings
Paper: $4   ISBN 0-913937-86-X
The Postulates of Re-evaluation Counseling
Paper: $2   ISBN 0-911214-93-3

INDONESIAN
Fundamentals Manual
Paper: $6   ISBN 0-913937-29-0

JAPANESE
Fundamentals Manual
Paper: $6   ISBN 0-913937-52-5
The Human Side of Human Beings
Paper: $4   ISBN 0-913937-78-9
How "Re-evaluation Counseling" Began
Paper: $2   ISBN 1-885357-33-8
The Liberation of Asians
by Cheng Imm Tan
Paper: $3   ISBN 1-885357-36-2

ITALIAN

Il Lato Umano Degli Esseri Umani
(The Human Side of Human Beings)
Paper: $4   ISBN 0-911214-73-9

*Manuale Elementare
di Rivalutazione Attraverso*
(Fundamentals Manual)
Paper: $6   ISBN 0-911214-74-7

16 Chapters from The Human Situation
Paper: $1 per chapter, available as pamphlets

*Linnea Guida per la Comunitá
di Co-Consiglio di rivalutazione*
(Guidelines)
Paper: $2   ISBN 0-913937-96-7

Il Piacere Della "Leadership"
(The Enjoyment of Leadership)
Paper: $3   ISBN 1-885357-21-4

*Stesura Riveduta delle Linee di Condotta della
Liberazione delle Donne Dichiarazione di Unitá*
(Women's Liberation Draft Policy)
Paper: $2   ISBN 1-885357-24-9

*Como dare ai Bambini un punto di partenza
vantaggioso a livello emotivo*
(How to Give Children an Emotional Head Start)
di Marjon Riekerk
Paper: $2   ISBN 1-885357-25-7

Lo Sfogo dei Primi ricordi Sessuali
(Counseling on Early Sexual Memories)
by Joan Karp
Paper: $3   ISBN 1-885357-00-1

*Cosa c'é di sbagliato nel sistema
di "igiene Mentale"*
**(What's Wrong with the "Mental Health" System
and What Can Be Done About It)**
Paper: $3   ISBN 1-885357-20-6

KANNADA

Fundamentals Manual
Paper: $6   ISBN 0-911214-79-8

Guidebook
Paper: $3   ISBN 0-913937-00-2

KISWAHILI

Fundamentals Manual
Paper: $6   ISBN 0-913937-79-7

LITHUANIAN

Fundamentals Manual
Paper: $6   ISBN 0-885357-16-8

MARATHI

The Human Side of Human Beings
Paper: $4   ISBN 1-885357-44-3

NORWEGIAN

En Teori Om Menneskelighet
(The Human Side of Human Beings)
Paper: $4   ISBN 0-911214-80-1

Lederskap Er En Fornoyelse
(The Enjoyment of Leadership)
Paper: $3   ISBN 0-913937-65-7

POLISH

The Human Side of Human Beings
Paper: $4   ISBN 0-913937-48-7

**The Distinctive Characteristics
of Re-evaluation Counseling**
Paper: $2   ISBN 1-885357-15-X

PORTUGUESE

O Lado Humano Dos Seres Humanos
(The Human Side of Human Beings)
Paper: $4   ISBN 0-911214-66-6

ROMANIAN

Latura Umana A Oamenilor
(The Human Side of Human Beings)
(rough draft)
Paper: $4   ISBN 0-913937-49-5

RUSSIAN

The Enjoyment of Leadership
Paper: $3   ISBN 0-913937-66-5

**The Postulates
of Re-evaluation Counseling**
Paper: $2   ISBN 0-911214-95-X

The Human Side of Human Beings
Paper: $4   ISBN 0-913937-50-9

**How to Give Children
an Emotional Head Start**
by Marjon Riekerk
Paper: $2   ISBN 1-885357-37-0

SHONA

Fundamentals Manual
Paper: $6   ISBN 0-913937-91-6

SPANISH

Guías para las comunidades de Co-Escuchas de Re-evaluación
(Guidelines for the Re-evaluation Counseling Communities)
Paper: $2   ISBN 0-913937-01-0

El Lado Humano De Los Seres Humanos
(The Human Side of Human Beings)
Paper: $4   ISBN 0-911214-27-5

Manual Elemental del Escucha para clases elementales del proceso de Re-evaluación
(Fundamentals Manual)
Paper: $6   ISBN 0-911214-83-6

La Situación Humana
(The Human Situation)
Paper: $7   ISBN 0-911214-29-1

Como Dar A Los Niños Una Ventaja Emocional
(How to Give Children an Emotional Head Start)
por Marjon Riekerk
Paper: $2   ISBN 0-913937-37-1

Como Pueden Los Padres Ser Escuchas De Sus Hijos
(How Parents Can Counsel Their Children)
por Tim Jackins
Paper: $4   ISBN 0-913937-74-6

Primer Taller Latinoamericano Preguntas y Demostraciones
(Transcript of the first Latin American workshop)
por Harvey Jackins
Paper: $5   ISBN 0-913937-70-3

Acomodando La Discapacidad
(Accommodating Disability)
por Marsha Saxton
Paper: $2   ISBN 0-913937-72-X

Qué Está Mal en el Sistema de "Salud Mental" y Qué Puede hacerse Acerca de Ello
(What's Wrong with the "Mental Health" System and What Can Be Done About It)
Paper: $3   ISBN 1-885357-01-X

El Gozo del Liderazgo
(The Enjoyment of Leadership)
Paper: $3   ISBN 0-913937-97-5

Pensando Logicamente Sobre Una Sociedad Futura
(Logical Thinking About A Future Society)
Paper: $3   ISBN 1-885357-12-5

Competición—Una Actividad Inhumana
(Competition—An Inhuman Activity)
por Perry Saidman
Paper: $3   ISBN 1-885357-13-3

Introduccion a la Co-Escucha
(An Introduction to Co-Counseling)
por Dan Nickerson
Paper: $1   ISBN 1-885357-17-6

TAMIL

The Human Side of Human Beings
Paper: $4   ISBN 0-913937-30-4

Fundamentals Manual
Paper: $6   ISBN 0-913937-16-9

TELUGU

Fundamentals Manual
Paper: $6   ISBN 0-911214-69-0

TURKISH

The Human Side of Human Beings
Paper: $4   ISBN 0-913937-81-9

SWEDISH

Det Mänskliga hos Människan
(The Human Side of Human Beings)
Paper: $4   ISBN 0-913937-45-2

Handbok I Omvärderande Parsamtal
(Fundamentals Manual)
Paper: $6   ISBN 0-911214-54-2

Människans Situation
(The Human Situation)
Paper: $7   ISBN 0-913937-12-6

The Upward Trend
Paper: $10   ISBN 1-885357-04-4

Hur Man Ger Barn Ett Känslomässigt Försprång
(How to Give Children an Emotional Head Start)
by Marjon Riekerk
Paper: $2   ISBN 1-885357-02-8

Riktlinjer (Guidelines)
Paper: $2   ISBN 1-885357-03-6

Hur Föräldrar Kan Parsamtala Sina Barn
(How Parents Can Counsel Their Children)
by Tim Jackins
Paper: $4   ISBN 91-971405-62

VIDEOCASSETTES

New videocassettes will be appearing.

BLACK & WHITE VIDEOCASSETTES:

■ DISCHARGING THE PATTERNS OF WHITE RACISM (1 hour, 20 minutes)

Four demonstrations from workshops on the West Coast of the United States, all related to the discharge of white racism. Two are demonstrations with persons oppressed by white racism. One is with a white person discharging the oppressor role of patterns of white racism. The final demonstration is of discharging the effects of white racism for Third World people who live outside of the United States. (#1)

■ RECLAIMING OUR POWER (1 hour, 20 minutes)

An early lecture and demonstrations on reclaiming one's power. Done soon after the realization first emerged of how important the powerlessness patterns instilled in early childhood are in supporting all the other distresses. (#2)

■ CHALLENGING THE CHRONIC PATTERN (1 hour, 26 minutes)

An early series of lectures and demonstrations on discharging chronic patterns. The visual and sound quality are very uneven but it is a priceless record of the important discussions and demonstrations when our understanding of chronic patterns was first being worked out. (#3)

■ COUNSELING ON CLASSIST OPPRESSION (37 minutes)

Two demonstrations on how to counsel about and discharge the patterns of classist oppression. One of them is with a working-class woman. The other is with a person caught in the oppressing role. (#4)

■ A YOUNG PERSON'S CHALLENGE TO ADULTISM (32 minutes)

A remarkable demonstration of discharging the oppression and mistreatment of young people. This young person is remarkably clear in his re-evaluation and rejection of the oppression. (#5)

■ COUNSELING ON SEXIST OPPRESSION (1 hour, 25 minutes)

A brief lecture and five demonstrations. Four of the demonstrations are with women discharging on the oppressed role in sexism. One demonstration is with a man discharging the distress that puts men in the oppressing role. (#6)

■ COUNSELING ON THE PATTERNS OF ANTI-SEMITISM (2 hours)

The theory for understanding and combatting anti-Semitism is discussed and there are four demonstrations. Two are with Jews discharging the distress imposed on them by anti-Semitic experiences. Two are with non-Jews (one an Arab) discharging to free themselves from the imposed patterns of anti-Semitism. (#8)

■ A RATIONAL POLICY ON SEXUALITY (45 minutes)

A lecture on sexuality. This is an important step in the development of theory and practice for dealing with the distresses connected with sexuality. (#9)

■ THE ORIGINS OF CLASSIST OPPRESSION AND THE REMEDY (1 hour, 25 minutes)

A lecture on the origins of and methods of dealing with classist oppression, the fundamental oppression which is the source of all other oppressions. (#10)

■ COUNSELING ON THE PATTERNS OF HOMOSEXUAL OPPRESSION (25 minutes)

The first demonstration is of discharging the oppression sustained by a person as a result of being homosexual in this society. The second demonstration is of discharging the homophobia and the patterns of oppressing homosexuals that have been imposed by the culture. (#11)

■ COUNSELING ON PHYSICAL HURTS (50 minutes)

Discussion of theory and practice of counseling on physical hurts. The necessity of discharging the painful emotion before attention can be successfully placed on the physical distress is particularly clear in the last demonstration. (#12)

■ THE OPPRESSION OF PHYSICALLY DIFFERENT PEOPLE (42 minutes)

A demonstration with a person who has been oppressed because she is disabled, discharging the internalized oppression. (#13)

■ THE FOUNDATIONS OF JEWISH LIBERATION (1 hour, 12 minutes)

Two moving demonstrations on the beginnings of liberation from oppression as a Jew and a demonstration leading to fierce commitment from a Gentile ally. A lecture to the workshop audience during the second demonstration is one of the clearest explanations of the role of anti-Semitism in world affairs available anywhere. (#14)

COLOR VIDEOCASSETTES:

■ TAKING CHARGE No. 1 (1 hour, 30 minutes)

A report by Harvey on the key issues facing the RC Communities in the 1980s. Those issues range from improving counseling at all levels to taking RC knowledge and skills into the wide world. The first demonstration is with an experienced counselor being helped to counsel with her attention completely outside of her distresses. The other demonstration is on the fight against attitudes of ageism. (#101)

■ TAKING CHARGE No. 2 (1 hour, 30 minutes)

Harvey talks about possible ways of defining the structure of the Communities and how we relate to each other in Re-evaluation Counseling. There are two demonstrations. One is on discharging fear of nuclear holocaust and the other is on using the women's commitment. (#102)

■ TAKING CHARGE No. 3 (1 hour, 30 minutes)

Harvey covers three frontier areas in the development of Re-evaluation Counseling. They include the ancient habit pattern of paying attention to our distress and the reliable technique for ending it. Second, the concept of counseling with the attention away from distress and a demonstration of that. The last part is both an explanation and a demonstration of the Wygelian leaders' group. (#103)

■ TAKING CHARGE No. 4 (1 hour, 30 minutes)

Harvey presents the details of building your own world community and how to use your leadership in proceeding to do it. The fears that immobilize us and keep our leadership from flourishing are discussed. There is a talk and four demonstrations on the frontier counseling of leaders: taking charge of everything, closeness, and resting. An activist's commitment is developed during a demonstration about both the making of a commitment and the fear of taking full leadership. (#104)

■ TAKING CHARGE No. 5 (1 hour, 15 minutes)

From chocolate to heroin, "There is no addiction that cannot be recovered from," a talk by Harvey. There are also two demonstrations. In the first a black woman counsels on "white" and attention away from distress, and in the second another woman promises to become a "shero" and see that everything works well. In the final segment Harvey answers questions about recovering from the distress of anesthesia and surgery. (#105)

■ A JEWISH COMMITMENT AGAINST ISOLATION (45 minutes)

The answer to the question, "What would be the universal commitment for Jews?" is worked out by Harvey in a demonstration with two people. It is a good example of the way that theory and practice continually evolve and develop in Re-evaluation Counseling, and it will inform and move people who see it. (#201)

■ NO LIMITS FOR WOMEN (2 hours)

These extensive demonstrations are some of the most advanced work toward re-emergence that has ever circulated within the Community. The extremely varied but similarly powerful directions and work of these three women will inspire anyone who views them. (#202)

■ COUNSELING WITH THE USE OF COMMITMENTS (2 hours)

Seven demonstrations illustrate the use and value of commitments in counseling. Commitments included on this program are: working class, Chicanas', men's, women's, parents', and United Statesers'. A talk by Harvey on the theory and use of commitments follows the first two demonstrations. (#203)

■ THE HUMAN SIDE OF HUMAN BEINGS: AN INTRODUCTION TO RC (1 hour, 30 minutes)

Harvey presents a detailed introduction to the theory and practice of Re-evaluation Counseling at a public lecture in Seattle, Washington, USA. A thorough overview of Re-evaluation Counseling can be gained by viewing this program. (#204)

■ THE WORLD OF WOMEN: A REPORT FROM THE NAIROBI WOMEN'S CONFERENCE (1 hour, 20 minutes)

Diane Balser, Barbara Love, Ann Neitlich, and Joke Hermsen report on their experience of taking RC to the United Nations' Women's Conference in Nairobi. Diane Balser summarizes the United Nations Decade for Women and the changes for women reflected in the four conferences sponsored during that time. (#205)

■ HOW A RATIONAL ORGANIZATION CAN GROW AND FUNCTION: A REPORT TO THE RC MONTREAL WORLD CONFERENCE (1 hour, 15 minutes)

At an RC World Conference, Harvey tells how RC has developed and spread around the world in thirty-five years. An exciting story. (#206)

■ SOUND FUNDAMENTALS AND ADVANCED PROGRESS IN RE-EVALUATION COUNSELING THEORY (45 minutes)

At the Montreal World Conference, Harvey relates how the most advanced concepts in counseling spring directly from the clarification of the fundamental concepts. He outlines specific frontier developments in Co-Counseling theory and practice. (#207)

■ DECISIVE COUNSELING (40 minutes)

What are the central elements of being excellent, decisive counselors? A report by Harvey at the Montreal World Conference. Three demonstrations are included. (#208)

■ THE WYGELIAN LEADERS' GROUP (35 minutes)

The simplicity, functioning, and effectiveness of the Wygelian type of leaders' organization is demonstrated by Harvey at the Montreal World Conference. The demonstration is with an international group of RC leaders in peace work. (#209)

■ WHY WOMEN MUST EMPHASIZE WOMEN'S ISSUES (1 hour, 5 minutes)

Diane Balser demonstrates the necessary priority of women's issues at a workshop. She works with several women on reclaiming their power. (#210)

■ SOME WORK ON WOMEN'S REPRODUCTIVE RIGHTS (1 hour, 5 minutes)

The beginning of a profound discussion of women's reproductive rights in a talk, with demonstrations and question-answering by Diane Balser at a women's workshop. (#211)

■ HOW PARENTS CAN COUNSEL THEIR CHILDREN (1 hour, 50 minutes)

Tim Jackins answers a large number of questions from parents at a gather-in for parents and allies of parents. (#212)

■ MEN'S LIVES: PANEL #1 (1 hour, 54 minutes)

Harvey counsels a panel of five men on what it's been like growing up male, from infancy to the present, in U.S. society: the isolation, violence, competition, and heavy expectations on men. The men's commitment highlights this revealing look at men's lives. (#213)

■ NO ANCESTORS, NO DESCENDANTS (53 minutes)

This videocassette presents the startling and logical perspective that we are not obligated to the past or the future and are completely free. It contains a short talk and several demonstrations, with explanations, by Harvey. It makes this important piece of theory easily understandable. (#214)

■ FRONTIER COMMITMENTS (2 hours)

You may well be inspired by this tape to decide for complete re-emergence. Exciting advanced theory presented by Harvey, combined with six demonstrations on the "frontier" commitments. (#215)

■ COUNSELING THE YOUNG AND THE VERY YOUNG (1 hour, 10 minutes)

Tim Jackins talks about and demonstrates counseling the very young. Patty Wipfler, Lenore Kenny, and Tim respond to questions about counseling young people. (#216)

■ BREAKING FREE FROM RACISM (1 hour, 40 minutes)

Harvey lectures and demonstrates new methods for white people to discharge racism and reclaim their full humanity. (#217)

■ PEOPLE OF COLOR AND BLACK PEOPLE: TWO PANELS (1 hour, 24 minutes)

At the North America/Oceania Continental Conference twenty-one counselors of color answer Harvey's question: What is it like to come to a conference like this and have to deal with being a minority in terms of the racism of this country and this continent? The black panel following answers the questions: What's been great and what's been hard about being black? How has RC been useful? How does RC need to change? (#218)

■ PROTECTING LEADERS AND HANDLING ATTACKS (2 hours)

Tim Jackins talks about why leaders get attacked and what to do about it. In this lecture at the August 1990 meeting of world RC leaders, Tim discusses how our fears get in the way of decisively handling such attacks and how to discharge these fears. (#219)

■ ADVANCED RE-EMERGENCE AND FRONTIER COUNSELING (1 hour, 55 minutes)

Harvey talks at the International Liberation Reference Persons' and Regional Reference Persons' Conference in Amherst, Massachusetts, August 1990, about planning for one's steady re-emergence. He emphasizes how to keep thinking while counseling on chronic patterns and how to use the frontier commitments. A definite pull-up-your-socks-and-go lecture. (#220)

■ MEN AGAINST SEXISM (1 hour, 35 minutes)

Charlie Kreiner counsels one man on the feelings that come up when he tries to discharge his sexism and a second man on his stereotypes of what women are "supposed to be like." Several women answer the question, "What is a part of your internalized oppression as a woman that men don't seem to understand and what would you like them to do differently?" Charlie provides simple, concrete techniques to deal with difficult material. (#221)

■ BATTLING INTERNALIZED SEXISM (1 hour, 20 minutes)

At a Northwest USA teachers' and leaders' workshop, Harvey counsels a woman on internalized sexism, using directions such as "Look up to me, Harvey" and "I have a female body." (#222)

■ ON CARING (FOUNDATIONS OF FAMILY WORK No.1) (1 hour)

Tim Jackins talks about showing caring as a foundation for all of our counseling relationships and as a key to doing family work. Tim and Chuck Esser talk about common distresses that people who do family work have to work through. Then Tim talks about where to put our time and attention to move things forward for children and families. (#223)

■ AN INTRODUCTION TO RE-EVALUATION COUNSELING AND FAMILY WORK (1 hour, 30 minutes)

At an open question night in Australia, Tim Jackins gives an introduction to Co-Counseling by talking about young children and how they heal from hurts. He describes RC family work and answers questions on a wide range of topics related to Co-Counseling and family work. (#224)

■ COUNSELING WITH ATTENTION AWAY FROM DISTRESS (2 hours)

At the International Liberation Reference Persons' and Regional Reference Persons' Conference in Seattle, Washington, USA, August 1995, Harvey explains the importance of counseling with attention away from distress. He talks about and demonstrates the Exchange of Roles, "Why Do You Love Me, Counselor?" and the "Understatement." (#225)

All videocassettes are available in NTSC (VHS), PAL, or SECAM formats. Please indicate the videocassette number and specify the videocassette format you need when ordering. Cost is $25.00 (U.S.) each, plus postage and handling.

ORDER FROM
Rational Island Publishers, P.O. Box 2081, Main Office Station, Seattle, Washington 98111 U.S.A.
Telephone: 206 / 284-0311 • Fax: 206 / 284-8429 • email: ircc@rc.org

AUDIO CASSETTES

Cassettes of Lectures by Harvey Jackins and Others — $10 each

- **An Introduction to Re-evaluation Counseling**
- **Loneliness and Learning in San Luis Obispo**
- **Social Change**
- **Affection, Love, and Sex at the University of Maine**
- Side A: **The Importance of Policy and Theory**
  Side B: **A Tentative Policy on Anti-Semitism**
- **The Oppressive Society**
- Side A: **How RC Started**
  Side B: **Radio Interview at Arlington, VA/ Discussion with Dr. Morris Parloff & staff at N.I.M.H.**
- Side A: **The Basic Skills of Being A Counselor**
  Side B: **The Inevitable Stages in the Development of Co-Counseling**
- **The Spectrum of Techniques**
- **Leadership (from the Reference Persons' Workshop)**
- **Being Effective Allies to the Very Young by Tim Jackins**
- **A Description of RC Work with Young People and Their Families by Tim Jackins**

Almost all RC literature in English is available on audio cassette at the same cost as the printed versions (or, on request, free) to persons with vision difficulties (blind, unsighted, etc.) and is ten dollars per cassette to sighted persons.